p. 47 51
p. 53 62
p. 69 68
75 78
81

BEHIND
THE
SCREEN

BEHIND THE SCREEN

The History and Techniques
of the Motion Picture

Kenneth Macgowan

A Delacorte Press Book
New York

To the memory of
ARTHUR RIPLEY
able and practiced film-maker
who became an inspired teacher

Contents

Studio Organization

The Problem of Censorship

The Masters of Film-Making

The Picture Reshaped

Preface

This book is a survey of many years and the work of many men. It is not a product of original research; its scope forbade this. A few researchers generously supplied materials. In the main it is an assemblage and sifting of published and sometimes contradictory facts, and of my own experience as a motion picture critic from 1914 to 1918, as a film producer in Hollywood from 1932 to 1946, and as a coordinator of film studies at UCLA from 1947 to 1956.

The writing of the book has been interrupted by collaboration on other publications, a sabbatical of travel in Europe, a Rockefeller grant to teach in Ankara, Turkey, and six months of illness. The manuscript would not have been completed if it had not been for the able and invaluable assistance of Robert G. Dickson. A special student at UCLA, he has had broad experience of different aspects of the film industry in his native Scotland. His wide reading, his historical knowledge, and his familiarity with the current film—plus his academic training abroad—fitted him to do a meticulous job of editing. The accuracy of my text, so often drawn from obscure sources, owes a very great deal to Dickson's probing and sagacious mind. He has saved me from a host of septuagenarian lapses.

I also owe a great deal to the detailed research in the first ten years of motion picture history that Gordon Hendricks, author of *The Edison Motion Picture Myth*, put at my disposal, and to his checking of the manuscript in the areas where he had special knowledge.

I am particularly indebted to Jean Vivié, Commission Supérieure Technique, Paris, for a long correspondence and many rare photographs, and to Rune Waldekranz of Stockholm for guidance as well as advertisements of early moving picture shows in Sweden.

Librarians and curators have—as always—proved uncommonly helpful: Harold S. Anderson, Edison Laboratory National Monument, Orange, N.J.; Eileen Bowser, Film Library, Museum of Modern Art; Betty Franklin, Academy of Motion Picture Arts and Sciences; George Freedley, Theatre Collection, New York Public Library; Richard Griffith, Film

Library, Museum of Modern Art; Shirley Hood, UCLA Department of Theater Arts (one of whose important contributions was finding Dickson); Ernest Lindgren, British Film Institute; Esther Leonard Shatter, Special Collections, UCLA; and Kate Steinitz, Elmer Belt Library of Vinciana, UCLA.

Through the help of these and others that I shall name, I have been able to present illustrations and factual material not accessible to the general reader. Among these are: the sketch by which Roget first pictured the effect of persistence of vision; Leonardo da Vinci's drawing of his proposed camera obscura; many aspects of the developing arts of photography and the moving picture, including Sellers' posed stills of 1861; aspects of the wide screen from the completely circular Cinéorama of 1900 to Gance's triple screen of 1927, and the experiments of Hollywood that were stopped by the depression; studios and theaters from 1896 to 1902 as shown in photographs and advertisements; theater programs when DeMille, Pickford, and Gish were on the stage; production budgets and schedules as developed in Hollywood; sketches made by Delmer Daves, Alfred Hitchcock, and Lewis Milestone as they planned set-ups; specially made drawings to illustrate certain techniques of modern production.

Many interviews and much correspondence have provided aid of many kinds. Among those in and about the industry who have contributed, I can thank only a few: John E. Allen, William Fadiman, Sol Halprin, John Hampton, Gerald McDonald, Kenneth MacKenna, Roger Manvell, Fred Metzler, J. K. Peterson, Paul Raibaud, Loren Ryder, Georges Sadoul, Douglas Shearer, Mogens Skot-Hansen, Earl Sponable, Raymond Spottiswoode, Seymour Stern, Rémy Tessonneau.

Among colleagues and graduate students at UCLA I am indebted to: Phil Babet, Al Baldecchi, Prof. Irving Bernstein, Prof. Ralph Cassady, Jr., Charles G. Clarke, Abe Fawal, Prof. Raymond Fielding, Prof. Richard Hawkins, Ray Kitchener, William Lieb, Michael Lonzo, Carlo Pedretti, George Voellmer, Serena Wade, Donald K. Worthen.

Frankie Porter made a valuable contribution in the creation of this book by her meticulous transcript of many of the chapters.

My gratitude to the members of the Dell Publishing Company for their assistance and especially to Richard Kennedy, who bore so patiently with me, despite delays and frustrations, until the successful completion of the book.

KENNETH MACGOWAN

Note to Book

Some of the dates in this book may be questionable and many of the financial figures only approximations. They are drawn from the few careful records that exist, but also—and of necessity—from the large body of myth and fantasy that makes up too much of the record of motion picture invention and the film industry. Dates in parentheses after the titles of films refer to the years in which they were completed. Usually these correspond to release dates.

Acknowledgments

Grateful acknowledgment is made to the following artists, authors, photographers and publishers for their permission to reprint the illustrations which appear on the pages indicated below:

George Allen & Unwin, Ltd., p. 213. From *A History of the Movies* by Low and Manvell.

Philip Babet, Photographer, Photo Lab Technician, Researcher and Illustrator, pp. 401, 414, 441.

Maurice Bessy, pp. 100, 102, 103, 109, 132. From *George Meliès, Mage* by Bessy and Lo Duca.

Chicago-Tribune-New York News Syndicate, Inc., p. 406. From "Gasoline Alley" by Frank King.

Columbia Broadcasting System, Inc., p. 382. Illustration by Robert Osborn from *Television News Reporting* by the News Staff of Columbia Broadcasting System, Inc. Copyright © 1958 by Columbia Broadcasting System, Inc. Reprinted by permission of Columbia Broadcasting System, Inc., and of the Publishers, McGraw-Hill Book Co., Inc.

Crown Publishers, Inc., pp. 166, 252. From *A History of the Movies* by Benjamin Hampton. Copyright 1931 by Covici-Friede. Used by permission of Crown Publishers, Inc.

Delmar Daves, Writer, Producer, Director, pp. 402, 434, 435, 457 bottom.

George Eastman House, pp. 31, 42.

Edison National Historic Site, p. 277. Reprinted by courtesy of Edison National Historic Site, National Park Service, U.S. Department of the Interior.

Les Editions Denoël, pp. 55, 63 top. From *Histoire général du cinéma* by George Sadoul.

Francis Faragoh Theatre Collection, p. 37 right.

Franklin Institute, Philadelphia, Pa., p. 45.

John Hampton, Silent Movie Theatre, pp. 20, 102, 164, 187, 190.

Hatton Press, Ltd., pp. 32, 54, 71. From *Living Pictures* by H. V. Hopwood.

Gordon Hendricks, pp. 88, 115, 117, 130, 144. From the collection of and by courtesy of Gordon Hendricks.

Hill and Wang, Inc., p. 431. From *The Cinema as Graphic Art* by Vladimir Nilsen. Used with the permission of Hill and Wang, Inc.

Alfred Hitchcock, p. 442.

Hollywood *Reporter,* p. 317.

Holt, Rinehart & Winston, Inc., pp. 36 top, 37. From *The Talkies* by Arthur Edwin Krows. Copyright 1930 by Holt, Rinehart & Winston, Inc. Copyright renewed 1958 by Arthur Edwin Krows. Reprinted by permission of Holt, Rinehart & Winston, Inc.

Journal of the Society of Motion Picture and Television Engineers, pp. 80, 84, 125, 428. From "Norman O. Dawn: Pioneer Worker in Special-Effects Cinematography" by Dr. Fielding, 1963. Reprinted by permission of the *Journal of the Society of Motion Picture and Television Engineers,* and of Norman O. Dawn.

Karl With Collection, p. 22 top.

Killiam-Sterling Film Collection, p. 146. From "The Fall of Babylon" by D. W. Griffiths. Reprinted by permission of the Killiam-Sterling Film Collection, Inc.

Raymond Kitchener, pp. 399, 427, 430, 433–440.

Jay Leyda, pp. 102, 348, 375. From *Kino* by Jay Leyda.

Librairie du Cygne, pp. 276, 63 bottom, 58 right, 57 left, 37 left. From *Le Cinéma des origines à nos jours* edited by Henri Fescourt.

Milton Luboviski, Larry Edmunds Book Shop, p. 138.

Metro-Goldwyn-Mayer, Inc., p. 391.

Lewis Milestone, pp. 385, 404, 438, 439. Reprinted by courtesy of Lewis Milestone.

Mirror Enterprises Syndicate, p. 91. Reprinted from the Los Angeles *Times* with permission of Mirror Enterprises Syndicate.

Museum of Modern Art Film Library, pp. 93, 124.

The New York Public Library, Belasco Collection, p. 162.

The New Yorker, p. 213 by Al Frueh. © copr. 1928, 1956 The New Yorker Magazine, Inc.

Oxford University Press, p. 453. From *The Cinema Today* by Douglas A. Spencer and H. D. Waley.

Prentice-Hall, Inc., p. 428. From *The Living Stage: A History of World Theater* by Kenneth Macgowan and William Melnitz. © 1955, by permssion of Prentice-Hall, Inc., Englewood Cliffs, New Jersey.

Paul Raibaud, pp. 472, 474. From *Promoteurs et réalisateurs du spectacle cinématographique sur écran large* by Paul Raibaud.

Robbins Music Corp., p. 148.

Charles Scribner's Sons. Illustrations pp. 46, 81 are reproduced with the permission of Charles Scribner's Sons from *Animated Cartoons,* pp. 36, 43 by E. G. Lutz. Copyright 1920 Charles Scribner's Sons; renewal copyright 1948 E. G. Lutz.

Martin Secker & Warburg, Ltd., p. 43. From *L. J. Daguerre* by Alison and Helmut Gernheim.

Fred Sersen, Director of Special Photographic Effects, p. 429. Reprinted by permission of Mrs. Fred Sersen.

Louis Sheafer, pp. 131, 142, 278.

Rudolph Sternad, Motion Picture, Production Designer, p. 405. Reprinted by permission of Mrs. Edna Sternad.

Earl Theisen, pp. 68, 73. From the collection of the Academy of Motion Picture Arts and Sciences.

University of California, pp. 40, 56, 76, 86, 279, 460.

Variety, p. 479.

Jean Vivié, pp. 57 right, 58 left, 126, 127, 254, 469. From *Historique et développement de la technique cinématographique* by Jean Vivié.

Rune Waldekranz, pp. 44, 122, 141, 157.

Walt Disney Productions, pp. 83, 118 left, 467. Reprinted by permission. All Rights Reserved.

A. A. Wyn, Inc., p. 240. From *Sergei M. Eisenstein* by Marie Seton. Reprinted by permission of A. A. Wyn, Inc. All rights reserved in the U.S.A. by A. A. Wyn, Inc.

Grateful acknowledgment is made to the following for permission to quote from their publications:

Charles Clarke, pp. 423–424. From *Professional Cinematography* by Charles Clarke. Copyright © Charles Clarke. Reprinted by permission of the author and of the publishers, The American Society of Cinematographers.

The Viking Press, Inc. "The Passionate Screenwriter To His Love" by Dorothy Parker. Reprinted by permission of The Viking Press, Inc. All Rights Reserved.

Quarterly of Film, Radio and Television (now *Film Quarterly*), "The Coming of Camera and Projector—Part I" by Kenneth Macgowan. Copyright © 1954 by The Regents of the University of California. Reprinted from the *Quarterly of Film, Radio and Television,* IX, 1–14, by permission of The Regents.

———, "The Coming of Camera and Projector—Part II" by Kenneth Macgowan. Copyright © 1954 by The Regents of the University of California. Reprinted from the *Quarterly of Film, Radio and Television,* IX, 124–136, by permission of The Regents.

———, "The Story Comes to the Screen—1896–1906" by Kenneth Macgowan. Copyright © 1955 by The Regents of the University of California. Reprinted from the *Quarterly of Film, Radio and Television,* X, 64–88, by permssion of The Regents.

Chapter

1

What Makes Hollywood Run?

T<small>HE</small> <small>MOTION</small> <small>PICTURE</small> <small>IS</small>, obviously enough, the only art created and developed wholly within historical times. Men were drawing pictures, carving sculptures, and making pottery in the Stone Age. They were composing lyric and epic poetry before they could write it down. The art of the fiction film, on the other hand, was almost entirely a product of the twentieth century, and what we call the "feature" developed only after 1910.

The Miracle of the Movies

The moving picture was very far from an art when men dropped a nickel in one of Edison's peep-show machines and saw girls dancing and cowboys busting broncos and prizefighters belaboring one another. Yet it was a fascinating and almost miraculous thing. We who have grown up in a world of movies can hardly conceive the amazement and the thrill that a man of the 1890's experienced. I can think of only one visual phenomenon that might today parallel the effect of those first movies. Imagine that you are looking at a picture in a newspaper, and that suddenly it takes on three dimensions without the use of special glasses.

No art form has ever fascinated so many people at the same time as the feature film. To dispose of mass competition in America, I need hardly say that the soap opera on radio was no art form, or that, in the main, television is essentially like film. In the early 1960's the popularity of the feature film was greater than anything now on the air;

it had a gigantic audience outside the United States. According to a report of the Department of Commerce, in 1961 there were 108,537 movie houses in 120 countries and territories across the world. They could seat 56,745,451 at a single performance; many more, of course, during the run of any one film.

Hollywood Still Dominant Abroad

World War I gave the United States an almost complete monopoly of movie production for four years. European film-making had only partially recovered when World War II dealt it a second blow, and renewed American supremacy. With peace, England, France, and Italy advanced once more. India had always led the United States in the number of feature films made each year; ten years after the war, resurgent Japan outdistanced India. Yet in the early '60s American movies filled 55 percent of the total film-playing time abroad. This was not quite as large a percentage as before, but through the spectacular nature of many of its pictures, Hollywood's income from overseas began, at last, to slightly exceed its profits from home rentals.

As in the past, the dominance achieved by our films continues in spite of the language barrier. Alien peoples throng to them even though they can't understand the spoken dialogue, and have to keep half an eye on superimposed subtitles. Unless they can see and hear films in which foreign actors match their words to the lips of the English-speaking players—such "dubbed" pictures are on the increase in a few countries—the members of this vast, world-wide audience gladly face the ordeal that we Americans must suffer when we see an Italian film and try to follow the action in the few moments left from reading each line of dialogue. In a sense, the moviegoer, in much of the world, is still seeing silent pictures, only there are ten times as many subtitles, and he cannot read them as he used to *between* scenes of silent action.

What Makes Hollywood Run?

You may say that Hollywood's conquest of the world, through two world wars, was a victory by default, but how did the American producers hold the advantages they had gained through lack of competition? Perhaps the answer is partly that the founders of Hollywood were, in the main, men who came from the masses and knew how to please without drawing on whatever imagination they themselves possessed. The level of the adult audience rose during the "talkie" period, but the number of juvenile moviegoers increased far more. In America today, the majority of spectators are children and adolescents. Various pollsters produce various figures. The highest is 52 percent under age twenty, 72 percent under age thirty. The lowest isn't so very much lower. Said screen writer Robert Ardrey: "A little child shall lead us." Has the child led Hollywood toward continued domination over the cinema world?

A Little Child Shall Lead Us

Some wag remarked bitterly, in the early days of television, that TV in two years had arrived at a mediocrity that radio had taken a quarter of a century to achieve. The same cannot be said of the movies. The ambitious struggle to achieve an audience made up exclusively of children has been long and arduous. It has been over such resisting bodies as Chaplin and Garbo and Goldwyn and Lubitsch, even Walt Disney. But the heights have been won. And the same John Ford who once gave adults "The Informer" must now give children "The Searcher[s]."

—Robert Ardrey, in *The Reporter.*

Has he kept our sights low enough to draw a bead on the underprivileged abroad? I think that in catering more or less to a youthful audience, Hollywood has gained and held a mass audience from Spain to Japan that operates, in the main, on the emotional and intellectual level of our juveniles.

Of course, the whole picture is not so simple and it has been changing in the nineteen-sixties. Hollywood has held its own abroad partly by dramatizing the obvious, exploiting the glamorous, and using the wide screen to capitalize on the spectacular. Meanwhile, foreign films have been invading our screen in greater numbers; in 1962 the New York State censor licensed 604 of them. While "art theaters" have increased in number, French and Italian explorations of sex, and splendiferous "dubbed" spectacles from Italy have invaded first-run houses. This has been due partly to the fact that the major film companies, no longer owning chains of theaters, are not compelled to produce enough features to fill them, and partly to the fact that exhibitors are looking for something "different" to compete with television. Some major and many independent producers are making "adult" films to compete in the world market as well as in America.

Once the Costliest Art

The art of the motion picture suffers grievously from the high cost of production. Until the coming of radio and television, no means of artistic communication was so expensive.

The high cost is partly inherent. A camera and film are more expensive than a typewriter and paper; brushes, colors, and canvas; chisels and a piece of marble. A novel or poem, a painting or statue, can be turned out far more cheaply than even a 16mm film. A piano costs less than a professional camera, and a composer can work with pencil and paper and the casual use of a borrowed instrument. A young film-maker or an older experimenter is severely handicapped by the cost of equipment. Even if he is a student at the one of the few universities that teach production techniques and furnish camera, sound stage, and editing equipment, the costs of film stock and laboratory work are high. While a student may make one form of animation quite cheaply by painting directly on film as Norman McLaren and others have done, or at considerably more expense make films ranging from the "nuts and bolts" type of educational film to fully dialogued fictional exercises, the cost involved is far more than that of the tools and materials of any other art. A film with dialogue means a layout of much hard cash. *A Time Out of War*, the prize-winning two-reeler made by Terry and Denis Sanders at UCLA in 1953, cost about $2,000; some other student films have run from $4,000 to $5,000.

The costs of professional film-making are fantastic. Even the most rigid economies, here or abroad, put a floor of $100,000 to $150,000 under a feature-length picture. A well-made Hollywood film without stars or an expensive story may cost upwards of $800,000, and blockbusters run from two or three million to more than ten million dollars.

A Mass Art

Such costs are the product of mass appeal and mass profits. As you will see later on, between 1915 and 1920 producers began to hike the salaries of stars and directors and even the price of stories. The huge profit from a successful film made Hollywood ready to pay through the nose for anyone or anything that seemed responsible for its popularity. This inflationary pattern has continued. By 1962, Hollywood was paying more than a million dollars a film for the services of Marlon Brando or Elizabeth Taylor, and $1,250,000 for *Camelot* and $5,500,000 for *My Fair Lady*. Supporting players, directors, and set designers were paid more than they could have earned in the theater.

Mass production, mass distribution, and mass consumption stamp the motion picture as the only art that had become big business before radio and television—if radio or television can be called an art. The conse-

HOW TO SEE A FILM. Perhaps, as Hitchcock says, he was not without selfish motives in insisting that audiences should see *Psycho* (1960) from the beginning. The excitements in the first part of the film would have been ruined for anyone who had come in later and discovered that the character played by Tony Perkins was a murderer who combined with telling effect an Oedipus complex and necrophilia. The continuous performance, bane of the movies, is unknown to the legitimate theater. There may be latecomers to *My Fair Lady* or *Hamlet,* but only by misadventure. Coming in at the middle of a movie is common, disadvantageous, and sometimes disastrous. *Enchantment* (1948) and *Happy Land* (1943)—otherwise excellent pictures—were failures because anyone who came in after the first ten minutes was completely befuddled by the frequent flashbacks to the past.

quences have not been wholesome. Around 1905, the movies were cater-
ing to a semi-educated mass audience; many who sat in the store theaters
had only just learned to read and some had trouble with the subtitles.
Within ten years, the level of the moviegoer was somewhat higher. Was
it high enough to justify the poet Vachel Lindsay when he wrote: "The
Man with the Hoe had no spark in his brain. But now a light is blazing"?
The bane of American movies, and to a lesser extent those of Europe,
India, and Japan, has been catering to a gigantic audience of fifty million
or more. It has hindered experiment and put a premium on the universally obvious. Yet there is always the chance that the experimental or
the obvious may prove to have universal validity in terms of high emotion. Then we have daring pictures such as *Citizen Kane* and *The Defiant
Ones,* or films of the broad and deep appeal of *Brief Encounter* and *The
Best Years of Our Lives.*

Hollywood "Too Slick"

The attack on Hollywood films is curiously divided, even contradictory.
The critic Dwight MacDonald inveighs against "the gigantism, the brutality, the tastelessness, the peculiar combination of unreality and dull-
ness." Others see too much glamor on the screen. Some of our film-makers
object to the technical perfection of the Hollywood product. It is "too
slick." Fred Zinnemann has attacked "this mania for perfection" at the
expense of everything else:

> It is important to forego this terrible itch for technical
> perfection; this uncontrollable need to put the industrial
> gloss over everything. They will take an interesting face,
> take away all the lines, and suddenly it looks like all other
> faces. This craving for technical varnish is the tail that wags
> the Hollywood dog.

Hollywood Too Remote

The general charge is that behind the brutality or glamor there is no content, no humanity, no concern with life. Many believe that this is due to
Hollywood's worship of what William James called the "bitch-goddess,
Success," which caters to the mass audience. Some, who are perhaps more
farsighted, assert that the emptiness is due to the isolation of the film
capital from the capitals of culture. As director Sidney Lumet put it, "all
the great centers of art have been centers of *other* things." Said Mac-
Donald:

> Hollywood is in the middle of a barbarically provincial
> non-city, three thousand miles from our cultural capital. . . .

It is as if all British films were made in Tanganyika. My modest proposal for improving the quality of our films is that the industry move back to where it started from, namely, Fort Lee, New Jersey, a short bus ride from civilization.

In the late nineteen-thirties J. B. Priestley wrote of Hollywood:

It is too far from the mainstream of life. . . . Producers of films should be inspired by the great spectacle of this [cosmopolitan] life, moved by it to compassion, laughter, and wonder, and a producer in London, Paris, or Moscow has this great spectacle roaring around him day and night, can dive at any hour into a vast invigorating sea of life, can bring up treasures from the deep. . . . Hollywood shows us the egoism of the artist but not his broad and rapturous humanity. It is too rich; it has been flattered by too many fools; and it is too remote and self-centered. And that, I concluded, is why it has done so well, and why it has never done any better.

Perhaps Hollywood was doing better in the fifties and sixties, and perhaps that was because so many of its films were "runaway" productions. American film-makers working in Europe may have profited as much from being free of the atmosphere and the control of the Hollywood studios as from contacts with the Old World. Some did not need to go to England, France, or Germany to touch a richer life than they had known in Beverly Hills. Elia Kazan and Lumet, and some less noted, found—or at any rate believed—that they could do better work in or around Manhattan than in Hollywood. It may be significant that certain television films made in New York—*Naked City* and *The Defenders*, for example—have seemed fresher and more vital than most of the Hollywood brand. Or was that partly due to giving us the atmosphere of true New York streets, and shooting in real rooms not much better lit than before the movie company moved in?

Topsy-Turvy Economics

Strange are the economic ways of the motion picture. They do not spring only from Hollywood. They are more or less common wherever films are shown. And they seem to violate the laws of supply and demand.

In the first place, demand works backward. When Americans developed a love for automobiles, Detroit's production lines rushed millions of new cars out of its factories. When our citizenry showed an interest in television sets, manufacturers made more and more of them. But, toward the end of World War II, when the public was thronging to the movie theaters as never before, film producers deliberately turned out fewer films. Each picture could play longer and make more money.

Here is where the factor of time comes in. A book publisher or a manufacturer of shoes doesn't care whether he sells more of his product on Saturday or Monday, the first week of March or the last week of September. He doesn't care if a shop is almost empty at one time of day and overcrowded at another. It is different with a movie theater and the maker and the seller of films. In the case of a theater, there are only so many hours in the evening, plus some matinees at downtown houses. Only so many people can attend any single showing. Hence some of those who fail to gain admission may not be able to buy seats later—unless the run is extended. The exhibitor has another trouble with this business of so-many-hours-a-day. Playing time is invaluable; once lost, it is irrecoverable. If a theater is dark for a night, the income it might have had is gone forever. In this fact lies the power that the projectionists' union has over the theaters and hence over the producers, who live by the theaters. Within limits, shoe stores could close down for a while, but shoes would go on wearing out and people would buy just as many new ones when they had the chance. But closing a theater through a strike—or a public disaster or a fire—means an irreparable loss of playing time. It can never be recovered.

During a period of box office prosperity, a bigger demand for entertainment meant a smaller supply of films. When the war was over and people could drive cars again, visit friends and distant places, or stay home and watch those new and miraculous television sets, business fell off in the theaters. Demand dropped and so did supply, but not for the proper reasons. The government had succeeded in forcing the producer-distributors of motion pictures to sell their chains of theaters. If they had still owned them when the box office sagged, they would have been forced to produce more films—more cheaply, of course—to keep their theaters prosperous. Instead, no longer owning theaters, they made fewer pictures. Also, in the competition for fewer patrons, they made them more expensively. The next economic vagary was the boosting of ticket prices. Ordinarily, when a manufacturer or a storekeeper has trouble selling shoes, he cuts his prices. The price of seats at the first-run theaters of the twenties was about seventy-five cents. In the fifties and sixties, it rose to at least a dollar and a half. And, as you will see later, highly successful films brought their owners incomes of over $4,000,000 instead of a third or a quarter that amount as comparable pictures had done in the past. The "blockbuster" was king.

The Drive-In, the Newest Theater

The post-war regression at the box office did other things to the movies. Hollywood turned to wide screens and curved screens. This was done to try to lure the public back to the theaters with something they couldn't see at home on "tinyvision." To make things harder for the industry, the frightened producers tried to cut costs by dropping their contract stars and directors, and then had to hire them back at higher salaries, and even finance independent productions for them.

Meantime, the exhibitors went through a maneuver rather like fewer productions and wider screens. They closed down a great many of the smaller theaters, reduced the seating capacity of some that they refurbished, and then developed still further a new kind of house—the outdoor theater, or drive-in. By 1962, the "hard top" houses had shrunk from roughly 20,000 to 15,000, while there were almost 6,000 drive-ins.

Historically the open-air theater goes far back. Before 1910 there were "airdromes." A trade paper thought they would become "a permanent feature of the entertainment situation." Just before World War I Marcus Loew drew 21,000 people to Ebbets Field in New York to see vaudeville and Thomas Ince's *Wrath of the Gods* (1914), and he tried the same policy in a Boston baseball park. But, beset by difficulties with the weather, open-air seating was unprofitable until the automobile could bring the patrons and house them comfortably. There were no more than two or three hundred drive-ins until the end of the war. Then they grew by leaps and bounds. In the early sixties, though only a third could stay open all year, they were producing 20 to 25 percent of our box office income. They had spread as far as South Africa. Most drive-ins "seat" about 500 cars—some around 2,000—with two to three

---

$1 For a Ticket, 25¢ For Popcorn, etc.

Ticket sales, including tax, 1961	$1,427,000,000
Refreshment sales, 1961	500,000,000

The ticket sales figure comes from the Department of Commerce. The refreshment sales total is an estimate of *The International Motion Picture Almanac; The Film Daily Year Book* of 1962 provided the analysis. Thus a quarter to almost a third of the audience's money goes for refreshments.

patrons in each. A drive-in occupies more land than a hard top, but thanks to the automobile it can operate on the outskirts where land is cheap. No parking fee, no baby sitter, and plenty of free rides for the active children have spelled prosperity for this new type of theater. It sells even more popcorn than a hard top and doesn't have to sweep up the floor after the show is over.

More Art Theaters—But Less Art?

A mayor of New York, with nice discrimination but not too much culture, once spoke of "art artists." Just as keen on precise distinctions, the film industry dubbed certain places of filmic entertainment "art theaters." At first these houses were few. Now we have about 500 in America. In the early days they were dedicated to foreign films that were too exceptional, too subtle, or too perceptive for general release. Occasionally, though not often, they showed avant-garde films, pictures devoted to the art of non-communication. In those days such houses were known in the trade as "sure seaters"; there was never a line at the box office. By 1960, things had changed. The art theaters had grown in patronage and therefore in number. Unfortunately, five hundred houses didn't mean a great increase in such films from abroad as *Carnival in Flanders* (1935), *Grand Illusion* (1937), *The Baker's Wife* (1938), *Open City* (1945), *Paisan* (1946), *The Bicycle Thief* (1949). A new trend was to the exploitation of sex. This could be blamed on the exposures of Brigitte Bardot and the "new wave" in France, the Italian excitations of Fellini, Antonioni, and Visconti, and the adult preoccupations of Britain's young film makers. America supplied some films that failed to get a seal from our self-censoring Production Code—*Private Property* (1960) and *A Cold Wind in August* (1961), for instance. And there was a flood of "nudies," cheaply made disclosures of the female body; they had their parallels in England as they had long had on the Continent.

For Forty Years an Ephemeral Art

If motion pictures—particularly Hollywood's features—have been vast in their appeal and worldwide in distribution, for forty years they were sadly ephemeral. From 1915 to 1955—when television began reviving them—their life was even shorter than the life of a successful Broadway play. The play might spend a year or two in a New York theater, and then go into print. Though a few films had long runs in four or five big cities, the rest played the first-run houses for a moderate length of time, spread out through second-runs and neighborhood theaters, and then disappeared to the one- and two-night houses in the sticks. Within eighteen months, most films were back in the vaults.

Even in the vaults their life was not too long. No one foresaw this fifty years ago when Sarah Bernhardt declared: "This is my one chance of immortality," and John Bunny justified his leaving the stage for the "flickers" by saying: "They offer a field for the ambitious which is not simply for this day and generation but for the future." Until a few years ago, all release prints as well as the precious negatives were made of a material—cellulose nitrate, very like gun cotton—that, in a few decades, shrank and deteriorated past usefulness. Only when film libraries took the precaution of duplicating or "duping" old negatives— which meant inferior copies—could the silent pictures be preserved. Fortunately, in the case of some very early films, the Library of Congress has positive prints that were made on paper for purposes of copyright; through the initiative of the Academy of Motion Picture Arts and Sciences, and the efforts of Senator Thomas Kuchel, our government is having negatives made. Because these enduring strips of paper preserve only images recorded before the new copyright law of 1912, we must still look at scratched and faded dupes of the silent features. Fortunately, the studios are now using a longer-lasting and non-inflammable base of cellulose acetate for all prints and negatives.

The Obsolescence of the Silent Film

Silent films suffer from more than physical deterioration. Compared with the talkies of thirty years ago, the great majority seem theatrical, obvious, puerile. Try to see, if you can, any famous silent film—except a comedy with Charlie Chaplin or Harold Lloyd, Raymond Griffith or Buster Keaton, Harry Langdon or Laurel and Hardy—and you will wonder why people thought it at all bearable, let alone great. Except for *The Birth of a Nation*, portions of *Greed*, the documentaries of Robert Flaherty and of Merian C. Cooper and Ernest B. Schoedsack, a very few Russian and German productions, and the work of the comedians mentioned above, I have seen no silent films during the past twenty years that matched my bemused memories of them. In support, I quote something that J. B. Priestley wrote in *Midnight on the Desert* in 1937:

Novels and plays, pictures and music of twenty years
ago, do not seem very different from the creations of this
year, but films of twenty years ago seem genuine primitives,
almost prehistorical. We take this progress for granted, but
it is a rare occurrence in our history, such a dazzling advance. It happened when the popular Elizabethan drama
went soaring from *Roister-Doister* to *Twelfth Night*.

It is a fortunate thing for men and women under thirty that, as Ernest
Lindgren has said, they "can have no clear recollection of watching
silent films." Spared the pain of recollection, they can believe in the
myth of cinematic wonders long departed.

Chapter

2

Time
and the Movies

I F HOLLYWOOD had not begun releasing its films to television in 1955, it would have been almost impossible for you to see many of the features mentioned in this book. In a few cities film societies and universities showed wretched dupes of silent pictures and 16mm prints on rent from Hollywood companies. Except for a few notably successful productions such as *Gone With the Wind* (1939), *The Best Years of Our Lives* (1946), and Disney's animated features, no producer realized that there might be an audience for reissues among the young people who have grown up since the films were first shown. Television not only brought old films to its screen; in a roundabout way it put them back in the theaters.

Television Revives the Oldies

To some, pre-1948 films seemed a glut on the video market. Television, Fred Allen said, was just watching an old movie in a washing machine window. Yet for the public it was a happy glut. They wanted more and more of the same thing. Starved for new films because Hollywood was producing fewer and fewer, exhibitors started to rebook old features. Pictures that seemed to have been run to death on television— *Little Caesar* (1930), *The Public Enemy* (1931), for example, were revived on theater screens and did quite well at the box office. In addition, studios that had held back some films from television made an interesting discovery. *Bambi* (1942), *For Whom the Bell Tolls* (1943),

13

and *Samson and Delilah* (1949) came out of hiding, and proved that there could be more money in a reissue than the $100,000 or $150,000 that might be had from television. But most producers—intent on the fast buck—went on selling their oldies down the river, along with films made in the fifties.

TV vs. Film

For a time many thought that the tiny area of the television set would be our only screen. They feared that the movie theaters would have to shut up shop. Whether or not this would happen, others were sure that the live show would disappear and the film would take over television. They prophesied—and time has borne them out—that except for current events, panel discussions, and a few spectacular shows, the bulk of television entertainment would be on film; later some foresaw tape. Programs would be better made, though more expensively.

Then came—long overdue—various kinds of screens and screen effects that TV could not equal. In the theaters 3-D films were a flash in the pan. They may have startled the movie audience by throwing spears at it, but they also laid an egg in its lap. Since 1952 the screens of the first-run and the bigger neighborhood houses—including the drive-ins —have concentrated on Cinerama, CinemaScope, Todd-AO and Ultra Panavision. Heaven only knows what other sizes and shapes and curves of screen are to come.

One thing is certain, however: the "smellies" have come—and gone. They had no effect on the battle between TV and film. Linking odor and entertainment goes back to at least 1868, when Rimmel's Vaporizers sprayed London's Alhambra Theater with perfume during a dance number in *The Fairy Acorn Tree.* I don't know what osmologist was responsible for a similar effect in 1952 when the Paris Opera revived *Les Indes Galantes,* but a Swiss named H. E. Laube devised a "console-type smell projector," with the hope that it would be used at the New York World's Fair of 1939–40 with a film called *Il Mio Sogno.* Twenty years later the American exhibitor Walter Reade, Jr., linked the Aroma-Rama of Charles Weiss to a travelogue about China called *Behind the Great Wall* (1959). In bitter competition, Michael Todd, Jr., lost part of the profits of *Around the World in Eighty Days* (1956) by producing a whodunit called *Scent of Mystery* (1960) "In Glorious Smell-O-Vision —the Process to End All Processes." It consisted of nothing more than the process of wafting numerous odors through a theater's air-conditioning system.

Requiescant In Pace

We cannot know how much more many men and women might have contributed to the progress of the motion picture if they had not died at or before the age of fifty.

James Dean	1931–1955	24		Jeanne Eagels	1890–1929	39
Jean Harlow	1911–1937	26		John Garfield	1913–1952	39
Laird Cregar	1916–1944	28		Larry Semon	1889–1928	39
Ross Alexander	1907–1937	29		John Hodiak	1914–1955	41
Carole Landis	1919–1948	29		Jeff Chandler	1918–1961	42
Vernon Castle	1887–1918	30		Ernie Kovacs	1919–1962	42
Wallace Reid	1892–1923	30		Thomas Ince	1882–1924	42
Maria Montez	1920–1951	31		Elissa Landi	1904–1948	43
Rudolph Valentino	1895–1926	31		Tyrone Power	1914–1958	44
Florence Mills	1895–1927	31		Gregg Toland	1904–1948	44
Kay Kendall	1927–1959	32		Grace Moore	1901–1947	45
Robert Walker	1919–1951	32		Roscoe Arbuckle	1887–1933	46
Carole Lombard	1909–1942	33		Alice Brady	1892–1939	46
Mabel Normand	1895–1930	34		Lon Chaney	1883–1930	47
Lilyan Tashman	1899–1934	34		Lowell Sherman	1885–1934	49
Lupe Velez	1910–1944	34		George Loane Tucker		
Renée Adorée	1898–1933	35			1872–1921	49
Marilyn Monroe	1926–1962	36		Jerry Wald	1912–1962	49
Irving Thalberg	1899–1936	37		Leslie Howard	1893–1943	50
George Gershwin	1898–1937	38		Robert Newton	1905–1956	50
John Gilbert	1897–1936	38		Mike Todd	1907–1958	50
Mario Lanza	1921–1959	38				

An Art That Lives in Time

The painter works in the two dimensions of canvas or paper, metal or lithographic stone; the sculptor in the three dimensions of stone, clay, or wood. The artist of the films has a fourth dimension. It is time.

In this respect the motion picture resembles the play, but the values that can make a film a work of art are more varied. Except for one, they all depend on the element of time. Even that one—the significant beauty of a photographic composition—can move in time if the camera moves, and moves skillfully. The art of pantomime depends on change of expression and on bodily movement. Acting develops in significance from moment to moment. So does the characterization that comes through dialogue. The screenwriter's plot and what he gives us in human understanding can exist only in terms of time. The director works in those terms, and never so clearly as when he joins the cutter in heightening the effectiveness of scenes through the relation of shot to shot. The organization of time is the essence of motion picture art.

The film and the screen have special qualities that may or may not contribute to the artistic value of a motion picture. They are unique qualities, however. One depends wholly on the camera, the other on the projector and the size of the screen.

From Slow Motion to Fast

The camera can play tricks with time. It can slow it down or speed it up. The limits are fantastic.

If a camera makes only one exposure every hour, the projector can show a plant growing from a seed or a bud unfolding into a flower in ten seconds of screen time. As far back as the eighteen-nineties, Biograph's camera exposed a frame of film every thirty minutes as it watched the demolition of the old Star Theater; the audience saw the building collapse in thirty seconds. This is called "time-lapse" or "single-frame" photography. It is the basis of animation in entertainment films and in television commercials. Animated cartoons are produced by taking pictures of a series of drawings one to a frame. In certain kinds of trick photography, objects can be made to move about, change shape, or disappear through the time-lapse technique.

At the other pole of time the camera can produce slow motion by increasing the speed at which it makes exposures. When such a film is projected at normal speed, a diver sails slowly through the air, or a prizefighter delivers a long-laborious punch. Beyond this lie fantastic camera speeds and visual slowdowns.

The other odd quality of the motion picture is its gargantuan expansion of space. This is due to the huge size of modern screens. On a frame of film about the size of a postage stamp, the camera reduces a six-foot man to no more than three-quarters of an inch in height, but the projector enlarges him to more than twenty feet on the screen. And, if we are seeing a close-up of his head, we are looking at what might be part of a giant 150 feet tall. In a motion picture theater, depending on the size of its screen, a 35mm frame of film may be magnified 50,000 to 300,000 times. Thus the motion picture projector becomes the world's most powerful microscope (short of the kind that uses electrons instead of light). Unfortunately this microscope lacks fine definition. But its field can be seen by hundreds instead of by one man.

What You Don't See on the Screen

There are other visual oddities about the motion picture. The camera records on film only about half of the action that goes on in front of it, for the shutter is usually closed 50 percent of the time. And so we see on the screen only half the action. Because the shutter of the projector is similarly closed, Roger Manvell has said, "for one-half of the time [that] an audience is seeing a film it is sitting in total darkness without knowing it." Actually there is no total darkness or there would be no moving picture. The eye remembers a brightly lighted object on the screen for about a tenth of a second after it has vanished. This is due to what scientists call persistence of vision—one static shot blends into the next, and we see apparent motion. We don't miss the unrecorded action, and we are conscious of no darkness. Since a motion picture is really a series of stills, Gilbert Seldes can write: "The only movement on the screen is one of which no one is aware—the movement of one picture off and another on." There are many movements within the projector, and the most interesting is the shutter's. It hides the movement of the film on the screen. It makes the darkness that we never see if the projection is perfect. When there is flicker on the screen, then we are "seeing" the shutter, or rather, its malfunction.

There are some other things upon the screen that the moviegoer seldom or never notices. One of these is the two sets of little circles—or in the case of CinemaScope, ovals—that appear in the upper righthand corner at the end of each reel. The first set signals the operator to be ready to change from one projector to the other, and when he sees the second he makes the change-over.

Audiences may see other things on the screen without being very curious about them. One of these is the "fade out" in which the end of one scene dims into darkness and then another slowly takes its place as the screen grows brighter. Another effect taken for granted is the "dissolve" that blends one scene into another by fading out the first while the next—superimposed over it—fades in at the same rate of speed. Later in this book you will learn how these effects are used and why.

Film History—a Dubious Record

Among the peculiarities of the motion picture is the distressing fact that its history is full of mysteries, confusions, and contradictions. Though the tools and the techniques of the new art form were developed within the last seventy years, the record of the invention of camera and projector is particularly cloudy. Nationalistic pride distorts the early history of the film. Also, the pioneer is either dead or has a faulty memory and "too much ego in his cosmos." Journalists and even critics have perpetuated errors and contradicted one another past all resolving. The trade papers of the industry have suffered a bit from journalistic haste and the irresponsibility of press agents.

Fortunately, the screen is blessed with three source books such as the theater sadly lacks: *The Film Daily Year Book of Motion Pictures,* running to over 1,100 pages; *The International Motion Picture Almanac,* almost as bulky; and *The Film Index,* another hefty volume. *The Year Book* lists, among other things, the feature films released since about 1915—by 1962 there were over 30,000 titles—and carries the credits for each picture of the past twelve months. *The Almanac* supplements *The Year Book* with a vast array of facts about the industry here and abroad, and 300 pages of biographies. In addition—and even more important —is *The Film Index,* edited by Harold Leonard and a Work Projects Administration staff. Its more than 700 pages and 8,600 entries list, group, and digest articles in trade papers, general periodicals, books, and pamphlets that deal significantly with film-making from the early nineteen-hundreds to the late nineteen-thirties. (It is a tragedy that the work was not continued year by year.) Except for this volume, the two annuals, the published listings of the Copyright Office of the Library of Congress, and the technical *Journal of the Society of Motion Picture and Television Engineers,* research materials are wretchedly inadequate and dangerously inaccurate. And so I am all too conscious of the errors I may be perpetuating instead of correcting.

Did America Lead in Feature Production?

The story of the introduction of the fiction film, and its development to feature length, is distorted by nationalistic fervor.

Because the Hollywood film has dominated the international screen since 1915, most Americans and many Europeans believe that the United States played a much greater part than it did in the early development of the motion picture. We in the New World were not solely responsible for the invention of the camera and the projector; Europeans contributed, too. We were not the first to record important news events; two Frenchmen shot the coronation of Czar Nicholas II in 1896.

It is far from safe to credit Americans with making the first films with stories. The Frenchmen Lumière and Méliès, the Englishmen R. W. Paul, James Williamson, Cecil Hepworth, and G. A. Smith, seem to have anticipated the American Edwin S. Porter, as well as his very minor predecessors; certainly the British films excelled ours for some ten years. We did not invent the basic techniques of storytelling; here the British and particularly Hepworth were ahead of Porter and anticipated some of the skills of D. W. Griffith.

The feature film was first successfully produced in Italy and France. The credit might have gone to J. Stuart Blackton and Vitagraph for producing *Les Miserables* and *The Life of Moses* in 1909–10; but the distributor released the former in four parts, and the latter in five, at a reel a week. (A reel was then about fifteen minutes long.) In 1912, while Griffith was still making one-reel, and occasionally two-reel, films, Italy brought forth *Quo Vadis?* in eight reels. The next year, when the Italians made two lengthy versions of *The Last Days of Pompeii* and the French made *Les Miserables* in twelve reels, Griffith had moved only as far as four reels with his *Judith of Bethulia*. By 1915, however, when *The Birth of a Nation* appeared, Griffith was leading the American film to its domination of the world screen.

Though it was the Lumière brothers of France who led in coverage of news events, the United States can claim priority in a related and very important field—the documentary feature. *Paul Rainey's African Hunt* displayed its eight reels of travel adventure in 1912. Robert Flaherty invented the true documentary film in 1922 with his *Nanook of the North*, and Merian C. Cooper and Ernest Schoedsack gave it epic quality three years later with *Grass*.

From Science to Filmic Fiction

Basil Wright, documentary writer and director, has called the motion picture the "child of the laboratory and the machine." Will Hays, first czar of Hollywood, spoke of his domain as an "art-industry." Between these two concepts lies the wide expanse of the unique human activity that the Americans call, rather lovingly, "the movies." I suppose it is rash to compare the range of the motion picture to the range of writing. Philosophy and lyric poetry do not lie within the scope of the movies. Yet the screen can go beyond fiction and news coverage to serve science and education.

Through slow- and high-speed photography and through the use of the X ray, the camera records and studies processes and states of nature that can't be so easily or so accurately analyzed by any other means. The camera can preserve a tribal life that will pass away. For classroom demonstration, the screen magnifies experiments in chemistry and phys-

ITALY'S FIRST SPECTACLES IN AMERICA. *Quo Vadis?*, produced in 1912, played legitimate theaters here as well as vaudeville houses. Later came *The Last Days of Pompeii*. It had already played the huge Gaumont-Palace in Paris, which had been remodeled from the old Hippodrome. (*Courtesy John Hampton.*)

ics. With the aid of animation, the film visualizes hidden processes that even the X ray cannot penetrate, and it clarifies all manner of relationships from mathematics to economics.

At its best, the fiction film has values beyond, though not above, those of the stage and the novel. These values are cinematographic—a six-bit word that some use for what is truly filmic. They are unique to the screen. They go beyond photography. They are something more than the ability to show sweeping landscapes or reveal visual intimacies. The filmic values of this art form include and utilize the skills of editing and the subtleties and power of directing that build upon those skills. And, of course, these values are not merely the values of the silent picture. The truly cinematographic film of today has inherited many of the virtues of the silent film, but it takes on far more stature through the values inherent in sound. I don't mean through music alone, which sets and enhances moods and action, or through the noises that accompany or dramatize human activity. The motion picture, at its most characteristic, uses all its resources to heighten the one basic value of the screenplay—character in action, which cannot live fully without expression through dialogue.

Between the scientific film and the motion picture's own unique and expressive art lie lesser things, all too many of which we see on the screen today. Forgetting the travelogue, the sports film, the cat-and-mouse cartoon, the comedy short, I must point out that too often the Hollywood feature—and this is not quite so true of the European product —is only a novel or a play given more or less filmic treatment but seldom a complete one. Like so many scientific films, this common type of feature is a record, but it is not an analysis, and it is almost never an expression of a new and special art.

Why Did We Make Pictures Move?

Man is the animal that invents. Discovery is not enough; he must create, too. He found natural fire, but he went a long step further when he invented a way to make a flame by rubbing two sticks together. Thousands and thousands of years have passed since then, and through all but a tiny part of this time inventions came very slowly indeed. The deadfall, the spear point, the bow and arrow, the boat, the basket, and the harpoon appeared in the long years of the hunting period that may have ended about 8000 B.C. With the discovery and development of agriculture, man multiplied his new devices. These involved the invention of writing and the spread of inquiry and knowledge from the days of

MOVIES IN JAVA. Among the peoples of Asia the shadow puppets, called *Wajang-Kulit,* anticipated the motion picture as a form of storytelling. Thrown on a screen, such shadows as these still re-enact old epics to the myriad voices of the *Dalang,* or puppeteer. (*Courtesy Karl With.*)

ON THE TURKISH SCREEN. Shadow puppets can still be seen occasionally in Anatolia. The two at the left are the chief figures, friendly rivals in many a farce, Hacivad and Karagöz. The first is full of highflown speech and fond of archaic words that his unschooled companion cannot understand; yet the show is called *Karagöz* in his honor. Other characters are victims of the pair. Here are two satirical portraits of elegant Turks at the turn of the century, who aped European fashions under the now-departed fez. (*From Siyavusgil's* Karagöz.)

the Sumerians to the Renaissance. Printing swelled the inventive activities of man far more in five hundred years than in the forty-five hundred that lay between the cuneiform stylus and Gutenberg's type. From the Revival of Learning through the seventeenth century, men's minds threw off many more new theories and machines. With the end of the eighteenth, these brought about the Industrial Revolution. Of all the centuries, the nineteenth must be called *the* century of invention. Spurred by the growth of manufacture, men created a still vaster number of more and more complicated and original devices for multiplying the goods and the enjoyments of life. As the century drew toward its close, the pace accelerated almost unbelievably. Railroad engines and steamships, harvesting machinery and sewing machines were followed by the telegraph and the telephone, steel and oil refineries, dynamos and incandescent bulbs, the typewriter and the phonograph, typesetting machines and armored ships, the streetcar, the bicycle, and the automobile.

It was in the nineteenth century and particularly in its last two decades that men invented and, to a great degree, perfected the motion picture camera and the projector. As in so many cases, the mother of invention was not necessity, but rather man's insatiable curiosity. Here as elsewhere, it is often difficult to fix the moment of invention, or even to know who out of many deserves the most credit. Here, too, it is not so important to know who first conceived something as to know who conceived it most perfectly. Because I know more about this particular complex of inventions than I do about the multitude of others in the past hundred years, I may make the mistake in the next two chapters of exaggerating the complexities and the difficulties of finding out how to make pictures move.

Chapter

3

When Pictures Began to Move—1825-1885

Tragedy and suffering beset the invention of the motion picture. Also folly and a touch of mendacity. An important pioneer took time out to kill his wife's lover. One inventor boarded a French train and was never seen again. Another committed suicide. One blinded himself in the course—and the cause—of research. A deaf man tried to invent talkies. The first exploiter of the movies didn't want to project them on a screen. A priest falsely claimed the invention of the oldest type of projector. Through much of the story, the end results were hardly more than toys, and even the most serious of the scientists contributed mainly to the art of entertainment.

Many Inventions—Rather Than One

No one man invented moving pictures, which for a long time meant moving drawings. They grew out of scores of accidents and observations, guesses and experiments, that go back through three centuries. Early or late, the record is full of coincidences and confusions. Far too often we have no idea of who first made a contribution of vital importance, because two or more men were working on the same thing at the same time and dates are obscure or disputed. Even if we ignore the long past and concentrate on the motion picture camera and the projector, we are not much better off. Out of a score of inventors, four or five men must share the major credit, and we have few facts on which to judge them. The pioneers of seventy years ago are all dead. They left no full records.

Yet this story of discovery and invention is not all darkness and confusion. We know what had to be done—and what *was* done—even
though we may not always know who first did it. And so we can list
the basic steps that led to the motion picture of today:

Projectors, beginning with the magic lantern.

The use of persistence of vision—the ability of the eye to
"remember" an image for as much as a tenth of a second.

Devices to view—and fuse—drawings of objects in motion.

Cameras, themselves devised from the camera obscura, to
replace drawings with photographs.

Flexible film instead of glass plates.

A number of important details, including fast lenses and fast
emulsions, ingenious shutters, devices to give the film intermittent movement, and other mechanical features of the motion
picture camera and projector.

The recording and amplification of sound on film.

Color on film.

Sound on magnetic tape.

The Mystery of the Magic Lantern

Of all the above, the magic lantern may seem the most basic and
important, yet it is not. This primitive projector was almost two hundred years old before anybody used it for anything but glass slides.
Without its aid, moving pictures could exist—and did exist—from 1832
to 1854. When the first successful projector of movies appeared in 1895,
it borrowed the light and the lenses of the magic lantern, but its prime
secret was the use of persistence of vision and the intermittent motion
of photographic film.

Confusion—and probably coincidences—begin with the magic lantern.
This seems natural enough, since it was invented three hundred years
ago. But certain film historians have compounded the confusion by
falling in love with the idea that it was the brain-child of a German
Jesuit, Father Athanasius Kircher. Properly known in his day as "doctor
of a hundred arts," he included among them a bit of mendacity. Whoever really invented the magic lantern—and it may have been one or
two or three men—Kircher did nothing of the kind. He merely claimed
the credit *ex post facto*. And no one can be quite sure who of two or
three men was the real inventor.

In 1646 Kircher published a book in Latin called *Ars Magna Lucis et
Umbrae* (The Great Art of Light and Shadow). Twenty-five years later, he

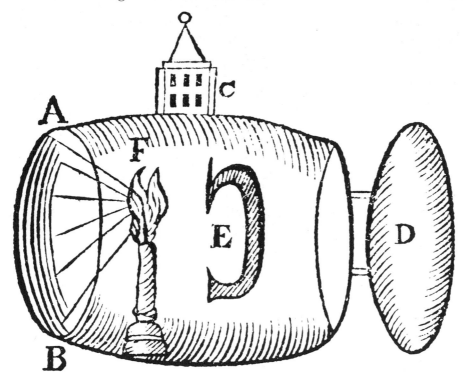

KIRCHER'S PROJECTOR. In 1646 the priest-scientist showed how letters painted on a concave mirror could be reflected on a wall. In this picture the mirror is marked AB. By the light from the candle (F), the letters on the mirror were projected through what he called a "window," which could be closed with a cover (D). C is a ventilator, and E a handle on this earliest of bull's-eye lanterns. Kircher used a lens only when the letters were painted on a flat mirror, and he did not describe or illustrate the use of slides until the second edition of his book twenty-five years later. Instead, he developed what seems to us a more difficult concept, the opaque projector.

brought out a second edition. Some film historians have made the mistake of looking at the new pictures and the new text in the 1671 book, and of not realizing that Kircher added them to the new edition. In 1646, he described and pictured a number of optical tricks, but he said nothing about the magic lantern. He had to wait until somebody else had put it on the market. So, in 1671, he wrote that a Danish mathematician named Thomas Walgensteen, "remembering my invention, produced a better form of the lantern I had described. These he sold with great profit to himself."

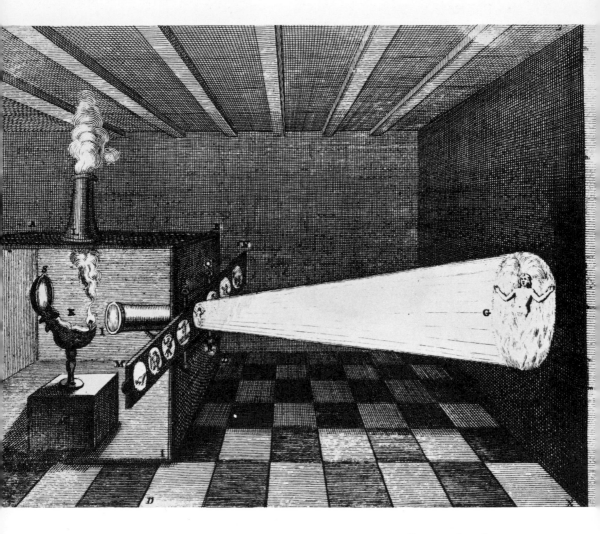

KIRCHER'S MAGIC LANTERN, 1671. This device, illustrated only in
the second edition of his book, showed no focusing lens in front
of the slide, only a mirror behind the light and a condensing lens
in front of it. The figure on the slide is right side up, like that on
the wall, instead of inverted.

To insure another sort of profit to Kircher, the good father not only
claimed to have invented the thing twenty-five years before, but added
a drawing of it, including a slide with eight painted pictures. Kircher's
"invention" seems to be a bungled imitation of somebody else's machine. It couldn't have done its job, for—as you can see above he
forgot to copy the lens that lies between the slide and the screen in all
proper magic lanterns.

17TH CENTURY MAGIC LANTERNS. Beginning with Francesco Eschinardi in 1666—five years before Kircher's second edition—a number of men wrote about true magic lanterns. Those that appear above are from a book by Joannes Zahn, published in 1685. The lantern at the bottom, which uses a circular plate instead of a slide, hints at a method for projecting moving pictures that was to be first used more than 150 years later. But Zahn, like other inventors or manufacturers of magic lanterns, never thought of employing persistence of vision to achieve the effect of motion.

Pepys Peeps at a Lantern Show

By the time Kircher's afterthoughts appeared, others besides Walgensteen had made magic lanterns; the first man was probably the
great Dutch scientist Christian Huygens in 1655 or 1656. Ten years
later, Samuel Pepys wrote in his diary: "Mr. Reeves . . . did also bring
a lantern with pictures in glass, to make strange things appear on a wall,
very pretty." If Pepys had lived more than his threescore years and
ten he could have seen the pretty pictures take on a bit more life. About
1710 he might have written: "Comes Mr. Reeves with a new manner
of lantern. It did make a cockroach leap into the open mouth of a man
asleep, very comical." The trick was simple enough. One slide showed
the man in bed. A second slide, with the insect on it, was shifted from
one position to another.

More than a century had to pass before scientists achieved, in 1832,
a better illusion, and then they did it without benefit of Kircher *et al.*
About 1850, when moving pictures—drawings, of course, not photographs—were first projected on a wall, a shutter had to be added to
the magic lantern, something that its makers never dreamed of. But
before we come to this device, there are other discoveries and inventions
to consider.

The Secret of the Movies—Almost as Old as Man

Of all the steps that I have listed in the progress toward the motion
picture as we know it, one is basic and essential. This is what science
calls persistence of vision. Without it, moving pictures—whether drawn
or photographed—would never have been thought of. Indeed, they
would have been impossible. Man took the century-long road to the
movie camera and projector only because he noticed that his eyes had
a trick of remembering, for a brief moment, whatever they saw. When
our optic nerves send an image to our brain, our brain "looks" at it for
a tenth of a second before it disappears, and sometimes longer. If
you'd like a demonstration—Leonardo da Vinci suggested it—gaze for
a moment at a bright light; then look away, and you will see a glowing
spot. The same thing occurs, though you aren't conscious of it, when
you watch any scene of movement. An "after-image" fuses with the
next. We may call this phenomenon a most happy flaw in our optical
system, for it makes the movies possible.

Man has been aware of persistence of vision for more than a hundred thousand years. When he first used fire, he must have swung a
burning stick and seen a radiant circle instead of a single flame. He

had to wait till 1833 to know for certain that a streak of light across the heavens is a "shooting star." It was about this time that scientists discovered how to use persistence of vision to make their fellows see figures in motion.

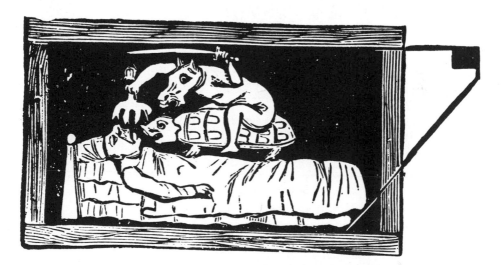

"COMIC SLIP SLIDES." As late as the 1890's makers of magic lanterns issued catalogues with a section devoted to trick slides. In the one above, a nightmare vision suddenly appears to a sleeping man. (*Courtesy Beaumont Newhall, George Eastman House.*)

"Things Are Seldom What They Seem"

Film historians seem to be even more confused about the first exploiter of persistence of vision than they are about the inventor of the magic lantern. Most of them believe that the celebrated compiler of Roget's *Thesaurus* made the first discovery that led to the motion picture. What Dr. Peter Mark Roget saw and reported in 1824 was curious and interesting, but not too important, and four years earlier someone known only as "J.M." had seen the same phenomenon and written about it in an English journal. Both of them noticed that the spokes of a moving cart seemed to bend and distort when seen through the vertical slats of a fence. Though neither man foresaw the moving picture, Roget knew that the trick depended on persistence of vision. He couldn't observe, of course, that the slats did what the shutter of the camera and the projector were to do some sixty years later.

THE FIRST SHUTTERS—WITHOUT CAMERAS. The palings of the fence through which Roget watched the wheel of a moving cart in 1824 might be called the earliest form of shutter. They distorted, however, the thing he looked at. As in his sketch above—which leaves out the palings—only the vertical spokes seemed straight. (*From the* Transactions of the Royal Society.) Five years later the Belgian scientist Joseph Antoine Ferdinand Plateau reversed Roget's phenomenon. He made a distorted object look normal. He drew a misshapen head on a disk, and then brought it back to human shape by viewing it through a slotted disk—a true shutter—which revolved at a different speed from the disk with the picture. Plateau called his device the Anorthoscope (distorted view). The illustration at the right shows only one of the three heads that appeared when Plateau used a disk with three slots. If he used four, he got four heads. (*From Hopwood's* Living Pictures.)

THE DAZZLING TOP. The movies use persistence of vision to make a series of still photos look like real things in motion. When scientists first began to play with this phenomenon, they produced quite the opposite effect. By moving real things they made them look like something else. Abbé Nollet seems to have been the first to demonstrate this scientifically. By revolving a group of disks with variously colored sectors, Nollet showed how he could blend and change their hues. Whether he originated the *Toupie éblouissante* (dazzling top) illustrated below, or a toy maker developed it from the French priest's ideas, a wire and a glass rod, bent and twirled, produced the illusion of a lamp and its shade. As the Optic Wonder it was mounted on a top.

Men had been playing tricks with persistence of vision before persistence of vision played tricks with "J.M." and Roget. More than 1,800 years ago, the Greek mathematician Ptolemy observed that a colored sector of a revolving disk tinted the whole surface. About 1765 the physicist Abbé Jean-Antoine Nollet bedizened Ptolemy's trick and discovered new ones. He and his followers demonstrated that if you twirled something on a pivot, it would take on a new shape; a disk would look like a sphere, and a bent glass rod like a lamp shade. Toys appeared that made the eye see one object in more than one place at the same time—an idea that I feel sure meant more to grownups than to children. The next toy did just the opposite. It made two things appear in the same place.

Sir John Spins a Shilling

In the case of this toy there is a good deal of confusion about who invented it, and when and how. The French are apt to credit a man whom they think a fellow-countryman, Dr. J. A. Paris, with the invention of a device called the Thaumatrope. Though Paris was actually a Londoner, some English prefer the geologist Dr. W. A. Fitton. The French think Paris made the toy between 1823 and 1826, but both men may have done it in 1820. There is a legend about the distinguished astronomer and physicist Sir John Herschel and how he played a trick on a friend. Herschel is supposed to have told him he could see both sides of a coin at the same time, and then spun a shilling to prove it. Later the scientist denied that the friend was Paris or that he himself invented the illusion. The friend tried the same trick on Fitton. Then Fitton pulled a new one. He drew a bird on one side of a cardboard disk and a cage on the other, spun the disk by a string on each side,

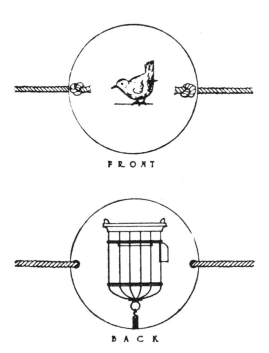

FRONT

BACK

TWO THINGS BECOME ONE. In the Thaumatrope (magical turning) there were two drawings on opposite sides of a pasteboard disk. The cage was inverted because it was seen from the back of the disk. When the device revolved, the cage appeared right side up with the bird inside.

and showed the bird sitting in the cage. If Fitton was really the inventor of the toy, Paris was more enterprising. He turned an honest penny—as well as a piece of cardboard—by marketing the device in London at the rather stiff price of seven shillings and sixpence; and he hired Cruikshank—famous later on as the illustrator of Dickens' novels —to draw some of the pictures. Paris' toy may or may not have been original, but by calling it the Thaumatrope he set the fashion of giving strange Greek and Latin names to a long series of devices for visualizing movement.

Roget's fence and Herschel's shilling started other experiments with persistence of vision. Between 1828 and 1831, Plateau of Brussels, a Frenchman named Aimé, and the British scientist Faraday reported some odd things they saw when they revolved a pair of notched disks. The front one, acting as a rudimentary shutter, played tricks with the appearance of both of them. In 1829 Plateau developed a true shutter (see page 32) to make a distorted object look normal. This slotted disk was to prove far more important than the vagaries of fences and shillings.

Moving Pictures at Last—But Without Photographs

Like the Thaumatrope, the next invention may seem no more than another scientific toy, but it was the first real step toward the motion picture. It didn't make a flat thing look like a solid one, and it didn't put two different things in the same place. Instead, it made a series of drawings look like a figure in motion. Here, at last, were moving pictures. They were only drawings, not photographs, but they had motion. Without camera, film, projector, or screen, this device produced the first animated cartoon.

Two men must share the credit. One was Plateau of Brussels; the other, Simon Ritter von Stampfer of Vienna. They worked quite independently but they invented the same device toward the end of 1832. It was a disk with a number of radiating slots; on the back were an equal number of figures drawn in successive stages of motion. The viewer spun the disk with the figures facing a mirror. Looking through the slots, he saw the figures move. Stampfer went a step further than Plateau. Although he marketed the disk that had to be seen in a mirror, he later proposed a handier type. This one had two disks revolving on a single axis. The viewer looked through the slotted disk and saw a figure moving on the other.

Plateau—the highest type of dedicated scientist—brought tragedy upon himself and mastered it. In 1829, his intense interest in optics led

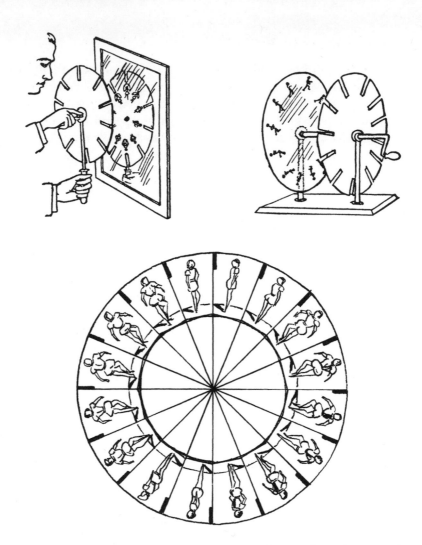

THE FIRST MOVING PICTURE MACHINES. The device that Plateau and Stampfer invented independently toward the end of 1832 resembled the drawing at top left (*from Arthur Edwin Krows's* The Talkies). In some versions slits nearer the center replaced the notches. When the toy was marketed, different sets of drawings on cardboard could be attached to the back of the metal disk. At the right is the double disk invented by Stampfer a little later (*also from Krows*). The third sketch is from one of the drawings furnished with Plateau's machine (*from* Films in Review). When Plateau and Stampfer named their devices, they helped set the fashion for classical terms that makes us accept words like cinematography, anamorphic lenses, Cinerama, and CinemaScope. Plateau called his the Phenakistiscope (deceitful view), and Stampfer used the term Stroboskop (whirling view).

him to stare at the sun for almost half a minute in order to test the effects of such a stimulus. The most important effect, unfortunately, was a growing blindness that became complete within fifteen years. Nevertheless he went on working out the problems of pictures in motion, relying on the eyes of others to check results. In 1849, when he was stone-blind, he used a glass disk for the figures; by putting a light behind it and hiding from view all but one of the slots, he was able to show moving pictures to a small group of people instead of only one. He even suggested using photographs, though he never attempted the formidable task of taking them.

Zoetrope—Most Popular of Movie Toys

Meanwhile another device for seeing drawings in motion had appeared. In 1834, William George Horner, distinguished mathematician, invented the Daedaleum. He named it after Daedalus (the legendary Cretan who is supposed to have made figures of men that seemed to move), but others marketed it as the Zoetrope or the Wheel of Life. Inside an upright pasteboard drum without a top, the viewer placed one

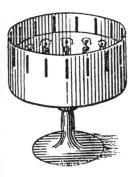

THE WHEEL OF LIFE. Probably the most popular of all the toys that played with persistence of vision, Horner's spinning cylinder of 1834 was appropriated and patented by a Frenchman in 1860 and by an American seven years later. The latter changed its name from the Daedaleum to the Zoetrope (life turning). In the drawing above at the left (*from* Le Cinéma: des origines à nos jours) you can see one of the many narrow strips of paper, each with different kinds of figures, that could be inserted in the cylinder. At the right are three out of twelve views of a monkey jumping over a fence from the back of a dog. (From a band made in the 1860's, *Francis Faragoh Collection.*)

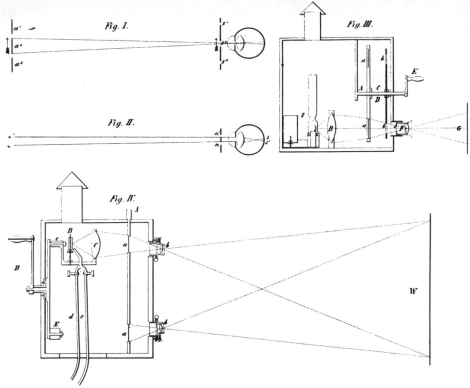

THE FIRST PROJECTORS. Uchatius' first and not too successful attempt to project drawings that seemed to move was probably as early as 1845. As in Fig. III above, he used the slotted disk of Plateau and Stampfer (b), but put his drawings on a glass one (a). He added a kerosene lamp and two lenses (B and F). The image on the screen (G) was too small and dim for the projector to be used as the teaching aid it was intended to be. The inventor might have employed a limelight, but the narrow slits in the opaque disk would still have limited the brightness of the pictures if they were thrown on a larger screen. So, in a second type of projector, which he revealed in 1853, he eliminated the shutter and achieved intermittent projection by revolving his light instead of the drawings. As shown in Fig. IV above, the drawings (a) were fixed in holes in a supporting surface (A); there were twelve of them in a circle. The limelight (B), with its gas pipes (d and e) passing freely through holes at the bottom, and a condensing lens (C), were counterbalanced by a weight (E), and turned by a handle (D). In front of each of the transparent drawings was another lens (b), and all twelve lenses could be so focused that the successive images would coincide on the screen (W). The drawings and a description of the projectors first appeared in a publication of the Vienna Academy of Science in 1853.

of a number of long strips of drawings. While the drum revolved on a pivot, he looked through slots in the upper part and saw, for example, a monkey jump over fence after fence or a juggler whirl a ball with his feet. If the Zoetrope was only a toy, it was a very popular one; I had one as a Christmas gift fully sixty years after it was first invented. Indeed, its popularity was so great that a tendency developed in later years to call all the disk devices Zoetropes or "zoetropic."

Movement at Last Projected

Thus far we have a magic lantern without continuous movement. We have twirling rods that create new shapes. We have a spinning toy that puts a bird in a cage. We have revolving disks and drums that show drawings in motion. But, until the middle of the nineteenth century, we have no machine for projecting these drawings.

The first device for throwing moving figures on a wall was developed between 1845 and 1853 by an Austrian artillery officer named Baron Franz von Uchatius. He seems to have anticipated Plateau's idea of using a glass disk with an opaque shutter. At any rate, he added a kerosene lamp and two lenses. The result was the first projection of moving pictures. But the combination of a weak lamp and a shutter with very narrow slits couldn't project a clear image larger than six inches square. So, in 1853, Uchatius used a powerful limelight, eliminated the shutter, and produced the odd machine that is shown on page 38. A resourceful inventor, he had developed "steel bronze" for cannons and used balloons for bombing Venice before he committed suicide in 1881.

It is interesting—and in a curious way prophetic—that an Austrian field marshal asked Uchatius to develop a projector as a means of military instruction. Thus, more than a hundred years ago, an officer recognized that moving pictures (even though they were only drawings at that time) could be a teaching aid for the army. They were to become a most potent weapon almost ninety years later, when inventors had added photography to projection.

Enter Photography

While disks and cylinders were making drawings move, artists as well as scientists were working on something that would banish drawings from the development of the motion picture. This, of course, was photography. One of its inventors aptly called it "a chemical and physical process that gives nature the ability to reproduce itself."

The story of photography is a long one, full of accidents, coincidences, and confusions. One essential was a camera. From an observation by Aristotle, it developed very slowly into the "camera obscura" of the Renaissance. At first this meant a "darkened room" in which a tiny hole in a blacked-out window threw an image of the outside world on the opposite wall. Late in the sixteenth century, the room had become a portable box with a lens, a diaphragm, and a mirror to turn the picture right side up. Essentially a true camera, it had to wait two hundred and fifty more years for someone to invent the means for making, developing, and printing photographs.

The secret lay in certain silver compounds that change color when light shines on them. As far back as 1614, an Italian doctor noticed that silver nitrate in contact with an organic substance turned dark on exposure to light. In the early eighteen-hundreds—the time when the

THE INVENTION OF THE CAMERA. The camera is not so new as many of us think. The basic idea goes back to Aristotle, who noticed that the image of the sun could pass through a small hole, and be seen on a surface behind it. Before the Arabian astronomer Alhazen died about 1040, he described how to use this principle for observing an eclipse, and other men, in the Middle Ages and the early Renaissance, followed him. Among them were Copernicus and Kepler, who named the device the camera obscura. Opposite top, is perhaps the first published picture of a camera obscura; it was used to observe an eclipse on January 24, 1544 (*from Gemma Frisius'* De radio astronomico et geometrico liber *of 1545*). Some forty years earlier, however, Leonardo da Vinci made a crude sketch of a camera obscura (below Frisius' drawings) in notebooks that were not published for almost 400 years. (*Courtesy Kate Steinitz, the Elmer Belt Library of Vinciana, resketched by Carlo Pedretti.*) He was the first artist to note that the "darkened room" could project "on a piece of white paper" an inverted view of a scene outside. In the sixteenth and seventeenth centuries the camera obscura became an adjunct of art as well as astronomy. By 1685, when the sketch opposite bottom appeared in *Joannes Zahn's* Oculus Artificialis Teledioptricus, someone had added a mirror to turn the view right side up; others, a lens and a diaphragm to improve the picture. Gradually the room had shrunk to a box, and anyone who stretched a piece of paper across the end could become an "artist" by sketching what he saw. A new device, our modern camera, was trying to grow out of the old one. After scientists discovered the proper photographic chemicals, the Latin word for "room" became the name of the apparatus with which laymen have taken millions upon millions of pictures.

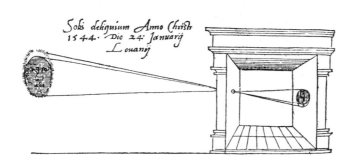

Solis deliquium Anno Christi
1544. Die 24. Januarij
Louanij

FIg Z

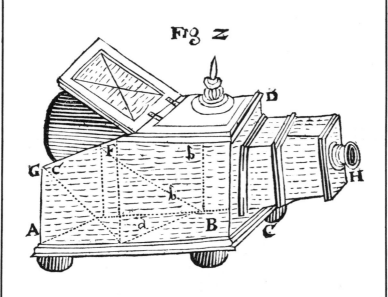

disks and cylinders were beginning to spin—men were experimenting with other silver salts. By using a camera they found that they could record on paper the lights and shades of a figure or a landscape. But they also discovered that their chemicals had an unfortunate habit of turning blacker and blacker as time went on. Someone had to learn how to "fix" these unstable substances.

Sometime between 1816 and 1822—such an authority as Beaumont Newhall believes it was 1816—a Frenchman with the unlikely name of Nicéphore Niépce made the first true photograph, but it soon faded into darkness.

In the eighteen-thirties the Englishman W. H. Fox Talbot created a

"PHOTOGENIC DRAWINGS." More than a hundred and sixty years ago Thomas Wedgwood, son of the noted potter, made the first attempt to reproduce nature through the effect of light on silver salts. He failed in attempts to use a camera. Dying at thirty-four, he got no further than making silhouettes of objects laid on sensitized paper. The results were what Herschel later called "negatives." Unfortunately, Wedgwood didn't know how to "fix" these images, and they could be safely looked at only "by the light of candles or lamps." Niépce, after failing in the same way with the first photograph made with a camera, copied engravings by laying them on stone or metal coated with a kind of asphalt used in lithography. Sunlight bleached and hardened this material—which would not fade or darken—while a solvent washed away the unaffected background. With a camera he produced in 1826 a crude photo on asphalt-coated pewter, which is still preserved. Niépce called his process heliography (sun drawing). Fox Talbot, who first succeeded in making permanent negatives and printing from them on paper positives, called the results photogenic drawings. Talbot's silhouette of a piece of lace, reproduced above, resembled the work of Wedgwood. (*Courtesy George Eastman House.*)

negative, in which light areas of the scene appeared dark, and dark areas light. He took his negative on a thin piece of paper, and, when he waxed the paper, it became transparent enough to make a positive print on another piece of paper.

Next came a scene designer named Louis Jacques Mandé Daguerre, who went into partnership with Niépce. Although he was quite untrained in science, he discovered in 1837 a new and highly successful method of photography. He created on burnished metal what he called a daguerreotype; the elder Oliver Wendell Holmes called it "the mirror with a memory." It preserved, each in a single copy, the image of our forefathers.

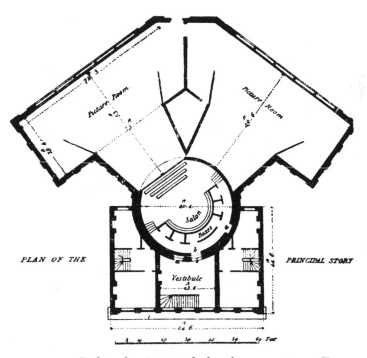

THE DIORAMA. Before he invented the daguerreotype, Daguerre devised a kind of changing view in a building he called a Diorama. By painting a daytime view of a scene on the front of a transparent drop and a moonlit view on the back, he could change from day to night by reducing the light from the front and bringing in illumination from the rear. The plan above is of the Diorama he designed for London in 1823. The circular portion where the audience sat revolved after the first spectacle to give them a second show. (*From Helmut and Alison Gernsheim's L. J. M. Daguerre.*)

Daguerre's method led only to the popular tintype of a century ago. Talbot's negatives—changing from paper to glass to film through fifty years—led finally to the Kodak camera and the modern motion picture.

Making Motion out of "Stills"

The first negatives on glass were made about 1847. Four years later an English sculptor and photographer, Frederick Scott Archer, perfected the "wet plate" process. These plates were hard to handle. Each one had to be prepared in a dark room just before it was used. This made

STILLS POSED TO SIMULATE ACTION. Two of the pairs of stereoscopic photographs that Sellers made in 1861 for viewing on a kind of paddle-wheel device. After the preparation and exposure of each wet plate, the producer of this early photographic motion picture moved the position of his children ever so slightly. (*Courtesy Rune Waldekranz.*)

rapid exposure impossible. The only way to photograph a figure in motion was to stop the motion. After one shot had been taken and another wet plate put in the camera, the figure had to move into a new position for a new photograph. This was simple enough in the case of a machine; in 1860 a Frenchman named Pierre Desvignes did it with a stationary steam engine, and viewed the result with the Plateau-Stampfer disks. A year later, Coleman Sellers of Philadelphia slowly and laboriously took a series of stills of his two children, one of them using a hammer. In 1870 another Philadelphian, Henry Renno Heyl, was bold enough to try this with a waltzing couple and an acrobat.

MOTION PICTURES THROUGH POSED STILLS. Some of the photographs that Henry Renno Heyl took in 1870. (*Courtesy the Franklin Institute.*)

The methods that the two Philadelphians used for showing their pictures were somewhat different. Sellers pasted his prints on a kind of paddle-wheel device. Each picture moved toward the eye long enough to satisfy persistence of vision and then moved away. The principle was a little like that of the "riffle book" whose bent-back leaves, when released by the thumb, showed a rapid succession of pictures that gave the impression of movement. Heyl projected his pictures by improving on Uchatius' first device. He mounted a cycle of eighteen photographs on a disk and passed them around mechanically in front of his light, while a shutter exposed them. Heyl must have had quite a bright light and a good lens, for on February 5, 1870, when he first showed his moving pictures, he is reported to have satisfied an audience of 1,500 people.

VIEWING PHOTOGRAPHS IN MOTION. An early attempt to take stills of people in motion was made by the English scientist F. H. Wenham in 1852, but the man who was photographed using a mortar and pestle said he "never worked like *that!*" When Sellers did a better job with his children at play, he had in mind two ways of viewing them. At the left is a device that he patented in 1861. It carried twenty-six photographs on an endless belt. (*From E. G. Lutz's* Animated Cartoons.) Actually he appears to have taken only six photographs—those of his two children—and to have shown them in the paddle-wheel device at the right. (*From Ben J. Lubschez's* The Story of the Motion Picture.)

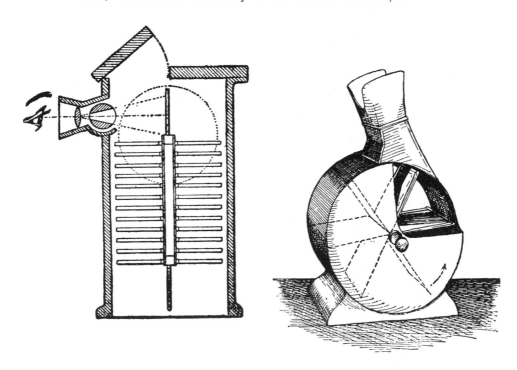

The Amazing Muybridge

A horse instead of a human being was perhaps the first thing to be photographed systematically in natural, unposed, and rapid motion. This developed as the result of a bet among race track buffs. The man who took the pictures—and later projected them—was the most picturesque and controversial figure in the pioneer stage of the movies. Again we come upon confusions.

The name of this man was odd enough—Eadweard Muybridge. Odder still, he made it out of Edward James Muggeridge, as he had been known before he left his native England. At the peak of his career, he looked somewhat like Walt Whitman ready to play King Lear. He had barely started his experiments in photographing motion when he killed his wife's lover, and was tried and acquitted. Except for this interlude, which, together with travel, occupied him for a year or so, Muybridge worked at his project in California between 1872 and 1879, and elsewhere into the eighties. Through much of this time, we find conflicts of opinion about why his project was financed and about how much aid he got and from whom.

A Bet—and Other Disputes

The various versions of how Muybridge became the first cameraman in movie history are as picturesque as the man himself. The most popular and perhaps the most dubious story is that Leland Stanford—a former governor of California, founder with his wife of Leland Stanford Junior University, and owner of a string of race horses—wagered someone in 1872 that all four feet of a trotter were off the ground at one point in his stride. According to this account, he bet $25,000 and then spent $40,000 on the Muybridge experiments to prove it. It is said to have been some of Stanford's friends who made the bet—you can take your choice between a $5,000 stake and $25,000—and the ex-governor obligingly agreed to decide the matter photographically. Stanford chose Muybridge to take snapshots of one of his horses. In 1872, according to the photographer, he settled the matter "in a few days," in spite of the fact that he had to use a heavy camera and wet plates that took minutes to prepare before each shot. This is supposed to have fired Stanford with a desire to make more studies of the horse in motion, and to spend anywhere from $15,000 to $25,000 in doing so.

The method Muybridge later used was to place a row of cameras along a track and set them off in rapid succession as the animal went by. But who was responsible for this idea? As far back as 1860, someone had suggested using a hundred cameras. Stanford's interest may have been heightened by a French book, *La Machine Animale* (Animal Mechanism), dealing in part with the movements of horses. It was written by a scientist named Marey, of whom you will hear more in the next chapter.

There has been a tendency to belittle Muybridge. Writers have called

MUYBRIDGE'S "STUDIO." On Leland Stanford's estate at Palo Alto, California, in 1878, Muybridge set up a battery of cameras in a long shed. Opposite them was a slanting background of white against which horses and other animals were photographed as they passed. At first he used twelve cameras, the lenses of which were twenty-one inches apart. The drawing above shows the battery when it was increased to twenty-four with only a foot between each lens. Sometimes he used four extra cameras so placed that they took oncoming or retreating shots, or could be centered on gymnasts whose movements were confined to a smaller area than the length of the track.

him eccentric and irresponsible, and credited other men with working out the technical problems. Actually Muybridge was a most expert photographer who had been employed by the United States government. Using wet plates, he had taken remarkable pictures of the West, some as large as seventeen by twenty-two inches.

The First Projection of Unposed Photos

The confusions and contradictions over Muybridge and his work increase when we turn to the question of who first projected unposed photographs of things in motion, and just when it was done. In 1880,

The Scientific American reported that on May 4 at a meeting of the San Francisco Art Association, Muybridge's "Zoögyroscope . . . threw upon the screen apparently the living, moving animals. Nothing was wanting but the clatter of the hoofs upon the turf." Supported by California periodicals, the report mentions pictures of a bull, greyhounds, deer, athletes, and even birds. Yet most histories of the early days of motion pictures ignore this showing and say that Parisians taught Muybridge the art of projection a couple of years later.

Film historians report, quite truly, that Muybridge's still photos made

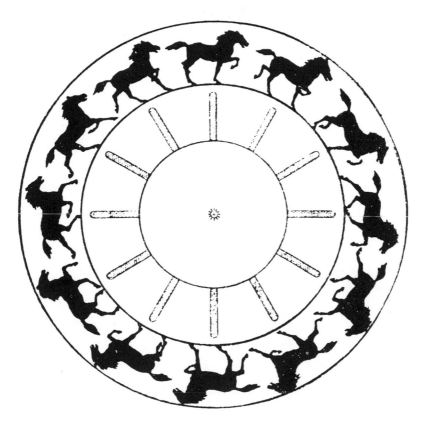

MUYBRIDGE'S HORSES ON PLATEAU'S DISK. Two years before Muybridge reached Paris in 1881, his photographs were already famous. They had appeared in French and British periodicals and been redrawn for use in the early moving picture devices. In 1879 *L'Illustration* sold strips for the Zoetrope, and the British magazine *The Field* drew crowds to its office window by mounting the horses in an improved version of this Wheel of Life turned by an electric motor.

THE HORSE IN MOTION. Here, in the second and third frames of a series taken in 1878, it is quite clear that all four of the horse's hoofs are off the ground at the same time. You can also see that each camera photographed a slightly different background. When Muybridge projected such pictures the visual effect must have been rather like a traveling shot of a rider or a stagecoach in a Western when a camera is mounted on an automobile moving parallel to the action. Muybridge used three methods of tripping the shutters—each for a different kind of motion. A swiftly moving horse broke a series of threads that set off the cameras. A sulky ran on metal rails connected electrically to the shutters. For slower-moving animals there was a machine like a music box to activate the shutters.

something of a stir when they were displayed and published in Paris in 1878. One American historian says that Meissonier—the French painter of cavalry horses in battle—was so excited by Muybridge's photographs that he got Stanford to send Muybridge to Paris in 1881, where Meissonier, according to this dubious authority, conceived the idea of having the photographs projected through a version of Uchatius' device. Another account says that Meissonier thought the pictures "didn't seem right," and rigged up a platform propelled on rails so that he could study a running horse. Still another version of the story has it that Marey —whose book had inspired Stanford—was the man who guided Muybridge toward projection. A French writer, however, tells us that the American brought his own projector to a meeting organized by Marey, which fits in with the record of the show in San Francisco.

In London, as well as in Paris, Muybridge triumphed. Lecture followed lecture before learned societies. When he spoke to members of the Royal Society of London, his audience included Gladstone, Huxley, Tennyson, and the man who was to become King Edward VII. In June of 1882 Muybridge returned to America for new triumphs and new work. From the spring of 1884 till the autumn of 1885, under sponsorship of the University of Pennsylvania he took some 30,000 dry-plate photographs of animals (including lions and kangaroos) in action, athletes, and nude young women skipping rope. At the Chicago World's Fair of 1893, he displayed 20,000 of those Philadelphia pictures—though probably not of the active young women—next door to the Midway show where Little Egypt demonstrated a different kind of motion.

Despite all the conflicts and confusions over Muybridge and his work, a few things are certain. There can be no question that his battery of cameras took the first systematic instantaneous photographs of successive stages of natural, unposed movements of animals, nor that these photographs were the first of their kind ever projected in public. In reviewing his first show in San Francisco, a magazine proclaimed with some truth: "Mr. Muybridge has laid the foundation of a new method of entertaining the people." When the writer went on to predict that "his instantaneous, photographic, magic-lantern zoetrope will make the round of the civilized world," his vision was not so clear. Other men and other devices were to give Little Egypt and many other moving figures global circulation.

THE ZOÖPRAXOGRAPHICAL HALL. Muybridge was as fond of Greek words as all the other moving picture inventors. He called his first projector the Zoöpraxiscope (life action view). When he was invited to the Chicago World's Fair of 1893 he exhibited his pictures in the Zoöpraxographical Hall. At his demonstrations in the '80's he showed separate still photographs of horses and other animals, and then the beasts in motion. The contrast must have been extraordinary, judging from an article in *The Illustrated London News* of 1882. Earlier, Muybridge had sent the writer stills of horses, and the Briton told how distressed he had been by "the unutterably hideous aspect of the attitudes assumed by the animal." But, when he saw the pictures projected "by a Magic Lantern Run Mad (with method in the madness) . . . the ugly animals suddenly became mobile and beautiful." Most, if not all, of the disks that Muybridge showed in Chicago were the result of the photographs he had made in 1884 and 1885 at the University of Pennsylvania in Philadelphia. There he stuck to his battery of cameras, but, besides twenty-four on one side, he added at each end of his field a vertical bank of cameras about three inches apart.

Chapter

4

The Pioneers of the Eighteen-Nineties

I_N EUROPE, Muybridge's galloping horses astonished and fascinated the men of science, and inspired a few of them—and some professional photographers—to join the experimenters who had been fruitlessly struggling for twenty years with the problem of recording motion. Yet when the problem was solved, in the decade after Muybridge returned to America, it was solved in quite a different way from the way of Muybridge. The solution involved one camera and one lens and—most important of all—a strip of film. The man who made the most effective camera was William Kennedy Laurie Dickson.

Many Ways to Moving Pictures

Muybridge left few fervent disciples behind him and perhaps only one imitator. The imitator, Ottomar Anschütz, used twenty-four cameras, but they were so tiny that he could group them all within a few feet of one another. He mounted his pictures on a revolving disk and by means of an electric flash showed them without projection.

The new experimenters, as well as almost all the veterans, had a reasoned feeling that they must use a single camera. Yet they used it in weirdly different ways. Some dropped plate after plate into position behind the lens. Some took photographs on the rim of a disk. One inventor made ten pictures of a runner on one plate. Others went mad for lenses and fastened anywhere from two to more than twenty on a single camera.

MULTIPLE CAMERAS AND LENSES. In the 1880's two Frenchmen developed a fondness for multiple lenses and cameras. During the last half of that decade Albert Londe used six, nine, and finally twelve cameras. (*From Hopwood's* Living Pictures.) His purpose was to record changes of expression on the faces of women in an insane asylum. With the camera below, he made six photographs about an inch in diameter on one plate. By 1892 he was photographing tightrope walkers and trapeze artists at the rate of twelve shots in a second and a half. To follow the movement in this illustration from *Georges Sadoul's* Histoire Générale du Cinéma, read from left to right on all three lines. Londe's pictures were made for study, not projection. Louis Le Prince, on the other hand, designed a complex of lenses on a single camera. No one can be sure that he used this device, for the record of his work is almost as baffling as the story of his death.

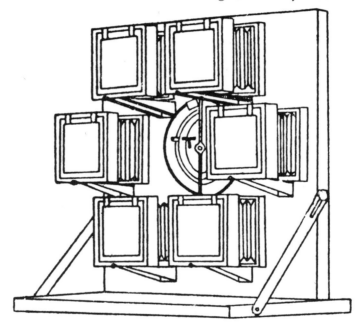

At first glance, that last operation may seem a bit unpromising; but along with the lenses went the pregnant notion of using a long strip of sensitized material instead of dry plates. At the start, this was paper; later celluloid, and finally film. By the time the proper vehicle was ready—close to 1890—most of the cameras had sloughed all but one lens and were ready to take moving pictures.

In his patent applications between 1886 and 1888, he gave himself plenty of leeway by mentioning "one or more lenses." In one device he proposed to use eight in one vertical bank and eight in another, with a strip of paper-backed emulsion behind each. There seems some evidence that he took short movies on paper with a one-lens camera in 1888, and demonstrated a projector before an official of the Paris Opera House two years later. Le Prince became the most dramatic figure in the history of the movies when he boarded a train from Dijon to Paris in 1890 and was never seen again.

Marey—an Inspirer Inspired

If Muybridge left no disciples behind him in Europe, he turned one scientist into an able and devoted explorer of all the possibilities of motion picture photography. He was Jules Étienne Marey, a physiologist at the University of Paris. There was a curious affinity between the two men. Born in the same year, 1830, and destined to die in the same

year, 1904, one was a professional photographer who turned to the scientific study of movement, the other a scientist who took up photography
to further his researches. It was the horse that brought the two together, and changed the path of their lives. Before Marey met Muybridge, he had been studying the gait of horses through pneumatic bulbs
fastened under their hoofs and connected by rubber tubes to a recording device. It was proper—all but inevitable—that the Frenchman who
may have inspired Stanford through his book *La Machine Animale*
should turn to photography after seeing Muybridge's pictures of horses
in motion.

In 1882, the year after Muybridge's Paris show, Marey tried two very
different methods of photographing motion.

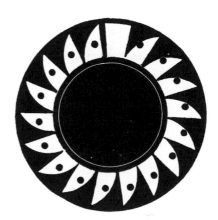

JANSSEN'S CAMERA, 1874. Above is the machine that Janssen set
up to photograph the transit of Venus across the sun. A clock-
work mechanism revolved and stopped both the disk and a circular shutter, taking a picture every seventy-two seconds. The
lens caught the image of the sun in a mirror outdoors. At the
right are the kind of pictures that Janssen's camera made. Actually it took forty-eight photographs on each of four disks. Here,
in an illustration from Marey's *Mouvement* (1894), the French
scientist seems to have arranged 17 of the images to show the
complete transit of the planet. (*Courtesy University of California
Press.*)

The first was an improvement on a device invented and used by the French astronomer Pierre Jules César Janssen in December, 1874. He had used a sequence camera to record the passage of Venus across the face of the sun. Curiously enough, he used only one principle of the modern motion picture camera—intermittent motion. For the rest he went back to the disks of Plateau and Stampfer and wedded them to the wet plate. Since all he wanted was an accurate record of the behavior of Venus crossing the sun, he never tried to develop a projector. Marey, with the dry plate at his command, invented what he called the "photographic gun." This mobile camera looked like a shotgun crossed with a revolver. In its muzzle was a lens. At the other end, above the gun grip and trigger, Marey had a cylindrical chamber in which a dry plate revolved. He developed this first of hand-held motion picture cameras in order to "shoot" birds in flight.

Marey's second try in 1882 may seem rather off-track. Changing Muy-

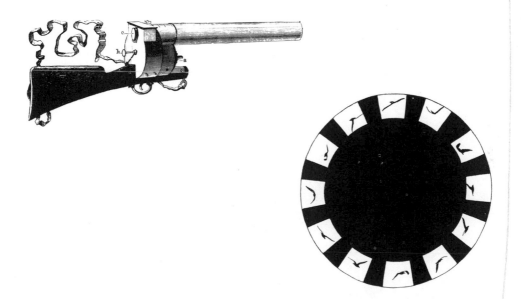

MAREY'S CAMERA. Because the dry plate had become widely available by 1882, Marey was able to take faster exposures than Janssen could. Marey's revolving plate made twelve pictures in a second. At the right is a positive print from one of Marey's plates (*from Jean Vivié's* Historique et développement de la technique cinématographique).

bridge's method, he photographed on a single plate many different stages of movement. To get as much definition as possible, he shot white figures against a black background. The purpose of what he called chronophotography was always exclusively scientific. "It is not the most interesting pictures," he said, "that are the most useful."

Within a few years, however, Marey was through with glass plates and overlapping figures. By 1887 he was using sensitized strips of paper in a camera with intermittent movement. When Marey showed his pictures and explained his method to Edison at the Paris Exposition in

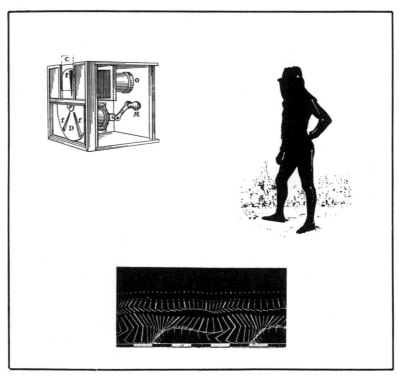

MOVIES ON A SINGLE PLATE. Employing one camera, Marey put all his pictures on a single plate. To a conventional camera, he added a circular shutter turned by a crank, which exposed the whole plate on each revolution. (*From* Le Cinéma: des origines à nos jours.) When he photographed a white-clothed man in motion against a black background, the overlaps were confusing. So he clothed his walker in black, and added white lines to define arms, legs, and feet, and put a dot on the hat. (*From Jean Vivié's* Historique et développement de la technique cinématographique.)

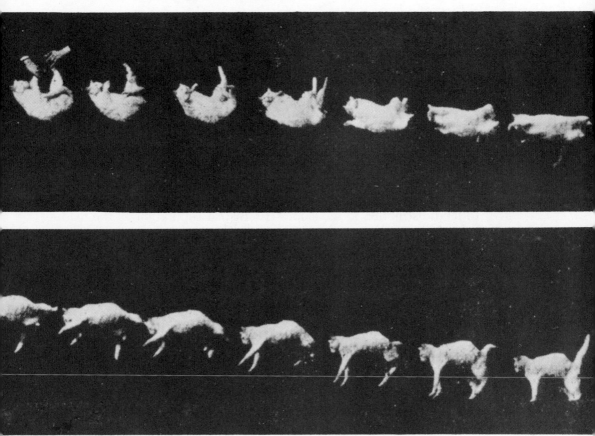

MAREY STUDIES MOVEMENT WITH FILM. When Marey began to use film instead of paper in a camera of his own design he was soon able to take as many as 120 pictures per second with shutter speeds as high as a thousandth of a second. It was invaluable when he made possibly the first experiment in slow motion—shots of a cat dropped back-downward and landing on its feet. (*From Jean Vivié's* Historique et développement de la technique cinématographique.)

the fall of 1889, he was using paper-based celluloid strips—something that the man from West Orange may have noted to his profit. Marey was soon combining his camera with a microscope. He was content, however, to mount his celluloid frames on the glass disk of Uchatius and Muybridge for leisurely scientific inspection. It was not till 1892 that he designed a modern type of projector.

Tragedy Defeats Le Prince and Friese-Greene

Following Marey come Louis Le Prince and William Friese-Greene. Between 1886 and 1888, Le Prince—a Frenchman working mainly in England and America—developed a very ingenious camera in which eight lenses made successive images on a band of paper, and then another set of eight lenses did the same to a second strip of paper parallel to the first. Then the same process was repeated. He seems to have turned to a single lens and had some success with it. Le Prince became the most dramatic figure in the history of the movies when, in 1890, he boarded a French train and was never seen again.

William Green acquired "Friese" through marriage, and added an "e" to lend distinction to his name. His British reputation as the leading pioneer is based on his claim that he took moving pictures on paper in 1887, and on celluloid two years later. So meticulous a student as Raymond Spottiswoode—English himself—doubts that Friese-Greene used his camera successfully before 1888. Spottiswoode also doubts that Friese-Greene's projector could or did work.

Nevertheless, Friese-Greene is an appealing figure, worth more space in this book than his camera should give him. He took stereoscopic motion pictures in 1889, though he had no means of projecting them. Toward the turn of the century he found no market for a color process very like the later Kinemacolor. Adversity pursued him. Although he owned numerous photographic galleries at one time, he landed in debtors' prison at the end of five years of designing motion-picture cameras. After twenty years of comparative obscurity, he fell dead just as he concluded a speech during a public dinner of industry leaders who had all but forgotten who he was. They found only one shilling and tenpence in his worn old purse. If his end was not so mysterious and intriguing as Le Prince's, it capped a life dramatic enough to furnish the plot for a British feature film in 1951 called *The Magic Box*.

Drawings in Motion Again

While Marey and a few others were struggling with the problem of photographic movement, another Frenchman busied himself with a very different matter—entertaining the public. Émile Reynaud shunned photography and devoted himself to projecting animated drawings. In 1877 he improved the Zoetrope, and soon turned it into a projector. About ten years later, he developed a very complex machine for entertaining a paying audience with fiction thrown on a screen. In 1892 Reynaud

AMONG THE FIRST MOTION PICTURES. In early June, 1889, Friese-Greene used his stereoscopic camera in Hyde Park, London. These two very worn frames are reproduced through the courtesy of his son, Graham H. Friese-Greene. The other frames—taken on celluloid like those in 3-D, but with sprocket holes—come from a film exposed in Chelsea. Note the perforations near the margins. So much change of position between the first frame and the next suggests that Friese-Greene's exposures were nearer three or four a second than the twelve he claimed. (*From* The Elizabethan.)

showed his Théâtre Optique in what we would call a dime museum, and by 1900 he had entertained, they say, about half a million spectators. His shows included three fables or comic episodes that lasted from five to fifteen minutes each. At first he drew his figures on bands of translucent material, and finally on film. He appears to have been the first to perforate celluloid or film before he used it. In 1896 he experimented with photographs; but he had no interest in science, and was quite content to make his mark as the first commercial producer and exhibitor of what we now call animated cartoons.

Film Solves the Problem

The paper negative of Fox Talbot was the first step in the advancement of still photography. Many years later, paper again led the way in the development of the motion picture, but only for a very few years. Transparent celluloid—put on the market in 1888–89—had an even briefer reign. Too thick and stiff to be used in sufficient lengths, it was replaced within a year by flexible film. This new, though somewhat similar plastic was the perfect medium for the motion picture. Hundreds of photographs—ultimately thousands—could be taken and shown in rapid succession. The public recognized the prime importance of this new material when it made "the films" a synonym for "the movies."

Bands of paper, celluloid, and finally film speeded up enormously the attempts to develop motion picture cameras and projectors. From 1886 to 1896, the experimenters are too numerous to catalogue. As to the leadership, chauvinism colors the choice. Thomas A. Edison and Thomas Armat for a long time took the bows in America; Le Prince, Marey, and the Lumières in France; the Skladanowsky brothers in Germany; and William Friese-Greene in England. Between 1886 and 1888, Le Prince, Marey, and Friese-Greene, in that order, led the pack patent-wise and photo-wise. Edison has been credited with the development of the first thoroughly efficient camera. Also, he won in the motion picture field, as he did elsewhere, a towering reputation. It seems to be out of proportion to his own personal and original contributions.

Edison—"Collective Inventor"

To the picturesque figures in the history of the motion picture—the blinded Plateau, the mysterious Le Prince, the murderer Muybridge, and the ruined Friese-Greene—we must add an equally remarkable American, the deafened Thomas Alva Edison.

Edison had only three months of formal education, yet he took out

REYNAUD'S COMPLEX PROJECTOR. Reynaud's machine, which projected his animated cartoons at the Théâtre Optique from 1892 to 1900, used large reels for perhaps the first time. They drew a long strip of colored sketches between a combination of mirror and lens that projected them as five- or six-foot images on a translucent screen. The audience, seated on the other side of the screen, saw not only these drawings but also painted backgrounds thrown by another lantern. Reynaud synchronized a musical score with his drawings. (*From Georges Sadoul's* Histoire Générale du Cinéma.)

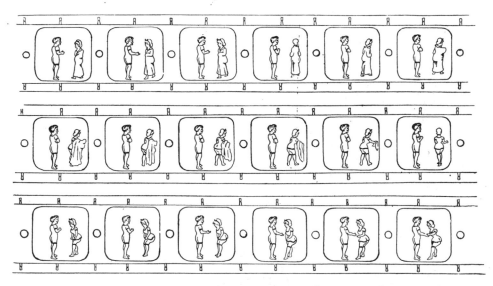

A REYNAUD CARTOON WITH PERFORATIONS. This is a redrawing of 18 frames out of 636 that made up a bathing comedy of 1894. The circles between the frames are the perforations that Reynaud used as early as 1889. Somewhat later, Dickson used a row of holes at one margin, then rows at each edge. (*From* Le Cinéma: des origines à nos jours.)

more than 1,000 patents during some sixty years of active work. He was able to do this for a number of reasons. Roger Burlingame in his synthesis of America's machine age, *Engines of Democracy*, points out that the Edison incandescent bulb was "not a basic invention. . . . it was an improvement by economic command of technic." According to Burlingame, Edison applied the same method to a host of widely different projects. And yet, as Burlingame says: "It is confidently believed by multitudes of Americans that he was the 'inventor' of the incandescent lamp, the electric railway, multiplex telegraphy, motion pictures, the storage battery, the stock ticker, and other matters with which he had even less to do. Edison was alert to all the stirrings of invention in Europe and America, and ready and able to make a success out of the failure of someone else. Like George Westinghouse, he practiced 'collective invention,' maintaining and guiding a large and efficient staff to work by trial and error on his projects."

Edison's method of work has succeeded in confusing the search for the inventor of the motion picture. Like many another writer, Terry Ramsaye, author of *A Million and One Nights*, asserted that there is no "motion picture film machine," since 1888, "that is not descended by traceable steps from the Kinetoscope." However true that may be, Burlingame added that "no basic part of the kinetoscope was original with Edison." So much for Edison's use and development of other men's ideas. His policy of collective invention has obscured until lately the major part played by the man to whom Edison, busy with "many inventions," entrusted his motion picture project—William Kennedy Laurie Dickson.

A Maze of Misstatements

Through many years of intensive research Gordon Hendricks has been able to provide in *The Edison Motion Picture Myth* some measure of Dickson's accomplishment. He has also done much to correct the distorted chronology of the Kinetoscope, and the errors as to dates and materials involved. These errors have fascinated many besides the present writer, and led them and their public astray. Their discovery must cast suspicion on the dates of many other men and their inventions.

Edison made many claims. Dickson was chary of dates when he and his sister first wrote about the invention of the Kinetoscope in an 1894 issue of *The Century Magazine*. But in the course of time he began to pin things down to dates about two years earlier than the evidence that Hendricks later drew, mainly from the copious files of the Edison

Laboratory National Monument of West Orange. For instance, Dickson claimed, in 1933, that he got hold of Eastman's new film at a meeting of the New York Camera Club in 1888; but Hendricks provides pretty convincing evidence that it was 1889. Edison's records show that Dickson bought Kodak film in September, 1889. Dickson says that when Edison examined the film as he was about to leave for Paris in August, 1889, he said: "Good, we can now do the trick—just work like hell." In 1933 Dickson gave out a fascinating tale about what happened when his employer returned. In one version Edison came to the factory the day he got back, October 6, 1889; in another, a week later. Anyhow, as the story goes, Edison was in for two surprises. Dickson had wangled a special photographic building at a cost of $516.64; and, using the new film, he showed Edison a talking picture on a screen. According to the young Englishman:

> I was seen to advance and address Mr. Edison from the small 4-foot screen; small, because of the restricted size of the room. I raised my hat, smiled, and said, "Good morning, Mr. Edison, glad to see you back. Hope you like the kineto-phone [they had been working on talkies]. To show the synchronization I will lift my hand and count up to ten."

What is Film?

Dictionaries derive the word from the Anglo-Saxon *filmen*, "a thin skin." They define the common, or nonphotographic variety as "a thin or light covering," "a very thin skin," "a membrane."

In photography, film is not a skin or covering. It is the base plus a coating of sensitized emulsion. Thus the skin has become the flesh.

Many have confused film with celluloid. They are alike yet different.

Celluloid—as invented by the Englishman Alexander Parkes in 1855, given its name by the Americans John W. and Isaiah Hyatt—was nitrocellulose (gun cotton) combined with camphor and alcohol.

This celluloid was transparent and strong but rather stiff.

Film—as processed rather differently by the Reverend Hannibal Goodwin in 1887 and by Henry W. Reichenbach for Eastman two years later—added fusel oil and amyl acetate (banana oil) to the substances in celluloid.

This film was strong and transparent yet most flexible.

According to this story, Dickson had developed a film camera and a projector by the fall of 1889. According to the records of Edison's plant, Dickson was still working on a scheme to make very tiny pictures on a cylinder linked to a phonograph recording machine. (Later Edison both affirmed and denied the existence of screen projection at this time.) Hendricks believes that if Dickson had already developed the peephole Kinetoscope (see page 71), he couldn't have used it for projection; further, the machine wasn't exhibited privately until May, 1891, or publicly until 1893. Though Dickson and other Edison employees have said that celluloid and Eastman film were used in 1888 and 1889, Hendricks states that the first moving picture wasn't taken until the fall of 1889, and none was made on film till 1891.

Why all these errors and inaccuracies, all these mistakes in favor of earlier dates for Edison's work? For a few years, it could have been a matter of egos. From 1897 through 1900 and on, Edison was involved in lawsuits against competitors. Did his witnesses commit perjury? Was Dickson's memory a bit faulty by 1933?

"YOU PRESS THE BUTTON." An advertisement in *The Scientific American* of 1889. By this time you could develop the film yourself instead of sending the camera back to Rochester. At first the camera had used "stripping film"; this was an emulsion supported by a strip of paper from which it could be removed and mounted on glass. In 1889 one of Eastman's technicians, Henry W. Reichenbach, developed a true film for the Kodak. Before, however, a clergyman and amateur photographer named Hannibal Goodwin had applied for a patent on the idea of flexible film, and some twenty-five years later his heirs and assigns got $5,-000,000 from Eastman as the result of a law suit. Eastman gave an amusing explanation of the name for his camera: "Philologically . . . the word 'kodak' is as meaningless as a child's first 'goo.' Terse, abrupt to the point of rudeness, literally bitten off by firm and unyielding consonants at both ends, it snaps like a camera shutter in your face. What more could one ask?"

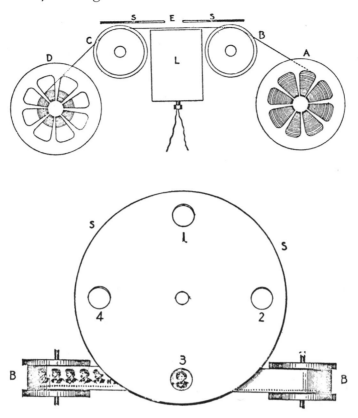

AN EARLY DICKSON-EDISON VIEWING DEVICE. In 1891 *Harper's Weekly* printed these sketches, "made by Mr. Edison for this article." The upper is viewed from above and the compartment L contains the illuminating bulb. S is the shutter, with E indicating one of the four apertures in it. These apertures are numbered 1, 2, 3, and 4 in the lower drawing. The film ran horizontally, as in Technirama and VistaVision cameras, but the picture was round, as in the first Kodaks.

Deaf Edison Foresees the Talkies

There was only one date in Dickson's magazine article of 1894. It appeared in the preface written and signed by Edison:

> In the year 1887, the idea occurred to me that it was possible to devise an instrument which should do for the eye what the phonograph does for the ear, and that by a combination of the two, all motion and sound could be recorded and reproduced simultaneously.

The idea may well have occurred to Edison in 1887. And, whatever the date when he set Dickson to work on it, the linking of sound and pictures obsessed him for twenty years. When he first showed his Kinetoscope to the public, he couldn't resist bragging:

> The Kinetoscope is only a small model illustrating the present stage of progress but with each succeeding month new possibilities are brought into view. I believe that in coming years by my own work and the work of Dickson, Muybridge [,] Marie [Marey] and others who will doubtless enter the field, that grand opera can be given at the Metropolitan Opera House at New York without any material change from the original, and with artists and musicians long since dead.

While most of the Kinetoscopes that swarmed over the country were silent machines, some of the machines that he sold to the penny arcades had earphones through which the lonely viewer heard a musical accompaniment—a strain from *Norma*, a singer's voice, or a band march.

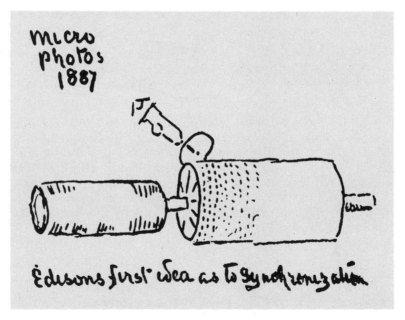

THE FIRST TALKIE MACHINE. To the left, in this sketch by Dickson, is the cylinder of the phonograph and, to the right, a larger cylinder covered with a spiral of photographs so tiny that the viewer had to examine them through a small microscopic eyepiece. In spite of Dickson's date of 1887, it is unlikely that the device took shape until some years later. (*Courtesy Earl Theisen Collection.*)

From a Cylinder of Celluloid to a Strip of Film

Because Edison wanted to "illustrate" his phonograph, he started Dickson on the task of recording pictures on the same kind of cylinder that his talking machine used. This meant a spiral of tiny photographs. These began at "pinhead size," one thirty-second of an inch, and had to be seen through a microscopic eyepiece. Later Dickson made quarter-inch pictures on a celluloid-covered cylinder. The results were not too sharp, yet Edison kept poor Dickson struggling with this drum-shaped abortion. After Edison had seen Marey's pictures in 1889, he decided to try another approach to motion pictures. However, Dickson kept on with the cylinder until the fall of 1890, according to Hendricks. At an Edison exhibition in the spring of that year at the Lenox Lyceum in New York, he tried the projection of pictures on a glass plate, possibly à la Anschütz. However, before this performance Dickson had been experimenting with celluloid strips, as Marey had done. He used rather short lengths joined together and notched along the top to drive them horizontally past the lens. Dickson wanted something more flexible. One of his stories was that he got a small piece of Eastman film at a meeting in New York in the summer of 1888, and another that in September of the next year he sent $2.50 to Rochester "for one roll Kodak film for which please accept thanks." However, Gordon Hendricks has proven that this material was for use in astronomical experiments and was not connected with Dickson's motion picture work. At any rate, Edison gave up imitating the form and movement of his beloved phonograph.

Contacts with Muybridge, Friese-Greene, and Marey

Muybridge may have exerted a certain influence on Edison. He talked with Edison on February 27, 1888, about using his Zoopraxiscope "in association with the phonograph." Edison, at different times, both denied and confirmed this. Toward the end of the year, he received a number of Muybridge's photographs. A second influence may have been Friese-Greene. According to Hendricks, he wrote to Edison on March 18, 1890: "Have sent you by same post a paper with description of Machine Camera for taking 10 a second which may be of interest to you." It is claimed for Friese-Greene that he wrote Edison in June, 1889, proposing a collaboration on talking pictures, and offering to send drawings.

Unquestionably, Marey's use of flexible film was not lost on Edison. From October, 1888, to November, 1889, Edison filed four caveats. (A caveat is a preliminary statement to register a priority of idea with the Patent Office.) The first three dealt with cylinders. The third,

MOVEMENT BY ELECTRIC FLASHES. Though, like Muybridge, Otto-mar Anschütz used twenty-four cameras, he could see no reason for stretching them along as many feet of track. His cameras were tiny and his lenses and shutters so fast that he could take, in three-quarters of a second, two dozen pictures of the leap of a horse. Under the patronage of the German army and the Ministry of Education he recorded military drills, troop maneuvers, and cavalry charges, as well as the exploits of gymnasts. He was con-tent to put his pictures in a Zoetrope turned sideways, or to mount them on a revolving disk and view them by flashes of light pro-duced by a Geissler tube. He showed his Electrotachyscope (electric rapid view) at the Chicago World's Fair of 1893 for the delectation of a small group of onlookers. His device was com-pleted early in 1887 and shown in Vienna and Berlin. He may have had as many as 96 pictures on his disks.

which proposed a glass cylinder, talked of projection by an electric spark, and the device was also to serve as a camera. This caveat was filed just after Edison left for Paris. In the last caveat, written a month after Edison's return, he wrote of film in "a long band," and of intermittent movement in his camera-projector.

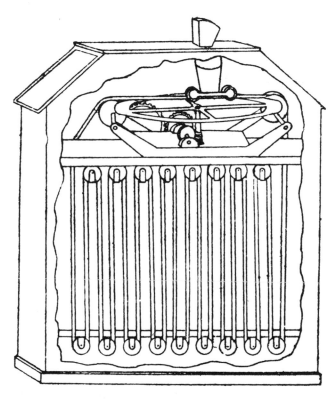

THE DICKSON-EDISON KINETOSCOPE. In this peep show about forty feet of film, joined in a loop and running over a series of spools, passed continuously above an electric light and below a magnifying glass, through which the viewer looked. Edison got the effect of intermittent motion through a very narrow slot in a shutter-like disk that revolved about forty times a second between the light and the film. On April 14, 1894, Edison's sales agents, Raff & Gammon, installed a battery of Kinetoscopes at 1155 Broadway, New York; and presently, several hundred were on display in the larger cities. In some cities, the spectator paid a quarter to see six machines, and attendants switched on the Kinetoscopes; soon Edison cut down on manpower by developing nickel-in-the-slot machines. Some Kinetoscopes added music. (*From Hopwood's* Living Pictures.)

Dickson as Producer

In spite of Edison's enthusiasm for his peep show, he was surprisingly slow in exploiting it. While Dickson was using the new camera in 1891, the Kinetoscope must have been taking shape, for Edison applied for a patent on it in that same year. Yet he waited till May, 1893, before demonstrating his box at the Brooklyn Institute, and he failed to deliver a battery of machines that his sales agents were to show at the Chicago World's Fair. There is some evidence that a single Kinetoscope appeared in the Edison exhibition there, but the first large-scale shipment from West Orange reached Broadway on April 14, 1894.

Meantime Dickson had been far from idle. He had become the first film producer in the entertainment world. When he worked with cylinders, the capers of employees had sufficed, but for the Kinetoscope Dickson had other and more impressive material—an organ-grinder and his monkey, a blacksmith at work, wrestlers, trained bears, a contortionist, boxing cats, and comic episodes in barbershops and in a Chinese laundry. Greatly daring, Dickson put the first "stars" on film—for instance, Buffalo Bill, Annie Oakley, the dancer Carmencita, and Sandow the Strong Man.

The Black Maria—Primeval Studio

Between the hazards of New Jersey weather and a camera as unwieldy as a grand piano, Dickson realized that he had to have an efficient studio. So he designed a special building that was finished early in 1893 at a grand cost, they say, of $637.67. It was a strange-looking structure covered with tar paper and affectionately called the Black Maria, another name for the "paddy wagon" of those days. A large section of the roof could be hauled up so as to let the sun hit the actors, who played against a black background. To keep the sun always full upon them, the whole studio could turn on a circular track.

From Perfection to Blunders

Although Edison was always commercially minded, he was a perfectionist at times, which caused him a bit of trouble in the case of the movies. Dickson's machines ran at a speed of about 40 frames a second—he often claimed 46. His camera accomplished this phenomenal speed through the perfection of the mechanism and the use of sprockets and perforations in the sides of the film. The idea of perforations wasn't new; but the success of the Kinetoscope made the size of each frame of picture, as well as the four sprocket holes at the side of each frame, the standard for many, many years. Until sound came, the only basic change in the Dickson pattern was reducing the speed of camera and projector to 16 frames a second. But Edison could take only about fifty feet of film on a roll because he devised no way of handling a heavier load.

Edison's devotion to electricity made difficulties. He insisted on driving his camera with an electric motor, and that required him to work close to a source of electricity, although he did use storage batteries.

In spite of Edison's passion for success, he missed the financial boat a number of times. When he met with delay in patenting the phonograph disk—his first and his final machines used cylinders—he said: "No matter, the disk phonograph will never amount to anything." According to Ramsaye, he refused to spend $150 to patent his motion-picture devices abroad: "It's not worth it." Perhaps his biggest blunder was to pass up the screen, for the first year or so, as a source of entertainment and money. Edison saw no future in that. He concentrated on his Kinetoscope—a peep show, a nickel-in-the-slot machine by which one person at a time looked at hardly fifty feet of film. When his financial partners urged him to develop a projector, he said, according to Terry Ramsaye:

EDISON'S STUDIO OF 1893. Designed by Dickson, who made this sketch forty years later, it was so arranged that part of the roof was opened to admit sunlight to the stage in the left end. The whole structure could revolve on a track to follow the sun. It was covered with tar paper, and called the Black Maria. (*Courtesy Earl Theisen Collection.*)

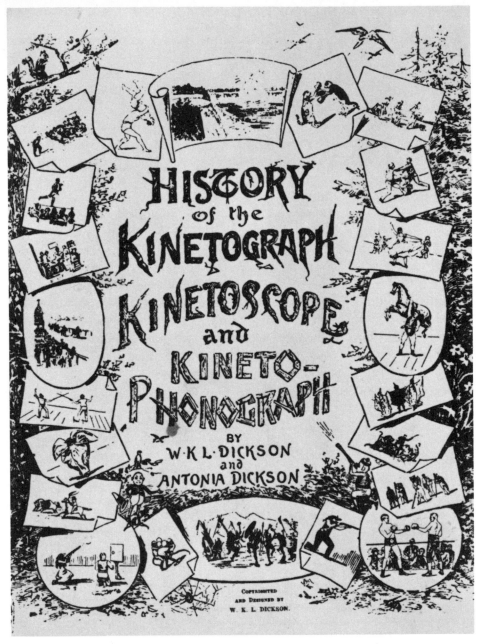

THREE NAMES FOR "EDISON'S" INVENTION. When, in 1895, Dickson and his sister published a booklet on the work he had done at Edison's, he was careful to use the term Kinetograph for the camera, Kinetoscope for the silent peep show, and Kinetophonograph for the peep show with sound. For the cover of this publication, Dickson drew various scenes, some of which he had shot with the camera. (*From* The Film Index.)

No, if we make this screen machine that you are asking for, it will spoil everything. We are making these peep show machines and selling a lot of them at a good profit. If we put out a screen machine there will be a use for maybe about ten of them in the whole United States. With that many screen machines you could show the pictures to everybody in the country—and then it would be done. Let's not kill the goose that lays the golden egg.

Ironically enough, when within a couple of years his peep show was losing its popularity, press and public applauded the "Edison Vitascope," a projector designed by other men and credited to the wizard for publicity reasons.

Projectors at Last

While Edison was launching his Kinetoscopes and Dickson was turning out films for these peep shows, at least a dozen other men were trying to make projectors, as well as cameras. Sometimes inventors made one machine do the double job of photography and projection; but they all used film, and they all had the same very sound—and obvious —idea about projection. Each picture had to be left on the screen long enough to make a bright, clear impression on the eye. A few of the inventors failed to realize that the best way to do this was to stop the film for a fraction of a second. Instead they let the pictures run by at breakneck speed and tried to "stop" the image with revolving lenses, mirrors, or lights that moved just as fast. Some even used two sets of pictures and a pair of lenses that moved up and down in turn. The result of all this optical trickery was an unsteady picture.

The only successful projectors used, like the camera, intermittent movement. Le Prince, Friese-Greene, and Marey hit on this basic idea in the eighties. For various reasons—death, poverty, or absorption in other things—these men never quite perfected their machines or promoted them properly. The vogue of the Kinetoscope set them thinking —and imitating. But they made a change in Dickson's machine that was quite as important as adding an arc light and lenses to throw the pictures on a screen. Instead of moving the film continuously, as the Kinetoscope did, they went back to the intermittent motion of the earlier inventors. That was how Dickson had taken his pictures, and that was how they had to be projected.

Le Roy, Projectionist Without a Camera

The case of an American with the surprisingly Gallic name of Jean Acmé Le Roy is a peculiar one. Most of our books about the movies fail

COMING!!

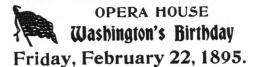

OPERA HOUSE
Washington's Birthday
Friday, February 22, 1895.

THE

Cinematographe
Novelty Co.

=== PRESENTING ===

LE ROY'S

MARVELOUS CINEMATOGRAPHE

SHOWING

WONDERFUL & ASTOUNDING
Pictures in Life Motion

ONCE SEEN NEVER TO BE FORGOTTEN

GEO. WOOD The Minstrel Man
Comedian and Singer

NEW YORK The Metropolis

100 VIEWS OF THE WONDER CITY

M'lle BINA The Second Sight Queen

DEXTER The Mystifying Australian

and other Features of Interest and Amusement.

Prices: 15c., 25c. and 35c.

LE ROY'S CLAIM. A committee of the Society of Motion Picture
Engineers accepted this advertisement as a fact, but it was probably printed some years later by producers outside the "movie
trust" who were attacking the patents of Edison and others in
court. It might even have been a product of Le Roy's ego. (*Courtesy University of California Press.*)

to mention him, yet some claim that he was the first man to show films commercially on a screen. Some French writers assert that he made a successful projector, exhibited it to a group of theatrical agents on February 5, 1894, and gave the first public exhibition of moving pictures in a New Jersey theater a year later. He made no camera, but was content to show Edison films to various clubs, social gatherings, and church groups till the summer of 1897. In 1930–31 a committee of the Society of Motion Picture Engineers studied what records there were, took depositions of "living eyewitnesses," and finally officially supported the claims of Le Roy. Unwittingly, the inventor himself cast doubt on the 1894 demonstration. The eyewitnesses didn't state what films they saw, but Le Roy's aging memory recalled one that wasn't made until 1895— *The Execution of Mary Queen of Scots.* A handbill advertising Le Roy's *"marvelous cinematographe"* at the Opera House in Clinton, New Jersey, on Washington's Birthday, 1895, should have proved this to be the first public showing of films on a screen, but the painstaking research of Gordon Hendricks has proved that no opera house existed in Clinton at that time. Whether or not Le Roy should take a bow for an early commercial projection somewhere else, neither his machine nor his work had any influence on the development of the motion picture. We know little about his projector, for he never patented it.

The Lathams and the Famous "Loop"

We know a good deal more about the next claimant, or rather, claimants. They are generally known as the Lathams, but, besides the former science teacher, Major Woodville Latham, and his sons, the group included an engineer named Enoch J. Rector, and Eugene Lauste, a rather remarkable French technician who had worked for Edison. The Lathams met Lauste in 1894. They had already met Dickson, and before Edison's English assistant left in 1895, he seems to have helped the Lathams develop a new camera. Also, Dickson may have had a good deal to do with designing their first projector, for the film ran continuously, just as in a Kinetoscope. To get more light through the swiftly revolving shutter, the Lathams used a larger film—about half as wide again as Edison's. On May 20, 1895, they installed their projector in an empty store on lower Broadway, and showed a four-minute film of a fight that they had staged on the sunlit roof of Madison Square Garden.

The Lathams made very little money out of their projector. Apart from their early projection, the Lathams do, however, merit recognition for a single feature of their otherwise inefficient machine. This was the so-

called "Latham loop," which became famous in patent litigation from 1902 till 1915. In the early cameras and projectors only a small amount of film footage could be rapidly jerked and stopped in back of the lens without tearing the film. A set of extra sprockets was added, providing a bit of slack in the moving film, and making it possible to use longer lengths of film. A loop of this sort had been used by Friese-Greene and Marey, but not with large reels.

Unprofitable Shows, but One Good Projector

The next attempt at projection was no more profitable than the Lathams', but it introduced two men who were to revolutionize the film business in America—C. Francis Jenkins and Thomas Armat. Jenkins, whose long and inventive life brought him to experiments with television, in 1894

No. 673.992.

T. ARMAT.
VITASCOPE.
(Application filed Feb. 19, 1896.)

Patented May 14, 1901.

(No Model.)

3 Sheets—Sheet 2

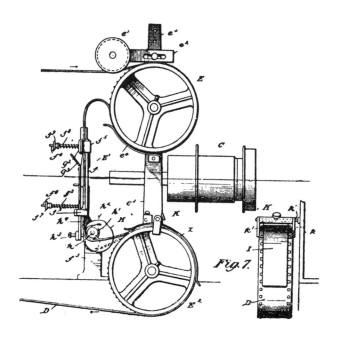

Fig. 7.

THE FAMOUS "LOOP". When cameras used only a short length of film—50 feet to 150—there was no problem about jerking each frame of film into place behind the lens and then jerking the next along. But the inertia of reels of greater length would tear the film. Rector is reputed to have solved this through what became known as the "Latham loop"; others before him, including Friese-Greene, had used a loop. When Armat "invented" the "Edison Vitascope" he added a loop to his projector, as you can see, to the left of the top sprocket. Armat's patent, as illustrated above, was applied for in 1896 but not granted till 1901.

conceived a camera with a continuously moving film and a circle of revolving lenses. He had developed a projector along similar lines, when he met Armat, a realtor with some interest in invention. The two went into partnership, out of which came a radically different projector. They set this up at the Cotton States Exposition at Atlanta in the fall of 1895, using some Edison films. Business was bad. Friction developed between the partners. Armat bought out Jenkins' interest. So much is certain.

What each partner contributed to the invention is still in dispute. The total result of their efforts was to play a great part in the future of the film.

Still another man gave film shows in that pregnant year of 1895—Max Skladanowsky of Germany. The films he projected at the Berlin vaudeville house, the Wintergarten, beginning on November 1, seem to have had as little success as those of the Lathams and Armat. They were hampered by a peculiar projector that required two lenses and two films. Again, there was no major contribution to the progress of the motion picture.

The Lumières Light Up the Screen

Of all the men who made projectors and cameras in the nineties, great credit must go to the brothers Louis and August Lumière. They weren't the first to project motion pictures, but they seem to have been the first to do it effectively. They began by fumbling with strips of sensitized paper—

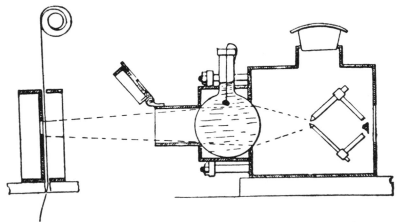

THE LUMIÈRE PROJECTOR. This schematic drawing of 1897 omits the focusing lens and the mechanism for moving the film, but it shows how the Lumiéres used a flask of liquid as a condenser that also protected the film from the heat of the arc. Where electricity wasn't available, they used an ether lamp. The Lumière projector served as camera and printing machine. Although the inventors adopted the film width and picture size of Edison, at first they used only one sprocket hole per frame instead of the four of the American's films. They reduced the number of pictures per second from the forty or so of Edison to ,sixteen, thus setting the standard speed for the silent era, and incidentally saving money for themselves. (*From The Journal of the Society Of Motion Picture Engineers.*)

something Edison wisely avoided—but they soon went to film. On February 13, 1895, they applied for a French patent, and in March they demonstrated their projector before the Society for the Encouragement of National Industry. After a few other showings, the Lumières took over the Salon Indien in the basement of the Grand Café on the Boulevard des Capucines. There on December 28 they charged Parisians one franc to watch the brief wonders of the Cinématographe. The first day's take was disappointing, but within a month, it is said, the Lumière brothers were making 7,000 francs a week. The next year, they turned a shop into a theater that exists today. Dr. Marey must have shuddered at the banalities of the first programs, but I'm sure he admired the technical skill of the men whose last name meant, appropriately enough, light, lamp, and intelligence.

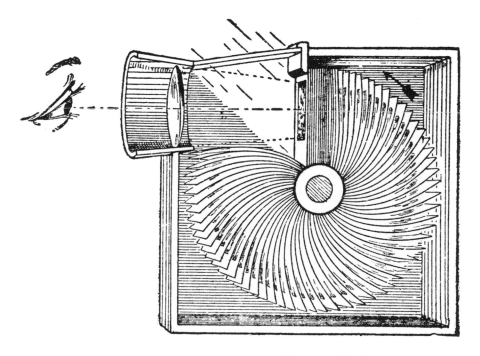

A FRENCH DEVICE LIKE THE MUTOSCOPE. The Lumière Kinora, invented and marketed in the late nineties, resembles the device developed by Dickson and Casler. They both go back to the riffle book of drawings that an Englishman named Linnett patented in 1868 as the Kineograph. But before them all was Sellers with his Kinematoscope. (*From E. G. Lutz's* Animated Cartoons.)

Projection Reaches England

Two Britons were hot on the heels of the Lumières, but never quite caught up. The stories of these men, Birt Acres and Robert W. Paul, are intertwined and a bit confused. Acres seems to have developed a camera first, and to have used it at the university boat race of March, 1895. Paul says that he designed a camera on "an idea due to Acres." His projector, the Theatrograph, as it was called, wasn't publicly shown until March, 1896, a month after the Lumière machine had invaded London.

Dickson and Another Peep Show

Dickson, who left Edison in 1895 and cooperated with the Lathams, was in a curious way responsible for the death of the Edison Kinetoscope and for Edison's surrender to the screen. Dickson approached a friend with the idea of making and selling riffle books of photographs (see page 83). This man and a group with whom Dickson became closely associated developed the idea into a new kind of peep show that they called the Mutoscope. Avoiding the patent rights of Edison, they made a camera that took pictures two inches high by two and three-quarter inches wide, printed them on pieces of light cardboard, and designed a peep-show machine in which the pictures flipped over rapidly after the customer put a penny—not a nickel—in the slot. It was proof of the enterprise of the American Mutoscope Company that it photographed the popular star Joseph Jefferson in several brief scenes from his great hit *Rip Van Winkle*. To this day, Mutoscope machines can be seen in penny arcades and amusement parks.

Dickson and one of his partners, Herman Casler, went on to produce a projector. This projector, which filled a very large screen at Hammerstein's Olympia Music Hall late in 1896, was only one of a flood of projectors that followed. By 1900 Paul counted up 566 patents for motion picture equipment in England, France, and Germany. Their names ran from Animatoscope to Zoplotrope and included such gems as Cinebibliographe, Heliocinegraphe, and Lapiposcope.

The "Edison" Vitascope, out of Jenkins-Armat

Early in 1896, the men who were distributing the Kinetoscope saw business decreasing. They heard of the Jenkins-Armat projector in Washington, had a demonstration, and persuaded Edison to manufacture it as the Edison Vitascope. To get Armat to disown his brain child, they wrote him:

. . . in order to secure the largest profit in the shortest time, it is necessary that we attach Mr. Edison's name in some prominent capacity to this new machine. While Mr. Edison has no desire to pose as inventor of the machine, yet we think we can arrange with him for the use of his name. . . . We should, of course, not misrepresent the facts to any inquirer, but we think we can use Mr. Edison's name in such a manner as to keep within the actual truth, and yet get the benefit of his prestige. The machine might be made with a plate upon which we could inscribe the words "Armat design" or something of that kind, and you understand that after we have disposed of our territory and the business is

FROM RIFFLE BOOK TO MUTOSCOPE. Open to page 113, the last of the Mickey Mouse drawings. Release the corners of the sixteen pages rapidly with your thumb and you will see the little figure move. This principle, patented in 1868, was used by Dickson's Mutoscope machines about twenty-five years later. (*Courtesy Walt Disney Studios.*)

fully established . . . we will then make it our business to attach your name to the machine as the inventor, and we are confident that you will thus eventually receive the credit which is due you.

So the Edison Vitascope opened at Koster & Bial's Music Hall in New York on April 23, 1896. There were dancing girls on the screen, ocean waves, prizefighters, and scenes from Charles Hoyt's play *A Milk White Flag*. And there was Armat in the balcony running the projector he had brought to Edison's attention. But it was to be many years before the public knew what he had contributed to the triumph of the American film, slight though that contribution was. Jenkins' contribution is still unsung.

FROM PROJECTION BOOTH TO SCREEN. The letterhead of the original distributors of the Kinetoscope carried a sketch of a music hall as it might appear when the Vitascope was on exhibition. Le Roy is supposed to have invented the first fireproof projection booth— refusing to patent or commercialize it. (*From Journal of the Society Of Motion Picture Engineers.*)

Chapter

5

The Screen Turns from Science to Storytelling

Hopes were high—and some of them fantastic—when Armat threw the switch of the "Edison" Vitascope and started the motion picture on its prodigious way. A newspaperman wrote: "Edison is a mighty ingenious fellow—and electricity in its application to the arts is in its infancy." After the first Vitascope show Charles Frohman, the "starmaker" of Broadway, said: "That settles scenery. Painted trees that do not move, waves that get up a few feet and stay there, everything in scenery we simulate on our stages will have to go. When art can make us believe that we see actual living nature, the dead things of the stage must go. . . . the possibilities of the Vitascope as the successor of painted scenery are illimitable." (This Broadway producer used no movie scenery in the remaining twenty years of his life; ironically, after his death a motion picture company bought Charles Frohman, Inc.)

Of all the prophets, Edison's bright young man Dickson saw the most effulgent future for his foster-child, this "object of magical wonder." "What," he asked in a pamphlet of 1896, "is the future of the kinetograph? Ask rather, from what conceivable phase of the future it can be debarred. . . . It is the crown and flower of nineteenth century magic, the crystallization of eons of groping enchantments." The vision of the future was apocalyptic:

> To the final development of the kinetographic stage, than which no more powerful factor for good exists, no limitations can possibly be affixed. The shadowy histrionics of the

85

near future will yield nothing in realistic force and beauty
to their material sisters. . . . Not only our own resources
but those of the entire world will be at our command, nay,
we may even anticipate the time when sociable relations
will be established between ourselves and the planetary
system, and when the latest doings in Mars, Saturn, and
Venus will be recorded by enterprising Kinetographic reporters.

EDISON'S NEW WONDER, THE VITASCOPE.

THE VITASCOPE IN KOSTER & BIAL'S. At the right, the screen, audience, and projection booth. At the left, the two projectors in
action, with 50-foot loops of film running over bobbins instead of
from reel to reel. (*Courtesy University of California Press.*)

The First Short Films

But, meantime, what were those reporters busy with? The first programs of Edison's Vitascope and the Lumières' Cinématographe tell the tale. Koster & Bial's Music Hall advertised the following:

Sea Waves	Venice, showing Gondolas
Umbrella Dance	Kaiser Wilhelm, reviewing his troops
The Barber Shop	Skirt Dance
Burlesque Boxing	Butterfly Dance
Monroe Doctrine	The Bar Room
A Boxing Bout	Cuba Libre

The newspapers reported that the umbrella dance was hand colored, and that the program also included *The Band Drill*, a scene from Charles Hoyt's Broadway success *A Milk White Flag*. The films that the Lumières showed at their premiere were no more remarkable, except for the first known fictional film, the little comedy *L'Arroseur arrosé*, under another title, *Le Jardinier*. These were short subjects indeed. None ran more than a minute.

The first movie program I saw wasn't nearly so full and varied but it amazed the young audience that sat in the basement of a church in St. Paul about 1897. We saw two short films. The first showed a half-dozen men diving into a pool; the other, two girls who leaped out of bed to have a pillow fight that ended with feathers filling the air. To add to the thrill of my first movies, at the end of each film the same scene was run backward. The divers came feet first out of the water and laded on the diving board, and the feathers went back into the pillows and the girls back into bed.

Between 1896 and 1906, films grew in number, length, and variety. Railroad trains, ocean waves, and card games lost their charms. Vaudeville turns disappeared, along with such products of the "naughty nineties" as Fatima in *The Coochee-Coochee Dance*. News events—foreshadowed by the shot of the German Emperor reviewing his troops—grew more and more popular, along with short travelogues and very short science films. Cameramen made advertising pictures. Tricks of lens and shutter spawned more elaborate fantasies. Comic episodes grew into rudimentary story films of several scenes. The discovery of what the skills of editing and camera work could do led finally to ten-minute dramas.

A Few Longer Films—for Fights, Religion, and Opera

Prizefights accounted for the first movies that lasted longer than Edison's fifty-foot pictures. In the summer of 1894, one of the Latham group

THE "PICTURE PLAY" BEFORE THE PHOTOPLAY. In 1894 and 1895, Alexander Black put drama on the screens of the lyceum circuit in what he called picture plays. He wrote and then recited from the lecture platform stories of between an hour and a half and two hours in length while he showed about three hundred lantern slides. Through the way he handled his camera, sets, and people, he achieved a curious, if limited, sense of movement. In each scene his background—whether an office or an alley in the slums—was absolutely static. Each photograph was taken from the same spot and the same angle—only his actors appeared in new positions. He used a magic lantern with an attachment to make one slide dissolve into the next, and thus the movement of his actors seemed a little less jerky. Black spent a great deal of care on his photographs, and induced distinguished people to appear in them. In his first picture play, *Miss Jerry,* above, the story of a girl reporter, his cast included Chauncey M. Depew, later to be Senator from New York. (*From* The Photographic Times, 1896. *From the collection of and by courtesy of Gordon Hendricks.*)

found out how to triple the length of the reels, shot a prizefight in Edison's Black Maria, and exhibited it in New York Kinetoscopes. In May, 1895, the Lathams showed a four-minute film of another faked fight, this time on a screen. Two years later Rector, divorced from the Lathams, used his Veriscope camera to film many thousands of feet of the Corbett-Fitzsimmons championship fight at Carson City. If he showed New York an hour and a half of the fight—as the "Dramatic Mirror" said he did—here in 1897 is our first feature-length film. Late in 1899, the American Mutoscope and Biograph Company installed some

---

The Measure of the Silent Film

After Edison gave up his attempt to project films at more than forty frames a second, all the film world ran on the standard gauge of Lumière:

16 frames	1 foot
1 foot	1 second
60 feet	1 minute
1,000 feet (1 reel)	about 16 minutes
1 reel	about 16,000 frames

---

400 arc lights to shoot the Jeffries-Sharkey fight at Coney Island. A Vitagraph crew sneaked in to make a rival film. I find no record of how long Vitagraph's version was, but the other went to the trade in 5,575 feet.

Until 1909, only three other American films of much more than one reel seem to have been released. An American representative of Lumière interested the theatrical firm of Klaw and Erlanger in photographing *The Passion Play* at Höritz, Austria—not Oberammergau. Rich G. Hollaman, proprietor of the Eden Musée in New York, and Albert G. Eaves, head of the well-known costume company, united to film the twenty-four scenes of the "Oberammergau" *Passion Play* on the roof of a New York building—not even at Höritz. When Hollaman and Eaves added their show to the waxworks and chamber of horrors of the Eden Musée in January, 1898, they employed a lecturer to guide the audience through the story—subtitles hadn't yet been invented—and to explain that the film had been made in Oberammergau. In spite of the fact that the New York *Herald* exposed this roof-top fraud, the *Passion Play* had enough success to induce its backers to make a two-reel film called *The Opera Martha,* to the tune of badly synchronized phonograph records.

Plagiarism and Copyright

Subjects ran in cycles—just as they still do in Hollywood—and this soon led to plagiarism. As audiences grew tired of rival versions of Niagara Falls, fire engines, and babies smearing their faces with porridge, producers turned to comic episodes, and then began to steal each other's plots. Lumière—from now on I shall ignore the less active brother Auguste in favor of Louis—made a film called *L'Arroseur arrosé*, or *Watering the Gardener* (1895), in which a boy stepped on a hose, the gardener looked into the nozzle to see what was wrong, and got a dousing as the boy walked away. An Englishman reproduced the episode and it is said that before long, there were ten versions in circulation. Producers not only pilfered plots. They stole prints, made "dupes," and sold them under new titles.

OBERAMMERGAU ON A NEW YORK ROOF. This advertisement from the New York *Herald* of February, 1898, does not claim that the film was made in the Teutonic home of *The Passion Play*; the newspaper had found it necessary to expose the fact that the picture's 2,100 feet had been photographed on the roof of a New York building.

LUMIÈRE REDIVIVUS. The old gag of *Watering the Gardener*, the short comedy film made in 1895, was reproduced sixty years later in the comic strip *Napoleon* by McBride. (*Courtesy Mirror Enterprises Syndicate.*)

Until 1912, the copyright law in America didn't apply to motion pictures on celluloid, but only to still photographs and printed words. In 1894, Edison assembled, on a single paper print, eighty-one frames of his very short film called *The Sneeze,* and entered it for copyright. When Rector shot the Corbett-Fitzsimmons fight, he tried the bluff of painting on the side of the prize ring—visible in every shot—the words "COPYRIGHTED THE VERISCOPE COMPANY 1897." Since words and still photographs *could* be copyrighted, some producers tried to protect their films by sending to Washington sets of cards on each of which frames from different scenes had been fastened.

Triumphs for Lumière

Lumière's camera-projector seems to have been the best equipment of his day, and his films among the most varied and interesting. After seeing some of the Frenchman's pictures, a man who had been showing Edison's wrote to the Vitascope Company: "You never saw living pictures until you see this machine. . . . It is ridiculous; the few films I brought from your place yesterday. There are not two good scenes in the whole lot. . . . You folks certainly will have to get a hurry up on your business or I would not give much for the chances on the Vitascope." And so, for a time, Lumière outdistanced all other film-makers and exhibitors. His showmen covered hundreds of cities and towns in Middle Europe and Russia as well as France; they even penetrated North and South America and the Far East. Lumière's hand-cranked machine was light, and, because he knew that most towns had no electricity, he used an ether lamp. When one of his representatives reached a new district, he announced that he would take moving pictures of the place and the people, and add them to the show. This not only advertised the new wonder. When the local pictures flashed on the screen, even the most cynical peasant was convinced that here was no trickery.

Lumière's men also made it their business to send back to Paris coverage of news events as well as pictures of town and countryside. Occasionally they scored quite amazing scoops. A Lumière cameraman recorded the coronation of Nicholas II of Russia in 1896. He was shooting when more than 5,000 people were killed in the rush for imperial gifts, but the police seized the film.

News—Faked and Genuine

Perhaps it was Lumière who began the business of faking news. One of his men exploited the Jewish populace of the Ukraine through what purported to be a film on the persecution of Dreyfus. Out of stock shots he spliced together a French military parade headed by an officer whom he called Dreyfus, a public building for the scene of his trial, and some warships to take the condemned man to his exile on Devil's Island. Since there were no subtitles on films in those days, the exhibitor

"THE UNSEEN WORLD'

(Copyright Title)

A Series of Microscopic Studies, Photographed by means of

The Urban-Duncan Micro-Bioscope.

The "UNSEEN WORLD" Series of Films are made to fit all Standard American Guage Projecting Machines.

The magnification of these Subjects as viewed from a Screen, with picture 20 by 25 feet in size. is 2,200,000 to 76,000,000 times, according to the extent of magnification on the Film which varies from 25 to 850 diameter.

Mr. F. MARTIN-DUNCAN, F.R.H.S.

MICROSCOPIC SUBJECTS.

2500 ... AMERICAN BLIGHT AND GREEN-FLY

The American Blight which has invaded so many English Orchards, and the Green-fly, the greatest pest of the Rose Garden, are shown greatly magnified, crawling about in search of food. The American Blight or Woolly Aphis presenting a very curious, untidy appearance, with bits of the woolly matter, which it has formed itself, stuck about its legs and body. *Magnified 25 diameters on film.* **Length 75 feet.**

F 2

VISUAL AIDS—c.1903. Dickson had used the motion picture to view microscopic slides, but such an adjunct to education was not thoroughly exploited until Charles Urban marketed the work of F. Martin-Duncan. Here is one page from an Urban catalogue. (*Courtesy Film Library of the Museum of Modern Art.*)

told his audience by word of mouth what he wanted them to believe. News faking became a habit on both sides of the Atlantic around 1900. Cameramen staged, at home, bits of the Spanish-American war, the Boer War, and the Boxer Rebellion in China. They faked the eruption of Mt. Pelée, and one producer advertised *The Great Corbett-Fitz-simmons Fight,* qualified by the words: "(in counterpart)."

Fakery continued into the new century, but there was more and more genuine coverage of news events. American cameramen recorded William McKinley during the 1896 campaign and at his inaugurations in 1897 and 1901; some shot such disasters as a great fire in Baltimore and the Galveston flood. Englishmen covered all manner of happenings from ship launchings and the Derby to the funeral of Queen Victoria. Though the British faked episodes of the Boer War, they also had cameramen actually at the front, and one of them photographed the surrender of General Cronje to Lord Roberts. Another took shots of a rebellion in the Balkans, and a man named Joseph Rosenthal made his reputation by covering the Russo-Japanese War in 1905.

Charles Urban—an American who became a leading English producer and distributor—was largely responsible for the improvement in non-fiction films. Beginning in 1903, he sent cameramen to the Alps, Canada, the Near East, and even Borneo to make what we now call travelogues. He turned out advertising films on whiskey, soap, cigarettes, and custard, but he also distributed science films—more than a score of short pictures taken by F. Martin-Duncan with the aid of a microscope, and called *The Unseen World.* In 1903, some of these played the music halls with great success. The climax of Urban's career came in 1911 when he produced through G. A. Smith's Kinemacolor—the first effective color process—a record of the crowning of George V as Emperor of India at the Delhi Durbar.

The Development of Silent Techniques

It takes many years for any art to find its way to full expression. Techniques develop very slowly at first. Then they quicken and multiply as one contribution begets another. From 1200 to 1400, European painters worked slowly and painfully upon the problems of draftsmanship, composition, and perspective. Then Renaissance art reached a sudden perfection. Beyond lay only refinements and amplifications.

The film-makers weren't as slow as the painters in discovering and perfecting the techniques that culminated in the talking picture of the nineteen-thirties. They had the skills of photography and of the theater

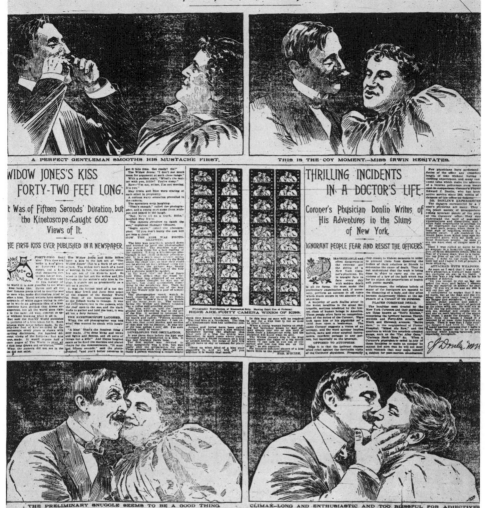

FAMOUS AS A KISS BUT NOT AS A TWO SHOT. Shortly after the introduction of Dickson-Edison movies at Koster & Bial's, Raff and Gammon filmed a brief moment from *The Widow Jones,* a comedy in which May Irwin—no Mae West—was being starred. Its forty-two feet were widely condemned as an affront to public morals. This shot is often wrongly referred to as the first close-up. It might better have been called the first two-shot. In these drawings from the New York *World* of April, 1896, the frames have been redrawn almost in the CinemaScope proportion.

to build upon as well as modify. More important, when an artist of the
screen—a director, I mean—developed a new bit of technique peculiar
to the motion picture, it was quickly known to his fellows. Films, unlike miniatures, murals, and oils, were duplicated by the hundreds. Any
experiment, any improvement in camera work, cutting, or direction,
was soon seen by film-makers in other countries. Yet in such an age of
technology as the twentieth century, the progress of the film still seems
slow. Automobiles, radios, refrigerators, and electric heaters developed
faster. For the first ten years, motion picture directors fumbled with
their cameras. It was almost by accident that they developed the simplest but most necessary of film techniques. It was another ten years
before Griffith could produce *The Birth of a Nation* as the feature film
swept across the screens of the world. It was a bit more than another
decade before the talkie came along and required the development of
still more skills. By the middle of the nineteen-thirties—forty years after
the first movies—directing, editing, and sound recording had at last perfected the means to tell a story in the full terms of this new art. Many
of these techniques apply, of course, to the documentary, the educational, and the travelogue film, but they are all essential to the fictional
movie.

Let me outline some of the basic steps in the development of storytelling techniques during the first ten years of the silent films. In the
beginning the director used the camera to record only a single episode.
The action took place only in a single setting. The camera was as fixed
as a spectator at a play. The next step forward was to photograph a
second episode of the story in another setting—but again with the fixed
camera covering all the action. This may have been the result of faking
news events that had covered months or years; Lumière's faked Dreyfus
film of about 1898 had to use a number of different scenes because there
was no other way of showing what had happened to him. Somewhere
along the line, a director discovered that he could pan his camera from
side to side, and even—this was really a great step forward—shoot two
scenes in the same setting and intercut them with scenes shot somewhere else. Along with fades, dissolves, and other lens tricks, this was
about as far as film techniques got between 1895 and 1905. The results
may not seem very impressive today, yet these were the materials that
D. W. Griffith was soon to develop, through deft editing, into true
filmic art.

Here I should point out that the length of a film has no necessary
bearing on technique. The feature film of many reels was an important

development, but all the essential techniques of film-making can be found in a short subject such as *La Cucaracha* (1934) or *A Time Out of War* (1953).

Who Produced the First Fiction Film?

It is as hard to say who first told a story on the moving picture screen as it is to identify any sole inventor of the camera and the projector. There was a shred of fiction in *Watering the Gardener;* it was only a single episode, yet it had suspense and climax. Because the joke was told in only a single shot, it lacked fluidity. Until the Library of Congress is able to restore more of those paper films, we shan't know when the little comedies and dramas were first made in more than one scene.

Plots Before and After Griffith's Advent

But we know how puerile the plots of the little pictures were before the days of Griffith and how puerile they remained even after he had begun to show other directors the way to reasonably good storytelling.

Here are the plots of two films of 1899 as outlined in sales catalogues:

> *Jones Gives a Private Supper.* This picture shows Jones entertaining three young ladies, after the theatre. They have a private room, and are evidently enjoying themselves very much. Jones sets up the wine freely, and the party becomes hilarious. The girls dance in turn for Jones, each vying with the other in executing novel and startling terpsichorean effects.
>
> *A Fair Exchange is No Robbery.* The coachman sleepeth. The broad piazzas look cool and nap provoking. Even the horse droopeth his ears and shutteth one eye contemplatively. All at once, the small boy! and with him the butler, whom he hath impressed as prime minister in the joke. Horse awakeneth and unhitcheth and leadeth away. Boy bringeth billy goat and fasteneth to the runabout. Coachman still sleepeth, boy doubleth in joy and butler shaketh. Dude cometh with lady, who entereth the wagon. Dude graspeth the situation, but not the joke. Awakeneth Jehu sasseth the dude, who scrappeth and bruiseth Jehu and his hat. Small boy weepeth for very joy.

Waiting for Méliès

Ignoring a very few faked films like the Dreyfus picture, it is very difficult to say who first used a series of scenes to tell a fictional story. Too few films made at the turn of the century still exist. The catalogues of most of the makers and distributors provide synopses, yet are these any more accurate, except as to story content, than current advertisements of films? But we do know quite a good deal about a man who turned out fiction films prior to 1900. And we know that, before the century was out, he shot a fairy story in twenty different scenes. This man was Georges Méliès of Paris.

Gorky Sees the First Films

Last night I was in the Kingdom of Shadows.

If you only knew how strange it is to be there. It is a world without sound, without colour. Everything there—the earth, the trees, the people, the water and the air—is dipped in monotonous grey. Grey rays of the sun across the grey sky, grey eyes in grey faces, and the leaves of the trees are ashen grey. It is not life but its shadow, it is not motion but its soundless spectre. . . .

When the lights go out in the room in which Lumière's invention is shown, there suddenly appears on the screen a large grey picture, "A Street in Paris"—shadows of a bad engraving. As you gaze at it, you see carriages, buildings and people in various poses, all frozen into immobility. . . . But suddenly a strange flicker passes through the screen and the picture stirs to life. Carriages coming from somewhere in the perspective of the picture are moving straight at you, into the darkness in which you sit. . . .

And all this in strange silence where no rumble of the wheels is heard, no sound of footsteps or of speech. Nothing. Not a single note of the intricate symphony that always accompanies the movements of people. Noiselessly, the ashen-grey foliage of the trees sways in the wind, and the grey silhouettes of the people, as though condemned to eternal silence and cruelly punished by being deprived of all the colours of life, glide noiselessly along the grey ground. . . .

It is terrifying to see, but it is the movement of shadows, only of shadows. Curses and ghosts, the evil spirits that have cast entire cities into eternal sleep, come to mind. . . .

This mute, grey life finally begins to disturb and depress you. It seems as though it carries a warning, fraught with a vague but sinister meaning that makes your heart grow faint. You are forgetting where you are. Strange imaginings invade your mind and your consciousness begins to wane and grow dim . . .

—From a newspaper review by Maxim Gorky after seeing the Lumière films at the Nizhni-Novgorod fair in the summer of 1896. *Translated by Leda Swan and published in Jay Leyda's* Kino.

Chapter
6

The Magic of Méliès
and of England's Editing

WHEN THE FIRST Lumière films appeared, Georges Méliès was thirty-four, a conjurer, and the proprietor of the Théâtre Robert-Houdin, a house devoted to sleight of hand and mechanical magic. The motion picture fascinated him. He fell in cinematic love at first sight. When the Lumières refused an offer of 10,000 francs for a camera, Méliès fabricated one from parts supplied by the English inventor and film maker R. William Paul. In April, 1896, when the Vitascope came to New York, Méliès was showing pictures at the Théâtre Robert-Houdin.

At first, I believe, Méliès didn't have the slightest idea of adding the magic of camera to the magic of the stage, though that was what he ultimately did. The mere photographing of daily life, comic episodes, or a conjuring trick was magical enough. He had his *Card Party*, his *Gardener Burning Weeds*, his *Place de L'Opéra*, and he stole the plot of Lumière's *Watering the Gardener*. In 1896 he made more than seventy-five 65-foot films, but it was only in his seventieth film that he began to make his camera do tricks. The one that he used in *The Vanishing Lady* was very simple. He merely stopped the camera while the lady ducked out. In his last film of 1896, *The Haunted Castle*, he added a theatrical setting to some visual hocus-pocus.

Photographic Tricks and a New Studio

Méliès knew how to use the illusions of still photography. He could produce ghosts by double exposure, and utilize mattes to make a man meet

99

his double. But Méliès also invented tricks that were possible only with film. He used fades and he possibly invented the dissolve. He developed slow motion as well as fast motion effects. And he knew how to use animation and miniatures effectively.

Méliès must have come upon some of his effects quite accidentally. For instance, when he was photographing a humdrum scene on a Paris street in 1896, he discovered that the camera could make transformations far more startling than those of the stage. Méliès had set up his tripod in the Place de L'Opéra, and was taking a shot of traffic when his film jammed and his camera stopped taking pictures. He corrected the trouble and went on shooting. When he developed and printed the scene, he saw an omnibus disappear and a hearse take its place. The registry of the two vehicles can't have been perfect, but the film told Méliès all he needed to know.

In the spring of 1897, Méliès built the first glassed-in film studio. This may have been partly to avoid the delays of bad weather, but it was mainly to add theatrical tricks to those of the camera that he had discovered. At one end of the building, which looked like a great

IN THE DEPTHS OF THE SEA. For one of his films Méliès created an underwater scene by shooting at a mermaid through an aquarium while, to the rear, sea monsters passed on wheeled platforms behind gauze curtains. Griffith is supposed to have said of Méliès: "I owe him everything." (Later C. B. DeMille declared that David Wark Griffith was "the teacher of us all.") (*From Bessy and Lo Duca's* Georges Méliès, Mage.)

greenhouse, he installed a stage equipped with traps, chutes, rigging, and capstans as well as drops and wings.

From Dreyfus to Fairy Tales and Science Fiction

Though Mél, now had a studio that he could use for a new type of production, he still followed to a great extent the current styles in films. In 1897 he made such shorts as *Peeping Tom at the Seaside* and *Dancing in a Harem*. He faked the news in what he called *actualités reconstituées*. Among these were *The Blowing up of the Maine in Havana Harbor* (1898), and *The Eruption of Mount Pelée* and *The Coronation of King Edward VII* (both 1902). Of course one piece of fakery had to be another *Dreyfus Affair*. This production of 1899 was his first long film, running to about 715 feet. More important, it was the first in which he—or probably any other film-maker—used as many as twelve different scenes.

In his next film but one, *Cinderella*, Méliès applied the same technique of many scenes—this time, twenty—to the sort of story that cried aloud for visual magic. During the rest of his career, he made many more fairy tale films, but he is best known today for a kind of science fiction laced with humor as well as fantasy. The two outstanding pictures were *A Trip to the Moon* (1902) in thirty scenes, and *An Impossible Voyage* (1904) in forty-three. Throughout both films, Méliès emphasized the satirical and the absurd. His scientists could have come out of the *commedia dell'arte*. The men who helped launch the rocket ship in *A Trip to the Moon* were chorus girls in tights, straight from the Paris revues. On the other hand, he treated the story of *Joan of Arc* (1900) with proper seriousness. It was, as his catalogue said: "A grand spectacular production in twelve scenes. About 500 persons enacting the scenes, all superbly costumed. Running time about 15 minutes."

The Virtues and Faults of Méliès

Méliès made three contributions to the screen. The least important was increasing the length of fiction films. *An Impossible Voyage* was 1,414 feet long, and *Cinderella* is supposed to have run to 2,000 before his distributor, the Pathé Brothers, had it cut to 410. Méliès' second contribution was the invention or development of almost all the optical maneuvers that we use today. His third distinction lay in turning so soon toward imaginative storytelling.

For all his enterprise with camera and settings—indeed because of

La grande Ourse.

FROM STAR GODDESSES TO MACHINES. In some of Méliès' films he
mingled fantasy and science fiction. He turned music hall beauties
into the constellation of the Great Bear. For _A La Conquête du
Pôle_, released in 1912, he created a huge piece of mechanism to
animate a giant. (_From Bessy and Lo Duca's_ Georges Méliès,
Mage.)

it—Méliès failed as a film-maker in one very important way. As he himself put it, he "set the cinema along the path toward theatrical spectacle." Resourceful as he was in camera tricks, he photographed what he called the "artificially arranged scenes" of his films from the point of view of a single spectator in a theater. They were indeed, as he said, "moving tableaux." Much more was needed before a story on the screen could be truly filmic. Characters had to move toward the spectator and away

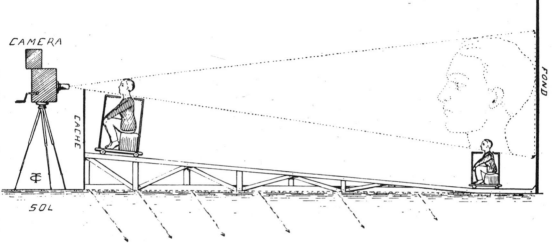

MOHAMMED COMES TO THE CAMERA. Méliès probably never moved his camera. In *L'Homme à la tête de caoutchouc* (*The Man with the Rubber Head*), which he made in 1901, he moved the man toward the camera in order to make the head seem to swell. (*From Bessy and Lo Duca's* Georges Méliès, Mage.)

from him, instead of sidewise. The camera had to move in or cut in to a close-up. (Once, in *The Man with the Rubber Head* (1901), Méliès moved a man's head *toward* the camera but only to make it seem to increase in size as if blown up by a bellows.) Above all, the director-cameraman had to break up a single scene into two or more shots. If Méliès did this at all it was only after men in other countries had shown the way. As late as 1901, when he should have shown an insert of a bloody key in *Bluebeard,* the villain's wife held up a foot-long prop, spattered with red.

Hard Work, Neglect, and Belated Honors
Méliès must be credited with a tremendous amount of work between 1896 and his retirement in 1913. He made almost 500 films. He dreamed

up those plots that he didn't borrow. He cast the actors and directed their performances. He conceived his tricks of camera and stage. And, for the more important pictures, he designed the scenery and saw to the costuming. Because his longer films had to be carefully worked out in advance of shooting, Méliès may be called the first man to write a scenario. He also made films of a noted singer named Paulus. One French authority says that these movies were synchronized with phonograph records. Another claims that Paulus sang behind the screen—which would at best hamper the distribution of the films, and hardly satisfy a singer's ego.

In spite of the early and worldwide success of Méliès' pioneering, his sales fell off after 1908 as his costs increased. His last year of full activity was 1908, and he ceased work in 1913. About ten years later he was reduced to selling toys and candy in a kiosk of a railroad station. There a journalist found him in 1929. The French film industry celebrated this discovery with a gala showing of some of Méliès' films, and he was admitted to the Legion of Honor.

Fantasy in England

The trick film and perhaps screen fiction might have come earlier if R. W. Paul had been able to finance a production of H. G. Wells' *The Time Machine*. When the book appeared in 1895, the producer had been fascinated by this story of a man's journey forward and backward through time. In October, 1895, Paul filed a patent on a very elaborate arrangement of swaying and wind-blown platforms upon which the spectators would sit as if within the time machine, while they viewed films and slides that would seem to carry them into the past and the future.

Perhaps it was just as well that Paul couldn't find the money for his project. *The Time Machine*—granted its success—would have stimulated storytelling, but it might have led English film-makers down the theatrical path that Méliès took. To be sure, some of them did use trick photography in many short films; G. A. Smith made *Cinderella and the Fairy Godmother* (1898) a year before Méliès' version. But there appears to have been no attempt at longish fantasy until 1903, when Cecil Hepworth put forth an 800-foot version of *Alice in Wonderland* in sixteen scenes. It is not surprising to read in a film catalogue of the time: "No pantomime or stage effect is introduced in this film; the whole of the various scenes having been produced in pretty natural surroundings." Since the beginning, English film-makers had been shooting fiction out of doors, and developing cutting and camera techniques that D. W. Griffith later perfected and added to.

England Discovers Editing Through Close-ups

From 1900 to 1905, England led the film world in creative experimentation. Her directors discovered that new ways of placing the camera and of editing film could produce more excitement than a series of tableau-like long shots. The English learned that film could be shot from more than one position in a scene, and these takes could be intercut. They discovered the "marines to the rescue" technique—cutting from one locale to another and then back again. They found out that characters could be followed from one setting to the next—which produced the "chase" picture.

The close-up came into motion pictures quite early, but was the only shot in the little films. Edison's very short film *The Sneeze* included the shoulders and chest of one of his employees. *The Kiss*, which stirred up a moral furor in 1896, was actually a two-shot of May Irwin and John C. Rice clear down to the waist. Before the turn of the century, Paul had a man's face grow larger and larger until it "swallowed" the screen, and James Williamson did the same thing in *The Big Swallow* of 1902. But none of these close-ups or close shots was cut into another set-up.

The film historian Georges Sadoul credits the Englishman G. A. Smith with discovering the art of editing film by using more than one cut in a scene. Certainly this scientific-minded man, who later patented Kinemacolor, went from a medium shot to several close-ups in 1900. Evidently he felt that he needed a special excuse for jumping from one shot to another. As the title, *Grandma's Reading Glass*, indicates, he found it in a magnifying glass. After a shot of grandmother at her sewing table and a little boy holding her reading glass, the boy focused it on such things as a newspaper, a watch, a canary, grandma's blinking eye, and a kitten. In 1902, Smith used a magnifying glass again in *At Last! That Awful Tooth!* But, in between, he had a moment of boldness. In *The Little Doctor*, Smith showed a close-up of a kitten's head during a scene in which two children gave it medicine. The film catalogues called such a shot a "short telescopic view."

Did a German Intercut Before 1900?

Like Sadoul, I believe that Englishmen were the first to shoot more than one angle of a scene, but there is a counterclaim on behalf of a German, Oskar Messter. About 1898, according to the French writers

Bardèche and Brasillach in their *History of the Film,* the director used five different shots of a file of women on bicycles in a short film variously called, in French, *Excursion* and *Promenade en bicyclette.* These writers say that the film used a long shot and a closer one of the line of bicyclists, then cut to their faces, to their feet and skirts, and finally to another shot of the full line of riders. But two other French authorities, René Jeanne and Charles Ford, assert in their *Histoire Encyclopédique du Cinéma* that there were no separate cuts. Like the train arriving at a station in an early Lumière film, the bicyclists merely rode up from a distance until they were close to the camera.

British Editing Makes Progress

Between 1901 and 1902, the English tried out three techniques essential to storytelling on the screen. One was a more elaborate use of close shots. Another was cutting away from one scene and, later, back to it again. Finally, there came the chase film, in which characters were followed from scene to scene.

In *Mary Jane's Mishap* (1901 or 1902), Smith showed a full shot of a maid in a kitchen and then, according to Sadoul, close shots of her trying to clean boots and light a fire, and of her comically distressed face. Then she puts kerosene on the fire, there is an explosion, and Mary Jane is blown up the chimney. Out come her shattered remains, to fall to the ground. Finally, according to a film catalogue quoted by Sadoul, "As a final warning to future Mary Janes a visit is paid to the cemetery [sic] where an old lady endeavors to improve the occasion by exhibiting the unhappy slavey's grave to other slaveys. But the gathering is scattered, for Mary Jane's ghost rises from the tomb in search of her paraffin [kerosene] can and having secured this desired article she retires again to her final resting place, a domestic cat being the sole remaining witness." All this in 260 feet.

Attack on a China Mission, made in January, 1901, was probably the first movie to use some of the elements of continuity and cutting that are as important to screen fiction as close-ups. This film of James Williamson's was made on English soil, though it dealt with the Boxer Rebellion in China. It began with the exterior of the mission and the forcing of the gate by the Chinese. Next, inside the compound, the Boxers killed the missionary while his wife and child and a young woman fled to the protection of the house. The wife appeared on a balcony, probably in the same long shot, and signaled off-screen for help. Then —and here we have something new in film-making—Williamson cut to a shot of armed sailors outside, then returned to the compound, and showed the sailors entering to rescue what remained of the missionary's family and to vanquish the Boxers. The film was 230 feet long.

Chases Produce Filmic Drama

The true chase—which because of its very nature can't help being cinematic—appeared first in English films. Among these were Williamson's *Stop Thief!* (1901) and, made by other men, *A Daring Daylight Burglary* (1903) and *The Robbery of the Mail Coach* (1903). From the last, Sadoul believes that Edwin S. Porter borrowed ideas for his film *The Great Train Robbery.*

There were more chases, comic as well as melodramatic, before the English film began to falter, and the French and American took over about 1906. The best picture of this kind—and perhaps the most skillfully conceived and edited film before the coming of D. W. Griffith —was Cecil Hepworth's *Rescued by Rover,* 425 feet long, which he made in 1905. The plot is a bit preposterous: a child is stolen by a beggar woman, the father's collie dog listens to the story of bereavement, jumps out of a window, tracks down the child without the aid of scent, and leads the father to the room where the child is hidden. What makes the film notable—aside from the fact that the dog was the first film character that didn't overact—is the continuity of the chase. The dog runs down a street, swims a stream, runs down another street, and finds the house where the beggar lives. Then Hepworth carefully reverses the action to get the dog back home. Just as carefully, he brings the dog and the father through the same settings. There is not the slightest error in direction of movement, not the slightest jar in editing. When the dog first ran down the street, Hepworth took two different shots; in the second he set his camera lower to suit the dog's height as it came into the foreground. At the end of the film there is even a cut from a long shot of the reunited family to a closer angle.

Méliès' Success Retards French Rivals

The French were slow in taking up the techniques of the English. For some years, Méliès was more active and successful in the fiction field then Lumière, Leon Gaumont, or Charles Pathé, and everyone copied his methods of shooting—with or without tricks. The camera stayed at one spot inside a studio set. It wasn't till 1905 that a chase film dragged French actors out of doors. This was André Heuzé's comic *Ten Wives to One Husband.* A better-known director, Ferdinand Zecca, used a close-up in 1901, but he liked studio scenery, and he imitated Méliès' trick films as late as 1909. Between those dates he reenacted history by telling the story of the revolt of the sailors on the cruiser *Potemkin* in *Rebellion, Mutiny in Odessa* (1906), and he capitalized on horror and murder in *The Victims of Alcohol* (1902) and *The History of a Crime* (1901). Zecca sensed that the film was for the proletariat and that the proletariat wanted the sensationalism of real life rather than magical fantasy. But Zecca played it safe, and gave the public every sort of fare.

The Film d'Art—Even Stagier Than Méliès

By 1908 Méliès was losing ground. *Humanity Through the Ages,* last of his artificial but ingenious spectacles, miraculously covered in 1,000 feet the history of the violence of man from Cain and Abel to a street fight of modern times, and concluded with "The Triumph of the Peace Congress." Few people cared. The masses were much more interested in the work of Zecca and some American directors. In spite of Méliès, French films were growing filmic. Then the blow fell. It was Film d'Art with its stagey productions. This first of highbrow motion picture movements was fathered by literary figures and the leading actors of the Comédie-Française. Film d'Art transferred a play to the screen with all the creative freedom of decalcomania.

Its initial production, *The Assassination of the Duc de Guise,* opened on November 17, 1908, to great acclaim. It was only 853 feet long and it was photographed by a fixed camera in a canvas set. But the scenario was written by the noted playwright Henri Lavédan; Le Bargy, a leading actor of the Comédie-Française of France, acted in it, shared in the direction, and recited poetry by Edmond Rostand at the première; there was special music by Saint-Saëns.

The film was a great success, and so, for a time, was Film d'Art. The group turned from history to novels and dramas. The middle class and the intelligentsia soon developed a perverse interest in stage plays and stage players. Directors and producers fell in line. Ready to please everyone, Zecca directed Le Bargy and Cecile Sorel in *La Tosca* (1909) for Pathé. Gaumont created the Film Esthétique to compete with the Série d'Art Pathé. Other producers in France and on the Continent went arty. The resulting films were as stagey as those of Méliès, but they had none of the photographic antics that had made Méliès popular with both highbrows and lowbrows in Europe and America. In 1911, Sarah Bernhardt starred in *La Tosca* and the distinguished comedienne Gabrielle Réjane in *Madame Sans-Gêne;* and the next year, the great tragedian Mounet-Sully in *Oedipus Rex,* and Bernhardt in *La Dame aux Camélias.* The Film d'Art movement ultimately failed financially as well as artistically, but not before Adolph Zukor had acquired Bernhardt's *Queen Elizabeth* (1912) on which to found the Famous Players. The great Eleonora Duse made no such filmic stir in America, but she was able to save an otherwise stagey production of *Cenere* in 1916 through a simple yet powerful naturalism that fitted the screen perfectly and contrasted with the flamboyant pantomime of the Divine Sarah *sans voix.*

A MÉLIÈS MAIN TITLE. At times, his company maintained a production line of fifty women, each of whom applied a single color to a portion of each frame.

Chapter
7

American Film-Making—
1902-1912

A<small>T LEAST ONE</small> American director was quicker than the French to appreciate what the English were doing. The man was Edwin S. Porter, now celebrated for his *Great Train Robbery* (1903). In the film *The Life of an American Fireman*, made late in 1902 or possibly in January of the next year, he adopted the shooting and editing techniques of G. A. Smith and James Williamson. Porter not only used the close shots of Smith and the intercutting of Williamson, he used them rather better. Yet he has been much overpraised for *The Great Train Robbery*, and he never equaled the work of Hepworth in *Rescued by Rover*.

In a sense *The Life of an American Fireman* was a chase picture. Fire was the antagonist. It threatened the destruction of a mother and child, while fire fighters raced to the rescue. There were British precedents. The first was probably R. W. Paul's *Plucked from the Burning* (c. 1898). This 100-foot film had only one scene and one set-up. Fiery death threatened but was defeated. In 1901 or 1902, Williamson used five scenes and 280 feet of film in *Fire!* The picture started with a policeman discovering a fire, then showed the man calling out the fire company, the fire trucks racing to the house, the interior of the burning building with a fireman saving a man through the window, and then more rescues as seen from outside.

111

The Life of an American Fireman

Some like to say that Porter saw and copied the Williamson film. He saw it, I feel sure, but he seems to have improved upon it in a very important way. In my opinion, *The Life of an American Fireman* was more significant than his *The Great Train Robbery,* which was slightly longer and much more successful at the box office.

The story of Porter's fire film is as simple and obvious as that of the English one. But it is told in more detail, and it closes with a new sort of editing. In the opening scene the fire chief is asleep. We know he is dreaming of his wife and child, for they appear vignetted in the upper corner of the scene. With our movie-oriented sophistication, we expect that these loved ones will be the threatened victims of a fire and that the chief will rescue them. But Porter had no subtitles to tell us that the wife and child in the burning house are the two that the chief dreamed about, and the faces are too vague to be identified. Next Porter introduces a close-up of a fire alarm box with a hand opening it and appearing to pull a lever. The third shot takes us to the dormitory of the fire fighters, who wake up, dress hurriedly, and slide down the pole to the floor below. It is obvious that Porter clipped these two shots— like some that follow—from stock footage. For, though we saw most of the firemen slide down the pole in the first shot, when we see the next, on the ground floor, they haven't yet appeared. Before they do show up, horses have charged out of their stalls and been hitched to the fire engines by other men. The next shot shows the outside of the fire house as the apparatus comes out. Then we see a number of machines rushing past the camera. This, too, is a stock shot, for the street is covered with snow. Now, however, comes a scene that Porter must have taken; the camera pans with a fire engine, stops in front of a burning house, and tilts up to the second story where, later on, the mother appears at a window. Then Porter cuts inside to a mother and child in a blazing room.

Now comes some remarkable intercutting of the rescue scene, about which there is considerable dispute. In an existing print, we see mother and child overcome by smoke; a fireman enters by a door, and carries the woman to a window where a ladder appears. Then, from the outside, we see him descend; the mother, becoming conscious, begs the fireman to save the child; he goes up the ladder and in through the window. Inside the room, he picks up the baby, and makes his exit. Outside, we see him descend, and reunite mother and child. Thus Porter seems to have intercut two shots of an interior with three of an exterior—for the first time, so far as I know, in the history of the movies.

A Dispute Over Porter's Editing

Some challenge this claim of intercutting. They do this on the evidence of a paper print of *The Life of an American Fireman* filed for copyright early in 1903. After the fire company reaches the building, this print shows the interior and the exterior scenes in continuous action with no intercutting. The fireman enters the room, opens the window, exits with the mother down the ladder, reappears and does the same thing with the baby; then other firemen enter with a hose. Outside, in another continuous shot, the man comes down the ladder with the woman, listens to her entreaties, goes up the ladder, and comes down again with the baby.

I don't believe that the evidence of the paper print is conclusive. In copyrighting the picture, the Edison company may have made a print from the negative when it was only partially edited. In assembling the negative, Porter would naturally start at the beginning. He would splice the opening shot to the close-up of the firm alarm box, then add the stock material, and the panning shot of the machines arriving at the burning house. At this point, in order to hustle out a print for copyright, someone—doubtless Porter himself—may have spliced on the unedited "rushes" of the interior scenes, which had been taken from one set-up, and then the exterior scenes.

Yet, in all fairness, I must add some evidence pro and con from the Edison catalogue. The action it describes doesn't wholly follow the present release print. It doesn't mention the interior shot in which the fireman rescues the baby and the firemen come in with the hose. After the mother begs the man to return for the baby, the catalogue reads: "He . . . rushes up the ladder, enters the window and after a breathless wait, in which it appears he must have been overcome with smoke, he appears with the child in his arms and returns safely to the ground." Thus the only intercutting indicated in the catalogue is from the outside of the house to the inside and to the exterior again as the fireman rescues the mother.

However, it is obvious from the copyright print that the director took just exactly the scenes he needed for intercutting. If he hadn't intended to intercut elaborately, why would he have shot the fireman returning through the window and rescuing the child, as well as other firemen entering to put out the fire with the hose? And yet a doubt remains. In the rest of his short films, Porter never used such intricate intercutting again.

The Great Train Robbery

There are few disputes about the editing of Porter's famous chase film *The Great Train Robbery*, which he made toward the end of 1903. He used no intercutting, and there are quite a number of identical prints. The picture was far more successful than *The Life of an American Fireman*, and it had a great influence on other film-makers and on the development of theaters for movies only. Yet the earlier film seems to have been more daringly conceived from the point of view of editing.

I think that the success of *The Great Train Robbery* was largely due to the fact that it was the first important "Western"—though it was shot in New Jersey. The other was almost a documentary, a crude reenactment of the dangers and thrills of a fire. *The Great Train Robbery*—obviously fiction but just as obviously exciting—exploited the violence of armed crime. The film started with two desperadoes slugging a station master. It involved murder in the express coach of a moving train, and the blowing open of a strong box. It turned into a chase on horseback and it ended with a gun battle between the good men and the bad. Audiences at *The Great Train Robbery* reveled in thrill after thrill, unaware that they were watching the picture with which the rise of the American film was to begin.

Some of the picture is quite ordinary. The interior scenes are shot in conventional stage fashion. The actors move right to left or left to right. Their gestures are theatrical. But once Porter is out of doors, we are almost in a modern picture. People move toward the camera and away from it. The camera itself rides on the top of a train as the bandits fight for control of the engine. When the train is stopped, and the passengers pile out and line up to be robbed, one man makes a break— directly toward the camera—and is shot dead. Through the window of the railroad station, Porter managed to create the illusion of a train coming to a stop, and, through the open door of the express car, a moving landscape. In two pan shots, he carried his bandits down off the engine and across the woods. For a fillip of excitement after the last scene of the story, Porter added a close-up of a bandit who aimed his pistol at the camera and pulled the trigger.

The important point about *The Great Train Robbery* is that Porter built up what was, for those days, an effective continuity of action

THE GREAT TRAIN ROBBERY—MADE IN NEW JERSEY. This advertisement of 1903 deftly dodges the question of where the film was shot. The illustration is from the scene in which an outlaw shoots at the audience. This could, as one circular explained, be used at the beginning or the end of the film. (*From the collection of and by courtesy of Gordon Hendricks.*)

through a dozen scenes. But he never used two different camera angles in any one setting. He cut back only once to an earlier locale—the station. He didn't intercut as he might have done quite often; in the chase of the bandits by the posse both groups rode by in the same shot. Yet the total effect was of true and mounting excitement—in the terms of those days. Compare it, for example, with *A Gentleman of France* of the same year—a reproduction in one setting and one camera set-up of a scene from a Broadway hit in which the star Kyrle Bellew fought a duel on a staircase.

Porter—One of Three Skillful Cameramen

Around 1900 America had three cameramen who were to win a certain repute in the early days of the new century. Gottlieb Wilhelm "Billy" Bitzer was the only one content to stick to lens work; he contributed much to Griffith's films through twenty years. J. Stuart Blackton was a director, too, and a producer through his partnership in Vitagraph with Alfred E. Smith and "Pop" Rock. Though Blackton made some successful feature films later on, not one of them contributed as much to the screen as the short films that Porter made after he became a director.

A skilled mechanic and electrician, Porter had been a projectionist before he went to work for Edison as a cameraman. All in all, he had seen or shot a goodly number of films. When he directed *The Life of an American Fireman* and *The Great Train Robbery,* he was still the cameraman, and he was quick to see how he could use old or new photographic tricks to heighten the illusion of his pictures.

He knew, for instance, that Méliès had often matted out different parts of two shots in order to create a composite scene that couldn't be directly photographed by a single camera. Thus, Méliès could make an actor meet and talk with himself in a scene. Porter used matte shots in *The Great Train Robbery* to show the train through the window of the railroad station, and the moving landscape through the open door of the express car.

Porter didn't originate the pan shot, which he used effectively in his best-known fiction films. There was camera movement as early as 1896, but it had been merely the accidental result of shooting from a trolley car or a moving boat. The Edison catalogue of 1901–02 bragged about the deliberate use of panning in a short film of a blizzard in New York City: "Our camera is revolved from right to left." In France, perhaps as early as 1902, Zecca had his camera follow actors across a studio set.

Whatever tricks of camera or editing Porter might use, he stuck close to what passed for reality. They say he admired and studied the work of Méliès. In *The Dream of a Rarebit Fiend* (1906) he rivaled the camera tricks of the Frenchman, adding perhaps a bit more realism.

Between Porter's films of fire and robbery, he made a 1,100-foot ver-

sion of *Uncle Tom's Cabin* with a prologue and fourteen tableau scenes
à la Méliès. Did Porter invent the subtitle by "inserting," as the catalogue
said, "announcements with brief descriptions" between the scenes of
Uncle Tom's Cabin?

EDWIN S. PORTER EN TABLEAUX. Between *The Life of an American
Fireman* and *The Great Train Robbery*—both essentially filmic
in treatment—Porter made a very stiff version of *Uncle Tom's
Cabin*. (*From the collection of and by courtesy of Gordon
Hendricks.*)

Imitators and Competitors

In the nineties Edison faced the competition of other inventors, and
soon the competition of other film-makers. Over in Philadelphia Sigmund Lubin faked *The Passion Play* and the Corbett-Fitzsimmons fight.
Just as Edison copied Lumière's *Watering the Gardener* as *The Bad
Boy and the Garden Hose*, Lubin took a leaf from Edison's book and
committed a number of similar robberies. J. Stuart Blackton and Alfred
E. Smith proved more serious and ingenious competitors. Smith, who
had done a spirit-cabinet act at club entertainments, proved an astute
inventor by improving the shutter of the projector, devising a refram-
ing device, and building his own projector and camera. Blackton, a

newspaper illustrator who did chalk talks in some of the shows where
Smith appeared, provided something approaching the first animated
cartoon when Edison photographed his act in the Black Maria. Teamed
together, Smith and Blackton set up a studio on the roof of a New York
building, made one-shot films such as *The Burglar on the Roof* and
Tearing Down the Spanish Flag in 1898. Smith cranked the camera

OFFSPRINGS OF REYNAUD. J. Stuart Blackton, newspaperman and
exploiter of "chalk talks," seems to have been the first to make
an animated cartoon for projection, his *Humorous Phases of
Funny Faces* of 1906. Two years later, the Frenchman Emile Cohl
made his first animated cartoon, *Fantasmagorie,* and then *Drame
chez les Fantoches,* upper left. Another newspaper cartoonist,
Winsor McCay, took his *Gertie the Dinosaur* (1909) on a vaudeville tour, acting as commentator. Walt Disney's first film about
Mickey Mouse, *Plane Crazy* (1928), was not seen until the second, *Steamboat Willie,* had been shown with sound, and a musical accompaniment added to *Plane Crazy.* The last frame is from
The Adventures of Prince Achmed, one of the charming silhouette films that the German artist Lotte Reiniger began to make
in the twenties.

while his partner played the lead in *Happy Hooligan,* a borrowing from the comic papers. Blackton made a trick film and, in *The Humpty Dumpty Circus,* an early American example of stop motion. After the turn of the century the Vitagraph company of Smith, Blackton, and Rock branched out more ambitiously. According to Smith's autobiography, it was in 1904 that they persuaded Mark Twain to let them make a short film out of his story *A Curious Dream,* which the author found "frightfully and deliciously humorous." About the same time Vitagraph filmed parts of two Broadway hits, *A Gentleman of France* and *Raffles, the Amateur Cracksman.* In 1909–10 it was the first Amercan company to give the screen four- and five-reel features—of which more in a later chapter.

Of course there were other competitors, and they grew in number. In 1909 Kalem, Selig, Essanay and representatives of Méliès and Pathé joined Edison, Vitagraph, Kleine and Lubin in the so-called film trust, the Motion Picture Patents Company. Against them stood a couple of dozen independents. Among these were Carl Laemmle's "IMP," which grew into Universal; William Fox, an exhibitor forced into production; and producers operating under such picturesque brands as Flying A, Rex, Nestor, Bison, Keystone, Thanhouser, Lux. There was another trade name to reckon with—Biograph, the last company to join the trust (also in 1909). Biograph, which had grown out of Mutoscope, was notable because of its director general, D. W. Griffith. And Griffith was notable not only because of the new filmic language that he created, but also for the quality of the stories that he drew from literary classics. It was his mastery of the motion picture that made it possible for him to use such materials, vary them with strong contemporary topics, and avoid to a great extent such puerilities as this Pathé plot of 1907:

> *A Fine Birthday Cake.* A gentleman is seen entering a confectioner's, where he leaves an order for a very elaborate cake with which he intends to surprise his wife on the anniversary of her birthday. The errand boy is quickly dispatched with the cake in a basket which he carries on his head. Going down a street, he meets another boy, and they stop under a balcony to exchange cigarettes. While they do this, a couple appears on the balcony above them, and take out the cake, substituting a pair of old shoes. The boy, unsuspecting, is soon on his way. He reaches the home of the customer, and lays the basket on a table. But when the man reaches for the beautiful cake and finds only a pair of old shoes, the boy receives a severe cuffing, instead of the tip he had anticipated.

Films of "Social Significance"

Except for Méliès, film producers after the turn of the century found their chief market among the undereducated. It was an audience that delighted in fast comedies and melodramatic chases. Fortunately, such material made directors experiment with new ways of editing and of using the camera to tell a banal story effectively. And films of this sort —with many outdoor scenes and very few trick shots—were cheaper to make than fairy tales or spectacular fantasies.

Porter and his first contemporaries—and, of course, Griffith a little later—were thoroughly commercial even while they experimented in filmic technique. Hence it may seem odd that so many pictures made between 1905 and 1915 had what might be called social significance. Typical examples were Porter's *The Ex-Convict* and *The Kleptomaniac*. Both dwelt on the plight of the poor and the privileges of the wealthy. Other early directors made films on the iniquities of slum landlords, corrupt politicians, and exploiters of labor. In many of Griffith's films between *A Corner in Wheat* (1909) and the one that began as *The Mother and the Law* and grew into the modern tale in the four-storied *Intolerance* (1916), he attacked the rich and championed the poor.

It is tempting to say that Griffith, as well as Porter and many imitators, turned out thesis films to flatter the vast audience of what we now call the underprivileged, an audience that grew by almost a million a year through immigration between 1902 and 1914. We must remember, however, that if the people who spent their nickels and dimes to see *The Ex-Convict* or *A Corner in Wheat* enjoyed attacks on social injustice, so did the more educated public that read magazines and books. In the first decade of the twentieth century, the celebrated novelist Frank Norris pilloried capitalists and wheat speculators in *The Octopus* and *The Pit*. Upton Sinclair exposed slaughterhouse conditions in his novel *The Jungle*. O. Henry sympathized with the shop girl, the convict, and even what he called "the gentle grafter." And Lincoln Steffens led a group of "muckrakers" through three national magazines.

Chapter

8

Store Theaters
and Greenhouse Studios

O<small>N BOTH SIDES</small> of the Atlantic in the first ten years of the movies, all manner of men made films, showed them, and sold, or finally, rented them. R. W. Paul, Cecil Hepworth, and A. E. Smith had a scientific turn of mind. Paul could make his own cameras. Hepworth invented the first machine for developing film on a rotary drum. Some, like G. A. Smith, the Briton, had been portrait photographers. Méliès and Blackton were draughtsmen as well as entertainers. Others had come out of vaudeville and the circus, where they had juggled, shown acts of magic, walked the tightrope, operated spirit cabinets, or run minstrel shows. In America, the furrier, the glove salesman, and the garment sponger were to appear later—and not as inventors, cameramen, or directors. They proved most capable, however. They made Hollywood.

Most of the earlier film-makers were also projectionists and showmen. At first, they installed their machines in vaudeville houses or music halls in the large cities. Some "bicycled" the machine and reels from one theater to another in the same town. Pretty soon the cameraman had a traveling show that moved from fair to fair. If he had a family, they were apt to go with him in the summer, help run the show, and even at times make new films. (All but two of the cast of *Rescued by Rover* belonged to the Hepworth family, including the dog.) Those were the days when men were proudly installing electricity in their homes, and a woman could be cozened into buying an "electric corset." So, naturally,

121

EARLY SHOWINGS IN SWEDEN. At the left, an early advertisement of
films in Sweden. "Living photographs" from Paris—presumably
Lumière's—were shown at the Summer Theater in Malmö on June
28, 1896. For some few years circuses were show places for motion pictures in Scandinavia. Thus in 1899 the Cirkus Madigan
in Gothenburg advertised Biograph films—whatever they may
have been—as "Edison's ideal in greatest perfection." (*Courtesy
Rune Waldekranz.*)

fairground shows in England and America were "electric theaters"—
"where you see all the latest life-size moving pictures. Moral and refined. Pleasing to the ladies, gentlemen, and children."

The Movies' Checkered Career in Vaudeville

The first American home of the movies was the vaudeville theater.
There they were received with open arms. Not very long after the April
opening of Edison's show at Koster & Bial's in 1896, Oscar Hammerstein
—later the patron of opera—booked films from the American Mutoscope
Co. and Rector into his new variety house. B. F. Keith, titan of vaudeville,
brought the Lumière machine to New York. By the fall of 1896 many of
the important vaudeville theaters were showing films.

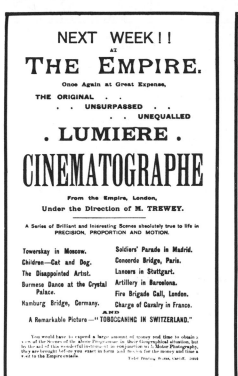

EARLY DAYS IN ENGLAND. Lumière at a provincial music hall in 1896. Two years later the Cheltenham Cricket Club of Gloucestershire used the movies to swell its treasury and allow a member to do some antic promotion. (*From Low and Manvell's History of the British Film.*)

But the days and nights of the movies in vaudeville were numbered. At first the motion picture was the headliner or almost the headliner, spotted two or three turns before the end. By 1900, however, the film had become so boringly repetitious that it was placed last on the program—the "chaser" that was supposed to clear out the audience before the next show. In that year, the strike of the American vaudeville performers' union (oddly called the White Rats) drove a number of theaters to rely entirely on pictures. But a whole evening of the usual short films merely demonstrated that the public had lost interest in this kind of entertainment. And when the strike was over, the houses went back to vaudeville, sometimes with movies as a chaser, sometimes without. Where was the film to find a fitter home?

"Store Theaters"—Here and Abroad

The favorite myth of too many film histories is that the movies found their way to a home of their own through the Nickelodeon that opened in Pittsburgh on Thanksgiving Day, 1905. This, so many think, was the first of the "store theaters" that were to sweep across the country. State Senator John P. Harris and his brother-in-law Harry Davis put a projector, a linen screen, and less than a hundred folding chairs into a vacant room in one of Harris's properties. Some say that the Nickelodeon opened with fifteen minutes of trivial films like *Poor But Honest* and *The Baffled Burglar*. Others claim that the reel-long *Great Train Robbery* kicked off the tiny theater to a career of success.

BIRTHPLACE OF A NAME IF NOT AN IDEA. The movie show that Davis and Harris opened in Pittsburgh in 1905 was not the first store theater, but it gave the name to thousands of similar houses. (*Courtesy Film Library of the Museum of Modern Art.*)

But the Nickelodeon was not the first store theater nor the first successful one. For the Lathams' public showings in New York in 1895 they used a storeroom, and beginning in August a relative of the Lathams did rather well, according to Terry Ramsaye, with a store in Norfolk, Virginia. In September, Jenkins and Armat had their show at the Cotton States Exposition in Atlanta. The following July, "Pop" Rock—later the partner of Blackton and Smith—opened the 400-seat Vitascope Hall in New Orleans with such Edison films as *The Corbett and Courtney Knock-Out Fight, Niagara Falls from the American Side, The Annabella Serpentine Dance, Coney Island, Shooting the Chutes,* and the now famous *May Irwin and John Rice Kiss.*

AN EARLY AMERICAN "STORE THEATER." After showing Edison films at West End, a summer park on the outskirts of New Orleans, "Pop" Rock and a partner named Wainwright opened Vitascope Hall at Canal Street and Exchange Place on June 26, 1896. (*The photograph from the Journal of the Society of Motion Picture Engineers; the advertisement from the New Orleans* Picayune.)

There were store theaters in Europe in 1896. Two days after the Lumières' representatives in Russia showed their films in a summer theater at St. Petersburg, May 17, 1896, they opened a store theater on Nevsky Prospect. In June they exhibited at the spring fair of Nizhni-Novgorod on the Volga. Then in a deal with two Moscow entrepreneurs, they installed their equipment in a small store on Kuznetsky Most, and showed their films there during the winter of 1896–97. Meanwhile in Paris, the Lumières had rented a theater for films and nothing but films. Opened in 1896 as the Cinéma Saint-Denis, it became the oldest movie house in the world. In Berlin, the Kino unter den Linden began film showings on September 19, 1896.

There were not only store theaters in the United States before 1905. There were theaters especially built to house the movies, something never suspected by the film historians. Gordon Hendricks tells me that his research has turned up a number of these, some as early as 1896, some a little later. They were located in Chicago, Toledo, Bergen Beach, Long Island and elsewhere.

THE OLDEST MOVIE THEATER? The Cinéma Saint-Denis in Paris, where the Lumières began to show their films in 1896. When another management took it over and changed the name to the Pathé-Journal, it became a newsreel theater. (*From Jean Vivié's* Historique et développement de la technique cinématographique.)

What Held Back the Dawn?

Why did most of these houses last so short a time and why weren't more of them built? Or more store theaters opened before 1902?

One explanation is aesthetic. The artistic level of the "little" films was low. Another deterrent gravely affected Europe and it may have affected America. This was the fire of May, 1897, that killed 180 people at the Paris Charity Bazaar. Of the victims, 130 were members of the nobility and people prominent in the social and political life of France. And the fire sprang from a Lumière projector, commingling ether and film—the projectionist lit a match as he refilled his lamp. The blow fell only a year after the debut of the Vitascope in New York and less than a year and a half after the first Lumière showing in the Grande Café. A salutary result of the holocaust was severe regulation of projection equipment. Another aftermath was public avoidance of film enter-tainment in any but the best built and best reputed variety houses.

More Theaters Again

The resurgence of the movies in America after the turn of the century may be laid to two things. These were the availability of equipment, and somewhat better films.

FILMS IN A MUSEUM AND A THEATER. At the left, the Musée Grévin, where Reynaud presented his animated cartoon, stories through the nineties. (*From the Archives du Musée Grévin, Courtesy Jean Vivié.*) (*From the Collection Sirot. Courtesy Jean Vivié.*)

As the popularity of moving pictures faded in the vaudeville houses, projection machines began to turn up in the penny arcades. These pleasure places had depended on coin-operated entertainment machines, at first the Edison phonograph, then the Kinetoscope, and in the middle of the nineties the Mutoscope. The arcades might have added projection rooms rather early if it hadn't been difficult at first to get equipment. Edison had made the Vitascope projector for Raff & Gammon, who put it into the vaudeville houses at a good profit. Equipment became much more plentiful when the White Rats lost their battle with the vaudeville chains, and many of the theaters went back to simon-pure variety. By 1902, enterprising owners of arcades could buy projectors at a very reasonable price.

Now we come to a man in Los Angeles named Thomas L. Tally. He didn't wait for the manna from vaudeville that fell after 1901. In August of 1896 he opened his Phonograph and Vitascope Parlor. At the back of the arcade he partitioned off a section to serve as a theater, and installed chairs, a screen, and a projector. The partition had holes in it through which patrons who were nervous about venturing into a darkened room in such a place could see the show. Tally charged ten cents to enter the projection room. There is some dispute about the fee for those who peeked. One authority says Tally charged them nothing, so as to prove that there was really a picture show going on. Another believes he made the timid pay fifteen cents, which sounds more likely.

In April, 1902, Tally took the great plunge. He closed down his arcade and opened a store theater on another street. Tally's Electric Theater showed some Méliès subjects as well as run-of-the-mill American films. At last he booked *The Great Train Robbery*, and with great success.

TALLY'S STORE THEATER. An advertisement on the first page of the *Los Angeles Times* of April 16, 1902.

Suspecting that he wouldn't find such a money maker every week or two, he closed the Electric Theater and toured the Porter film through the West.

Yes, there were a few store theaters before the Nickelodeon burgeoned in 1905, but there were to be 3,000 of them within two years and 10,000 by 1910. Some had such monikers as the Bijou Dream and the Gem, but many bore the name that was such a happy combination of the price of admission with the impressive Greek word for a hall of music. This is said to go back to the 1880's when a Bostonian used the term for one of those strange and depressing exhibitions of oddities called "dime museums." At any rate, the cheap admission price that Nickelodeons advertised by their very name, plus the better one-reel films that came along, spelled success—a big success—for these theaters.

In Europe the pattern was somewhat the same. When the English music halls tired of films, the fair shows took up the slack. On the Continent, audiences gradually forgot about the Charity Fair. In 1903 Berlin had a permanent theater called Das lebende Bild (The Living Picture). Two Electric Theaters opened in Moscow. By 1908, Paris had three newly built theaters—the Louxor, the Electric Palace, and the Omnia-Pathé, and within three years the Hippodrome had been converted into the Gaumont-Palace, seating 5,000 people.

"Make a Small Fortune"

Obviously there was plenty of money to be made in America's store theaters. The chairs were almost as cheap as they were uncomfortable. Of course, the front of the building had to be made over, with a box office in the middle, an entrance door on the right, and an exit door on the left, but that was probably the most expensive item. A projector—and they used only one—could now be bought for as little as seventy-five dollars. There had to be a magic lantern and slides to advise the audience, "One moment, please, while we change reels" and "Ladies, kindly remove your hats," but the theaters got a small income from slides advertising local merchants. To pep up business or fill in while the projectionist changed reels, some theaters added a singer whose ballads were illustrated by lantern slides. By and large, costs were low enough to justify an advertisement by Lubin who made equipment as well as films:

> You are bound to make a small fortune.
> Buy now and get in the push.

Ladies & Gentlemen PLEASE REMOVE YOUR HATS.

NO SMOKING OR SPITTING ALLOWED
Order Board Of Health.

Positively NO WHISTLING, STAMPING OR LOUD TALKING Allowed in - This Theatre.

Why don't you TRY THIS MADAM

SIGNS OF THE TIMES. Each of the nickelodeons that followed the turn of the century had to supplement its single projector with a magic lantern. At first the management needed only a slide reading: "One Moment, Please, While We Change Reels." Supply houses soon began to offer slides like these above. Then came colored illustrations for the songs that the man at the piano rendered between reels. Louis B. Mayer is supposed to have warbled occasionally at his Orpheum Theater in Haverhill, Massachusetts, where he became an exhibitor in 1907. (*From the collection of and by courtesy of Gordon Hendricks.*)

At first, shows lasted only about fifteen minutes. Over the years, they grew longer. The cost per day is hard to arrive at. This depended on the number of films on the program and whether the bill was changed daily or less often. For some time, the exhibitor had to buy films instead of renting them. Black-and-white prints cost from ten to twenty cents a foot. Films that were hand-colored cost as much as thirty cents a foot. These prices didn't worry the exhibitors so much as the fact that they soon had a stock of used films on hand. Hence they began trading with one another, and the word "exchange"—along with a new economic concept—was born. Then came companies that bought films from the pro-

THE MOVING PICTURE AUDIENCE OF TO DAY

MOVIEGOING IN 1910. In a full-page story on Sunday, April 17, 1910, the New York *Herald* pictured the audience of the day, and commented: "Right off the reel it might be well to state that a large part of the population is moving picture mad, and if you don't believe it just separate yourself from ten cents and drop into any one of the 750-odd places in this city where the drama is now being elevated through the medium of films. . . . Thousands of persons keep complete records of the pictures they have seen, and woe be to the film impresario who tries to ring in an old one on them." (*Courtesy Louis Sheaffer.*)

ducers and rented them to the theaters. Ultimately, of course, producers became distributors through offices still called exchanges.

Producers, Too, Made Money

In the years between 1900 and 1910, story films grew longer and costlier, more popular and more profitable. And, of course, the producers as well as the exhibitors made money. *Rescued by Rover* cost seven pounds, thirteen shillings, and ninepence to produce—about $35 at the exchange rate of 1905. When the film proved a success, Hepworth sold each print for ten pounds, twelve shillings, and sixpence. As the negative wore out, he made two more versions, and finally disposed of almost 400 prints at a handsome profit. Porter's *The Dream of a Rarebit Fiend* cost a good deal more to make—$350—and brought in $30,000. Alfred E. Smith writes in *Two Reels and a Crank* that the capital of Vitagraph when it started business in 1896 was $936. Two years later, it showed a profit of $4,750; in 1907, a quarter of a million; and in 1912, $924,782.

Economic changes also touched the camera and the projector. At first, men like Edison and Lumière wouldn't sell or lease the means of making pictures. When Lumière refused to sell a camera to Méliès, even for ten thousand francs ($2,000 at that time), he said, "It is just a scientific novelty of the moment; there is no future in it." It's more likely that he didn't want to part with a golden-egged goose. Paul and others, however, were ready enough to sell, and soon all manufacturers fell in line. A few of the men who made projectors tried to keep control of them by leasing their use on a sort of state's-rights basis. When Edison made his own Projecting Kinetoscope in 1896, he began to sell it outright. The present-day pattern slowly established itself.

MÉLIÈS'S STUDIO. Looking from the well-equipped stage toward the glassed-in walls and ceiling. (*From Bessy and Lo Duca's* Georges Méliès, Mage.)

A ROOFTOP STUDIO. Here on the Morse Building at 140 Nassau Street, New York, J. Stuart Blackton and Alfred E. Smith made their first films. (*Sketch by Blackton from* Two Reels and a Crank, *Smith's autobiography.*)

Studios—With Sun and Without

The motion picture camera was dependent on sunlight for the first half-dozen years of its life. To be sure, Dickson claimed that in the first studio at the Edison plant he sometimes used four parabolic magnesium lamps, or the light of twenty arcs, in addition to opening the studio roof to the rays of the sun. Four laters later Méliès had the first studio of glass.

In between, film-makers worked on the roofs of city buildings. Blackton and Smith made many Vitagraph films on a rooftop stage that could turn with the sun. The English liked to work in natural settings, but by 1898 they were beginning to build raised stages, about fifteen by thirty feet in area, with glass roofs, changeable rear and side walls, and doors at the front against inclement weather. Another had a track to move the camera to a close shot. And one stage revolved on a central ball-and-socket and on outer wheels; when the wheels were removed, the studio floor could rock like a ship.

It is rather odd that Edison—developer of the incandescent bulb and privy to other illuminants—should have remained a cinematic sun worshipper, and built a $10,000 glassed-in studio in the Bronx in 1905. Across the Hudson in Fort Lee, Samuel Goldwyn used this type of studio as late as 1917. Since mercury-vapor lamps had quite eclipsed the sun, workmen covered the outside of the glass with black paint. When the sun and the rain cracked it and washed it off, they painted the inside. When I worked there I can remember how flakes of paint—loosened by the heat of the sun—drifted slowly down like sable snow, and had to be swept up off the floors of the sets twice a day. Out in California, film-makers built interiors on outdoor platforms, and filtered the sunlight through muslin awnings overhead. In a barroom scene of *Keno Bates, Liar*, a William S. Hart two-reeler of 1915, you could see a tablecloth flapping in the breeze. It was in 1903 that Biograph moved to an indoor studio at 11 East 14th Street, New York, and began to use artificial light.

By 1915, the motion picture had found its salvation in the fiction film. In the previous ten years it had developed its primary tools—cameras, projectors, and studios—and it had learned most of the essential secrets of directing and editing. It was waiting for the advent of the man who would bring the silent film to perfection—David Wark Griffith. As it happened, he began his creative work with Biograph, and thus he was soon able to add controlled light to the other skills that he was to perfect.

A BRITISH STUDIO c.1900. In the neighborhood of temperate Brighton, film producers built a number of glassed-in studios, which could be opened or shut. Here is G. A. Smith's with a setting for *Mary Jane's Mishap*. (*Courtesy National Film Archive, British Film Institute.*)

Chapter

9

The Age of Griffith

IN THE YEARS from 1896 to 1906, moving pictures changed into moving stories—moving in physical action, of course, rather than in deep emotion. Between 1906 and 1916, "came the dawn"—memorable words of a forgotten screen writer—the dawn of the feature film, the film star, the first distinguished director, the first picture palaces, and the place called Hollywood.

Those were also the years that created and broke the monopoly of the Motion Picture Patents Company, ruined half its producers, and gave us Adolph Zukor's Paramount, Carl Laemmle's Universal, and the enterprises of William Fox and Warner Brothers. The Motion Picture Patents Company expected to control the manufacture and use of cameras and projectors. Through an exclusive contract with Eastman, the only large American manufacturer of raw film stock, the "trust" forced the independent companies to depend on foreign film. To take care of distribution, it made the General Film Company out of 57 exchanges. Through a licensing system, the distributing arm tried to make theaters show only the movies made by members of the Patents Company. The "trust" used other repressive measures against its lively and progressive competitors. There were court injunctions. Sheriffs seized cameras. So did "goon squads," who also infiltrated mobs of extras and broke up shooting by staging fights. But still the independents produced films and sold them. Laemmle and Fox led the fight, and Zukor and the Warners were in at the death.

Hegira to Hollywood

One way or another, the Motion Picture Patents Company may be credited with making Hollywood the movie capital of the United States. A
legend of the film industry is that the independents discovered Southern
California as a haven of refuge. It was far from New York and close to
Mexico. In moments of stress, cameras, films, and the persons of the
producers could find sanctuary south of the border. Now it is true that
a number of the independents moved west, but so did as many of the
monopolists. Even before William Selig joined in the Patents Company,
he sent a producing unit to California toward the end of 1907. They had
finished the interior scenes of *The Count of Monte Cristo* (1908) in
Chicago and moved west to shoot the exteriors—with a different principal
actor behind Edmond Dantes' beard—on the shore of the Pacific. Soon
an independent producer set up headquarters in a vacant grocery store.

More and more producers, monopolists as well as independents, felt
the lure of West Coast weather. There was no need for electricity in

BEFORE THE MOVIES CAME. About 1905, land was cheap not very
far from Hollywood and Vine. (*Courtesy Milton Luboviski, Larry
Edmunds Bookshop.*)

sunny California. All summer, and except for a few rainy days, all winter, interiors could be shot out of doors with only muslin overhead to kill the sharp shadows. California and the neighboring states offered another attraction as potent as their sunshine. Los Angeles was close to a great many different kinds of landscapes that could not be enjoyed in the East. From San Diego to San Francisco and eastward to Arizona there was almost every variety of mountain, valley, lake, seacoast, island, desert, countryside, and plain that a story might call for. Much of the seacoast was barren of habitation; where there were houses, a type of local architecture sometimes provided Mediterranean atmosphere. Westerns, popular even before the days of the first feature films, could be shot in Griffith Park or San Fernando Valley without leaving Los Angeles County.

All manner of men came to make films. Broncho Billy Anderson—born Max Aronson—had appeared fleetingly in *The Great Train Robbery*, but went on to become the first popular star in Westerns, and made a fortune by turning out a one-reeler every week from about 1908 till 1914. Early in 1910, Griffith began the policy of taking Biograph players to Los Angeles for the winter months. There Jesse Lasky, Samuel Goldwyn, and Cecil B. DeMille made their first picture three years later. Others followed, and the strange concept of Hollywood was born. At one time, studios stretched west to Santa Monica and to Santa Barbara, north into the San Fernando Valley, and southeast to Balboa on the Pacific. Even today, the studios of half the leading companies lie outside the present limits of that little village whose name grew to be a symbol of American film production.

The Days of Small Costs and No Publicity

Long before the courts finally disposed of the Motion Picture Patents Company in 1917, it was dying of its own ills. These were the by-products of monopoly—inefficiency and resistance to change. The chief dogma of the Patents Company and General Film was that the public wouldn't enjoy films longer than one reel or, later, two. One of their producers, Vitagraph, thought differently as early as 1909. It had made *Les Misérables* in four reels and *The Life of Moses* in five, but General Film sent them out a reel a week. Most of the monopolists preferred small pictures made quickly and cheaply. So did some of the independents—but only for a time. They were the men, later joined by Griffith, who brought the feature film to the screen, and opened the way for the huge motion picture theater.

Today it is hard to believe that in the first decade of the century the motion picture industry avoided publicity. But the trust and some of its competitors tried to keep down salaries by not advertising, even on the film itself, the names of their actors or directors. The public had to identify Mary Pickford by the name of the character she played, "Little Mary." Some of the anonymous players were so popular with their audience that astute independents began to recognize the value of advertising their names. "The Biograph Girl" suddenly became Florence Lawrence when Laemmle lured her away from the older company in 1910 and made her the first screen star. When Griffith left Biograph in 1913—after horrifying his employers by making a four-reel film called *Judith of Bethulia*—he bought a full page in *The New York Dramatic Mirror* to advertise the fact that in five years he had directed and/or supervised a great array of outstanding films for Biograph. The days of anonymity were over. The stage was to give stars to the screen while the screen developed far more popular players of its own.

Griffith, the Reluctant Director

At first and for about two years, the screen meant nothing more to Griffith than a fairly dependable income. Acting on the stage had brought no security. He can't have made much out of his poems and stories, though some appeared in national magazines. His one play had been a flop. Following that failure in 1907, he tried to sell Porter a scenario based on *La Tosca*. Balked in that, he began to act for Biograph. In the middle of the next year, when the studio's director, Wallace "Old Man" McCutcheon, fell ill, Griffith was loath to take his job. In *When the Movies Were Young*, his wife, Linda Arvidson, quotes him as saying: "Now if I take this picture-directing over and fall down, then you see I'll be out my acting job." Before he would agree to direct his first film—that was in June, 1908—Biograph had to promise that he could go back to acting if he failed as a director.

Griffith's hesitation was only natural. At that time—in spite of Porter—the art of the screen was either absurd or hidebound. There were no American pictures as well made as *Rescued by Rover*. The settings were poor. Crudely painted outdoor sets mingled with real exteriors, as in the first film in which Griffith acted, Porter's *Rescued from an Eagle's Nest* (1907). The pictures that played the nickelodeons were a sorry lot. Their very titles were bad enough: *Bandit King, The Need of Gold, The Crooked Banker, The Path of Folly, The Football Craze, Engaged to Another, The Cowboy and the School Marm.* Before 1914, most of

Luftens konung på
människojakt.

Kungsörn, som röfvar ett barn.

Rescued from an Eagle's Nest IN SWEDEN. The first of the seven
films in which Griffith acted for Biograph was advertised with
two catch lines: "The king of the air on a man hunt" and "King
Eagle steals a child." (*Courtesy Rune Waldekranz.*)

Griffith's sound as dubious—*The Red Man and the Child, Fools of Fate,
Behind the Scenes, Money Mad, A Fool's Revenge, The Drunkard's Refor-
mation, A Baby's Shoe, The Sheriff's Baby, Just Gold.* A few directors
made one-reel condensations of such things as *Parsifal, As You Like It,*
and *Dr. Jekyll and Mr. Hyde.* Against the fears of Biograph, Griffith
tried his hand at such material. In his first year of work he filmed novels,
short stories, plays, and poems, by Tennyson, Dickens, Jack London,
Shakespeare, Stevenson and Tolstoy.

A Stage Actor the First to Understand the Screen

Griffith's choice of material wasn't so important as the techniques he
developed for filming it. Whether he tackled highbrow or melodramatic
stories, his great contributions to the screen lay in more natural yet vivid
acting, better story organization, and, above all, the invention or the
perfecting of the means for photographing and editing along truly filmic
lines. Since Griffith came from the stage to the screen, it is all the more
remarkable that he should have been the first director to understand
fully the possibilities of the silent film and to develop its true and special
techniques.

COLUMBIA

Washington's Leading Theater.

TOMORROW EVENING AT 8:15
Thursday and Saturday Matinees.

FIRST PERFORMANCE ON ANY STAGE OF A NEW AMERICAN PLAY
IN FOUR ACTS ENTITLED

A FOOL AND A GIRL

BY DAVID WARK GRIFFITH.
PRODUCED UNDER THE DIRECTION OF MR. HACKETT.
COMPANY INCLUDES:

JOHN W. DEAN,   FRANK WUNDERLEM,
DOUGLAS J. WOOD,   J. CLENEAY MATHEWS,
H. S. HADFIELD,   MISS FANNIE WARD,
MISS ALISON SKIPWORTH,   MISS HELEN MAR,
AND OTHERS.

NEXT WEEK
CHARLES FROHMAN PRESENTS

DUSTIN FARNUM
IN THE BIG AMERICAN PLAY,

THE RANGER

BY AUGUSTUS THOMAS.
Entire Production and Excellent Cast Direct From Its Run at Wallack
Theater, N. Y.

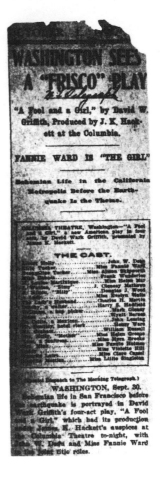

WASHINGTON SEES
A "FRISCO" PLAY

"A Fool and a Girl," by David W.
Griffith, Produced by J. K. Hackett at the Columbia.

FANNIE WARD IS "THE GIRL"

Bohemian Life in the California
Metropolis Before the Earth-
quake Is the Theme.

THE CAST.

WASHINGTON, Sept. 30.

The Wild Duck.

LOOK—how beautiful he is !
    Swift his flight as a bullet
As he comes in from the sea in the morning.
For the wind is from the sea in the morning.
See ! He is bound for the hilltops,
The gold hilltops, the gold hilltops.
There he will rest 'neath the flowers,
The red flowers—the white and red,
The poppy—the flower of dreams,
The crimson flower of dreams.
There must he rest in the morning.
Happy wild duck ! Happy wild duck !
For the wind is from the sea in the morning.

So will he rest 'neath the roses,
The red roses, the love roses,
And their petals will fall around him,
Sweet and warm around him,
Closer and closer around him,
Warmer and warmer around him,
Till even in the day-time the stars shall be shining.
Happy wild duck ! Happy wild duck !
For the wind is from the sea in the morning.
There by the roses bloom the lilies, the flowers of peace,
The white flowers of peace,
Red and white together, red and white and red,
Waving and blowing together,
Blooming and waving together
On the gold hilltops in the morning,
For the wind is from the sea in the morning,

GRIFFITH AS PLAYWRIGHT AND POET. For many years the ambition of the greatest of silent directors was to write successful plays. The only one produced, *A Fool and a Girl,* opened September 30, 1907, in Washington and closed after a week. The above advertisement is from a Washington newspaper. (*Courtesy Louis Sheaffer.*) Before he found his true vocation, Griffith turned out many a verse, such as this excerpt (below) from *Leslie's Illustrated Weekly* in 1907.

In his very first year, Griffith broke all the rules he could find. They were as hidebound as they were absurd. Scenes usually began with an entrance or ended with an exit. Directors never used more than one angle in a scene. They stuck to medium shots, following the dictum of Charles Pathé: "Will you gentlemen never learn that in the cinema an actor must be photographed so that his feet touch the bottom of the screen and his head the top?"

As Griffith used the camera, it was no longer a recording machine turning out a finished film in one shot or making a series of different one-shot scenes to be spliced together. He made his camera give him a set of images that he could shape into a complex scene or sequence. The best effects that he achieved came from the relation of one shot to another. Griffith didn't invent the close-up, but he knew how to use it in a new way. He dared to move the camera while action was going on; he put it on an automobile so that he could follow a galloping horse. He was the first to take extreme long shots of beautiful landscapes or widespread action. Also, he and his cameramen, Billy Bitzer and Arthur Marvin, created new lighting effects—sometimes, perhaps, by accident. As early as 1909, they developed the illusion of firelight, and used back-lighting. They also originated certain techniques—backlighting and reflectors to kill shadows—that are better for romance than reality, and often plague our screen today.

More Drama Through the Close-Up

In Griffith's initial film, *The Adventures of Dollie* (1908), instead of merely moving from one setting to another, he cut at one point to a spot we had already seen. This had already been done by Williamson in *Attack on a China Mission* and more elaborately by Hepworth in *Rescued by Rover,* but it was not common practice in America, and it hinted that the new director was ready to experiment. His next step, far more radical, came in *For Love of Gold,* which he made a couple of months after *Dollie.* He made two set-ups of the same scene and in the second of these, forgetting Pathé, he placed his camera so close to the two actors that they had no feet and—what Griffith was after—the audience could read in their faces the distrust they felt of one another.

Within four months, Griffith introduced two truly revolutionary types of editing in one picture, *After Many Years,* adapted from Tennyson's *Enoch Arden.* They were more important than the intercutting of parallel action that he was to develop, if not invent, and to use so effectively in *The Birth of a Nation.* This was because these types of editing applied

FORM NO. 1326   BULLETIN No. 151. RELEASED July 14, 1908

THE ADVENTURES OF DOLLIE

HER MARVELOUS EXPERIENCE AT THE HANDS OF GYPSIES

LENGTH, 713 FEET.   PRICE, 14 CENTS PER FOOT.

GRIFFITH'S FIRST FILM. Though he used only a single set-up for each scene in *The Adventures of Dollie*, at one point the director cut back to a location he had previously used. It was a daring innovation in American film-making that may have been anticipated only by Porter in *The Life of an American Fireman*, although that is open to question. In Griffith's early days at Biograph he is supposed to have said of the movies: "They can't last, I give them a few years. . . . Nobody is ever going to know I ever did this sort of thing when I am a famous playwright." (*From the collection of and by courtesy of Gordon Hendricks.*)

to more important matters than last-minute rescues. One has been used in all pictures for some fifty-five years, the other in a very great many. In *After Many Years,* he went further than in *For Love of Gold* to make sure that the audience was fully and intimately aware of the emotion of a character. Instead of cutting just a little closer to a figure, he introduced a true close-up. He followed a medium shot of the heroine with a shot of her brooding face. Then came the second device. From the close-up, Griffith cut to the object of her thoughts, her husband on a desert island. Since Griffith's day, many a director has thus cut—or, rather, dissolved—to what a character is thinking about. Here, in two shots following one another, filmic artistry was born. Here was a creative mind applying imagination and psychological intuition to means of communication that no film-maker had yet understood.

Griffith Intercuts the Chase

The Adventures of Dollie was released July 14, 1908. By June 10, 1909, when *The Lonely Villa* appeared, Griffith had developed yet another of his special tools for film-making. This was the intercutting of shots of parallel action, and it was to be hailed in later years as the director's own invention. As film historian George Pratt has pointed out, Griffith had done this in five earlier films, the first time in *The Fatal Hour*, released in August, 1908. Also, says Pratt, directors at Vitagraph and Pathé had used the same technique in two pictures made before *The Fatal Hour*. In *The Lonely Villa* Griffith intercut parts of scenes that were taking place at the same time. After establishing that robbers were holding a mother and her children at gun point, he cut to the husband rushing home to save them. Then he alternated shorter and shorter shots, increasing the excitement and suspense.

Thus Griffith perfected a type of last-minute rescue that he was to use often and effectively. At the climax of *The Birth of a Nation* (1915), he interlaced shots from four pieces of action—the men and women besieged in the cabin, the heroine Elsie being forced into an interracial marriage, the Negro militia rioting in the streets, and the clansmen riding to rescue Elsie and relieve the cabin. Thus Griffith intercut shots that another director might have used to build separate scenes or sequences. In *Intolerance* (1916), Griffith used intercutting not only *within* the film's four separate stories, of ancient Babylon, first-century Judea, Renaissance France, and the America of his day. He also intercut *between* the four stories and he often interjected between them the symbolic vision of "the cradle endlessly rocking."

The Cutter's Secret—E Pluribus Unum

Until the coming of war in *The Birth of a Nation*, Griffith's editing was as unhurried as the life he pictured. Then, when the drama quickened, so did his cutting as he developed more complex sequences. Scenes made up of a medium or long shot and a closer one gave way to scenes involving many more angles. From such scenes, the director went to longer and more elaborate sequences. For instance, in the meeting of the Negro-dominated legislature Griffith opened on a long shot of the empty chambers. Then—perhaps too obvious a trick—he dissolved in the legislators at their desks. After that, he went to close shots of various figures, then to a balcony, and back to individuals and a long shot or two.

Griffith's mastery of this kind of editing is best demonstrated in the scene of Lincoln's assassination. Here we have the actions and reactions of a half-dozen people fused with longer shots of the auditorium and the stage of Ford's Theater. In this scene Griffith used at least fifty-five cuts. After an establishing shot of eighteen feet (running only eighteen seconds) no cut was longer than twelve-and-a-half feet. Seventeen were three feet or less. Of course it was in the last-minute rescue at the rushing climax of *The Birth of a Nation* that Griffith used the shortest cuts. He got down to shots that have to be counted by frames—one foot and eleven frames, one foot and one frame, and a shot of only fourteen frames, or less than a second.

D. W. GRIFFITH'S

Tremendous Spectacle

"THE FALL OF

BABYLON"

Produced Personally by
David Wark Griffith
CREATOR OF
"The Birth Of A Nation"
"Hearts Of The World"
"The Mother And The Law"
AND OTHER NOTABLE MASTER
PRODUCTIONS

A PURPLE ROMANCE OF
ANOTHER DAY

(BASED ON THE BABYLONIAN EPISODE IN "INTOLERANCE")

125,000 PLAYERS IN THE PRODUCTION
7,500 HORSES
THE GREATEST PICTURE WHICH THE WORLD'S GREATEST MA-
STER OF PICTURE-MAKING HAS TURNED OUT." - - Los Angeles Times.

THE MAN AND A SMALL PART OF HIS WORK. After the failure of *Intolerance*, Griffith made a feature out of the most spectacular section of the gigantic picture. The statistics seem a bit exaggerated, but the portrait is rather good.

A New Syntax of Expression

Though Griffith experimented from the first, it took him five years of very hard work to develop the full artistry of *The Birth of a Nation*. Between 1908 and 1913 he directed or produced more than 450 one-reel and two-reel films and went on to the four-reel spectacle, *Judith of Bethulia* (released in 1914). In all this work he was analyzing a new medium and a new area of audience-reaction, and he was guessing audaciously and successfully at the means that would achieve his ends. He was learning and demonstrating how emotion could be stimulated and satisfied through the visual impressions and associations created by the skills of camera work and editing. He developed and all but perfected a new means of expression. He did not invent all the words of this new language of communication, but he found out how to put them together and give them vastly greater meaning. As Terry Ramsaye has admirably expressed it, although Griffith did not provide a whole new vocabulary, he gave the screen its syntax.

The virtuosity of Griffith was more than uncommon. Besides directing and cutting, and also supervising other directors, he conceived story ideas and knew how to adapt the work of others. Frank Woods, one of the first scenario writers, had only to suggest *Enoch Arden* to Griffith, or *The Clansman*, the novel by the Reverend Thomas Dixon, Jr., which became *The Birth of a Nation*. According to tradition, Griffith never worked from a written script until he made his first talkie, *Abraham Lincoln* (1930). Even with *Intolerance*, he is said to have carried in his head each of the four stories and all the angles he needed. However, I am inclined to suspect that he made notes from time to time and wasn't above looking at them before the day's shooting began.

Music Wed to Editing—or Vice Versa?

The motion picture was never a truly silent art. Except for the short-lived shows of the Lathams and of Jenkins and Armat in 1895, there was music at even the earliest shows in America. Vaudeville orchestras had always underscored the silent feats of acrobats and jugglers. They could never have failed—and they didn't fail—to make an expressive noise when the Vitascope flickered. When one or more are gathered together, man abhors the vacuum of silence. Else why did the humble owner of a humble store theater go to the expense of a piano player and an upright? The silent films required more than just noise. They needed interpretation. And so, even before pipe organs and orchestras graced the motion picture palaces, publishers issued special sheets of music sup-

148

APPASSIONATO № 1
For Deep emotion, intense or tragic situations

Piano

Erno Rapee
and William Axt

8 bars from APPASIONATO #1—By Erno Rapee and William Axt (Capitol Photoplay Series) Copyright 1923/Copyright Renewal 1951 Robbins Music Corp. New York, N.Y. Used by permission.

FAMOUS FOTOPLAY SERIES
VALSE PASSIONNÉE
Desire - Ecstasy - Vampire

Piano

DOMENICO SAVINO
Orch. by the Composer

8 bars from VALSE PASSIONEE—By Domenico Savino (Famous Photoplay Series) Copyright 1927/Copyright Renewal 1955 Robbins Music Corp. New York, N.Y. Used by permission.

posed to be appropriate to various dramatic or comic scenes—for instance, "Hurry No. 2 (For scenes of great excitement, duels, fights, etc.)."

Today nobody knows just when Griffith began to take a special interest in music for the screen. He may have heard that the distinguished composer Saint-Saëns wrote a score for that one-reeler of Film d'Art *The Assassination of the Duc de Guise.* At any rate, the musical accompaniment that he provided for *The Birth of a Nation* was so filmic—closely wedded to the successive images—that it drew the attention of all the movie world. It was no original composition, and probably better for that reason. Griffith and Carl Breil supplied a couple of new tunes, but for the rest they found memorable themes that fitted particular scenes and became leitmotivs. The most famous was "The Ride of the Valkyries," which they borrowed from Wagner to whoop up each shot of the galloping clansmen.

I believe that Griffith's classic was the first picture *conceived* as more than a silent film, that the director saw the possibilities of music as he shot and cut. I first realized this when I viewed the film in a theater that ran a silent print with phonograph records. The sustained melodies couldn't approximate the swiftly varying score that Griffith had sent out to each theater, for his had been a blend of a great many musical themes, some short, some long, and many of them recurrent. Because no one record could fit the differing moods of even a few scenes, I found myself conscious of what seemed the over-length of many scenes, and realized that they could never have run so long, and been so effective, without the music designed for them. I even found myself wondering if the cutting hadn't been designed to some degree in relation to the music.

Griffith's Way with Actors

For about five years, no one equalled Griffith in the discovery and development of notable acting talent. Some of his players may have given obvious performances; as late as 1919 he let Donald Crisp play the heavy in *Broken Blossoms* with absurdly violent overemphasis. But even before *The Birth of a Nation,* Griffith showed what was then an unexcelled talent for handling actors. This was due in part to his policy of careful and thorough rehearsals before shooting began. Unhappily, the performances of many of those that he found or trained are now only dimly remembered; we seldom see films with his wife, Linda Arvidson, or with Arthur Johnson, Blanche Sweet, Wallace Reid, Robert Harron, Spottiswoode Aitken, Bessie Love. Some, like Lionel Barrymore, Mary Pickford, and Donald Crisp went on to new careers on the stage or

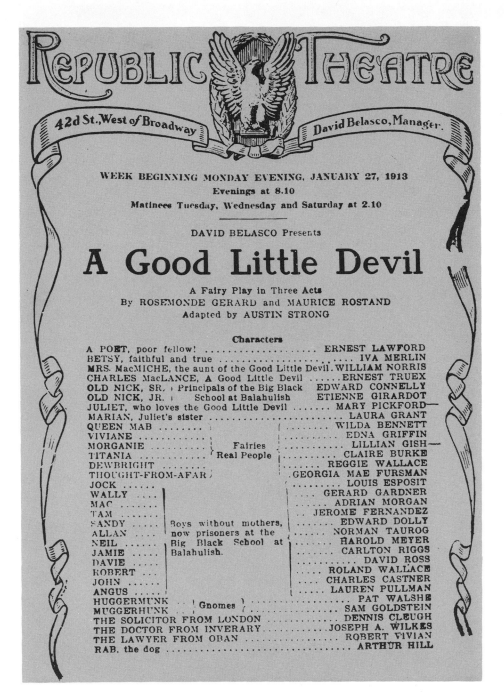

REPUBLIC THEATRE

42d St., West of Broadway

David Belasco, Manager.

WEEK BEGINNING MONDAY EVENING, JANUARY 27, 1913
Evenings at 8.10
Matinees Tuesday, Wednesday and Saturday at 2.10

DAVID BELASCO Presents

A Good Little Devil

A Fairy Play in Three Acts
By ROSEMONDE GERARD and MAURICE ROSTAND
Adapted by AUSTIN STRONG

Characters

A POET, poor fellow! .... ERNEST LAWFORD
BETSY, faithful and true .... IVA MERLIN
MRS. MacMICHE, the aunt of the Good Little Devil. WILLIAM NORRIS
CHARLES MacLANCE, A Good Little Devil ...... ERNEST TRUEX
OLD NICK, SR. ⎱ Principals of the Big Black ⎰ EDWARD CONNELLY
OLD NICK, JR. ⎰ School at Balahulish ⎱ ETIENNE GIRARDOT
JULIET, who loves the Good Little Devil .... MARY PICKFORD—
MARIAN, Juliet's sister .... LAURA GRANT
QUEEN MAB .... ⎱ ⎰ .... WILDA BENNETT
VIVIANE .... ⎰ ⎱ .... EDNA GRIFFIN
MORGANIE .... ⎰ Fairies ⎱ .... LILLIAN GISH—
TITANIA .... ⎰ Real People ⎰ .... CLAIRE BURKE
DEWBRIGHT .... ⎰ ⎱ .... REGGIE WALLACE
THOUGHT-FROM-AFAR ⎰ ⎱ GEORGIA MAE FURSMAN
JOCK ...... ⎱ ⎰ .... LOUIS ESPOSIT
WALLY .... ⎰ ⎰ ... GERARD GARDNER
MAC ...... ⎰ ⎰ ...... ADRIAN MORGAN
TAM .... ⎰ ⎰ .. JEROME FERNANDEZ
SANDY ..... ⎰ Boys without mothers, ⎰ ...... EDWARD DOLLY
ALLAN .... ⎰ now prisoners at the ⎰ ...... NORMAN TAUROG
NEIL ...... ⎰ Big Black School at ⎰ ...... HAROLD MEYER
JAMIE ..... ⎰ Balahulish. ⎰ ...... CARLTON RIGGS
DAVIE .... ⎰ ⎰ .... DAVID ROSS
ROBERT .... ⎰ ⎰ ... ROLAND WALLACE
JOHN ...... ⎰ ⎰ .... CHARLES CASTNER
ANGUS ..... ⎰ ⎰ ..... LAUREN PULLMAN
HUGGERMUNK ⎱ Gnomes ⎰ .... PAT WALSHE
MUGGERHUNK ⎰ ⎰ .... SAM GOLDSTEIN
THE SOLICITOR FROM LONDON .... DENNIS CLEUGH
THE DOCTOR FROM INVERARY............JOSEPH A. WILKES
THE LAWYER FROM OBAN .... ROBERT VIVIAN
RAB, the dog .... ARTHUR HILL

MARY PICKFORD AND LILLIAN GISH ON BROADWAY. In 1913 these
players, one of them already a screen star, appeared in a David
Belasco production.

screen. Revivals of *The Birth of a Nation* and *Intolerance* in art theaters and by film societies have let us know and cherish other talents that Griffith shaped. We see the true, if mid-Victorian, romanticism of Henry Walthall and his quick flashes of humor. Lillian Gish and Mae Marsh still compete in gaiety and pathos. The comedy of Constance Talmadge lives again.

Griffith's Defects and Limitations

Griffith's shortcomings are all too evident. They stand out in his best films almost as much as in his poorest.

Some, the least important, lay in the use of technical tricks that are long outmoded. One of these was the iris to concentrate attention without cutting to a close-up. Into normal black-and-white film stock—he cut scenes in blue, sepia, or red tints; this was to provide a poor impression of moonlight, lamplight or sunset. In *Broken Blossoms,* he introduced soft focus close-ups that jarred with the hard shots before and after them. Diffusion—and not too much of it—is now largely reserved for female stars a little past their prime.

Griffith's more important defects were psychological, a curious phenomenon in a man who understood almost instinctively the psychology of eye and brain in relation to a new medium. In certain areas, Griffith's mind was shallow and obvious, his emotions sentimental or even maudlin. He saw life through Victorian opera glasses. Heroines were blonde and fragile, villains darkly sadistic. In spite of his personal kindliness and consideration, he valued himself—or at least his ideas and his prejudices—too highly. He set himself up as historian-philosopher. In his subtitles he became pontifically authoritative, and thoroughly muddled. Early in *The Birth of a Nation* he pictured the South as about to be destroyed by Republican victory, and later in the picture he idealized Lincoln in this absurd line of printed dialogue: "We will ask mercy from the Great Heart." In the same picture he interrupted the flow of action at least three times to explain that a historical scene we were about to see was "an exact facsimile" of a famous painting or of the event itself. In *Intolerance* he injected learned footnotes from *The Encyclopaedia Britannica,* and then went on to give his heroines such names as "The Dear One," "Brown Eyes," and "Princess Beloved."

Great Moments from Griffith

In spite of Griffith's limitations as a thinking and feeling man—and because of his skill as an artist of camera and cutting—he gave us some unforgettable moments. Most of these were due to new and daring skill in cutting. No one can forget a certain moment in the modern story in *Intolerance*. Vsevolod Pudovkin, the notable Russian director, has described it:

> Here there is a scene in which a woman hears the death sentence passed on her husband, who is innocent of the crime. The director shows the face of the woman: an anxious, trembling smile through tears. Suddenly the spectator sees for an instant her hands, only her hands, the fingers convulsively gripping the skin. This is one of the most powerful moments in the film. Not for a minute did we see the whole figure, but only the face and the hands. And it is perhaps by virtue of this fact that the director understood how to choose and to show, from the mass of real material available, only these two characteristic details, that he attained the wonderful power of impression notable in this scene.

In *The Birth of a Nation* there are many similar evidences of Griffith's fine abilities. Against the racial bias of *The Birth of a Nation,* we must set the romantic vigor with which he pictured the battles of "the lost cause." Against a scene in which Lillian Gish and a dove indulged in osculatory maneuvers while "The Little Colonel" pondered how to substitute his lips for the beak of the bird, we must set the poignant homecoming of the hero. First the empty street. Then the worn figure moving slowly to the steps of his ravaged home, and the eager, pathetic greeting of his little sister, so beautifully played by Mae Marsh. Finally, as the man is entering the house, comes an encircling arm about his shoulders —we know it is his mother's, though we never see her. War and homecoming were simple things that Griffith understood. Whenever he held his emotions to such levels, he gave us much. We found imagination in *Intolerance;* beauty and terror, as well as banality, in *Broken Blossoms;* and many, many fine scenes in almost all his maturer pictures.

As Griffith Fades Away

The last fifteen years of Griffith's life as a director were sadly mixed, both in value and in evaluation. Critical estimates of Griffith ranged from adulation to scorn. On the basis of *The Birth of a Nation* and *Broken Blossoms,* many critics said he was a genius whose work would never be equaled. In between these two films came the failure of *Intolerance,* a brilliant effort in which a great technician overplayed his hand. Jove had unquestionably nodded, and when the celebrant of the Ku Klux

Klan—who spelled Negro with a small "n"—launched a press campaign as the high priest of tolerance, many a critic saw him as a victim of something close to megalomania. Through *Hearts of the World* (1918), *Broken Blossoms* (1919), *Way Down East* (1920), and *Orphans of the Storm* (1922), Griffith's reputation wobbled between the poles of genius and crass commercial adroitness.

In the ten years after *Broken Blossoms*, Griffith made at least fifteen pictures, most of which were so disappointing to both critic and box office that all but two or three of their titles have been forgotten. When, on top of this, Griffith tried his hand at a talkie in *Abraham Lincoln*—doing no worse than most of the silent directors who were trying to master sound in 1930—the poor man was done for. He made one more film, *The Struggle* (1931), for United Artists, the group of independents to which he belonged. Thereafter, although he won high praise for *Abraham Lincoln*, Hollywood studios ignored him even while they built their pictures on the broad basis of what he had taught them.

To see *The Birth of a Nation* is to see Griffith at his peak, to see how great a contribution one man made to the art of the screen, and to see why he gave us no more than he did. This best of the silent films—one of the few dramatic films that are bearable today—makes us see not only the limitations of Griffith, but also the limitations of that "silent art" whose demise was so violently mourned when sound came in. Griffith was too much a part of the silent motion picture to survive it as a director. But he still survives—and brilliantly—as the man who made the silent screen speak.

Chapter

10

The Coming of the Feature Film

WHAT WAS THE FIRST feature film? Who made it? And when?

Most moviegoers of today would probably pick Griffith's *The Birth of a Nation* of 1915. Because I was a motion picture critic on a newspaper around that time, I happen to know that the idea of the feature film was born some three years earlier. Griffith himself had finished at least four features before he started his epic. And prior to 1915 more than fifty features had been made in Europe and America.

The Feature—Five Reels at One Showing

I think we had better begin by defining the feature film. In the first place, it doesn't have to last two or three hours like the blockbusters of the sixties. On the other hand, the French picture *Queen Elizabeth*, which launched Adolph Zukor and Famous Players in 1912, cannot qualify as a feature; it was only three reels long, though the distributor later advertised it as four. Zukor himself was rather slow in accepting the trade dictum that a feature ought to fill at least five cans, each can holding about 1,000 feet of film. He made at least two five-reelers in 1913, but among his movies of that year and the next were a dozen shorter films, three of which were only three reels long. Zukor—and some other producers of such short features—could hardly plead that the story material was scanty, for almost all were based on novels or plays. Though five reels got thoroughly established by 1914 as the rock-bottom minimum for the kind of feature that was called a "program picture," there were more and more "specials" that ranged from 6,000 to 12,000 feet.

It may seem absurd to add to the definition of a feature film that all of its five or more reels have to be shown, one after the other, at every performance. Yet we must recall the case of J. Stuart Blackton and *The Life of Moses*, made in 1909. So far as I know, this Vitagraph production was probably the first film of feature length, but the public never saw it as a five-reel movie. The short-sighted resistance of the "trust" and its booking office was so great, that though Vitagraph was one of the member companies, they sent it out, as I have said in the last chapter, one reel at a time for five weeks. Whatever the merits of *The Life of Moses* —and the three "stills" I have seen seem from a stage production with such things as mountains painted on a backdrop—Blackton deserves the credit for producing the first feature that could have met the test of the five-reel yardstick. Moreover, he himself intended it as a continuous show.

From Shorts to a Feature in a Single Year

Except for Vitagraph, the resistance of the members of the trust to films longer than one reel was bitter and uncompromising—and suicidal. Even 2,000-foot movies upset the monopolists. In 1910, when Biograph discovered that Griffith had made a two-reeler called, ironically, *His Trust*, the company cut the film in two, and sent it out successively as one-reel shorts called *His Trust* and *His Trust Fulfilled*. The studio tried to do the same thing with his *Enoch Arden* (1911)—an expansion of his 1908 *After Many Years*—but, as more and more such dismembered films appeared, exhibitors got into the habit of holding up the first reel and showing it with the second. This quiet revolt of the exhibitors was significant. It signalled the turning of the tide. It foreshadowed the destruction of the film trust, hoist on its own petard. By 1912 some members of the trust were making three-reelers, an independent had turned out a feature, and the Continent had sent us the first of a series of spectacles.

In Europe there was no patent monopoly to dictate the length of films. Italy took the lead. In 1911 a company in Milan devoted five reels to *Dante's Inferno*, and in August this film became the first feature to be road-shown in American theaters. Italian directors, turning history into screen spectacle, were as prodigal of film footage as of extras. Enrico Guazzoni's *Quo Vadis?*, made in 1912, opened at the Astor Theater on Broadway on April 21, 1913, at $1.50 top, and ran off eight or nine reels to a special orchestral accompaniment. That year Italy turned out two

QUO VADIS?

vari ej mindre än **5000 människor** och **30 Lejon** medverkat.

"5,000 PEOPLE AND 30 LIONS." Thus Sweden hailed the Italian spectacle of 1912 when it was first shown there, appropriately enough in the Lorensberg Circus in Stockholm. (*Courtesy Rune Waldekranz.*)

versions of *The Last Days of Pompeii*, Ambrosio's in six reels and Pasquali's in eight. From the rather short and quite static products of Film d'Art, France plunged ahead in 1913 to *Germinal* in eight reels and *Les Misérables* in twelve. With *Cabiria*, the same year, Italy matched *Les Misérables* in length and outdid the French film in lavish spectacle. It seemed that the Italians would dominate the film world with what one of their critics called "such solemn, terrible, and overwhelming images." Then came World War I and an end to their dreams of cinema conquest.

An American Feature Before Queen Elizabeth

As the trust weakened and the independents prospered, more and more American companies were able to produce and exhibit three- and four-reel films. At last, late in May or early in June, 1912, H. A. Spanuth, a now-forgotten independent, made film history that few remember by showing New York critics the Broadway star Nat Goodwin in a true feature, *Oliver Twist*. Its five reels were shown, unsegmented, at every performance. Here was the forerunner of the program pictures that were to meet the five-reel test-gauge of the feature film.

Whether or not *Oliver Twist* was shown publicly before Zukor's *Queen Elizabeth*, the American film was overshadowed by Zukor's importation.

We shall never know if the Dickens film was as stagey and unimaginative as the French movie, but Zukor's had the advantage of a great international star, Sarah Bernhardt. The actress was old and lame and shorn of her golden voice. But she was still Bernhardt, and Zukor took pains to exploit star and film to the limit of his ingenuity. Also, he planned to follow this up with the organized production of other films displaying "Famous Players in Famous Plays."

Zukor—From Penny Arcades to Broadway

In 1903 Zukor had begun his film career as one of the partners in a penny arcade that offered "Automatic Vaudeville" to the denizens of Union Square, then the heart of the New York theatrical district. The next year, the group added the Crystal Hall upstairs, where they showed fifteen minutes of films for ten cents. Dropping out of the partnership, Zukor enlisted the aid of the Broadway producer William A. Brady, and installed one of *Hale's Tours* in a shop near the arcade. When this simulacrum of a railroad trip proved a "one-shot" attraction, Zukor cannily added *The Great Train Robbery* to the end of Hale's travel film and found that business picked up. Convinced that the public wanted action pictures, he tore out the expensive equipment that imitated a train in motion, and turned what had been a store into the Comedy Theater in 1906. While he showed short films there and in other cities, his mind turned to the possibilities of longer pictures as a sounder investment. He soon imported a three-reel, hand-colored Pathé 1908 production of the Oberammergau *Passion Play*.

Zukor Enlists Both Stage and Screen

Getting the facts of the film history of only fifty years ago is no easy matter. The story of how Zukor obtained the American rights to *Queen Elizabeth* in 1912 is one of many examples. In 1926, Terry Ramsaye said in his voluminous and valuable history, *A Million and One Nights,* that Zukor and two partners bought the rights for $18,000. Some twenty-five years later, Zukor himself stated in his book *The Public Is Never Wrong* that he had put up $40,000 to finance this French production by Louis Mercanton.

To launch *Queen Elizabeth* in proper style and to advise on the production work that was to follow, Zukor enlisted the stage producer Daniel Frohman. The picture was shown to the press and "a distinguished audience" at the Lyceum Theater on the afternoon of July 12, 1912, blessed by a Broadway accolade: "Daniel Frohman presents *Queen Elizabeth.*"

When Zukor organized the Famous Players Film Company, the tone of his publicity suggested that he—like the men of Film d'Art—believed he had to depend for success on stage stars and stage plays. But he knew there was an art of the film that the French had not grasped, for he offered the post of director general to Griffith at $50,000 a year, and when he refused, Zukor hired Porter of *The Great Train Robbery.* He added to his staff J. Searle Dawley, who had had experience in directing short films as well as plays, and he engaged as press agent B. P. Schulberg, who was later to head Paramount production on the Coast.

At first Zukor concentrated on actors with stage reputations. His initial production, made late in 1912, starred James O'Neill—the father of Eugene O'Neill—in *The Count of Monte Cristo,* which the actor had played for almost twenty years up and down the country. Selig was first in the field, however, with a version starring Hobart Bosworth. In *A Million and One Nights* Terry Ramsaye states that the Famous Players film had to be shelved until "the Selig version should have been forgotten by the exhibitors." Their memories must have been short, for the O'Neill film was in release within a year. The first Famous Players production to reach the screen was *The Prisoner of Zenda* (1913) with James K. Hackett, who had made a hit in the play. Then, in 1913 and 1914, came a procession of stage stars in films made from stage plays and a novel or two. Among the actors were Mrs. Minnie Maddern Fiske, Henrietta Crosman, and young John Barrymore, all from the American stage, and Lily Langtry and Cecilia Loftus from the British.

In Zukor's first year of production he discovered that a screen actress could be more effective and more popular than the best player the stage could offer. The actress was Mary Pickford. On Broadway she had played a child in two of David Belasco's productions, but she was essentially a silent screen actress, well trained by Griffith in her Biograph days. Beginning with *A Good Little Devil* (1913), her first Famous Players production, Mary Pickford was to prove more successful than any of Zukor's stage stars. Through *Tess of the Storm Country* (1914), *Rebecca of Sunnybrook Farm* (1917), *Pollyanna* (1920), and a number of other films, she had a series of successes that vindicated Zukor's belief in the feature film—and Miss Pickford.

Longer Films for Bigger Theaters

Of course there were other producers making features besides Zukor —and some before him. Late in 1912, the Kalem company released a six-reel film, *From the Manger to the Cross,* which Sidney Olcott had

Famous Players Film Company
ADOLPH ZUKOR, President
124-130 WEST 56TH STREET

DANIEL FROHMAN
MANAGING DIRECTOR

NEW YORK___July 1,___ 19 16

Mr. James O'Neill,

PAYABLE IN NEW YORK EXCHANGE
TERMS NET CASH

Pequot Ave.,

New London, Conn.

"THE COUNT OF MONTE CRISTO"

Total Sales		$45539.32
Costs		
Raw Negative	$4105.75	
Talent	1025.00	
Hotel & Travel	83.35	
Costumes & Props	142.00	
Miscellaneous Expenses	1228.47	
Extraordinary Expenses	51.40	
Raw Positive	13882.37	
Advertising	1674.80	
Legal Expense	2450.20	
Royalty & License	1397.22	
Burden	1215.44	
Total Costs		27256.00
Profit		$18283.32
ROYALTY: 20% thereof as per contract		$3656.66
Cash previously paid	$3500.00	
Balance	156.66	
	$3656.66	$3656.66

CORRECTING THE RECORD ON MONTE CRISTO. Though film histories say that Famous Players had to shelve its James O'Neill version because a rival film had beaten it to the screen, Louis Sheaffer in researching for a biography of Eugene O'Neill came across records that show the Zukor film was released in San Francisco and elsewhere in November, 1913, and had grossed almost $45,000 by the end of the year. Though as shown by this statement of 1916, Famous Players charged in almost $14,000 for prints, physical production costs came to only a little more than $13,000. The profits on a modest investment were rather good. O'Neill sued the rival producers for infringing the rights to his own dramatization of the old novel and won a favorable decision.

directed in Palestine. During the next year *Traffic in Souls*, directed by George Loane Tucker, in six reels, opened in a rather small theater, Joe Weber's, but it was soon playing in nearly thirty New York houses. In 1914 Colin Campbell finished *The Spoilers*, at least two hours long. By the end of 1913, so many features had been made—even England had a 7,500-foot version of *David Copperfield*—that producers and distributors could take over Broadway theaters and even think of building new and bigger houses.

Early in 1914, the Blackton-Smith-Rock company had enough long films to lease the Criterion Theater on Broadway, a legitimate house of modest capacity, and rename it the Vitagraph. Much more important,

THE FIRST "RUNAWAY" FEATURE. This film, made by Sidney Olcott for Kalem, was distributed by the exchanges of the Motion Picture Patents Company early in 1913—a sign of the collapse of the film trust's policy against feature films. (*Courtesy John Hampton.*)

the supply of features was now so abundant that Mitchell L. Mark, who started with penny arcades, had no qualms about building the 3,300-seat Strand. This first of America's big new theaters opened in April, 1914, with Selig's nine-reel production of *The Spoilers*, still remembered by some because of the super-colossal fight between William Farnum and Tom Santschi. The success of the Strand, which charged from ten cents to fifty cents a seat, had much to do with the building, during the next three years, of many new theaters that seated more than 1,200 movie-goers.

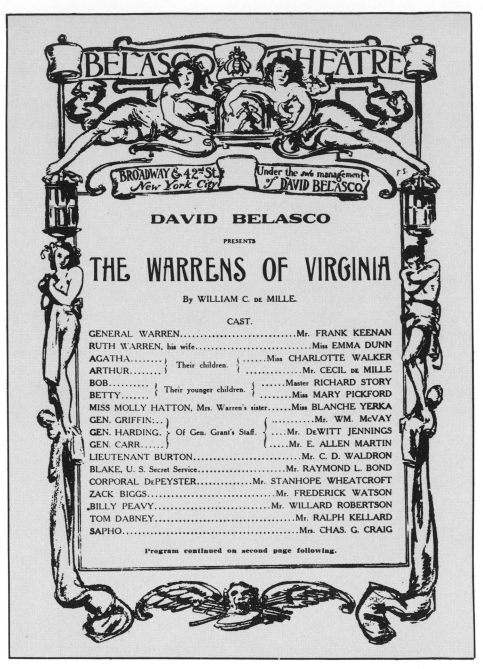

BELASCO THEATRE

BROADWAY & 42nd St. New York City

Under the sole management of DAVID BELASCO

DAVID BELASCO

PRESENTS

THE WARRENS OF VIRGINIA

By WILLIAM C. de MILLE.

CAST.

GENERAL WARREN..........................		Mr. FRANK KEENAN
RUTH WARREN, his wife........................		Miss EMMA DUNN
AGATHA........	*Their children.*	Miss CHARLOTTE WALKER
ARTHUR........		Mr. CECIL de MILLE
BOB.........	*Their younger children.*	Master RICHARD STORY
BETTY.......		Miss MARY PICKFORD
MISS MOLLY HATTON, Mrs. Warren's sister		Miss BLANCHE YERKA
GEN. GRIFFIN:..		Mr. WM. McVAY
GEN. HARDING.	*Of Gen. Grant's Staff.*	Mr. DeWITT JENNINGS
GEN. CARR.....		Mr. E. ALLEN MARTIN
LIEUTENANT BURTON........................		Mr. C. D. WALDRON
BLAKE, U. S. Secret Service....................		Mr. RAYMOND L. BOND
CORPORAL DePEYSTER.............		Mr. STANHOPE WHEATCROFT
ZACK BIGGS...............................		Mr. FREDERICK WATSON
BILLY PEAVY...........................		Mr. WILLARD ROBERTSON
TOM DABNEY............................		Mr. RALPH KELLARD
SAPHO................................		Mrs. CHAS. G. CRAIG

Program continued on second page following.

"C. B." AND LITTLE MARY ON BROADWAY. On December 3, 1907, DeMille (then de Mille) and Mary Pickford appeared in Belasco's production of a play by William C. de Mille with a much more distinguished cast. (*Courtesy Belasco Collection, New York Public Library.*)

Go West, Young Men—Lasky, DeMille, and Goldwyn

Hollywood meant very little to the feature film until close to the end of 1913. Then a West Coast actor sent to New York a seven-reel film that made quite a stir, and New York sent to Hollywood the first of three partners who were to set their mark—a very big mark—on modern production. The actor was Hobart Bosworth and the film was Jack London's *Sea Wolf*, a Pallas Pictures feature, which Bosworth produced and starred in. The three men were C. B. DeMille, Jesse L. Lasky and Samuel Goldfish. They came to Hollywood as partners, they became allies of Zukor, and each of them ended as an independent film-maker of note.

Lasky, a vaudeville producer, had created in the Folies Bergères of New York a cabaret that was, unfortunately, ten years ahead of its time. Sam Goldfish—to be known as Goldwyn after January, 1919—had been a glove salesman, and for some time his job was raising capital by selling pictures before they were finished. DeMille, after some years as a minor stage actor and playwright, was to find his niche in Hollywood as a producer and director of spectacles. Since DeMille had had no experience in film-making (neither had his partners, for that matter), he spent a few days at the Edison studio, and then hired Oscar Apfel, who had directed some short films. From December 29, 1913, and into January, Apfel took care of camera angles for the effective cutting of Lasky's first film, *The Squaw Man*, while DeMille looked out for the emotional responses of the actors. Apfel knew how to shoot interiors on outdoor "stages" with muslin curtains overhead. For dressing rooms, offices, and a cutting room, they used a barn at Vine Street and Selma Avenue, which was later moved to the present Paramount lot and proudly displayed as the original "studio" of that producing organization.

Stars—Bought or Made to Order

Like Zukor, Lasky and his partners played it safe for a time with famous players and famous plays. Their first film starred the stage actor Dustin Farnum in *The Squaw Man*, a Broadway hit in which, by the way, William Faversham originally starred. Later in 1914, the Jesse L. Lasky Feature Play Company followed up the success of this six-reel picture with film versions of plays and novels such as *The Virginian* ("When you call me that, smile"), *The Call of the North*, and *Rose of the Rancho*, one of a group of Broadway successes that they bought from Belasco. For most of the films, Lasky signed noted Broadway players such as H. B. Warner, John Barrymore, and Robert Edeson. Later, Lasky tried to exploit opera stars, successfully with Geraldine

ADVERTISING IN EVOLUTION. This full-page ad in the trade papers for *Brewster's Millions* was far from reticent about the artistic standing of its producers. A little later in 1914, however, display sheets for another Lasky film described it merely as a "highly interesting" picture, and when Lasky brought *Joan the Woman* to New York two years later, he set an example of good typography in advertising that was quite unknown to Broadway play producers. (*Courtesy John Hampton.*)

Farrar, disastrously with Enrico Caruso. But like Zukor, Lasky discovered that there were screen stars, too. He took Blanche Sweet away from Griffith, and signed Bessie Barriscale.

William Fox proved that stars could be made as well as bought. Owner of a chain of New York theaters and a film exchange, he went into production in 1914 with *Life's Shop Window*. He developed one of his players, Stuart Holmes, into the first "wolf" of the screen. (I remember how, in a later picture, this "love pirate"—to slip back into the argot of the movies fifty years ago—lured the object of his desire toward a round bed.) The most amazing feat of the Fox organization (actually the work of the director Frank Powell) was the presentation of the unknown

Theodosia Goodman as Theda Bara in *A Fool There Was* (1914) from Burne-Jones via Rudyard Kipling and the playwright Porter Emerson Browne. This was one of forty absurd films in which, within three years, Theda Bara played the first and most notable "vamp" in screen history.

Some Prospered—Some Didn't

"It isn't much credit to us," wrote Lasky in *I Blow My Own Horn,* "that we were successful. So insatiable was the public appetite for this new form of entertainment it seemed impossible to have a failure in those first years." I'm afraid Lasky had forgotten the financial crises that Goldwyn and Zukor had to weather, and the failure of all but a few of the companies of those days.

Of course, for a time at least, the feature film looked like a gilt-edged investment. Old companies such as Vitagraph, Pathé, Laemmle's Universal, and Reliance and Majestic under Mutual followed Famous Players and the Lasky organization into the land of plenty, while a score of new producing units cropped up. But, in spite of Lasky's happy experience, where are the new ones now, and some of the old ones, too? Names like Popular Plays and Players, Oliver Morosco Photoplay Company, Paralta Plays, Quality Pictures, Dyreda Films, All-Star, Selznick Picture Company, Pallas Pictures, World, and even Triangle are forgotten or only vaguely remembered. Bosworth's and Morosco's companies were absorbed into Lasky's, and Lasky's into the Famous Players-Lasky Corporation, and even that company—by various stages—into

---

New York Stars With Famous Players-Lasky—1913–15

Edward Abeles	Henry Dixey	Lily Langtry *
Maclyn Arbuckle	Marie Doro	Cecelia Loftus *
John Barrymore	Robert Edeson	Victor Moore
Donald Brian	Dustin Farnum	Carlotta Nillson
Ina Claire	William Farnum	Florence Reed
Marguerite Clark	Geraldine Farrar *	Charles Richman
William Courtleigh	Max Figman	Lou Tellegen *
Laura Hope Crews	Minnie Maddern Fiske	Lenore Ulric
Henrietta Crosman	Pauline Frederick	Charlotte Walker
Arnold Daly	James K. Hackett	Fannie Ward
Hazel Dawn	Elsie Janis	H. B. Warner
Gaby Deslys	Bertha Kalich	

* Farrar came from the Metropolitan Opera House, Langtry and Loftus from the English theater, and Tellegen from the French.

Paramount Pictures, Inc. Metro Pictures is remembered only as the company that Loew's saved from bankruptcy, along with the Goldwyn-less Goldwyn company, by a merger with the lively and prosperous unit of Louis B. Mayer and Irving Thalberg. The World Film Corporation—creature of the Broadway producer William A. Brady—is gone with Vitagraph, Pathé and Mutual. Lewis J. Selznick, with all the impetuosity of his son David O., said that motion picture production "takes less brains than anything else in the world." Perhaps he had enough brains but the wrong kind, for Zukor lured him into partnership as the Select Pictures Corporation, and took his name off the screen.

Lasky's "Supervisors" and His Writers

Let us now return to Lasky's saga of success. The story of his company is worth some study as an example of well-organized growth—backed by Zukor's mastery of distribution.

The demand for features was so great that the Lasky company made twenty-one in its first year. Famous Players added four more directors; one of them, James Kirkwood, doubled now and then as an actor. Following *The Squaw Man,* Apfel ground out eight films "like sausage,"

A Rosy View of Paramount Circa 1915

Paramount, gross total rentals per picture, average,		$100,000
Paramount charge for distribution, 35 percent		35,000
Producer's share		65,000
Producer's average costs:		
Negative	$25,000	
Positives, trade-press advertising, etc.	10,000	
Total costs,	35,000	35,000
Producer's net profits, average per picture		$30,000

Zukor was producing fifty-two pictures a year, and therefore, the optimists insisted, he must be making at least a million and a half dollars net profit a year; moreover, these calculations did not include foreign sales, which were good for $10,000 to $20,000 a picture. The Lasky Company was producing twenty-six features a year, and the optimists allotted to Lasky one-half the profits credited to Zukor.

—Benjamin B. Hampton in *A History of the Movies.*

Lasky says, "one every three or four weeks." Meantime DeMille made only two. He was more painstaking, and his shooting schedules "stretched from five to six to seven and then eight weeks." Yet in an emergency in 1915 he directed two at the same time, *The Cheat* with the not too facile stage star Fannie Ward and a striking Japanese actor, Sessue Hayakawa, and *The Golden Chance* with Wallace Reid. DeMille accomplished the miracle by shooting with one company in the daytime and the other at night.

After 1917, when Lasky was in charge of the 104 productions that Famous Players-Lasky had to make each year, he put "supervisors," later called associate producers, in charge of one or more films. Some of these men—Lucien Hubbard, William Le Baron, Howard Hawks, and Louis "Buddy" Lighton—later became well known as writers, producers, or directors.

Lasky, like most producers then and now, relied chiefly on plays and novels as the source of his story material, but he had to find writers to adapt them into what executives and directors, with their love of Latin, called "scenarios." The first was C. B. DeMille's elder brother, William C. De Mille. (In private life C. B., like W. C., was "De Mille," but some hasty writer of advertising copy once forgot to press the space bar of his typewriter and "DeMille" became official.) William planned to spend only three months on what he called "the galloping tintypes," but he was to remain in Los Angeles to become a director, and to end his life as a revered teacher of drama at the University of Southern California. Lasky soon hired as story editor Frank Woods, who had been helpful to Griffith in finding material.

With so many films to make each year and the supply of plays dwindling, Lasky decided to cultivate the kind of fiction that Hollywood calls—with no reflection on Shaw or O'Neill—"originals." Though Lasky had to pay upward of $10,000 for a stage play, he found writers on his own staff who would give him a new story for a $250 bonus. Hector Turnbull, who had followed William C. De Mille as story editor, turned in the plot for *The Cheat*, and Jeanie MacPherson—at first an actress and later one of Hollywood's noted writers—dreamed up *The Golden Chance* especially for Wallace Reid. This was a small start in a development vital to making the film a creative art—the writing of original scripts directly for the screen, just as dramatists write for the stage. Like the Elizabethan theater, the movies have usually taken their stories from other media. Unfortunately Hollywood's adapters have not all been Shakespeares.

Beauty—Out of Belasco by DeMille

In 1914, C. B. DeMille began to reform the designing and lighting of movie sets. Not for nothing had he worked in the Belasco Theater and noted how the producer and his staff achieved realism and, at times, beauty. By hiring Belasco's stage designer and lighting expert, Wilfred Buckland, DeMille gave Hollywood its first art director. With the aid of this artist of the theater, solid, illusive sets—whether a cabin, a saloon, or a palace—were no problem for DeMille. But the expressive, dramatic lighting of Belasco was another matter, for out in Hollywood DeMille and Buckland were working under tremendous handicaps.

To come anywhere near the stage effects of Belasco, the direction and intensity of light had to be controlled, and this was very difficult on the primitive outdoor stages of the period. Like Belasco, Griffith had been able to use artificial illumination at the old Biograph studio in New York. But because rain comes to Los Angeles only about forty days a year, and never in the summer months, the new Hollywood companies economized by taking advantage of the weather. Sunlight was cheaper than electricity, and open-air platforms cheaper than roofed-in buildings.

DeMille faced a dilemma. He wanted to do away with flat, overall illumination. He wanted to achieve realism and at the same time dramatize the mood of a scene through shadows and highlights—something that Griffith and Bitzer had occasionally achieved in New York. How was DeMille to get away from the daylight glare of the open-air stages? He took the first step in *The Warrens of Virginia* (1915) by using black velvet hangings to exclude the California sun from night-time scenes, and reflectors to control its direction. Soon DeMille and Buckland were using arc lights. Since electricity was the key to the kind of effects that DeMille wanted, it seems rather odd that when the Lasky company got prosperous enough to afford a roof over its artistic head, it built one of glass. Until such conservatories were blacked out with paint, or replaced by the modern type of studio, DeMille and Buckland, as well as those who tried for similar lighting effects, still did their work under great difficulties. But they did it, and they did it splendidly.

"Rembrandt Lighting"

Two of the best examples of DeMille's reforms in settings and lighting came in the last months of 1915: *Carmen* with Geraldine Farrar and *The Cheat* with Sessue Hayakawa. In Lasky's autobiography, he recalls how the shadowed lighting of a film—it seems to have been

The Warrens of Virginia—caused Goldwyn to wire from New York that he would have trouble selling a picture in which "you couldn't even see the characters' faces half the time." According to Lasky, "Cecil pondered a few moments. Then he dismissed it with: 'Tell him it's Rembrandt lighting.'" Goldwyn thereupon "hiked the rental fees for that picture."

Let me quote from a review I wrote of *A Romance of the Redwoods* (1917), which DeMille made with Mary Pickford:

> Light becomes atmosphere instead of illumination. Coming naturally from some window, lamp, or doorway, it illumines the center of the picture and the people standing there, with a glow that in intensity, in volume, or in variety of sources has some quality expressive of the emotion of the scene. In *A Romance in the Redwoods* . . . under a small, single source of light, the walls of the cabin and the faces

"REMBRANDT LIGHTING" AND HISTORICAL SPECTACLE. DeMille and Belasco's designer, Wilfred Buckland, brought the drama of shadows and ornate production to *The Woman God Forgot* (1917), with Geraldine Farrar as Malinche, Wallace Reid (right) as Cortes, and Raymond Hatton as Montezuma.

of the actors are filled with staring shadows to match the terror of the episode enacted. Under ordinary, clear studio lighting, the same scene takes on the cold grayness of the morning that follows. When comparative peace and security reign again, the cabin is warmed into mellow evening lamp-light by the use of two or three brilliant sources of illumination.

The poor prints we have today of the pictures made more than forty years ago still preserve the stilted acting, the overwrought pantomime, but these scratched, duped, and bleached-out copies give little evidence of the visual drama that I have described. We must rely on memories and the words that some of us wrote in those days. They tell us that physical production—settings, lighting, and photography—of Hollywood films reached a high level of artistic accomplishment in the decade between the Lasky company's huge greenhouse and the coming of sound.

Chapter

11

The Triangle of Griffith, Ince, and Sennett

BY THE SUMMER OF 1915, when Zukor and Lasky had laid the foundations of what was to become Paramount Pictures, three other men were planning an even more imposing edifice. They were Harry E. Aitken and the partners Adam Kessel and Charles O. Bauman, who released through a company called Mutual. Aitken had lured Griffith away from Biograph to supervise his Majestic unit. In the Reliance company, Kessel and Bauman had a rising young producer-director named Thomas H. Ince, and they controlled Mack Sennett with his Keystone Comedies. Aitken, Bauman, and Kessell left Mutual and took their considerable assets with them. These they united in a new and gargantuan project in both production and distribution, the Triangle Film Corporation. It was the most ambitious, promising, and potentially creative organization in the history of the silent screen—and the most disastrous.

Double Bills from Griffith and Ince

Triangle had a truly impressive program. Its films were to be produced by three of the outstanding film makers of the day. One production unit was to be headed by Griffith, and another by Ince, while on the third point of the triangle Sennett was to balance adroitly. In addition, the company signed up some two dozen stage stars, ranging from Beerbohm Tree and Taylor Holmes to Marie Doro and Billie Burke, and from DeWolf Hopper and William Collier to Raymond Hitchcock

171

Triangle's Stage Actors—1915–16

Sam Bernard	Eddie Foy	Willard Mack
Mary Boland	Jane Grey	Tully Marshall
Billie Burke	William S. Hart	Frank Mills
Frank Campeau	Raymond Hitchcock	Polly Moran
William Collier	Taylor Holmes	Truly Shattuck
Julia Dean	DeWolf Hopper	William H. Thompson
Elliott Dexter	Joe Jackson	Beerbohm Tree
Rozsika Dolly	Thomas Jefferson	Sarah Truax
Marie Doro	Orrin Johnson	Helen Ware
Douglas Fairbanks	Frank Keenan	H. B. Warner
Dustin Farnum	Wilfred Lucas	Joe Weber
Lew Fields		Henry Woodruff

and Eddie Foy. In some of the biggest cities, Triangle took over and redecorated "legitimate" theaters, and presented its films at "legitimate" prices—then two dollars for the best seats. A large orchestra played a classical overture and accompanied the films with special musical scores.

Few remember that Triangle spread the sorry business of the "double bill" across the nation, but at least the company made no "B" pictures in our meaning of the term. Although the films were no more than five-reel program features, they were carefully made, and boasted stars of the screen as well as the stage. Each bill—which ran a week at the special Triangle houses instead of only a few days—included one feature from Griffith's unit and one from Ince's, with a two-reel Keystone thrown in. The opening performance at the Knickerbocker Theater on September 23, 1915, drew an audience of Broadway's "first nighters" as well as the leaders of filmdom. The opening bill included *The Lamb*, from Griffith, with Douglas Fairbanks and Seena Owen; *The Iron Strain*, from Ince, with Dustin Farnum, Enid Markey, and Louise Glaum; and Sennett's *My Valet*, with Raymond Hitchcock, the Broadway comedian, as well as Mabel Normand and Sennett himself.

Super-Supervisors for Triangle

The basic policy of Triangle was that Griffith, Ince, and Sennett should *produce* pictures, rather than direct them personally. They were called director generals, and they combined the status of Lasky with that of his "supervisors" when he had to turn out 104 pictures a year. While Lasky hired lesser men to ride herd on scripts, directors, and cutters, Triangle made into supervisors three of America's four leading directors.

It is hard to say whether Sennett always could or did separate super-vision from direction, but on the whole, the plan worked well. In the old Biograph days, Griffith had been in charge of more pictures than he could possibly direct. In California, before Triangle got under way, Ince had supervised a number of features, as well as a lot of two-reelers. The failure of the venture can't be laid to the three director generals.

Ince—Model of the Modern Producer

Ince may have liked to direct pictures, but he seems to have pre-ferred directing directors. With a love of power went an equal love of sound organization, careful preparation, and thorough execution. I have seen studio records of some of his short films and one feature. They list the director, the cast, and the dates of shooting, shipment,

---

Some Triangle Screen Players—1915–16

Spottiswoode Aitken	Louise Fazenda	Mabel Normand
Mary Alden	Dorothy Gish	Seena Owen
Roscoe Arbuckle	Lillian Gish	Eugene Pallette
Bessie Barriscale	Louise Glaum	Charles Ray
Mae Busch	Mildred Harris	Wallace Reid
Jewel Carmen	Robert Harron	Mack Swain
Chester Conklin	Walter Long	Constance Talmadge
Josephine Crowell	Fred Mace	Norma Talmadge
William Desmond	Enid Markey	Henry B. Walthall
Minta Durfee	Mae Marsh	Clara Williams

---

and release, and they give the number of feet of action and of titles. The total cost is broken down into fifteen or twenty items, and then given per reel and per foot. Finally, there is a complete shooting script.

More than anyone else, Ince was responsible for developing the thor-ough and detailed scenario (now called a "continuity") that became common practice in Hollywood. He wouldn't let a director "shoot off the cuff," which meant developing scenes and sequences from a sketchy outline. Ince worked closely with his writers—C. Gardner Sullivan was the best of them—until he could approve a shooting script. He gave his director this complete blueprint of a picture and insisted that he follow it in every detail. Years later, men like Irving Thalberg, Darryl F. Zanuck, and David O. Selznick adopted the Ince policy when they managed big studios. Considering that Ince supervised the writing, directing, and editing of all his Triangle films, the number he produced is remarkable. In 1916 and 1917, he was responsible for sixty pictures each year.

There is a good deal of confusion about just who actually directed some of Ince's productions. One authority says that W. S. Hart was responsible for eighteen of the Ince pictures in which he appeared, and all but one of the seventeen for Triangle. Another says that various directors were in charge. In Hart's autobiography, he credits an ex-cowboy, Clifford Smith, as co-director with him after his first few films. As to other films besides Hart's, Ince sometimes added a certain confusion by announcing first that a film was "produced and directed by Thomas H. Ince," and later, merely "produced" by him. "Produced and directed" may have seemed strange and even a bit egotistic to Hollywood in those days. It didn't know that some day it would read such credits as: "Colossal Pictures Present an I. M. Pretentious Production, *Dead Leaves*, Produced by A. Minor Factor, Directed by I. M. Pretentious."

Griffith's Directors and Writers

Griffith was as busy as Ince, though for a shorter time. In the six or eight months before he became completely absorbed in *Intolerance*, he supervised around forty pictures for his unit. Among the best and busiest of his directors were Christy Cabanne, who made eight films, Allan Dwan, who took care of six, and John Emerson, Broadway actor and playwright, who directed six. These men and W. S. Van Dyke, Raoul Walsh, Jack Conway, and Chester and Sidney Franklin—all working under him—suggest that Griffith had better judgment than Ince in choosing directors, or felt that he had to depend more on what he called his "sub-directors."

Three-quarters of Griffith's pictures were made from original stories written expressly for the screen. He himself supplied eleven original stories, seven under the pseudonym of Granville Warwick. One of his early discoveries, Anita Loos—who was to write the best seller *Gentlemen Prefer Blondes*—had the aid and encouragement of Frank Woods, Griffith's story editor, and of her future husband, John Emerson, in developing a talent for oddly amusing plots and witty subtitles. As director and writer, Mr. and Mrs. Emerson were responsible for some of Douglas Fairbanks' successful pictures after he left Triangle.

Were Stage Stars the Ruin of Triangle?

Although Griffith and Ince saved money—and did the screen good service—by developing original stories, Triangle nevertheless came close to financial disaster within two years, and was out of business by 1919.

Since almost all its films were well written and well directed, why did the company fail so quickly?

The stage actors usually take the rap. It is true that they were unknown to the great bulk of movie audiences. Almost all of them seemed unsuited to the screen; without the spoken word, their stage personalities were lost. And their salaries were frightfully high. But, if these actors were a major liability to Triangle, why does nobody blame the man or men who picked them out and paid them too much? Was it Aitken, Kessel, or Bauman—the managerial brains—or should Griffith, Ince, and Sennett share some of the blame?

There can be no question that the salaries paid to the stage stars added greatly to the costs of production—and in two ways. Paying Beerbohm Tree $100,000 for six months' work, and signing Joe Weber and Lew Fields at $2,500 each per week and DeWolf Hopper at $1,500 were samples of Triangle's inflationary policy. Such salaries were bad enough, but when screen players heard about them, they insisted on getting on the gravy train, too. In 1913, screen players like Clara Kimball Young and Blanche Sweet, Francis X. Bushman and J. Warren Kerrigan, had been happy enough if the paycheck ran from $200 to $600 a week. Two years later, they had not only heard about the big salaries paid stage stars, but had discovered that the studios had to depend on the screen stars for effective performances and financial success. So they demanded more money and they got it.

From $2 to 25¢

The high cost of both stage and screen actors wasn't the secret of Triangle's failure, for Paramount and other studios also paid through the nose. No, something else accounted for the sad fact that after the first flurry of interest in Triangle's bold and ambitious program, the public grew chilly, and looked elsewhere for its entertainment. The debacle of Triangle was indeed spectacular. Exhibitors in thousands of theaters began to cancel contracts. The income of the company's own theaters was too meager and their expenses too great. Even though they were in the largest cities, moviegoers willing to pay two dollars for a couple of "program" pictures and a two-reel comedy weren't plentiful enough to fill a theater through a week's run. So the masters of Triangle made the most violent reversal of form known to the economic history of the screen. Within two months they dropped the admission price in their own houses to ten, fifteen, and twenty-five cents, and showed only one feature, with a Sennett comedy, each half-week.

CHESTNUT STREET OPERA HOUSE
2d WEEK, by Popular Demand—2 & 8 P. M.
LILLIAN GISH in
"THE LILY AND THE ROSE"
WILLARD MACK in "ALOHA OE"
Raymond Hitchcock in "The Village Scandal."
"A Janitor's Wife's Temptation."
PRICES 25c, 50c. A Few at Night, $1, $2.

Chestnut St. Opera House
CHESTNUT ST., Below ELEVENTH
Phila's. Most Perfectly Appointed Photoplay Theater
CONTINUOUS (Noon until 11 P.M.)
OF THE WORLD-FAMED
Griffith-Ince-Sennett
Master Productions
AT THESE NEW PRICES
10c, 15c,
25c
TRIANGLE
Symphony Orch.
Beginning
Monday
at noon
With a Change of
Bill Every Thursday
Mon., Tues, & Wed.
"The Winged Idol"
with HOUSE PETERS
and KATHRINE KAELRED
"The Submarine Pirate"
A Screamingly-Funny Keystone Comedy with
SID CHAPLIN and PHYLLIS ALLEN.
Thursday | "Jordan is a Hard Road"
Friday & | with DOROTHY GISH and FRANK CAMPEAU.
Saturday | "STOLEN MAGIC," with Raymond Hitchcock
EDUCATIONAL TRAVEL PICTURES AND OTHERS.

THE FALL OF TRIANGLE. On Saturday its theater in Philadelphia charged a $2 top for two features and two Sennett comedies. The next Monday it advertised split-week bills at 10¢, 15¢, and 25¢. (*From the Philadelphia* Evening Ledger, *November, 1915.*)

Program Pictures Doomed by Longer Features

In spite of Triangle's starry crown—supervisors Griffith, Ince, and Sennett—its failure would probably have been inevitable, even if the company hadn't loaded itself down with expensive and ineffective stars. With its modest program pictures, Triangle was moving against the current of the American screen and of Europe's before the war. Between Zukor's beginnings in 1912 and the five-reel releases of Triangle in 1915, there had come portents of a new order. The public had developed a taste for longer and more spectacular films. In 1913, *Traffic in Souls* in six reels and *The Sea Wolf* in seven were outstanding successes. The next year, *The Spoilers* did even better with nine reels. Italy had already sent us spectacles that culminated in *Cabiria* (1913), which lasted a full three hours. Then, in March, 1915, came *The Birth of a Nation.*

Oddly enough, it was this twelve-reel spectacle that seems to have lured Aitken, along with Griffith and Ince, into the mistaken belief that millions of Americans would pay the equivalent of more than $5.00 in today's money for a very different kind of entertainment—two five-reel program pictures. Aitken, who had helped finance and distribute *The Birth of a Nation,* must have been fascinated by the crowds, both in New York and on tour, that paid Broadway theater prices for the best seats. Unfortunately, he seems to have ignored two important facts about this film. It was a towering spectacle that lasted two and three-quarter hours. Also, it wasn't embarrassed with stage stars. I suppose I am not the one to scoff at this mistake of the otherwise astute Aitken, for I remember with what enthusiasm I looked forward to the launching of Triangle, and praised its films.

Three Stage Actors Become Money Makers

In spite of the trend toward longer films, one may argue that Triangle could have been a success if more of its stage actors had been as effective on the screen as Douglas Fairbanks, Sr., W. S. Hart, and Frank Keenan. For after the company stopped producing new films in 1919, many features in which these actors had appeared were reissued under new titles—some of them three or four times—as late as 1923.

Ironically enough, these three actors hadn't been as prominent on Broadway as Triangle's galaxy of stage stars. Crag-faced Keenan had been merely a character actor, but Ince's production of *The Coward* (1915) made him a screen star along with Charles Ray, who had played a few parts for Ince at Reliance. A pleasant and rather bumptious young leading man turned into the fabulously athletic, thoroughly likable, and enormously successful "Doug." Finally, there was the sadly heroic Hart. He had met Ince when they acted together in a Broadway failure called *Hearts Courageous,* and, a year before Triangle was born, Hart had gone west to work for his friend at seventy-five dollars a week. Ince may have paid him no more than three hundred dollars in the Triangle days, but he put him into stories that pretended to some emotional substance, and made Hart a famous player of strong silent men in strong and—inevitably—silent pictures. Even seventeen features with Hart and thirteen with Fairbanks in less than two years couldn't save Triangle from dissolution. The laughter of the gallery gods of Broadway must have greeted the news, in 1917, that Zukor had taken over all its assets —Griffith, Ince, and Sennett, Fairbanks, Hart, and "Fatty" Arbuckle. Emerson, Loos, and Woods.

Griffith's Epic Opens New Vistas

If *The Birth of a Nation* was responsible for the founding of Triangle, it had another effect and a more lasting one. Griffith's film might be called the *Hernani* of the American screen. It turned our leading directors toward romantic spectacle, just as Victor Hugo's drama turned French playwrights toward romance that was as spectacular as the stage of 1830 could manage to produce.

There had been European spectacles before Griffith's, but none had been successful enough to lure American film makers into competition. Since 1912, Italy had been exploiting history, building huge sets, filling them with thousands of extras, and turning out long films. *Quo Vadis?*, *The Last Days of Pompeii*, and *Cabiria* had had considerable success in our legitimate theaters, but that was before the feature film had opened the regular movie houses to long pictures. Even Griffith's four-reel spectacle *Judith of Bethulia* (1914) hadn't won the popularity that its all-star cast of Henry B. Walthall, Blanche Sweet, Mae Marsh, and Lillian and Dorothy Gish warranted.

The tremendous success and the huge profits of Griffith's epic stirred American film makers. Produced at a cost of about $110,000, it was undoubtedly the most profitable picture ever made. Its world gross may have been between $30,000,000 and $50,000,000. Whatever the figure, you must multiply it by two and a half if you compare it with the returns from *Gone With the Wind* and *Around the World in Eighty Days,* films made in times of inflation.

The Birth of a Nation *Breeds Spectacles*

Griffith's Civil War picture played an enormous part in establishing the importance of the American film during World War I, and in improving the directing and the editing of our own movie-makers. But its success led some of them into making spectacles of little merit that are now forgotten. Impetuous Herbert Brenon had worked aquatic wonders with Annette Kellerman in *Neptune's Daughter* (1914), exhibiting her in toe-dancing slippers, as well as in her one-piece bathing suit. For Fox's *The Daughter of the Gods* (1916), he remodeled part of the island of Jamaica into a Moorish city complete with imported camels.

The immensity of World War I called for super-productions—especially while America was debating whether she should play a part in it. Late in 1915, Blackton drew millions to the box office with the "preparedness" polemic *The Battle Cry of Peace,* and made a star of Norma Talmadge. The next year, Brenon hated war-makers and exalted peace in *War Brides* with Alla Nazimova. Ince, also preaching pacifism, went spectacular in *Civilization* (1916). The next year, in *Joan the Woman* and *The Woman God Forgot,* DeMille was to find his métier in historic spectacle. Incidentally, it is rather interesting that DeMille promptly gave up supervising the Lasky output, while Ince kept to his old policy.

Intolerance—*Huge yet Human*

The greatest of all screen spectacles before the days of CinemaScope and Todd-AO was to come, of course, from Griffith. Off and on, he spent the better part of two years and at least $425,000 on *Intolerance.* It ran for about three and three-quarter hours—but not nearly as many weeks as *The Birth of a Nation.* He used thousands of extras in the four interwoven stories, as well as many huge sets. The walls of Babylon, some ninety feet high, were crowned by a roadway on which chariots could pass, while above them soared lofty towers.

Though *Intolerance* was a financial failure, it demonstrated two of Griffith's distinguishing virtues. One was his editing, of which I have spoken in an earlier chapter. The other was his ability to humanize history. Italian film-makers set up a kind of *ménage à trois* between the stage, the picture gallery, and the art photographer, often achieving beauty and majesty but seldom or never human expressiveness. There was more of Jesus in the few minutes that Griffith gave Him in *Intolerance* than in all the two and a quarter hours of *Christus,* an Italian film of 1917.

Eccentric Costs and Profits

As for economics—simple enough in the days of the nickelodeons and their short movies—the coming of the feature and the spectacle turned the film industry into a monetary madhouse.

Length had very little to do with cost or profit. In 1913, George Loane Tucker made the six reels of *Traffic in Souls* for $5,700, while Edwin S. Porter spent between $40,000 and $50,000 on his four-reeler *The Prisoner of Zenda.* Tucker's film had no star, but it grossed almost $500,000; I doubt that the $5,000 paid to the Broadway star James K. Hackett helped Porter's picture to bring in anything like as much money

as Tucker's. In 1914, at least two producers were playing for high stakes
on some films, and making profits. The Lasky company may have spent
around $40,000 on *The Squaw Man,* and when Zukor sent Edwin S.
Porter and Hugh Ford to Rome to direct an eight-reel version of *The
Eternal City,* with the stage star Pauline Frederick, he risked $100,000.

Ince was much less reckless with money, but his costs went up and
down. Early in 1915 he could make short films for not much over $1,000
a reel, but in midsummer he had to spend $25,502.74 on a five-reeler
called *The Criminal,* with Clara Williams and William Desmond, whose
weekly salaries of one hundred and two hundred dollars seem modest
today. Some of Ince's Triangle productions were surprisingly cheap,
partly, perhaps, because he avoided using many of the stage stars. In
the summer of 1915, *The Disciple,* Triangle's first Hart feature, cost
only about $8,000, according to the star. Two years later, when Hart
was getting at least $1,000 a week, *The Desert Man* cost $29,835.17.

During 1919, when Allan Dwan was supervising productions for Triangle, he was able to hold costs down to a range of from $9,650 to $15,-
920.46 with minor stars. At about the same time, he directed productions
for Douglas Fairbanks and Norma Talmadge costing more than $30,000,
and Fox was spending between $25,000 and $60,000 in filming uncopy-
righted novels. In 1919, Hobart Henley, who had left stardom to direct,
made *Gay Old Dog* for $44,498.35.

In the field of the long spectacles there were wide differences in investments and returns. Little more than a year after *The Birth of a Nation,*
Ince turned out *Civilization*—almost as long, though not as elaborate
—for about $100,000, a little less than the cost of Griffith's epic. Ince's
pacifist film made only seven or eight hundred thousand dollars because
America was at war within ten months of its opening.

Authors Become Assets

One factor—but a small one—in the increased cost of features lay in
the prices paid for plays and novels. Back in the days of the one-reelers,
Vitagraph could get the rights to the Broadway hit *Raffles, the Amateur
Cracksman* merely by putting the name of the stage producer on the
screen. A couple of years later, the Kalem company made *Ben-Hur*
without consulting the author of the novel or the producers of the play,
and ultimately paid $25,000 for its carelessness. Within ten years, the
value of screen rights was pretty firmly established. Lasky is said to
have paid $5,000 for *The Squaw Man.* He gave Belasco $100,000, plus
50 percent of the profits, for ten plays, and made only nine of them.

Some Broadway hits could be had for five or ten thousand dollars, but by 1918 a magazine story called *Virtuous Wives* brought $15,000, and in 1920 Griffith is said to have paid $175,000 for the play *Way Down East*, which hadn't seen Broadway for fifteen years.

Screen Salaries—from $26,000 a Year to $520,000

Because the years from 1915 to 1917 were to set Hollywood's economic pattern for decades, it may be well to return once more to big salaries for stage stars, and to add a note on even bigger salaries for two screen luminaries.

There were other companies besides Triangle that bought expensive Broadway talent. Some are dead now, but Paramount still flourishes. The success of Zukor and Lasky lay partly in finding stage stars like Pauline Frederick and Marguerite Clark, and partly in making fewer program pictures and more films like *The Eternal City, The Cheat, Joan the Woman,* and Geraldine Farrar's *Carmen.* The triumph of Zukor and Lasky lay mainly in exploiting the silent star Mary Pickford. Another example of a player who won an enormous success without a stage reputation was, of course, Charlie Chaplin. When Mutual lost Griffith, Ince, and Sennett it won another year of life by signing the other outstanding screen star of that era, Chaplin.

The financial story of those players foreshadows the financial battles that were to be fought over other box office draws of later years. "Little Mary," the anonymous star of Biograph days, went to Famous Players in 1913 at $500 a week. Soon it was $1,000. The next year, a producer offered her $4,000 a week, for a limited number of weeks, to appear in a serial, *The Diamond from the Sky.* Zukor managed to keep his ever-more-popular star by paying her $2,000 every Saturday. That wasn't the end, of course. By June, 1916, he had to offer her $10,000 plus 50 percent of the profits on her films. Chaplin, who had started with Sennett at $150 a week in 1914, got $1,250 the next year, and beat Pickford by a few months in signing a contract at $10,000 per week and a bonus of $150,000. Financial jealousy accounted for Miss Pickford's share in the profits.

Chapter

12

What a Photoplay Editor Saw — 1915-1917

IT WAS MY GOOD FORTUNE to be a motion picture critic in Philadelphia through the burgeoning years from 1915 to 1917. I watched the growing success of the Zukor and Lasky companies, the birth and death of Triangle, Vitagraph's growth and decay as a maker of features, and the steady industry of Fox and Universal. In the Stanley Booking Company of Philadelphia I saw the beginnings of the theater chains that were to be taken over later by the big producing companies. And perhaps I took the art of the silent screen much too seriously as I weighed the merits of Griffith and Ince and some other film-makers.

The Boom Years of the Feature Film

By 1914 nobody questioned the ascendancy of the feature film. Even the trust accepted it—far too late. The output was phenomenal. In 1915 the Paramount group began to make 104 features a year. So did Triangle. Fox, Universal, and companies now dead swelled the output until there were 687 new features available in 1917, and 841 the next year. Spurred on by the success of the Strand in New York, and the road shows of big films in "legitimate" houses, exhibitors built hundreds of new "first-run" theaters. New producing and distributing corporations appeared. What was left of the Patents company—Vitagraph, Lubin, Selig, and Essanay—consolidated as V.L.S.E., and then vanished. W. W. Hodkinson, a pioneer in clean, attractive nickelodeons and an exchange

manager who had handled Famous Players and Lasky products, came
out of the west with a remarkable idea. Turning his back on the state's-
rights method of selling pictures, Hodkinson created, in 1914, the first
successful distributing organization covering the whole country. It was
known as Paramount Pictures. As conceived by Hodkinson, the company provided only financing and distribution; it did not produce or
exhibit. This foresighted attempt to set up a simon-pure marketing organization ended when the Zukor interests took over Paramount three
years later, having ejected Hodkinson, and proceeded to buy and build
theaters. In 1917 more than twenty-five owners of some hundred theaters formed First National Exhibitors Circuit to finance and distribute
features. Zukor replied by building more new theaters and continuing
to buy old ones. Fox and Universal continued as producers and distributors—and Fox grew in stature as a theater owner.

The Philadelphia Story 1915

By November, 1915, my newspaper, the *Evening Ledger,* had developed
an eight-page tabloid "Amusement Section," in which I covered drama
and books as well as movies. It carried the advertisements of fifty film
theaters owned or booked by the Stanley company. In one issue I note

FEATURE FILMS AND THEATER CHAINS—1915. There were enough
full-length films by this time to fill more than forty Philadelphia
theaters. Here are some of the advertisements placed by the
Stanley Booking Company, which was soon to control an important chain of theaters in Pennsylvania.

that all but four or five were playing features, and only two were showing the same film. I don't know how many independent houses existed, but *The Birth of a Nation* was at the Forrest Theater, where plays normally appeared, and Vitagraph's *The Battle Cry of Peace* was at the Metropolitan Opera House, built by Oscar Hammerstein. The Chestnut Street Opera House was advertising the last week of the Triangle's Griffith-Ince double at two dollars top.

There must have been some nickelodeons left, for I wrote, "whether the admission price is 5¢ or 50¢ . . ." *The Battle Cry of Peace* had some reserved seats at one dollar, but it was a "special." A quarter was the top price even for a first-run house like the Stanley. A maneuver of Zukor's indicates that this was true in New York. In 1915, he leased the Broadway Theater and, because it was within two blocks of the Metropolitan Opera House, he called it "the home of the grand opera of motion pictures." Such a grandiloquent title would suggest high prices at this first-run house, but you will note a kind of financial anticlimax at the end of the following announcement: "Owing to the enormous salary which it has been necessary to pay Miss Pickford in order to secure her services, all future releases will be first released to big city theaters charging a minimum price of twenty-five cents." In 1919, before Loew's, Inc. had added production to theater ownership, Marcus Loew declared that fifty cents was the limit the public would pay.

The Movies Adopt a Classy Pseudonym

Of coure the film-makers of 1915 took the movies rather seriously. So did owners of the newspapers, who were happy to find that the producers as well as the theaters would advertise. And we aestheticians of a new art were very serious indeed. An odd result of all this was an attempt to banish the vulgar term "movies" and substitute a loftier word. Just before Essanay acquired the ungentlemanly Chaplin, it decided to offer a prize of twenty-five dollars for the proper pseudonym. So great was the desire of the movie-makers—and the movie critics—for dignity, that everyone decided to accept the winning word, and to produce, advertise, and discuss the "photoplay." The oldest of our fan magazines has borne that title since 1914.

And so I was Photoplay Editor of the Philadelphia *Evening Ledger*. I don't know whether I liked the fancy title, but I went to the movies with almost the enthusiasm with which I attended plays, and I tried to detect and appraise each advance in the art of the screen. So did Gilbert Seldes, then music critic on the paper. In reviewing *Die Walküre* he amused himself and his readers by congratulating Wagner on his superior use of the *leitmotiv* from the Clansmen's ride in *The Birth of a Nation*.

Sidney Drew and John Bunny vs. Charlie Chaplin

There were two kinds of films that we paid little attention to. One was the serial and the other the short comedies of Mr. and Mrs. Sidney Drew and of the globular John Bunny and the angular Flora Finch.

Mr. Drew might be the brother of John, and he was certainly going to be the uncle of Lionel, Ethel, and Jack, but up to the end—which came about 1917—he clung to the one-reeler as the ideal length and preferred "sentimental human comedy" to slapstick. Like Drew, John Bunny had a respectable background. I had seen him play an excellent Bottom in Annie Russell's stage production of *A Midsummer Night's Dream*. But he and Flora Finch were no match for Chaplin and Mabel Normand, who deserve a chapter to themselves. We were all for the slapstick of Sennett and Chaplin and the longer the better. Our only objection to the six reels of *Tillie's Punctured Romance* (1914) was that, because Sennett had made it before he quite understood Chaplin's box office potential, the producer starred Marie Dressler in too much footage.

The Birth of the Serials

As for the serials, I regret to say that we went to laugh at them, much as audiences now laugh at so many of the silent films that were never meant to be risible. Today I find as much skill in some of the serials as in many of the features of 1916—and a good deal more excitement. In these cinematic tapeworms, there were absurdities, of course, that matched alliterative titles like *The Perils of Pauline, The Hazards of Helen,* and *The Exploits of Elaine,* but many of the serials were as elaborately produced as any Hollywood "special," and often more truly filmic.

In those Philadelphia days when the serials were growing in number and popularity, we had no idea of how they had evolved. We hadn't learned to discriminate between what we can now call "series" and true serials In both cases, the same group of chief characters and actors appeared week after week in one-reel or two-reel films. The plot of each short in a series was a separate and a complete episode in which dangers or difficulties came to a happy ending. In the true serial, on the other hand, the plot was as continuous as the chief characters, and at the end of all but the last of the short films, the heroine—or sometimes the hero— was left in dire extremity. Then the words "To be continued" flashed on the screen. In the course of time, this suspense gimmick earned for the serials the name of "cliff-hangers," but the writers of the early stories called them "Blue Jeans" after the title of the popular melodrama in which the heroine was left bound to the railroad tracks as the express train approached. Here, in terms of the screen, we can see the birth of radio's "soap opera."

A Series That Might Have Been a Serial

The earliest of the series films may have been England's *Mirthful Mary* back in 1905. Crime reared its fascinating head in 1908 when the French —often seizing on American detectives—made *Nick Carter,* and other series. The first and most notable American series was *What Happened to Mary,* which started production in 1912. Each monthly installment was complete in itself, but the story of Mary, who began as a foundling escaping from a children's asylum, carried the heroine through various troubles on her way to happy young womanhood. Frank Leon Smith, author of some of the early serials, points out that *What Happened to Mary* could have been a true serial if the happy ending of each episode had come in the middle of it, with the troubles of the next one interrupted by the fade-out. In another way, *What Happened to Mary* was closely related to the serial. The story of each episode appeared in a periodical, in this case *The Ladies' World.* The idea of serialization in print was basic to the first of America's true serials, *The Adventures of*

THE FIRST AMERICAN SERIAL. A trade paper advertisement of 1914. (*Courtesy John Hampton.*)

Kathlyn (1913), and to many that followed. Week by week, the Chicago *Tribune* printed the plot of the current installment in order to draw new readers from the patrons of the nickelodeons.

There is some dispute as to whether America or France produced the first true serial. Certainly the series of films about Fantomas, master criminal of Paris, came to the screen a little ahead of Kathlyn. Also they have an essential feature of most American serials—the menace of an arch-villain from start to finish. On the other hand, *Fantomas* (1913), was released here in multiple-reel installments and Fantomas was triumphant in each. No cliff-hanging for him.

Expensive Writers and Actors

The output of American serials has been surprisingly large, and investments and profits were quite considerable in the early days when the producers hired well-known writers and players. Statistics begin only in 1920, when the first rush was over; but between then and 1957 *The Film Daily Year Book* lists about 375 serials. Almost all of these were made up of two-reelers, and they came in ten to thirty installments. In 1914, when features could be made for $35,000, the twenty-six episodes of *The Million Dollar Mystery* are said to have cost $125,000 and grossed nearly $1,500,000. As for the actors, Billie Burke got more than $150,000 for appearing in *Gloria's Romance* (1916). Arnold Daly, a pioneer of Shaw's plays on Broadway, and also Lionel Barrymore, appeared in some of the episodes of *The Exploits of Elaine* (1915).

Warner Oland—once dedicated to the translation and production of the plays of Strindberg and later renowned as Charlie Chan—became a popular villain. Kathlyn Williams, Helen Holmes, Pearl White, and Ruth Roland either made or consolidated their reputations in serials. Among other screen actors who appeared in serials were Henry B. Walthall, Antonio Moreno, Creighton Hale, Sheldon Lewis, and Tom Santschi. Popular novelists were responsible for some of the stories. Harold MacGrath wrote *The Adventures of Kathlyn* and *The Million Dollar Mystery* (1914), and Rupert Hughes wrote *Gloria's Romance*.

The history of the serial was of small concern to us photoplay editors. We were much more interested in what looked, for the moment, like an aesthetic reform that the serials were to work in the handling of dialogue subtitles. In 1915, Sigmund Lubin of Philadelphia put out *Road o' Strife*, with the handsome Crane Wilbur. In this serial all dialogue appeared in white letters on some dark portion of the background. Thus, as in a foreign film at an art theater today, the screen action was continuous, never interrupted by subtitle cards. We hoped to see the idea applied to feature films, but, alas, the only record I can find of its later use was in a French serial *Judex*, made in 1916 or 1917, depending on which authority you accept.

Thar's Gold in Them Thar Westerns

In some ways serials were often what we now call cinematographic, but Westerns were far more so—telling the story with the fullest use of camera and editing. Violence followed violence against the contrasting peace of the Great West. There was swift riding and there was swift editing. I think that Ince can be credited with adding better technique to Westerns and also more truth. Before him, they had been mostly cheap and phony —whether American or, quite surprisingly, made in France.

Between 1908 and 1915, Max Aronson, who had appeared in *The Great Train Robbery*, made almost 400 one-reelers under the name of "Broncho Billy" Anderson. The early Westerns, blown up into feature length by Tom Mix, a genuine cowboy, and by W. S. Hart, a reasonable facsimile thereof, were to lead to James Cruze's spectacular *The Covered Wagon* (1923), John Ford's authentic re-creations, and on to *The Gunfighter* (1950), *High Noon* (1952), *Shane* (1953).

W. S. Hart—the Authentic Man of the West

The phrase "a reasonable facsimile" is hardly fair to Hart. Mix, with his brilliant horsemanship, could ride rings around the former Broadway thespian, but Hart was a better actor. Also, he insisted on authenticity in his pictures of the West. In the late eighteen-seventies, when he was eight years old and there were still many Indians in Minnesota, he had learned to speak Sioux; before his father took him East in his early teens, he had been a ranch hand. He felt so keenly the virtues of the old frontier life that he attacked *The Covered Wagon* for showing a wagon train bivouacking in the trap of a box canyon, and cattle crossing a turbulent river while burdened with heavy neck yokes. (They were yoked only when they pulled the wagons.) These, he said, were "errors that would make a Western man refuse to speak to his own brother."

At the peak of Mix's career, he was even more popular than Hart. From 1917 to 1928, he and his current horse—Tony, Old Blue, or Tony, Jr.—are said to have appeared in over sixty Fox features. His short films go back to 1910 with Selig—further than Hart's, but Hart's rise was swifter. Under Ince's skillful handling, Hart developed in 1915 from an actor in two-reelers into one of Triangle's two most important stars.

Soon Hart and Fairbanks rated salaries second only to those of Chaplin and Miss Pickford.

Like Fairbanks, Hart had a photogenic face and one that fitted the pictures he made; yet no two men could have been more different. As the title of one of Hart's own films described him, he was "the silent man"—until his guns spoke. The first and perhaps one of the greatest "deadpan" actors of the screen (which will pay millions for the practiced inertia of a Gary Cooper or a Humphrey Bogart), he had a face that could turn from the inscrutable to the menacing or the gentle in, and through, the flick of an eye. His favorite character was often known by the title of one of Fairbanks' films, *The Good Bad Man* (1916). Then the man Hart played was some kind of outlaw or fugitive who couldn't help being heroic in a crisis. The French critic, Louis Delluc wrote: "I think that Rio Jim [the French called him that, just as they called Chaplin Charlot] is the first real figure established by the cinema." Of

HART AS AN "INDEPENDENT"—1920. A trade paper advertisement of "A William S. Hart Production," released by Paramount. (*Courtesy John Hampton.*)

course Hart's films were escapist fare for the moviegoer of 1915. The very names of his characters were wondrously flavorous—Mr. "Silent" Haskins, "Draw" Egan, "Blaze" Tracey. The titles of many of his pictures—*The Passing of Two-Gun Hicks* (1914), *"Bad Buck" of Santa Ynez* (1915), *The Desert Man* (1917), *The Narrow Trail* (1917), *Tumbleweeds* (1925)—spoke of the hard-bitten but romantic West. These titles cried to the audience, "Go West, young man," and the films took them there. Yet often there was a sting of irony or even tragedy in the end of some of the tales.

The Immortal "Doug"

There was no irony and, of course, no tragedy in the films of Fairbanks. Of all the stars in feature pictures, he was the king of romantic comedy in 1917. His only rival was Charlie Chaplin, who, except for his activities in *Tillie's Punctured Romance*, didn't venture into features until the nineteen-twenties. By that time, Fairbanks was adding spectacle and romantic comedy to the derring-do of men like Robin Hood, D'Artagnan, Zorro, and a certain thief of Bagdad. But in his first five years as a star, he was the gay image of contemporary youth. Past thirty, he was still the Great American Boy.

Fairbanks had a physical vitality particularly suited to the screen. When I saw him on the stage, I was annoyed by his bouncing breeziness; his exuberance seemed overbearing. A creature of superb animal energy,

---

Making a Feature Out of Shorts

When Mix joined Fox in 1917 the years with Selig paid off, and he became a top-liner right away. Whereupon Selig, realizing the commercial value of Mix *features*, attempted to create some of his own by re-editing the old Mix shorts. Some of these "reconstructions," like *Twisted Trails*, are still in circulation, and show, if not cohesion, considerable ingenuity. One whole reel of *Twisted Trails* is from a film in which Mix did not even appear, and was used to establish the predicament of the heroine (Bessie Eyton) in running away from an unwanted marriage. An old reel of Mix footage established *him* as a wandering cowboy. Then a title was inserted to announce that "Thus were the twisted trails of the boy and girl joined together." Whereupon Tom met Bessie and the rest of the film consisted of one of their old co-starring two-reelers!

—"Tom Mix," by George Mitchell and William K. Everson, in *Films in Review.*

a born athlete, and a trained gymnast, he had the amazing good fortune of escaping the confines of the stage and bursting forth in an art where nothing was physically or technically impossible. It was in his very nature, however, to take no advantage of camera tricks, and to use no double. He was always his own stunt man. Griffith is said to have looked coldly on this bouncing ball of energy, and turned him over to John Emerson, Anita Loos, and Frank Woods to make what they could of him. Griffith even suggested that the actor belonged in Mack Sennett's unit, and there is a record of a two-reeler that he made on the Keystone lot. I don't remember seeing it, but I know that Fairbanks and Sennett were poles apart in humor. They both achieved effects that seemed impossible, but Fairbanks did it within the realm of plausibility. He was a flying saucer in a very real world. He was a Méliès who didn't have to stoop to photographic tricks.

With a happy exuberance of spirit and body, Fairbanks created a man called "Doug," who lived in the best of all possible worlds. Or at least it was the best after he had put some things straight by satirizing hypo-chondriacs, "bean-can nobility," New Thought eccentrics, and publicity lovers. There were graver dangers, of course, and there was always suspense, but his audience knew—and was happy to know—that nothing could go permanently wrong as long as "Doug" was there.

Memories of Forty-Five Years Ago

Of course there were other actors besides Fairbanks and Hart, the Gishes and Mae Marsh, Charlie Chaplin and Ben Turpin, Henry B. Walthall and Mary Pickford, but how little I remember of most of them! Florence Lawrence and Maurice Costello, of Biograph and Vitagraph fame, had faded away. Theda Bara's *Salome* of 1918 can have been no worse than Alla Nazimova's absurdly mannered version four years later, but I have charitably forgotten Bara's Biblical vamp along with the Juliet she essayed in 1916. I remember Wallace Reid best for his blacksmith in *The Birth of a Nation* and Constance Talmadge for her somewhat overdrawn comedy in *Intolerance*. Norma Talmadge, Clara Kimball Young, and Blanche Sweet remain lovely faces and little more. Charles Ray and Frank Keenan are still vivid but mainly because of *The Coward*. The talkie *The Broadway Melody* (1929) has erased the Bessie Love of ten years earlier. Mary Miles Minter, Vivian Martin, and Anita Stewart seem pale copies of Mary Pickford, and Francis X. Bushman remains only another profile beside John Barrymore's.

If Hart and Fairbanks are my happiest and most vivid memories of the early days, it is because each was not so much an actor as a character. Perhaps it is not high art to play the same role in every picture, but at least their roles were vivid and unique. There could have been no other such Silent Man, no other Americano.

"What's in a Name?"

Many screen players and a few directors, too, have followed the happy habit of the stage, and rid themselves of surnames like Langhanke and Dukinfield. Here, below the names of two men illustrious in the theater, are some of the transfigurations achieved by men and women whose careers began in the silent era. On page 312 you will find specimens from the time of the talkies.

John Henry Brodribb	Sir Henry Irving	Leatrice Joy Zeidler	Leatrice Joy
Jean Baptiste Poquelin	Molière	Arthur Stanley Jefferson	Stan Laurel
Arthur George Brest	George K. Arthur	Augusta Appel	Lila Lee
		Otto E. Linkenhelt	Elmo Lincoln
Lucile V. Langhanke	Mary Astor	Maximilien Levielle	Max Linder
Mario Bianchi	Monty Banks		
Theodosia Goodman	Theda Bara	Juanita Horton	Bessie Love
		Myrna Williams	Myrna Loy
Elisabeth Blythe Slaughter	Betty Blythe	Bela Lugosi Blasko	Bela Lugosi
Isidore Itzkowitz	Eddie Cantor	Bartolomeo Pagano	Maciste
René Chomette	René Clair	Juliet Shelby	Mary Miles Minter
Claudette Cauchoin	Claudette Colbert	F. W. Plumpe	F. W. Murnau
Jack Krantz	Ricardo Cortez	Donna Dooley	Nita Naldi
Marta Maria Lilitte	Lil Dagover	Appolonia Chalupec	Pola Negri
Marion Douras	Marion Davies	Ramon Samaniegoes	Ramon Novarro
Ernest L. Brimmer	Richard Dix	Signe Auen	Seena Owen

"What's in a Name" (*Cont'd*)

Lillian Bohney	Billie Dove	Gladys Marie Smith	Mary Pickford
Germaine Saisset-Schneider	Germaine Dulac	Winifred Shaunessy de Wolf Hudnut	Natacha Rambova
Douglas Elton Ulman	Douglas Fairbanks, Sr.	William Deane-Tanner	William Desmond Taylor
Jacques Frédérix	Jacques Feyder	Maurice Thomas	Maurice Tourneur
W. C. Dukinfield	W. C. Fields	Rodolpho Alfonzo Rafaelo Pierre Filibert Guglielmi di Valentina d'Antonguolla	Rudolph Valentino
Sean O'Feeney	John Ford		
Greta Gustafsson	Greta Garbo		
Samuel Goldfish	Samuel Goldwyn		
Marianna Michalska	Gilda Gray	Erich Oswald Hans Karl Marie Stroheim von Nordenwald	Erich von Stroheim
Ehrich Weiss	Harry Houdini		

Chapter
13

The Lure of the Primitive Screen

$\mathbf{A}$s I write about the screen of almost fifty years ago, I am conscious of the words of Joel, minor prophet of the Old Testament, "your old men shall dream dreams, your young men shall see visions." The dreams that I still cherish of the wondrous films of 1917 too often vanish when I get a disillusioning look at one of them. And what about the visions I had in those days—faith in the power of the silent screen, belief in its new and vibrant beauties, utter confidence in its potent future—all this set down in cold print by a young man in his twenties? Viewing the work of Griffith and Ince, Hart and Fairbanks, Pickford and Chaplin, the spectacles and the program pictures, I wrote that we were watching the film "in its first campaign for the conquest of the minds and emotions of man." Why did the art of the screen seem so important then? What did I see that could justify such apocalyptic fervor?

Compensations for Crude Plots

Certainly the virtue of the movies I reviewed didn't rest in what they told us about human beings. The silent screen flattened out the play, cut down the stature of the novel, and distorted an author's material for the sake of popular appeal. (Perhaps I should mention that in the Theda Bara version of *Carmen*, Don José, instead of surrendering to the police, committed suicide by jumping off a cliff on horseback.) Sometimes, to be sure, writers and directors conceived new stories that fitted the new medium. But even as I hailed the campaign for the minds and emotions of man, I had to recognize and deplore "the crude plots, the ugly crime, and the silly happiness . . . the disjointed mediocrity" that filled and dominated the screen.

Then why did young men—and some older ones, too—see something more in the movies than "galloping tintypes"? Why was the screen so fascinating in spite of all its fictional crudities? What did we find in this popular amusement that made us hail it as the eighth art?

Aside from the fun and the excitement we got from new personalities —from Chaplin, Fairbanks, and Hart, for example—I think that our faith in the future of the screen grew from its progress in two technical fields. These were the ability to tell stories in a new and effective way, and the expressive beauty that the camera often achieved.

Two Styles of Storytelling

As we all know, a motion picture can be developed from a novel or from a play. In either case, however, the script will use *both* the narrative and the dramatic method of telling the story. It may lean more heavily on one, but it will employ the other to some degree. This was as true in the formative years of the feature film as it is today. There were many kinds of stories, but only two ways of telling them. The narrative method dominated in Griffith's pictures, the dramatic in Ince's. I find that in some of my articles of the period I analyzed rather thoroughly the fictional methods of both men, and pointed out that the differing ways in which they told their stories seemed related to the kind of stories they liked.

Ince preferred strong, masculine tales. When he wasn't making melodramas of the West, he turned out films like *The Coward*, with simple but forceful emotional conflicts. He had little interest in comedy, and he seldom let sentiment spill over into sentimentality. Griffith's interests and his tastes were more varied. He could be brutal and violent—remember how he lopped off the head of a Babylonian warrior in *Intolerance*— yet he also liked stories and acting that were gentler and more naturalistic than Ince's. Griffith was fond of moralizing and sentimentality, and he had a keen interest in poetry. We saw him turn Poe's "Annabel Lee" and "The Tell-Tale Heart" into *The Avenging Conscience* (1914), which I rather recklessly called "his least known and best photoplay." At his saccharine worst, he could perpetrate that scene in *Intolerance* when the

Princess Beloved put a rose in a little cart that two doves in harness drew toward Belshazzar.

Considering their diverse tastes, it was natural enough that Ince should lean toward the dramatic method of storytelling and Griffith toward the narrative. The films of Ince were direct and tight-knit. Within the bounds of realism, he strove for theatric effect, yet his scripts were often as logical and well made as Ibsen's dramas. I felt that Ince and his writers, such as C. Gardner Sullivan, Monte Katterjohn, and J. G. Hawks, "pushed the art of screen storytelling furthest," even though Griffith's "school of photoplay writing is vital and perhaps more important because of its natural humanity." Griffith's stories had a tendency to wander— partly, perhaps, because he liked to work without a formal script—and I grew annoyed at his tendency to drag a chase into so many of his films. In the scripts of Ince, I found that "the action is pared down to the bone, and then fleshed with exact and appropriate details." It was no surprise to me that in 1923, when he chose to turn away, for the moment, from melodrama and obvious conflicts to produce *Anna Christie*, his style proved well fitted to O'Neill's play.

Two Types of Subtitles

The differing ways in which Griffith and Ince used the subtitle were characteristic. The film-maker of the silent days could interrupt a scene with one or more lines of printed speech, or he could introduce a scene with a descriptive sentence or two. Of course all directors used both methods, but Ince preferred dialogue. When he introduced a descriptive subtitle, he did it to set a mood or indicate a change of character. Then, characteristically, he would pare down a sentence to a phrase. We read, "Filled with indecision," instead of "Rio Jim is filled with indecision." Sometimes Ince grew a bit corny, as in *Square Deal Sanderson* (1919): "With the killer light in his eye." On the whole, Griffith seemed to dislike interrupting a scene with lines of dialogue. He preferred to describe or interpret the action that he was about to show; and sometimes he described action that he *should* have shown. I wrote that Griffith "loads into long descriptions at the beginning of new scenes enough explanation to get around any lack of clearness in the subsequent action." At one point in *The Birth of a Nation*, he missed what could have been a scene of some impact when he used a mere subtitle, "Against the brother's warning she goes alone to the spring," instead of showing the "Little Colonel" telling his young sister of the danger she would face if the "renegade" Negro Gus found her alone.

"Rembrandt Lighting" à la Ince and Griffith

In a previous chapter, I credited C. B. DeMille with bringing Belasco's technician Buckland to Hollywood in 1914 and developing shadowed lighting in solid settings. Before Ince found a similar art director in Robert Brunton, a British stage designer, he had shown in a Hart film, *The Ruse* (1915), a woman's head lit only by a street lamp outside her window. Ince liked to mask the sides and sometimes the background of a room in shadows, in order to concentrate attention on action in the center. Griffith had an unfortunate trick of doing this with an iris which cut down the area covered by the lens. In an outdoor scene, we saw the action within a black circle. Indoors, the circle might be lost in the dark-colored walls of the set; in *The Birth of a Nation,* for instance, we saw Lincoln and his secretary alone in what seemed a pool of light. But in the next scene, when the mechanical shadow of the iris had disappeared, we suddenly discovered that other actors had been lurking in the room.

The reforms of DeMille and Ince in lighting spread rapidly. Oscar Apfel, who taught DeMille the techniques of directing and editing, carried the gospel of contrasting light and shadow to the Morosco Company and *Peer Gynt* (1915). I wrote of one scene, "tense faces were shadowed with a drama that lay deep in the lines of lips and eyes, and leapt out with each slightest movement."

Germany's New Stagecraft Comes to the Screen

While Hollywood was accepting "Rembrandt lighting" and improving upon it, producers and directors in the East were to adopt the theories and the practices of the new stagecraft of Germany. Working from the theories and designs of Adolphe Appia and Gordon Craig, men like Max Reinhardt were using scenery in the theater that combined simplicity with suggestion and that was dramatized by light. As World War I began, the new stagecraft came to New York through the work of the designer Robert Edmond Jones and the producer Arthur Hopkins.

When Allan Dwan produced and directed *Panthea* in the East late in 1916, he made a palatial dining room out of a few pieces of furniture highlighted against a shadowed background—only one of a number of excellent effects that he achieved by wedding economy of materials with imagination. This was a clean break with the heavy, solid scenery and sculptured lighting of DeMille and Ince, which stemmed from the realism of Belasco. Dwan was adding to the new stagecraft the fresh and potent powers of the lens.

When the Lasky company was prosperous enough, in 1916, to be able to pay Samuel Goldwyn some $900,000 to "include him out," that man of enterprise and taste started his own organization in partnership with Arthur Hopkins, two other Broadway producers, Edgar and Arch Selwyn, and the successful playwright Margaret Mayo. Hopkins had a number of ideas about film reforms. One of them—unfortunately disastrous—was to revolve the camera at the center of an arc, stopping to shoot scenes of action against small groupings of props and set pieces. Behind the actors and these indications of locale was a great cyclorama of black velvet. This eliminated or restricted editing, and there was an added failing. Photographically the effect that Hopkins wanted was ruined by the fact that the "color," or value, of the background changed from scene to scene. Because each scene had to be lighted separately, the black velvet looked a little lighter or darker in one scene than in another. Hopkins must be credited, however, with an excellent suggestion that Goldwyn accepted with enthusiasm. This was to hire well-known artists to design settings along modern lines, and to serve as co-directors. One of them, Hugo Ballin, soon began to direct on his own, but not until he had shown movie people how to create a corner of Sherry's restaurant out of a few tall pillars and some heavy draperies. His settings for Mary Garden in *Thaïs* (1917) were an admirable example of good design skillfully and discreetly applied. When he created elegant modern rooms, they were quite bare of bronze statues, carved picture frames, devitalized polar bears, and the other gimcracks of "realism."

Close Shots Used More Effectively

Apart from what the director, the set designer, and the cameraman could do to emphasize drama pictorially, the man with the megaphone, the puttees, and the cap with the visor turned to the back—then and for many years the uniform of the director—could add dramatic effects unique to the film. This lay in the use of close-ups of objects, shots not always called for in the script. Griffith and others had done this to some extent, but it became common practice toward the beginning of the nineteen-twenties. Let me dwell on an example from a scene in Dwan's *Panthea*, where he deals with a Russian police raid on a house. In reviewing the film, I wrote that he "shows not only the approach, the groups on both sides of the door, the violence of the entry and the scattering of the dwellers, but as the police charge upstairs after the hero, Dwan smashes it home to us with a sudden flash of feet pounding the steps. Again he uses that close-up expedient—and with even greater,

THE YEARS OF THE EGGHEAD. When Samuel Goldfish formed his
own company late in 1916, he got more from his new Broadway
partners, the Selwyn Brothers, than the "wyn" to replace "fish"
in the name he adopted somewhat later. Goldwyn, with his flare
for distinguished collaborators, acquired the works and/or services of popular playwrights, novelists, and stars. Though he didn't
mention the artists he had hired to design—and, in some cases, to
direct—his productions, he boldly pledged his company to a policy
that would be considered a bit suspect in Hollywood forty years
later.

because characterizing, effect—when, after the officer has shot the hero, he kicks him over with his spurred boot to make sure he is harmless. Dwan catches in his close-up of the kicking boot not only the beastliness of the act, but a curve in the boot itself and in the direction of the blow that are amazingly characteristic of the hard, perky, Prussian-like little officer." I added: "It is things of this sort . . . which will give photo-plays some of the quality of observation and character that make litera-ture."

All this may sound as if I believed that the films of 1917 were vastly better than *The Birth of a Nation*. Obviously they weren't. Biologically speaking, Griffith's was a sport; he never again equalled or even approached *The Birth of a Nation*, nor did anyone else in the silent era.

The Lure of the Screen Even in 1910

Why were so many of us such enthusiastic students of the screen in those days? Here and there, some of the pictures showed new skills in directing, writing, editing, and production, and there were a dozen film-makers who could do with considerable success in 1917 what only two or three could accomplish in 1915. Over and above this, however, were certain things that made the screen seem powerful and exciting to many of us. Of course there were plenty of highbrows who cocked a snook at the screen, as there were also quite a number who mistook it for an altar. Between 1910 and 1916, I can recall four Americans, notable then or now—a philosopher, a psychologist, a sculptor, and a poet—who tried at some length to explain why this newest and crudest of popular enter-tainments meant so much to them. And also, as they thought, to the future of mankind.

I was still an undergraduate when Horace M. Kallen, a young man teaching philosophy at Harvard, analyzed the extraordinary interest that he felt in watching the screen. This was in 1910, when the movies were at dead center. Photographs in motion no longer had the lure of novelty, and they had yet to show the flashing power of Griffith's Civil War epic. Fumbling with bits of fiction in the most obvious way, repeat-ing the absurdest clichés of pantomime, still innocent of the full skills of directing and editing, these ten-minute films had a basic fascination. Kallen described the peculiar pleasure he experienced in receiving and interpreting the signals flashed from the screen. For him it was "an exertion delightful and absorbing." Here, too, was art, said Kallen, and an art superior to that of the theater. If he erred in his comparison of screen and stage, at least he had a philosophical argument for seeing a potential art in the movies. They met the test of the "aesthetic paradox," which means that an object, a person, or an emotion can become art when it is presented in a different medium. The actor on the screen loses his corporeality, and so do his surroundings. By the magic of the camera they become altered and ordered. Something new has been added to reality.

To See a New Art in Growth

In 1916, the psychologist Hugo Münsterberg, also at Harvard, wrote a fair-sized book, *The Photoplay, a Psychological Study*. He was stirred, with good reason, by the opportunity of watching a new art in growth: ". . . for the first time the psychologist can observe the starting of an entirely new esthetic development, a new form of true beauty in the turmoil of a technical age, created by its very technique and yet more than any other art destined to overcome outer nature by the free and joyful play of the mind."

Watching and analyzing this new art, Münsterberg waxed ecstatic as he explained the unique qualities of the film:

> The massive outer world has lost its weight, it has been freed from space, time, and causality, and it has been clothed in the forms of our own consciousness. The mind has triumphed over matter and the pictures roll on with the ease of musical tones. It is a superb enjoyment which no other art can furnish us. No wonder that temples for the new goddess are built in every little hamlet.

Fortunately, I was then a young and relatively uneducated man, and thus incapable of the psychological fervors of Münsterberg. As for the theater, I had loved it too long and too deeply to agree with Kallen that the art of the screen—particularly the silent screen—was superior to the art of the stage. But I did feel in the movies a kind of power that the stage can never have, a power that goes beyond the mere fascination of watching movement. Barring a few exceptional films and the signs of technical progress that they bore, the lure that the screen of almost fifty years ago held for many of us lay in visual beauty, linked (all too seldom) with episodes of human significance. With this went the hope, and indeed, the belief, that the screen would bring aesthetic experience to millions who had never seen or liked a better painting than "The Stag at Bay."

The visual appeal was undeniable. George Grey Barnard, the distinguished sculptor, said that he had a sense of discovery in watching the most ordinary moving pictures. He found delight in following them with their endless combinations of masses and flowing surfaces.

Some of the distinguished lovers of the screen went a bit overboard in praising it as a pictorial art, and analyzing it into categories. In 1915, Vachel Lindsay followed the success of his poem "The Congo" by writing a book called *The Art of the Moving Picture*. He said that the ripe photoplay is the art museum, plus action. He found three types of films: the photoplay of Action, the photoplay of Intimacy, the photoplay of Splendor. He saw the first as sculpture in motion and cited *The Spoilers*. He illustrated the second—the "intimate and friendly" film—with *Enoch Arden,* remade by Christy Cabanne in 1915 under Griffith's supervision, the comedies of Mr. and Mrs. Sidney Drew, and Mary Pickford. Of course the "photoplay of Splendor" included spectacles like *Judith of Bethulia* and *Cabiria*.

Screen Beauty—How and Why

I myself saw beauty on the screen as a natural and almost inevitable product of the camera. If the amateur with a Brownie or a Graflex takes enough pictures, a few are bound to be good, to be more than mere records. The cinematographer, working day after day with his new kind of camera, began by achieving accidental beauty. Then, if he had any feeling for the pictorial, he analyzed what he had done and began to explore the fuller possibilities of the new medium. Some of the expressive beauty that I saw in 1917 may have been sheer happenstance: "the rounding of a valley into view, the poise of a shoulder against a background, the proportions of a house to its frame of trees or even to the edges of the picture, the flare of shadow cast by a single point of light, or just the reflection and diffusion of a cross light under a summer pier." More and more, as the years went by, the screen excited and satisfied us with new displays of expressive dramatic beauty. We came to see, as did the film-makers first of all, that the beauty and significance of the silent screen were more than the beauty and significance of a photograph, for the movie was a photograph in motion. Furthermore, it was a succession of such photographs. Its greatest vitality and its highest expressiveness lay in the relationship of each picture to the one before.

I think that there were reasons why the triumphs of the camera seemed so important. They were an anodyne for the acute distress of most movie plots; they relieved us just a little from the boredom of stories stupidly rehashed. Furthermore, though we didn't realize it then, visual beauty and pictorial vitality were bound to be of paramount importance in the silent film, since there were no spoken words to create characters, to express ideas, and to make it possible for the screen to show us more than a shadow of the fullness of life.

Some critics felt that the silent films, even without the living vitality of speech, held a promise of infinite progress for the vast audience of the undereducated who thronged to the movies. Münsterberg wrote that "their influence is one of the strongest social energies of our time . . . the greatest mission which the photoplay may have in our community is that of aesthetic cultivation. No art reaches a larger audience daily, no aesthetic influence finds spectators in a more receptive frame of mind." Lindsay said: "The invention of the photoplay is as great a step as was the beginning of picture writing in the Stone Age. And the cavemen and women of our slums seem to be the people most affected. . . . The Man with the Hoe had no spark in his brain. But now a light is blazing."

Visual Power in a Film of 1915

The way Lindsay puts it may seem a bit highflown, but I saw a film in 1917 that dramatized this blazing light, and showed at the same time how far even the silent screen could go in conveying an idea. Released in Germany early in 1915 as *The Golem,* it was marketed in America two years later as *The Monster of Fate.* It was based on a Jewish legend about a giant of clay who comes to life when a magic scroll is inserted in a sort of hollow button on its chest. The distinguished German actor Paul Wegener played the towering Golem magnificently, both in this version and in a second, which he also directed, in 1920. While the earlier film had its crudities—after all, this movie was made when the feature film was in its infancy—*The Monster of Fate* had an unforgettable sequence that showed how the visual power of the screen could dramatize the visual power of beauty over brute man.

The old legend is told in terms of the day. An antiquarian brings the clay giant to life, and uses him as a servant and for the guarding of a daughter, who wants to run away to the castle of a young nobleman. The young woman arouses the curiosity of the Golem and then a sort of passion. When she escapes from the house and he follows her, the Golem discovers in the world outside something that is for the moment—but only for the moment—more wonderful than the discovery of passion. The clay giant lumbers across the square of the village, stopping to stare in wonder at its Gothic buildings. He reaches a brook, and with a grin of amazed pleasure splashes through the water. On the other side he finds a flowering bush. Halting, he takes a blossom in his hand. Forgetful of the girl whom he is pursuing, he stares at the flower and accidentally brings it close enough to his nose to smell its odor. Another of the beauties of life is caught on the broad and elementally stupid face of the creature—all this in varied medium shots and close-ups. The Golem drops the flower, and we and the camera follow him cross country after the girl. We climb a slight rise of ground to a wooded crest. We stare through a circle of shadowing boughs toward a cathedral city raising its spires to God. Suddenly, up from the foreground, comes the bulk of the monster. The body rises higher and higher, the head tilts back, the shoulders lift, the arms spread out from his sides in a gesture of astonished wonder that encircles our own view of the cathedral. Then the Golem is off again on a quest that will lead ultimately to his death and the death of the girl.

In this sequence, the creative team of director Stellan Rye, writer Henrik Galeen, cameraman Guido Seeber, and Wegener drove home, as perhaps no other art could do so well, the arresting significance of the beauty of life. Using light and shadow, the selection and composition of scenes, and above all a script that progressed clearly, logically, and imaginatively, these men created one of those rare motion pictures that made watching the screen of 1917 something of an adventure.

Chapter
14

The Art of Chaplin and Lesser Comics

I T IS HARD TO FIND the proper place in this book for the story of Charles Spencer Chaplin. The career of the greatest figure of the silent films runs counter to the changing pattern of the screen from 1914 onward. When Griffith had given up making two-reelers, the Strand had opened in New York and feature films were burgeoning, Chaplin was beginning his fabulous career in short comedies, most of them less than fifteen minutes long. While *The Birth of a Nation* was leading Hollywood toward two-hour-long spectacles, the great comedian was triumphing in two-reelers. Except for supporting Marie Dressler in *Tillie's Punctured Romance* (1914), he didn't appear in a feature film until 1921. Ten years later, when Hollywood was making nothing but talkies, Chaplin stuck stubbornly to pantomime and produced what was perhaps his best film, *City Lights*.

It was impossible to inject into the story of the growth of the feature film this man who insisted on making fame and fortune in short comedies. If I had left Chaplin to the nineteen-twenties—when at last he joined Hollywood in making features—I would have had to include his films of 1914 through 1920, and write about other shorts in which his later rivals began their careers. Then there is the matter of Mack Sennett and his Keystone Comedies. Of course, I might have discussed them in relation to Triangle, but they seem inseparable from the talent of Chaplin, to which, quite accidentally, they gave birth.

207

How Chaplin Came to Hollywood

If anything about Chaplin is sobering, it is the thought of how close the screen came to not finding him, and also how close Sennett came to losing him. As far back as 1910, when most film-making was centered in New York, Chaplin appeared there in *The Wow Wows*, one of Fred Karno's English vaudeville acts, complete with trained dogs, a quick-change artist, jugglers, acrobats, and ballad singers. *Variety* said at that time: "Chaplin is typically English, the sort of comedian that the American audiences seem to like, although unaccustomed to. His manner is quiet and easy and he goes about his work in a devil-may-care manner, in direct contrast to the twenty-minutes-from-a-cemetery make-up he employs. . . . Chaplin will do all right for America, but it is too bad that he didn't first appear in New York with something more in it than this piece." The film folk ignored him.

Later, it was only a series of happy accidents that brought Chaplin to Hollywood and Keystone—and kept him there. To begin with, Karno might never have sent another of his turns—such as *A Night in an English Music Hall,* in which Chaplin played a drunk in evening clothes—to tour America. Next, Mack Sennett and his comedienne Mabel Normand, seeking relaxation—as Sennett recounts it—might have gone to another theater rather than the one where Karno's troupe was playing. If, some time later, Sennett hadn't begun to worry about the salary demands of his star Ford Sterling, he might not have thought again of the English comedian. Sennett had trouble recalling the comic's name; was it Champion, Chapman, Chapin, or even Kincaid? The producer, then in Hollywood, solved that problem by wiring his bosses, Kessel and Bauman, to locate the man who did a particular line of business in *A Night in an English Music Hall.*

So Chaplin came to Keystone. But how close he also came to leaving the screen and going back to England! His first film, *Making a Living,* put Sennett in a black mood. Why was the vaudeville clown so much less amusing on the screen? There is a story that, before Sennett had read a trade paper review hailing Chaplin as "a comedian of the first water," the producer wanted to cancel his contract, but that Kessel thought it worthwhile to gamble on Chaplin's modest salary. The actor himself was very low. According to Sennett in *King of Comedy,* Chaplin told Chester Conklin, Mister Walrus of the Keystone troupe:

> I'm going to get out of this business. It's too much for me. I'll never catch on. It's too fast. I can't tell what I'm doing, or what anybody wants me to do. At any rate, I figure the

cinema is little more than a fad. It's canned drama. What audiences really want to see is flesh and blood on the stage. I'm not sure any real actor should get caught posing for the flickahs.

The Clothes That Saved Chaplin

Chaplin stayed in Hollywood because of a pair of oversize shoes, a small derby hat, Fatty Arbuckle's baggy trousers, a skimpy cutaway coat, and the kind of mustache that later added a touch of absurdity to Hitler. Again according to Conklin, Chaplin collected these items in a dressing room while the other comedians played cards on a rainy day. When Sennett got one look at the new Chaplin shuffling, sliding, and skittering, his heart rose and he sent him off to the local version of Coney Island to make a picture in the costume that was to become his alter ego. The plot of *Kid Auto Races at Venice* was nothing more than Chaplin blundering in the way of a dummy camera that was pretending to shoot the contest. Released on February 7, 1914, it shared a reel with a factual film called *Olives and Their Oil*. After nine more pictures in two months, Chaplin found himself co-directing with Mabel Normand. Henceforth, he was pretty much on his own as director and writer.

Not Always the Tramp

In some of the seventy-nine films that Chaplin has made, he has worn costumes other than the one that became his trademark in 1914. In two or three he was a man of wealth. In one he showed himself briefly without make-up or special wardrobe. Twice he impersonated a woman for some minutes, and once he played a bona fide wife all through a short. He has donned the clothes of a number of professions from sailor to waiter. If anyone remembers him, in his older films, without his famous habiliment, it is probably as the Spanish soldier in his burlesque of *Carmen*, the minister in *The Pilgrim*, the policeman in *Easy Street*, or the soldier in *Shoulder Arms*. But the expression he gave to his face, his arms, and his legs dominated any costume he might slip into. Pants, jacket, and derby might be gone, but the art of Chaplin remained. It was an art of personality plus precision and comic inventiveness.

Keystone—the Screen's Commedia dell'Arte

Another art, the art of Keystonerie, is not to be sneered at. By the time Chaplin arrived in Hollywood, Sennett had evolved a form of slapstick far better fitted to the silent screen than was any other kind of comedy or, perhaps, any sort of drama short of the Western and the spectacle. In certain ways, Keystone was close to the Italian *commedia dell'arte* of the seventeenth century. Sennett's plots were just as skimpy. There was almost as much improvisation. Each actor—Hank Mann, Mack Swain, Chester Conklin, Fatty Arbuckle—was a special character; in costume and mannerism he was as set and inflexible, as defined and enduring, as Pantaloon, Punch, The Doctor, or The Captain. On the faintest thread of plot, the Keystone players hung a series of gags and extraneous episodes corresponding to the *lazzi*, or varieties of comic stage business, that made the Italians famous.

The Comic World of Mack Sennett

Keystone comedy expanded beyond the *commedia dell'arte* insofar as the screen expands beyond the stage. If the Italians had had a movie camera, they would have done just the sort of things that Sennett and his gag men did. These pioneers of a new kind of screen humor imagined and executed the most fantastic—and convincing—of comic incidents. They made the impossible seem probable, for it all happened in an otherwise logical world. Keystone autos tore and slithered around real streets; they did not, like the cars of Méliès or Paul, plumb the heavens or ride the rings of Saturn. The imagination that was Keystone seized upon realities and turned them into wild and hilarious absurdities. Crooks robbed a bank with a vacuum cleaner. A flood swept into a house and carried off a man in a bathtub. An automobile with its right-hand wheels on the sidewalk cut down a row of telephone poles. Sennett took advantage of whatever happened to be going on in Los Angeles. An oil well "came in," and he sent his actors there with a few gags. He learned that a reservoir was to be drained for cleaning; so some of his comedians played scenes in a boat, and went back some days later to work in the bared mud.

Censorious folk of almost fifty years ago—who seldom went to the movies—believed that Keystone Comedies were nothing more than pie-throwing contests. The lustier and the more astute of us enjoyed the art of these ballistics, and we observed that in what the players did, there was more than custard that met the eye. I'm not thinking of the Keystone Bathing Beauties or the curvaceous Gloria Swanson or the piquant Mabel Normand. Before Sennett discovered the possibilities in pulchritude, he relied heavily on chases, usually presided over by the Keystone Cops in their antique helmets. His films had the intellectual irreverence that makes satire, and the preposterous exaggeration that takes the sting out

of it and leaves only hilarity. I cannot say, as W. S. Gilbert did of Beerbohm Tree's *Hamlet*, that Keystone pictures were funny without being
vulgar; but, if you look in a dictionary, say the *Century*, you will find
that the word "vulgar" comes from the Latin *vulgus*, a multitude, and
is defined as "of or pertaining to the common people," and "common; in
general use," before you come to the meaning, "offensive to good taste."

Chaplin's Path to Pathos

Some critics have spread the delusion that Chaplin was out of key with
Keystone, that he couldn't match the tempo of the other actors. This
springs from Chaplin's words, "It's too fast," and not from a fresh look
at those comedies of 1914. Chaplin was physically more agile than any
of Sennett's people—when he wanted to be. But he knew something that
Sennett never learned—the value of comic deliberation. And, also, of
pathos.

When Chaplin left Sennett he did not, in a sense, leave Keystone. He
took with him the better part of it. Completely his own master, he added
new values as he worked more and more carefully. It is significant that
as his salary went up the number of his films went down and their
quality improved. In 1914 when Sennett paid Chaplin $125 a week
(another authority says $150), later raising it to $250, he appeared in
thirty-five films, directing almost two-thirds of them. In the year when
Essanay paid him $1,250 a week, he turned out only fourteen short films.
As he went on earning more and more, his output steadily decreased.

Theodore Huff, in his thorough biography and analysis, *Charlie
Chaplin*, traces the growth in his characterization and his technique as
he made fewer and better films. In all his Keystone Comedies, Huff
points out, Chaplin appeared "as a basically unsympathetic, though
engaging, character—a sharper, a heel, an annoying blunderer, a thief,
an obnoxious drunk, who is cruel, sometimes to the point of sadism."
When Chaplin worked for Essanay, the character he played became more
sympathetic, while he added better plotting and subtler pantomime.

With *The Tramp*, in the spring of 1915, Chaplin injected a note of
pathos. At the end of the film, the little tramp loses the girl he has come
to love, and, as Huff points out in his *Index to the Films of Charles
Chaplin,* "we see Charlie, back to the camera, walking dejectedly down
the long road." But, before the fade-out, the moment of pathos dissolves
into the eternal blitheness of the comic spirit. "Suddenly he shrugs, flips
up his heels and ambles quickly toward the horizon as the scene irises
out." In various ways this mood of sadness—accepted, reconciled—was

Chaplin's Output and Intake as Actor and Director

This list shows how the number of Chaplin films decreased each year as he spent more time and care on them. Until he joined United Artists, he had appeared in only two feature films, *Tillie's Punctured Romance* (1914) and *The Kid* (1921). He wrote and directed *A Woman of Paris*, but played only a walk-on in one scene.

Release dates	Company	No. of films	No. of reels	Approximate earnings
Feb. 1914 to Dec. 1914	Keystone	35	45½	$125 to $250 per week
Feb. 1915 to Mar. 1916	Essanay	14	26	$1,250 per week
May 1916 to Oct. 1917	Mutual	12	24	$10,000 per week plus $150,000 bonus
Apr. 1918 to Feb. 1923	First National	9	25½	$1,000,000 plus profit-sharing

Features Made for United Artists

Oct. 1923	A Woman of Paris	8 reels	Known only to Chaplin and his partners in UA
Aug. 1925	*The Gold Rush*	9 reels	
Jan. 1928	*The Circus*	7 reels	
Feb. 1931	*City Lights*	87 minutes	
Feb. 1936	*Modern Times*	85 minutes	
Oct. 1940	*The Great Dictator*	126 minutes	
Oct. 1947	*Monsieur Verdoux*	123 minutes	
Oct. 1952	*Limelight*	138 minutes	

Made Independently

Sept. 1957	A King in New York	105 minutes

to appear again and again in Chaplin's maturer films. It mounted in effectiveness from the ending of *The Kid* (1921), through the dinner party in *The Gold Rush* (1925) to which his adored one never came, and reached its climax in certain scenes with the blind girl in *City Lights* (1931).

CHAPLIN IN *The Circus.* Said *The New Yorker* in 1928: "As the nearest child, mounted policeman, ship chandler or banker can tell you, Mr. Charlie Chaplin has come back to town, after two awful, lost years, and is to be seen at the Strand Theatre in a very funny picture." (*Drawing by Al Frueh* © Copr. 1928, 1956 The New Yorker Magazine, Inc.)

Chaplin's Glad Gags

Chaplin gained greatly when he made his tramp sympathetic and added a touch of passing pathos, yet the success of his silent films came mostly from the physical "business" and the comedy gags that he invented and then executed so deftly. Like the *lazzi* of the *commedia dell'arte*, this vital element in Chaplin's art had little or no relation to plot. The gags had to fit the occasion or the locale—that was all. To fall down while carrying a tray of food, turn over on the floor, and get up without spilling the dishes, Chaplin had to be waiting on table in *Shanghaied* (1915). In *The Idle Class* (1921), we see Chaplin standing in front of a photograph of his departed wife, his back shaking with apparent grief; because the film involves a party, the actor can turn around and let us see that he is mixing a cocktail. The plot of *Laughing Gas* (1914) has nothing to do with the way the comedian enters the dentist's office, looks the patients over, carefully removes his gloves, rubs his hands, and then goes about his menial job of carrying out the cuspidors. In *The Gold Rush*, he had to be starving in order to cook an old shoe, eat the laces like spaghetti, and suck the nails as if they were juicy bones, but he could have starved elsewhere than in the Klondike.

In Chaplin's splendid concession to sound—this occurred in *City Lights* —we saw and heard him hiccoughing with a strident tin whistle in his windpipe; the gag paid off all the better because he was trying to listen politely to a very bad singer at a musicale. A gag in the same picture is a beautiful example of comic deliberateness and at the same time, of humor based on escaping disaster instead of suffering it. In the sidewalk outside the shop of an art dealer, there is the top of an elevator that drops down into the basement now and then. To Sennett this would have been only a means to quick and violent exits for unsuspecting victims. Far otherwise with Chaplin. Looking out from the shop, we see Chaplin standing innocently on the elevator and examining—not so innocently, yet with the air and the eye of a connoisseur—a nude statue of a girl in the window. As he steps forward off the elevator, for a closer look, the elevator descends. When he steps back, still intent on the *objet d'art*, the platform elevator returns to the sidewalk level and supports the lover of the beautiful. The episode is played with a leisurely deliberation befitting Chaplin's pose as a *cognoscente*.

Pantomime of Ideas As Well As Dexterity

Chaplin seldom threw pies—and never, I think, received one. Most of his gags were far subtler. Consider how he lavished on a single scene of *The Pawnshop* (1916) a rich array of *lazzi* that depended on a satiric idea rather than physical movement. Gilbert Seldes, the first of the intelligentsia to appreciate the art of Chaplin and write brilliantly about it, recorded in *The Seven Lively Arts* exactly what happened in the film when a customer offered Chaplin a clock in pawn.

> Charlot [the French name for Chaplin's character] looks at it; then takes an auscultator and listens to its heartbeat; then taps it over crossed fingers for its pulmonary action; then taps it with a little hammer to see the quality, as with porcelain; then snaps his thumb on the bell. He takes an auger and bores a hole in it; then a can-opener, and when he has pried the lid off he smells the contents and with a disparaging gesture makes the owner smell them, too. He then does dentistry on it, with forceps; then plumbing. Finally he screws a jeweler's magnifying glass into his eye and hammers what is left in the clock, shakes out the contents, measures the mainspring from the tip of his nose to arm's length, like cloth, squirts oil on the debris to keep it quiet, and, lifting the man's hat from his head, sweeps the whole mess into it and returns it with a sad shake of the head.

From his facial pantomime in *The Pawnshop* and from many another film, we know that Chaplin could have been a Marcel Marceau if he had cared to play solely to the intelligentsia. He preferred a more obvious attack, and he brought back a richer prize. In comic imagination, in satiric ingenuity, he outstripped Marceau. In physical dexterity, Chaplin had no rival. He could carry eleven chairs looped around his neck and right arm. He roller skated divinely in *The Rink* (1916). No fall was impossible. With it all went the most perfect timing, the most effortless precision. Whether he was involved in the broad comicalities of Keystone or in humor linked to pathos, he had the deadly precision of an expert accountant adding up a column of figures, or the ease of a Pavlova executing a glide. And all in the terms of comic inspiration.

Success and Its Fruits

Charlie Chaplin was twenty-four when he turned some ill-assorted old clothes and a touch of genius into an image that was soon to be world famous. From the screen it spread to comic strips, took the form of a doll, christened a dance, and—almost a generation before Mickey Mouse —proliferated into many of the other sidelines that now both advertise and enrich a figure of the entertainment world. Chaplin was twenty-six when he signed a contract for $670,000 a year. Before he was thirty, he had contracted to make eight films for a million dollars.

Now what did Chaplin contribute to the screen besides untold hours of joy for millions upon millions of moviegoers? What did he leave behind him beyond reels of film that are slowly deteriorating? What effect did he have on the screen today?

Though Chaplin was the first and perhaps, as Shaw said, the only genius of the silent film, the answer has to be—very little. I think this was due to the advent of sound. If the screen had remained mute, Chaplin could have been a creator born ahead of his time and destined to have a profound effect on the later course of a growing art. Through the last dozen years of silence, Chaplin was an innovator who couldn't be effectively copied, and in this short span of time, no one appeared who could improve upon him. At his peak, he triumphed in a kind of rueful, gentle comedy that Sennett was wise enough not to try to duplicate. At a lower level, there were plenty of imitators. In America they ranged from Billy West to a man named Charles Amador who had to be restrained by law from calling himself Charlie Aplin. Germany had a Charlie Kaplin. Of course these men could copy only the outer image— the clothes, the make-up, the shuffle. No one could hope to match the special, creative spirit within.

But somewhere between the venal copycats and the genuine article, there were a number of men who seem to have drawn their comedy from Chaplin's. Oddly enough, they chose the better part, though not quite the best. In the main, they ignored much of the slapstick, but they never dared try complete pathos. In between, they became new versions of "the little man" menaced by life and somehow triumphing over it. Perhaps, however, there was no conscious or even unconscious imitation. Perhaps the work of these men—and of Chaplin himself—was merely the natural reaction to the complex and baffling, overorganized yet unmanageable, world that was taking shape at the start of the twentieth century.

The Comedian—Like Portia—Faces Life

Among the comics I am thinking of, the outstanding were Harold Lloyd, Buster Keaton, Harry Langdon, Stan Laurel, and to a certain degree Roscoe Arbuckle and Oliver Hardy. With the possible exception of Laurel and Hardy, their type of humor was peculiar to the screen because it needed the intimacy of the medium close shot. The comic stars of the stage had been stronger personalities, more vigorous men, actors like Harrigan and Hart, Francis Wilson, and DeWolf Hopper, who could drive a comic point to the last row of the gallery. This type, which includes men like W. C. Fields and Danny Kaye, seems better suited to talkies than were those silent comics. There were a few sad clowns in the circus from Grock to Emmett Kelly, but neither they nor Jimmy Savo of vaudeville and revue conquered the screen.

Harold Lloyd and the others I have named had only one thing in common. Outwardly handicapped or inwardly insecure, beset with troubles, harassed by the strong, perplexed by all about them, they faced their fate and had the ingenuity or the luck to win through. In other respects, they were highly individualized. Harold Lloyd, after some experiments with grotesque characters called "Willie Work" and "Lonesome Luke," abetted by producer Hal Roach, found that an ordinary suit of clothes plus horn-rimmed glasses could turn him into an eager but foolhardy weakling, who to his own surprise could survive anything from lions and bullies to hanging from the hands of a clock a hundred feet above the street and getting entangled in the awnings of a skyscraper. Clad in baggy coat and pants, frozen-face Keaton braved as many physical dangers as Lloyd and with no more expression than a somewhat ascetic Sphinx. Stan Laurel, a British-born actor who had understudied Chaplin in *A Night in an English Music Hall,* faced life with a nervous but hopeful simplicity that survived all the troubles that the foolish optimism of Oliver Hardy thrust upon him. For a time, Harry Langdon came closest to rivaling Chaplin. He had less physical dexterity, but his mask of infantile innocence could switch from bland hopefulness to pathetic and puzzled apprehension as troubles descended upon him. Fatty Arbuckle, with his vacant helplessness, and Hardy with his absurd and disastrous rodomontade, fitted—despite their physical bulk—into the pattern of the little man in the big, big world.

Some of Sennett's Nurslings

Sennett, who fired Lloyd because he didn't realize how funny he would be, nurtured the careers of Langdon and Arbuckle, as well as Chaplin and Normand, only to see them leave him for the greener pastures of the feature film. Among his Keystone troupe there were a number of comedians who all but qualified as "little men." These were courageous Ben Turpin with his hopelessly—and profitably—crossed eyes; imperturbable Hank Mann, with the haircut of Elihu Root and eyes of Theda Bara; Chester Conklin, as falsely fierce as his mustache; Edgar Kennedy, master of the "slow burn"; Charlie Chase; Slim Summerville; and that former elephant-tender Wallace Beery—they were wide of the Chaplin pattern yet very funny. Among Sennett's gag men was Raymond Griffith, who went on to be the "Silk Hat Harry" of just fame.

Some of the comics—Laurel and Hardy, W. C. Fields, and, to an extent, Harold Lloyd and Buster Keaton—were able to move into the talkies. The best of the others were stopped in their tracks. Sennett and many of the lesser producers of two-reel comedies seemed to have had a premonition that words were going to take the place of gags and comic action. For, around 1925, they began to inject subtitles like these: "As crooked as a corkscrew hiding behind a pretzel." "The restaurant was so small they had to serve condensed milk." "The great wide open spaces where men are men and women are scarce."

The Prime Comedienne

Women seemed ill-fitted to the broad comedy of the silent days. Marie Dressler came to her real success only in the talkies. So did some of Sennett's Bathing Beauties—Gloria Swanson, Carole Lombard, and Bebe Daniels. Louise Fazenda and Polly Moran survived sound. But the one real comedienne of the great days of Sennett was Mabel Normand. She might have said, "He that is without humor among you, let him first cast the pie." For, though Mabel did cast a pie or two before she deserted shorts to make her best feature, *Mickey* (1918), she was so full of high humor that she never had to resort to physical violence to hold her own with the best of the comics. Robert E. Sherwood was a motion picture critic and not yet a playwright when he wrote of Mabel Normand: "Once a year, perhaps, she steps forth to remind us that she is still the first comedienne of the silent drama. . . . You can't imagine this irrepressive gamin doing anything stupid or dull or obvious on the screen."

Here Today—But—

When Chaplin first won fame, we used to see outside the theaters that played his comedies a great cut-out of his figure, with the legend: "I am here today." Ten years later, when Chaplin was winning stupendous success, Seldes wrote, "like everything else associated with his name it is faintly ironic . . . that particularly transient announcement . . . 'I am here today,' with its emotional overtone of 'gone tomorrow.'" Yes, it was ironic in its day, but it was also prophetic. The great comedian and so many of his fellow comics were to expire, like a modern Laocoön, entangled in the coils of a sound track.

Chapter
15
Germany and Scandinavia
Take the Lead

U<small>NTIL WORLD WAR</small> I, the history of the motion picture was written in France and Italy, England and America. East of the Rhine there were no inventions of importance, no productions of notable merit. With the end of the war, Germany was to assume on the screen something of the commanding position that she had held in the theater for a generation or more.

The pre-war start was modest enough. About 1910 a few Germans began to transfer plays to the screen in the stiff fashion of the French Film d'Art, and some tried to achieve a more filmic quality with stories of a fantastic sort. The two techniques were as far apart as their material, yet one man seems to have had an influence in both fields of action, especially through his actors and designers. This was Max Reinhardt, the outstanding director and producer of the German stage.

From Reinhardt and His Co-workers

In 1910, Reinhardt is said to have made a film in the lifeless manner of Film d'Art. He directed *A Venetian Night* in 1913, and *The Isle of the Dead* the next year, but he never created in terms of the screen. On the other hand, some of the men who had worked closely with him in his Berlin theaters followed a different path when they entered the movies. The poet-playwright Hugo von Hofmannsthal, who had adapted *Everyman* for Reinhardt from medieval sources, wrote the script for a dream fantasy, *The Strange Girl* in 1913. That same year an actor trained by

219

Reinhardt began developing a series of short comedies of everyday life; he was Ernst Lubitsch. Another actor, F. W. Murnau, became a noted director. Paul Wegener, a member of Reinhardt's company, seems to have breathed some cinematic life into a version of *The Student of Prague* in 1913.

Such sinister and supernatural make-believe as *The Student of Prague* —which had its roots in the "Gothic romance" of the Teutonic stage a century before—was to be one of the three major trends in German films after the war. Other directors followed this lead, and many added elements of the expressionism that was to sweep the German stage. This bizarre movement owed nothing to Reinhardt, but the other trends, costumed spectacles and bitter realism, drew much from the example and the methods of the great stage director. Adding certain technical advances, German film-makers and German films were to win international repute and to influence Hollywood production during the twenties.

A War-Born Industry

When World War I closed Germany's western frontier, and only Scandinavian films were available, the German film boomed. In 1913 there were only twenty-eight producing companies; by 1919 there were 245, including the giant Ufa. Ufa had been created in 1917 when the government intervened to consolidate a number of companies, including the Danish Nordisk, and to supply about a third of the new firm's capital. Until then, the armed forces had seen to it that films were made of German military triumphs; some of these were sent to America on neutral ships as early as the fall of 1915. In 1917 the army provided 500 movie houses for the soldiers on the western front, and 300 for the eastern. When Ufa became essentially a private corporation after the war, it built many theaters in Germany and acquired others in countries that had been neutral.

Ufa Launches the German Spectacle

The first major effort of Ufa was to rival the gargantuan Italian film *Cabiria*. The German picture was Joe May's *Veritas Vincit* (1918); to provide plenty of sets and costumes, it traced the transmigration of two loving souls through three historic ages. It was Lubitsch, however, who was to bring to the screen the skills needed to make period films both striking and convincing. Under the leadership of Reinhardt, the German theater had learned to build and light scenery in the ways of the new stagecraft. Its settings created both beauty and illusion out of fine design,

whose simplicity often suggested off-stage grandeur. Lubitsch expanded
such settings until they filled the screen with convincing magnificence,
and he discovered how he could adapt stage lighting to make motion
picture photography more effective. From Reinhardt's mammoth production of *Oedipus Rex* in a circus building, Lubitsch learned to handle
screen crowds as they had never been handled before. He added something filmic to mob vitality. The English critic Miss C. A. Lejeune described his work:

> Lubitsch had a way of manipulating his puppets that
> gave multitude, and in contrast, loneliness, a new force. No
> one before had so filled and drained his spaces with the
> wheeling mass, rushing in the figures from every corner to
> cover the screen, dispersing them again like a whirlwind,
> with one single figure staunch in the middle of the empty
> square.

In America Lubitsch is known best for his comedies, and it was with
comedies that he began his screen work in Germany. Beginning in 1913,
he played a Yiddish clothing-store clerk in a series of short comedies—
many of which he later directed—that made him as popular in Germany
as dapper Max Linder in France or Harold Lloyd in America. In 1918,
he directed his first feature-length drama, *The Eyes of the Mummy*,
with Pola Negri and Emil Jannings, and in the same year he made both
his own and Miss Negri's fame with *Gypsy Blood*, a version of *Carmen*.
The Oyster Princess (1919), in only four reels, crudely satirized the
American businessman. When Lubitsch turned to spectacle, some saw
anti-Allied propaganda in the distorted history of his *Passion* (1919)
and *Deception* (1920), dealing with Madame du Barry and Anne
Boleyn respectively, and also in Dimitri Buchowetski's *Danton* (1920)
and Richard Oswald's *The Affairs of Lady Hamilton* (1921). But there
were many more spectacles, from Lubitsch and others, that couldn't be
accused of trying to make enemies or influence peoples.

Caligari *and Filmed "Expressionism"*

The impact on Hollywood and its public was tremendous when Lubitsch's *Passion*, *Gypsy Blood*, and *Deception* reached America in 1920
and 1921, but another picture won greater acclaim among critics and
intelligentsia. This was *The Cabinet of Doctor Caligari*, produced in
1919 and imported by Goldwyn in 1921. The film was a thing of strange
distortions, distortions of the mind and distortions of flat scenery with
painted angles and shadows. The script by Carl Mayer (who was to

have a marked influence on German film makers) and Hans Janowitz
was highly spiced with somnambulism, murders, and maniacs. The direction of Robert Wiene and the acting of Werner Krauss, Conrad Veidt,
and Lil Dagover completed the bizarre fascination of *Caligari*. Like the
expressionist writing and decor through which many of the plays and
stage productions of the early twenties tried to escape from realism into
a stylized presentation of emotion, *Caligari* and a number of other German films had their roots in a certain macabre Teutonic occultism and
morbid romanticism of the early nineteenth century.

Other types of German expressionism appeared on the screen: F. W.
Murnau's Jekyll and Hyde film, *Janus-Faced* (1920); Wiene's *Genuine*
(1920); the second *Golem* (1920) which, with its distorted medieval
ghetto, had none of the qualities that I ascribe to the early version in
chapter thirteen; Fritz Lang's *Destiny* (1921), Murnau's Dracula film,
Nosferatu (1922); Fritz Wendhausen's *The Stone Rider* (1923); and
Paul Leni's *Waxworks* (1924), as well as the second version of *The
Student of Prague* (1926).

Various Kinds of Realism

Films of this sort tapered off into a kind of realism with psychic and
morbid overtones. Among these were director Leopold Jessner's *Back-
stairs* (1921), Lupu Pick's *Shattered* (1921) and his *New Year's Eve*
(1924), Arthur Robison's *Warning Shadows* (1922), and Karl Grune's
The Street (1923).

Fritz Lang, the only active survivor among the German directors,
set himself apart from the rest through a wider range of interest and
accomplishment. His *Destiny* was a mixture of fairy tale, symbolism, and
historical spectacle. (Siegfried Kracauer, who has written with such
understanding in his book *From Caligari to Hitler*, claims that Douglas
Fairbanks drew some of the effects in *The Thief of Bagdad* (1924) from
a Chinese episode in *Destiny*.) In *Dr. Mabuse, the Gambler* (1922),
Lang set an almost documentary story of a super-gangster in an atmos
phere of unreality that suggested something of *Caligari*. A year later,
he mounted the legendary *Siegfried* in settings of stark grandeur.
Metropolis (1926) wasted the amazing scenic effects of a city of the
future on a stilted story, tinged with horror, of a revolt of slave laborers.
In his film *The Spy* (1928) he dealt again with an eccentric mastermind
involved in entanglements à la Hitchcock. Lang won his greatest success
with his first talkie, *M* (1931), an ingenious and imaginative piece of
utter realism. His final picture in Germany, *The Last Will of Dr. Mabuse*

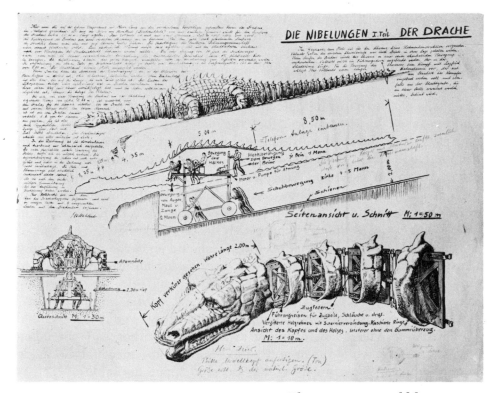

FROM RICHARD WAGNER TO FRITZ LANG. The composer would have loved the dragon that German technicians developed for Lang's *Siegfried*. This sketch shows, in part, the elaborate articulations of the reptile's body and how it was put into motion by a crew of men concealed within it. (*From the* Archive of the Cinémathèque Française. *Courtesy British Film Institute.*)

(1932), was, as he put it, "an allegory to show Hitler's processes of terrorism." Unfortunately, Lang misjudged the Fuehrer's timetable of triumph, for the film was finished just before Hitler took over, and thus was not released in Germany at that time.

The Last Laugh—at a Happy Ending

The historic spectacle, the expressionistic film, and a kind of psychotic realism developed in Germany during the first years of the nineteen-twenties, a period of national tensions. Then, with the false stabilization of the Republic, came pictures more conventional in outlook but produced with a technical skill more effective than that of Hollywood. The most important of these was Murnau's *The Last Laugh* (1924). Its distinction lay partly in its story, partly in the excellent acting of Emil Jannings and direction of Murnau, but to a great extent in the way that the writer, Carl Mayer of *Caligari,* suggested the camera should be kept in motion.

Mayer's plot is simple but affecting. We meet a dignified old doorman who is exalted by the uniform that the hotel provides. Because of his age, the man is demoted to the menial position of washroom attendant. Humiliated at home as well as at work, he sinks into unconscious sleep in a corner of the washroom. Perhaps because American films with happy endings had become popular—Germany's had been almost invariably tragic or tragi-comic—Mayer and Murnau tacked on a final sequence in which Jannings was dining sumptuously in the same hotel. The will of an American had specified that his fortune should go to the man in whose arms he died, and the man had been the washroom attendant. Up to this final sequence, the story had been told without subtitles—something already done by Pick in *New Year's Eve* and Grune in *The Street*— but now came a subtitle explaining that the story would have ended here with the fellow slowly pining away, if the author had not taken pity on the forsaken old man and added an epilogue in which he made things happen as, unfortunately, they do not happen in real life.

The Moving Camera Writes

The sensation of *The Last Laugh* was a technical one, and it must be credited to script writer Carl Mayer and cameraman Karl Freund, not to Murnau, the director. Again and again Mayer conceived scenes in terms of camera movement. Murnau accepted the idea, and cameraman Karl Freund found ways of carrying it out.

Moving the camera wasn't new to the screen before Mayer used it, at first tentatively in *Shattered* and in *New Year's Eve.* Griffith had put his machine in the back of an automobile. He had had his camera swoop down to a close-up in *The Avenging Conscience.* He had begun a Babylonian sequence in *Intolerance* with a long shot of the gigantic set for Belshazzar's Feast, and by means of an elevator in a moving tower, descending a ramp, he had brought the camera down and into a close shot of Prince Belshazzar. (Griffith could have made the great edifice still more impressive if he had drawn back from the prince to an ever-widening shot of the huge set, but the equipment was too heavy to work against gravity.) Lubitsch (like the Italians) had never been wedded to a fixed tripod. In previous films, most camera movement had been panning or tilting, but in *The Last Laugh* the camera moved forward or backward, as well as up or down, in scenes of considerable length. Normally such scenes would have been built up out of a number of separate shots. Personally, I am against the too common distractions of camera movement, but there were spots in *The Last Laugh* where it was highly effective. One of these, in the first scene of the film, took us down in the elevator, through the busy foyer of the hotel and out to the doorman on the sidewalk.

Making a shot like that was a triumph of makeshift ingenuity in the days before camera cranes and dollies. Freund has described how he and his camera were mounted on a tricycle in the descending elevator, and rolled out into the lobby and through the door of the hotel. In another scene, the camera rode on a fire ladder, anticipating the modern crane. It also traveled on overhead cables. In a scene where the porter was drunk, Freund achieved the subjective camera—the eye of the character—by strapping a light camera to his chest and staggering around the set. The utter mobility that Murnau and Freund achieved impressed the film makers of Hollywood even more than it did the directors in Berlin. Basically, the movement wasn't willful or freakish, as in Laurence Olivier's *Hamlet;* it served more successfully the dramatic purposes of the author.

Carl Mayer—Inspirer of Movement

Carl Mayer's scripts were meticulously detailed. They indicated every shot. They prescribed, for example, all the camera movements in *Shattered, New Year's Eve,* and *The Last Laugh.* In order to visualize action and movements as he wrote, he used a camera view-finder, a device that shows what area a shot will cover. Directors welcomed the aid he gave them in opening up the possibilities of the camera, and they kept him on the set through all the shooting. He became, in all but name, a co-director. All in all, he seems one of the most remarkable men in the German film industry of the nineteen-twenties, certainly the outstanding writer: Beginning as a collaborator in *Caligari,* he worked on many of the most celebrated pictures made between 1919 and 1926. Yet, though his career sounds like a success story, only *The Last Laugh* won wide popularity. His "screen poems," writes Kracauer, "met with little response outside the circle of the intellectuals."

Down-to-Earth Realism

With 1925, German film-makers began to turn away from the bizarre and the exotic, and to concentrate on a literal kind of realism, sweetened sometimes by a happy ending. Perhaps the success of American films—

and the chance of going to Hollywood at fat salaries—had something to do with this. Perhaps it was a change in the temper of Germany as the Dawes Plan began to stabilize the country's economy. Also, new directors appeared to take the place of those who had been snapped up by Hollywood.

In *The Joyless Street* (1925), the Austrian G. W. Pabst filmed a bitter novel of Vienna in the days of inflation. With a cast headed by the Reinhardt actor Werner Krauss, Greta Garbo fresh from Sweden, and the ever-popular Danish actress Asta Nielsen, Pabst drew a brutal picture of middle-class degradation and the sadism of the profiteers. With *The Love of Jeanne Ney* (1927), adapted from another novel, Pabst was ready to mingle passion and horror and then top it off with a happy ending not in the book.

Variety (1925) brought success to another newcomer. Written and directed by E. A. Dupont, this brutally passionate film told the story of the love triangle of three trapeze performers at the Berlin Wintergarten. The acting of Emil Jannings was as powerfully persuasive as Dupont's interpretation of life in a cheap café and the sordid hotel in which his people lived. The camera—again in the hands of Freund—followed the action with the greatest skill and imagination. Those who saw *Variety* can never forget how the camera, once more subjective as in the drunken scene in *The Last Laugh*, swung with the trapeze, and looking down at the swaying audience, visualized the temptation of the cuckold to drop his rival to his death.

There were also the films that Paul Czinner—not quite Teutonic—made with Elisabeth Bergner and various noted actors such as Jannings and Veidt. *Nju* (1924) was as neurotic as the Russian play from which it came, but *The Violinist of Florence* (1926) and *Donna Juana* (1928) had tenderness and even at times naïveté.

To complete the picture of the silent screen in Germany, I should mention the flood of pathological sex-films at the end of the war, such as *Lost Daughters, Hyenas of Lust* and *The Girl and the Men;* and also the Alpine films made by the geologist Dr. Arnold Fanck, the most striking of which was *The White Hell of Pitz Palü* (Germany, 1929), made under the supervision of G. W. Pabst.

One of the lesser miracles of the German film at its best was the array of stars from the stage, and the film actors who played with equal skill: Jannings, Wegener, Krauss, Veidt, Fritz Kortner, Albert Bassermann, Ernst Deutsch, Negri, Garbo, Nielsen, Henny Porten, Dagover, Lya de Putti, and Anna Sten.

A GUINNESS IN PETTICOATS. Henny Porten, perhaps the most popular German actress of the nineteen-twenties, anticipated the English actor who played eight different characters in *Kind Hearts and Coronets* (1949). In Porten's film *The Adventure of Sybille Brant*, released in 1925, she appeared in two chief parts, rich in contrasts, and she played three minor roles as well.

Scandinavian Directors

In the first years of World War I, two directors of unusual qualities appeared in Sweden—Victor Sjöström (renamed Seastrom in Hollywood) and Mauritz Stiller. Both made a number of pictures based on the works of the great Swedish novelist Selma Lagerlöf. Both gave their films a pictorial sweep that they drew from the wide landscapes of their country. Seastrom was the greater director, but Stiller found or developed better players—Greta Garbo and Lars Hanson, who were to work in Hollywood, and Jenny Hasselquist, who became Sweden's outstanding screen star. Seastrom and Stiller began to make films in the same year, 1912. In 1917 came Seastrom's first notable picture, *The Outlaw and His Wife,* as well as *The Girl from the Marsh Croft,* the latter based on a Lagerlöf novel. It was after the war, however, that these two Scandinavians did their best work. In *Thy Soul Shall Bear Witness* (1920), from another Lagerlöf story, Seastrom added what seemed then a vivid sense of the supernatural. Stiller reached his peak in the last film that he made in his native country, Lagerlöf's *Story of Gösta Berling* (1923), with Greta Garbo.

Important film-making in Denmark began in 1910 when Peter Urban Gad directed Asta Nielsen in *The Abyss*. Directors had the advantage of being able to use the excellent actors of the Royal Theater. In the earlier years of World War I, one company alone is said to have made some three hundred long and short films. Toward the end of the conflict, Ufa absorbed the chief Danish company, Nordisk. Both Gad and Miss Nielsen worked in German studios. The gifted actress appeared under the direction of Svend Gade (not to be confused with Peter Urban Gad) in *Hamlet* (Germany, 1920), a version based on a thesis that made the Prince of Denmark a woman in disguise. When Nordisk was reconstituted after the war, A. W. Sandberg filmed a number of the novels of Dickens, and he also made two of Denmark's most popular pictures, *The Clown* (1916) and *The Four Devils* (1920).

Another Dane, Carl Dreyer, far outshone Sandberg. Except for his naturalistic *The Master of the House* (1925), his earlier films got scant circulation in America. His fame as a silent director rests on *The Passion of Joan of Arc* (1928). This film, made in France with Falconetti, was an extraordinary assemblage of close-ups with comparatively few medium shots or two-shots. He gave the trial of Joan great poignancy, though he himself felt the lack of the complete drama that he could have achieved if good recording of spoken dialogue had been available then. Today, *The Passion of Joan of Arc*, like *The Last Laugh*, still seems a fine picture, while Murnau's *Nosferatu* is often absurd and hardly ever moving, and Buchowetski's *Othello* (1922) and Lubitsch's *Deception* are disappointingly obvious.

Hollywood Discovers Foreign Directors

It was early in the nineteen-twenties that American film-makers, film critics, and to some extent filmgoers, awoke to what was going on in Germany. *Caligari* was a success only with the critics and highbrow moviegoers, but Lubitsch's two historical films, quickly followed by his *Gypsy Blood*, were popular enough to arouse the acquisitiveness of American producers. Mary Pickford brought Lubitsch to Hollywood to direct her *Rosita* (1923) for United Artists. Following Lubitsch came Victor Seastrom and in the mid-twenties, Murnau, Dupont, Leni, Buchowetski, Stiller, and others. Germany and Sweden thus lost their best directors to Hollywood. Also, Ufa lost to Hollywood, for a time, its equally distinguished producer Erich Pommer, who had done so much to cultivate Carl Mayer and guide Germany's best directors.

The Fate of the Aliens in Hollywood

There was a considerable gap between what the Germans had done abroad and what they accomplished in the alien atmosphere of Hollywood. They weren't asked to make historical spectacles, and, as a matter of fact, most of them weren't interested in that kind of film. American producers didn't believe that their public would care for the other two types upon which the Germans had concentrated—bizarre and morbid fantasy, and tragic realism. Leni had some success with *The Cat and the Canary* (1927) though its comic exaggerations go badly with the pictorial atmosphere of fantastic horror that he tried to give this version of the popular American mystery play. Except for Lubitsch and to a slight extent Murnau, the Germans were defeated, and they returned to Europe. Dupont, after a failure with *Love Me and the World Is Mine* (1928) at Universal, had as futile a stopover in London.

Murnau, whose *The Last Laugh* had a greater effect on Hollywood technique than any other single foreign film, left Germany after the release of his pictorially ingenious version of *Faust* (1926). At Fox, where he first worked in America, he had no such actors as he had gathered together for his Teutonic swan song: Emil Jannings, William Dieterle, the Swedish star Gösta Ekman, and the famous French diseuse Yvette Guilbert. In *Sunrise* (1927), with Janet Gaynor and George O'Brien, Murnau again used the moving camera with great skill; many still remember the long trucking shot across the misty marsh. Murnau got Carl Mayer to write the script of this adaptation of Hermann Sudermann's novel *A Trip to Tilsit,* but he could not induce Mayer to leave Germany and work with him in an American studio. Mayer also collaborated on Murnau's second picture, *Four Devils* (1928), which had already been filmed in Europe. After quarreling with the Fox executives over a semicompleted picture, Murnau formed an independent company with that genius of the documentary film, Robert Flaherty. They went to the South Seas to make *Tabu* (1931). Flaherty retired from the project, and Murnau was killed in an automobile accident shortly after his return to Hollywood.

Neither of the Swedish directors fared too well. Stiller, who brought over Greta Garbo and Lars Hanson, was taken off his first Garbo picture for MGM, *The Temptress* (1926), and replaced by Fred Niblo, who had just directed *Ben-Hur.* Under the supervision of Erich Pommer at Paramount, Stiller, replacing von Stroheim, made only a fairly successful film in *Hotel Imperial* (1927) with Pola Negri. Hung from an overhead trolley, his camera moved through the lobby and the four rooms on each side of it. He died in Sweden after completing in Hollywood *The Street of Sin* (1928), which Pommer did not supervise. The film was more distinguished for its players—Jannings and Olga Baclanova—than for its script by Joseph von Sternberg. Seastrom proved somewhat more adaptable. His only memorable pictures, however, were *The Scarlet Letter* (1926) and *The Wind* (1928). In both, he had the services of Lillian Gish and Lars Hanson, and to these pictures he brought some of the lyricism that had distinguished his work in Sweden. After two more films, Seastrom returned to his native land to make talkies. Some thirty years later he won world-wide acclaim for his acting in Ingmar Bergman's *Wild Strawberries* (1957).

Lubitsch's Outstanding Success

The only foreign-trained director who made a definite success with silent films in Hollywood was Lubitsch. His mastery of actors, as well as camera, continued, and his skill with comedy expanded in the era of sound. He adapted himself amazingly well to the problems of American production. His training as an actor under Reinhardt, added to his instinct for filmic effects, enabled him to draw fresh and sometimes remarkable performances out of silent screen actors like Florence Vidor, Monte Blue, Marie Prevost, Adolphe Menjou, and Rod La Rocque, as well as Maurice Chevalier, Herbert Marshall, Greta Garbo, Miriam Hopkins, Claudette Colbert, and Gary Cooper in the time of the talkies. In his first American picture, *Rosita,* Lubitsch carried Mary Pickford through her first maturely emotional scenes. (Miss Pickford later commented, "*Rosita* was the worst picture, bar none, that I ever made.") After *Rosita,* Lubitsch very wisely turned to comedy with *The Marriage Circle* (1924). He made only one spectacular production, *The Patriot* (1928), the tragedy of Czar Paul and Count Pahlen, brilliantly played by Emil Jannings and Lewis Stone. Lubitsch carried over into sound, and developed through dialogue, an ability to achieve witty subtleties that pleased both the critical and the mass audience. The range of Lubitsch's work from 1915 to 1946 included almost every form of screen expression—farce and high comedy, spectacle and drama, satire and fantasy.

Chapter
16

Russia's
Film Revolution

IN 1925, THE SILENT FILM of Germany reached its climax with *Variety*. That same year Eisenstein began to break new ground in *Potemkin*, and in 1926 Pudovkin followed him with *Mother*. In story content and in production methods, there was even a greater difference between German and Russian film-making than there had been between American and German. Contrasted with the expressionist bizarreness and the morbid realism of the Germans, the Russians produced what looked like hopeful reality. Forswearing the studio skills of German directors, their finely conceived settings and lighting effects, and their highly trained actors, Soviet film-makers went out of doors or into real buildings, and drew their casts, as far as they could, not from actors but from the Russian people. In place of the moving camera, they developed a new kind of editing.

Films of Vigorous Propaganda

All this came about because the Communist party decided to use the screen as a means of propaganda, a way of making the common people believe that the October Revolution of Lenin and Trotsky had brought them an enduring and heroic way of life. In 1918, Lenin recognized the power of the screen. He said: "For us, the most important of all the arts is cinema," and, "the cinema must and shall become the foremost cultural weapon of the proletariat." (In our own time, Nikita Khrushchev has said, "There is nothing to compare with the cinema in its power of

231

Rare Agreement

There exists today no means of influencing the masses
more potent than the cinema.
—Pope Pius XI.

The cinema must and shall become
the foremost cultural weapon of the proletariat.
—Nikolai Lenin

---

impact on human minds and hearts and in the breadth of audience it reaches among the people.") Lenin had to wait almost ten years before Russian directors told with full effectiveness the story of the October Revolution. Meantime, he placed all film production under the Commissariat of Education, and he used an American film for more general propaganda.

The film was *Intolerance*. Some prints of Griffith's picture, found in Berlin and expropriated, were re-edited, duped, and distributed through Russian theaters for perhaps ten years. As Seymour Stern has pointed out in *An Index to the Creative Work of David Wark Griffith*, the Babylonian story became a warning against priest-rule, and the medieval a tragic picture of the collaboration of church and state. With new subtitles, the modern plot showed American capitalism oppressing the workers. The part of the film that dealt with Christ was sometimes omitted, and sometimes edited to show that the "bandit nations of the West" ignored His teachings.

Lenin's statements and the manhandling of *Intolerance* highlight the obvious fact that all Soviet film productions until Stalin's death were propagandistic—except the purely educational pictures made for school use. They preached the Revolution and distorted history. For example, because Trotsky was demoted after Lenin's death in 1924, and was on his way to expulsion from the Communist party, he doesn't appear in Pudovkin's film on the October Revolution, *The End of St. Petersburg* (1927), and his part is obscured in Eisenstein's *Ten Days That Shook the World* (1928). In the earlier historical films, the Czars and their generals were all villains; after the purges of the late thirties, some of them became nationalist heroes—even Ivan the Terrible in Eisenstein's last picture. Yet, despite the overriding emphasis on propaganda, the Russian films were, in the main, far more exciting entertainment—even for noncommunists—than any propaganda films made in the West. This was because the directors and writers had a flaming belief in their revolution, and an eager desire to develop new ways of conveying their belief.

From Newsreels to Documentaries

Recognizing that the old regime had left the Soviets no powerful directors, Lenin said: "The production of new films, permeated with communist ideas, reflecting Soviet actuality, must begin with newsreels." So the first film-makers concentrated on such pictures. Dziga Vertov headed a group of cameramen, called collectively the Kino-Eye, whose ideal was to record all Russia on film, and let an editor-director make productions out of the material. This led to documentaries, beginning with Vertov's thirteen-reel *Anniversary of the October Revolution* (1918). It also led to manifestoes against the fiction film.

When there was more than enough available raw stock to take care of the newsreels and Kino-Eye's documentaries, groups began to experiment with comedy. FEX, or the Factory of the Eccentric Actor, brought from its theater into the movies some of the expressionist methods that had grown up in playhouses like Taïrov's Kamerny Theater during the Czarist regime.

Movie Schools Study American Films

Lev Kuleshov, the first theorist of Russian editing, organized a kind of workshop-school. Its first production, *On the Red Front* (1920), mixed re-enacted scenes with newsreels. Kuleshov turned to comedy with *The Extraordinary Adventures of Mr. West in the Land of the Bolsheviks* (1924). He struck a firm dramatic note a couple of years later in *By the Law* (1926), from Jack London's grim story *The Unexpected*. Aside from his theories, Kuleshov contributed most notably to Russia's film progress when he turned Pudovkin from chemistry to motion pictures by showing him *Intolerance*.

It was America, not Germany, that inspired and schooled the first Russians who made notable fiction films. They learned from Griffith, and later, from others, the mastery of film editing. Leonid Trauberg, speaking for himself and his coworkers, was to write to Griffith that "under the influence of your pictures such as *Broken Blossoms, Dream Street, Way Down East, Orphans of the Storm* and others, our style has been created." Other American films came into Russia after the end of the civil war. Henry King's *Tol'able David* (1921) made a great impression about three years after its American release. In one of the film schools, Eisenstein's students ran a print—too old for exhibition—until it literally wore out, while they measured and analyzed every scene and every cut.

Cutting Instead of a Moving Camera

Russia's film-makers were far less interested in the moving camera of the Germans than in American film-editing. They never wholly abjured movement, for Eisenstein trucked his camera the length of the great steps in his most important scene in *Potemkin,* and in this same scene he had one of the crewmen running, leaping, and falling with a camera strapped to his waist. But, by and large, the Russians disapproved of movement because it reminded the audience of the camera. The British critic and film maker Raymond Spottiswoode says that in the two and a half hours of Eisenstein's *Ten Days That Shook the World* "there were hardly a dozen moving shots." The Russians not only preferred a static camera, but also straight cuts from shot to shot. Up to 1935, when Spottiswoode wrote *A Grammar of the Film,* he could find only three dissolves and no wipes in the whole of Eisenstein's silent work. As a matter of fact, dissolves were not too plentiful in American films of the nineteen-twenties, for they had to be made in the camera and could not be added during editing.

Editing and "Montage"

The reason for the use of straight cuts in Russia lay in the editing theories of Kuleshov, Pudovkin, and Eisenstein. These theories began with the familiar and the obvious. "The foundation of film art is editing," said Pudovkin. Porter may have had a glimmering of this idea; Hepworth understood it, and Griffith practiced it early and brilliantly. The Russians, however, pushed the art of editing past the point of assembling and integrating a series of progressive shots that told a straightforward screen story. At first they called it the "American cut." Later they gave their method of editing the name "montage."

Here I must clear up some possible misunderstanding. American film makers spoke and still speak of "editing" or "cutting"; they are commonly the same thing, though some like to feel that editing is creative and cutting mechanical. The French call editing "montage," which in this case means "putting together." The Russians took over the French expression, and used it to cover their own special contribution to editing. Unfortunately, Hollywood adopted the term in the early thirties and applied it—quite differently from the Russians—to short sequences made up of symbolic dissolves that set a mood at the beginning of a picture or, more often, bridged a gap of time and a development of events. Slavko Vorkapich, specializing in this work, provided such montages as that in *The Conquerors* (U.S. 1932) which symbolized the boom and bust of the late twenties; in this case he dissolves over one another such shots as smoking chimneys, cattle on the way to market, the busy stock exchange, happy faces, stacks of coins piling higher and higher and then toppling down through shots of stricken faces and smokeless chimneys. Russian montage, as you will see, was quite different and it was more powerful.

Film Tricks with Time, Space, and Emotion

We are always in danger of giving the Russians too much credit for their montage. Basically, they developed a great deal of it, perhaps the better part, from American practice. Indeed, Seymour Stern has cited example after example of how Russian directors used effects of camera-work and cutting that had appeared in earlier films by Griffith. The Russians, however, carried analysis and theory much farther than anyone else had done and developed some new ways of gaining power from cutting.

The pioneer Kuleshov and his pupil Pudovkin saw two inherent values in any film shot. One lay in what a shot expressed by itself; the other in what it came to mean when joined to another. The second and far more important value was known to Griffith, though I do not believe he ever wrote about it.

The first and simplest effect of cutting can be to play with the relations of time and space, something that the West had known and practiced for many years. Kuleshov demonstrated this to his students by splicing together seven shots taken at separate places and at different times—a man walking from right to left, a woman walking from left to right, the two meeting, shaking hands and looking at something, a view of a big building with steps (actually the White House in Washington), a shot of the couple leaving their original meeting place, and then the two ascending a similar flight of steps. Before Kuleshov explained the editing trick, his students believed that they were looking at a scene taken in one locale.

A much more important effect of adding one shot to another can be emotional. The Russians studied this principle more consciously than any other film workers, and developed it more elaborately. Along with Pudovkin, Kuleshov showed by means of short bits of film just how the emotional content of one shot may be affected by another. In one experiment they used a close-up of a man whose face, as Pudovkin has written, "did not express any feeling at all," then added a shot of a bowl of soup on a table. In another, they took out the shot of the bowl and replaced it with a dead woman in a casket. For a third experiment, they substituted a child playing with a funny toy bear. Pudovkin wrote:

> When we showed the three combinations to an audience which had not been let into the secret, the result was terrific. The public raved about the acting of the artist. They pointed out the heavy pensiveness of his mood over the forgotten soup, were touched and moved by the deep sorrow with which he looked on the dead woman, and admired the light, happy smile with which he surveyed the girl at play. But we knew that in all three cases the face was exactly the same.

Pudovkin's Montage

The montage of the Russians went farther, in a certain direction, than the cutting of the Americans. The Russians put great emphasis on the use of contrasting yet related shots. Though Pudovkin usually built a scene out of fairly intimate angles, he liked to interject quick cuts of contrasting people or objects in order to dramatize, through a kind of symbolism, an emotion felt by one of his characters.

The intercutting of diverse scenes goes far back in screen history. Even Porter used it occasionally, and the modern story in *Intolerance* intercut the miseries of the poor with a banquet of the rich. Pudovkin did this at times in *The End of St. Petersburg*.

Pudovkin's use of symbolic shots, cut into the midst of an emotional scene—such cutting is one aspect of montage—is clearly illustrated in his distinguished film *Mother* (1926), inspired by Gorky's novel. These shots are carefully prepared for. A mother visits her rebel son in prison, slips him a note, and leaves. Then a title tells us, "And outside it is spring," and we see shots of a river and a stream, some geese, a happy boy, a baby on the ground, a mother picking him up, and the prisoner's mother walking home across the fields. The total effect is happiness in spring. Then we are in the cell again, where the prisoner reads the note, which tells him of a plan for his escape. I am indebted to Ernest Lindgren and his admirable book *The Art of the Film* for a detailed description of how Pudovkin then injects other very brief cuts of the joys of freedom as expressed in such scenes of spring as he has already forecast:

> The shots which follow are a large close-up of his eyes, very short (8 frames); a medium shot of him sitting on the

edge of the cell bed; a close-up of gushing and foaming water; a close-up of his hand tightly gripping the edge of the bed; a medium close-up of his body on which the shadows of the prison bars form a pattern; swirling water of a stream in flood (39 frames); another (14 frames); four brief close-ups of a child laughing (4 frames, 6 frames, 20 frames, and 8 frames); two shots of swirling water (14 frames and 13 frames); a baby laughing (27 frames); a splash subsiding into turbid water (32 frames); a close-up of the son's eyes (11 frames); turbid water (14 frames); the son sitting on the edge of the bed (16 frames); a close shot from the rear, of the son jumping up (13 frames); a large close-up from above, of a mug on a table, and a hand coming forward to clutch it (9 frames); a close shot of the son hurling the mug on to the floor (21 frames); a close shot of the mug bouncing on the floor; a second shot of the mug bouncing; it rolls to rest. The son then bangs on his cell door in sheer exhilaration, until the guard looks in through the observation port and orders him to be quiet.

Eisenstein's Potemkin

In Eisenstein's first film, *Strike* (1925), he used rather obviously a contrasting and symbolic scene: he cut from the shooting down of workmen to the slaughter of an ox. In his next and most notable picture, *Potemkin*, he used no such editing as Pudovkin's and no shots of the kind that Lindgren has listed in *Mother*. Eisenstein told a straightforward story of a naval mutiny of 1905, but he introduced a typically Russian device of rhythmic cutting. In some sequences the shots were long and the tempo slow and ominous. In others the cuts were unbelievably fast. Sometimes they increased in speed within a sequence. He used some visual tricks; one was to show shots of three different statues of a lion—the first crouched, the second rising, the third erect and roaring—in order to give the effect of a single animal in movement.

The greatest distinction of *Potemkin*, aside from Eduard Tisse's striking photography, lay in the enormous array of well-chosen shots superbly edited into the scene on the high, broad steps of Odessa. From the opening shots·of the mass of citizens—many of them brilliantly differentiated —who were assembled there to cheer the victory of the mutinous sailors, to the slow, relentless march of the Cossack soldiers down the steps, killing and sweeping away the mob, the scene became under Eisenstein's shooting and editing what Roger Manvell in his book *Film* has called "one of the most influential few minutes in cinema history." It showed film-makers everywhere a way of dynamic cutting more exciting than anything that even Griffith had done. It is interesting that whereas scenes in many other films last for a shorter time on the screen than they would in reality, the action of these few minutes on the steps would, as Manvell points out, have actually been over in a far shorter time if Eisenstein's camera had merely recorded a long shot of the happy crowd and the descent upon them of the soldiers.

Eisenstein's Theories and Methods

In Eisenstein's next film, *Ten Days That Shook the World,* he was miles away from the imaginatively rapid realism of *Potemkin.* Among his early scenes was the destruction of the statue of the czar; when in the film the Kerensky government assumed power, Eisenstein ran the film of the statue backward to visualize his thesis that czarism had come to life again. In the film's vicious satire on Kerensky, the director launched into a new way of shooting and editing. While Kerensky walked up the steps of the Winter Palace, Eisenstein cut in shots to ridicule what he considered the vanity and incompetence of the man. Statues seemed about to place garlands on his brow. While he waited at a door, a toy peacock wagged its head, spread its tail, and seemed to dance. Kerensky was then depicted with his head bowed and one hand in his jacket, and the director cut to a statue of Napoleon in the same attitude. All through the film Eisenstein was attempting to impress on the spectator not just the story of the "ten days," but their ideological background. "While the conventional film directs *emotions,*" he wrote, his method of montage "suggests an opportunity to encourage and direct the whole *thought process* as well." When a tank seemed to climb up Kerensky's desk and crush a plaster-of-Paris Napoleon, Eisenstein felt that he was liberating "the whole action from the definition of time and space."

Of course Eisenstein went beyond derision and eccentricities in *Ten Days That Shook the World.* He dramatized with the power of fast cuts and slowly mounting scenes the gathering force of the Revolution, and its final triumph. In his glorification of the tractor and of the collective farm in his often humorously lyrical film *Old and New* (1929), also called *The General Line,* he used all his skill as a director-editor, as well as his political ideology.

Eisenstein As Doctrinaire

Eisenstein's theories were often as doctrinal and absurd as his montage was sometimes hard to follow and understand. A former engineer, architect, and stage director, he is reported to have said, "I approach the making of a motion picture in much the same way that I would approach the installation of a water system," and he also said that film-making is "primarily a mathematical problem that could and should be solved by mathematical methods." He saw Karl Marx's dialectical materialism as the method for proper film-making. To him, as he put it, "montage is socialistic."

Eisenstein pursued his free film ideology until it led him to the extreme of comparing filmic expression to the ideographs of the Chinese: ". . . the picture for water and the picture of an eye signifies 'to weep'; . . . a dog + a mouth = 'to bark'; a mouth + a child = 'to scream.' " After such theorizing, and after the accomplishment of *Potemkin*, it is odd to hear that Eisenstein once called himself "a bourgeois at heart." We must remember, however, that Eisenstein was a complex character capable of many and divergent enthusiasms. Marie Seton, his English biographer, calls this student of all the arts and sciences a romantic and gentle cynic.

His cynicism may well have been fed by his adventures in Hollywood and Mexico. In 1930 he wrote two scripts for Paramount, one based on Dreiser's *An American Tragedy*, the other on the story of Sutter, who was ruined by the discovery of gold on his California estate in 1848. Both subjects were ultimately filmed by others and from other scripts. Late in 1930, financed by the Upton Sinclairs, Eisenstein went to Mexico to make a picture that was to be called *Que Viva Mexico!* and was to cover Mexican history from the time of the Aztecs and the even earlier Mayas of Yucatan, to the present. Through fourteen months, he and Tiss shot some 150,000 feet of film. (One authority says as much as 234,000 feet was shot.) Then the Sinclairs found it impossible to continue the project. Parts of Eisenstein's brilliantly photographed footage were ultimately edited, through Sol Lesser, into *Thunder Over Mexico* (1933) and by Miss Seton and Paul Burnford into *Time in the Sun* (1939). Numerous short subjects also used the Mexican footage.

Pudovkin vs. *Eisenstein*

Though Pudovkin and Eisenstein both served the purposes of Soviet ideology, they were highly different in a number of ways. Pudovkin created through emotion, Eisenstein through the mind. The first was lyric, the other epic. Pudovkin's hero was an individual, Eisenstein's was the masses. Pudovkin showed more interest in a story than Eisenstein did. Though Eisenstein had worked in the theater for a time, it was Pudovkin who became more concerned in developing individual acting, and who used many professional players. It is curious that though Eisenstein depended so much on reason, it was Pudovkin who made educational films, such as *Mechanics of the Brain* (1926), which dealt with Pavlov's experiments in conditioned reflexes.

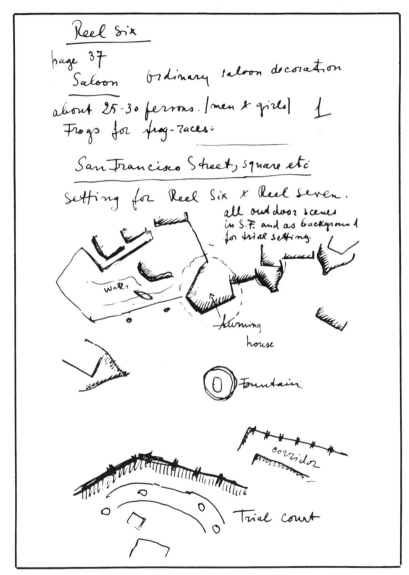

AN EISENSTEIN SKETCH. For *Sutter's Gold*, which the Russian director planned to make for Paramount, he indicated on this page the need for "Frogs for frog-races," as well as a saloon and men and girls. (*From Marie Seton's* Sergei M. Eisenstein.)

Other Russian Directors

There were other Russian directors, of course, many of them. They learned from Pudovkin and Eisenstein, as these men had learned from American films and from the ideas of Kuleshov. Though they all accepted the same sociological and political base, there was variety in their approaches and technique. Abram Room in his first notable film, *Bed and Sofa* (1927), blended comedy with a sympathetic treatment of the woman's problem during a shortage of housing, all on an intimate, emotional level. Directing for a film studio in the Ukraine, Alexander Dovzhenko fused many poetic images, as well as powerful realism, into a political film, *Arsenal* (1929); he used horses that spoke via subtitles, and he directed questions at the audience. His *Earth* (1930) had lyric qualities. In *Fragment of an Empire* (1929), Friedrich Ermler got comedy as well as propaganda from a man who loses his memory during World War I, and recovers it ten years later to find himself living under the revolution.

"Away from Realism to Reality"

In the silent days, an American director could pick a girl off Hollywood Boulevard, make her give an effective performance, and even build her into a star. As long as her voice wasn't heard, she could succeed through pantomime and directorial tricks. For some ten years after the Revolution, Russian directors used almost no trained actors and no studio scenery. Until the coming of sound, Eisenstein and most Russian directors employed real soldiers, real workmen, even real czarist generals. "Away from realism to reality," said the director of *Potemkin*. Instead of working in a studio with professional actors, he preferred to go "to the original place and person." As late as 1930, and in Hollywood where sound ruled, Eisenstein was saying, "I think that the art of acting is a thing that ought to be left on the stage," and he was searching filling stations for a man to play the boy in *An American Tragedy*. Pudovkin, on the other hand, came slowly to depend more and more on professional players for important roles.

Sound Kills Montage

Sound was bound to put an end to the use of the "original person." And it was just as certain to destroy the Russian method of montage. Yet, in 1928, Eisenstein, his assistant G. V. Alexandrov, and Pudovkin signed a statement accepting sound as a boon to "an imperfect film method, working only with visual images." They weren't giving up montage, however, and they weren't accepting synchronized dialogue. They didn't like *"talking films,"* which meant sound "on a naturalistic level." They said that such use of sound would "hinder the development and perfection of the cinema as an art," and threaten "to destroy all its present formal achievements." These men, who stood to the left in Russia's film industry, wanted to use sound, first, in order to escape what they called the "impasse" of the subtitle and the "insert" (the close-up of a letter or other explanatory object), but mainly as another tool of montage. Sound, whether noise, dialogue, or music, must be used only as a counterpoint to visual images.

Contrapuntal sound was all very well in theory, but it failed in practical application. Pushed to the full, it became puzzling on the screen. But when the sound came from a source that the audience was familiar with, it was effective because it was really naturalistic. In Nikolai Ekk's *The Road to Life* (1931)—a straightforward story of the regeneration of the "wild boys" who roamed the country—when the young hero died, the escaping steam from the engine of the railroad train on which his body had been borne to the scene was like a great sigh matching the mood of the crowd that mourned his heroic death.

Other directors—lesser men than Eisenstein and Pudovkin—used sound as everyone is doing today. Dialogue made propaganda more effective, for it could present social theories more directly and fully. No longer need a film like *Ten Days That Shook the World* be loaded down with three hundred subtitles to express ideas that Russian montage couldn't convey. Also, the public liked realistic talkies. They thronged to *Chapayev* (1934), directed by the Vasiliev brothers; Yefim Dzigan's *We from Kronstadt* (1936); and the flood of dialogue films that followed.

The End of Eisenstein and Pudovkin

In the statement on contrapuntal sound that Eisenstein, Pudovkin, and Alexandrov had signed, they had expressed the fear that montage without sound would end in "meaninglessness and reactionary decadence." Communist party officials, however, condemned the use of contrapuntal sound, and condemned its users for pursuing "barren intellectualism." Due to government condemnation, Eisenstein and Pudovkin became, for a time, merely "artistic supervisors" and teachers. Later they were allowed to direct films again. Pudovkin turned to synchronized dialogue with films like *Suvorov* (1941), glorifying Russian history. Eisenstein did the same with *Alexander Nevsky* (1938) and two parts of *Ivan the Terrible* (1944 and 1946); when he died in 1948 he was trying to finish the third part of his exaltation of that Czar. *Alexander Nevsky* was full of beautiful and exciting shots, particularly in the battle of the mounted knights on the ice; *Ivan the Terrible* seemed handsome but slow and operatic, with bits of dialogue replacing subtitles.

It had taken ten years for the Russian directors to learn how to tell the story of the revolution and perfect their technique of montage. They had only a few more years in which to practice the new and exciting art of montage before sound killed it forever.

Montage vs. *Human Emotion*

It may be argued that even if sound hadn't made Russian montage unusable, the technique could not have had too long a life. In 1933, Dalton Trumbo wrote:

> The Russians, for all their power, are intolerably camera-conscious. Elaborate montage and sublimated symbolism impede their pictures. . . . In America one is irritably aware of watching a star; in Russia it is the cinematographer [he might better have said the director-editor] who hogs the show. It seems plausible to believe that Russian pictures succeed among Russians chiefly because they lack serious competition.

Russia's directors could have discarded the more extreme elements of their montage without injury to their work. After all, the Russian cinema, for all its political emphasis, could be simple, straightforward, and highly successful in its depiction of human values. No one who saw *The End of St. Petersburg* can forget the homely old figure of the workman's wife carrying a lunch pail through the marble corridors of the Winter Palace of the Czar to the spot where her husband was on guard with his rifle.

Chapter

17

Hollywood's Gilded Decade

W ITH EUROPE AT WAR, America had been free to shape the course of the motion picture. From 1914 through 1919 our film companies developed practices and policies that were to dominate the making and showing of movies until the advent of sound. By the time America entered World War I, the pattern was well set. Through the next ten years it grew in scope and pervasiveness.

The Pattern of a Decade

From 1917 to 1927, the star system continued more or less dominant. Salaries went up and up. Longer and more spectacular films also increased the costs of production. First the exhibitors and then the film companies built new and larger theaters, and admission prices increased. To ensure bigger profits, the major producers expanded their distributing systems, and built up chains of theaters. Economically, Hollywood mirrored the expansive pattern of the nineteen-twenties. In its films, Hollywood reflected and exaggerated the frenzied tempo and the frenetic temper of that booming decade.

In the techniques of film-making there were changes and improvements, of course. Some came from abroad, and came rather late. Just as Europe, before the war, had led America to the feature film, so did Europe, when peace came, show America new ways of using the camera and editing film.

Before we consider such matters, as well as the kind of pictures that

America, Great Britain, and France were making in the decade before sound, we must pay some attention to the economics of film-making and distribution. They affected and will always affect the kind and quality of the pictures. The post-war spirit of the roaring twenties gave a special coloration to the Hollywood output, but this was not so important as the ways in which Hollywood and the theaters had learned to operate. For these ways still continue, and they affect the screen even today.

Hollywood's Unique Inflation

In the matter of salaries, Hollywood has always been as extravagant as its musicals and its epic spectacles, and as eccentrically amusing as some of its screwball comedies. It seems to have been working on an economic theory that might be called the Law of Undiminishing Returns. If a film is unusually successful, the studios are ready to believe that everyone who had much to do with it should be bound with chains of gold. This applies all down the line from stars to supporting players, directors, writers, cameramen, and, of course, producers. The result is a towering inflation unmatched in America's expanding industries. It began even before the first post-war boom. It slackened only a little in the depression. It surged upward with World War II, and it continues in spite of television's attack on the movie box office, or, as we will see later, because of this.

Though almost everyone in the studios has profited in some degree from mounting salaries, the stars have given us the most amazing and sometimes the most amusing demonstrations of this unique inflation. When the industry agreed to pay Mary Pickford and Charlie Chaplin at least two-thirds of a million dollars each in 1916, they seemed to be special cases. Perhaps they were, as performers. But as box office assets, they were merely portents of things to come. There were to be more and more stars who would be paid huge salaries because they could draw huge audiences. Like Chaplin and Pickford, some were to be given a share of the profits of their pictures. And, like these two, later on they might be set up in business with corporations of their own.

High Salaries for All—Profit Sharing for Some

In 1926, Gloria Swanson—then as popular and potent as Mary Pickford had ever been—was so eager to be her own producer that she turned down a fantastic offer from Paramount to renew her expiring contract. She had been getting $6,500 a week, a tidy sum when the income tax was only ten years old. The studio offered her $15,000—as much in salary

The Golden Stars

In *Comedy Films,* John Montgomery lists the estimated weekly earnings, in British pounds, of the most popular stars of 1926. Here these
are converted to American currency at the 1926 ratio of £1 to $4.85.
Because Tom Mix's contract called for a weekly wage of only $10,000
(some say $17,000!), one is tempted to cut all these figures in half.
But perhaps "earnings" included a share of film profits.

Harold Lloyd	$40,255
Charlie Chaplin	$30,555
Douglas Fairbanks, Sr.	$24,250
Gloria Swanson	$19,400
Mary Pickford	$19,400
Norma Talmadge	$19,400
Tom Mix	$19,400
Thomas Meighan	$12,125
Marion Davies	$10,185
Lillian Gish	$ 9,215
Colleen Moore	$ 8,245

alone as the pay and the bonuses given Chaplin and Pickford in 1916.
Finding Swanson still intent on being her own producer, Paramount
raised the offer to $900,000 for three pictures a year. And with it was
to go 50 percent of the profits of her films. I dwell at some length on these
sordid details because they are symptomatic of Hollywood inflation and
because Swanson's decision and its consequences reflect what happened
to some other overambitious stars, though not to all who set up as producers. Her decision may have been due in part to vanity, fed by a
triumphal visit to Europe and marriage to a marquis. But she certainly
knew that, as Lewis Jacobs states in his book *The Rise of the American
Film,* William S. Hart had made $2,225,000 from nine films in two years.
Swanson's aspirations were shattered, for the moment, when her first
production, *Queen Kelly,* written and directed by Erich von Stroheim,
was too poor to be released. Nobody knows just what astronomical incomes stars like Fairbanks, Pickford, Chaplin, and Harold Lloyd made
from the profits of their own producing corporations, or how much stars
other than Swanson suffered from incompetent management of their
companies.

Directors like Henry King, Edwin Carewe, James Cruze, Hobart Henley, and Marshall Neilan, who became producers in the twenties, had
both failures and successes. I doubt that they made as much as Thomas

Meighan, Pola Negri, or Colleen Moore, who as wage slaves of the studios were content to work for upwards of $7,000 a week. Tom Mix was very, very happy in 1925 when, they say, he got a paycheck of $10,000 every Saturday for keeping Fox out of the red. Lesser stars received between $2,000 and $5,000 weekly, according to the late financier and sometime film producer Ben B. Hampton in *A History of the Movies*. Even writers found that if their names were on enough successful pictures, their agents had little trouble in getting them $1,500 to $2,500 a week when their contracts ran out.

Contracts Rewritten by Agents

Hollywood inflation had its comic aspects when a new star or a young featured player was suddenly able to excite the interest of millions of people who had hardly known of his existence. This brings us to a couple of curious Hollywood phenomena, the agent and the so-called "seven-year contract." The matter of the agent is simple enough. For the past few decades he has been busy raising his clients' salaries because he gets 10 percent of what they earn. The seven-year contract developed in the early thirties from a four-year arrangement. It is nothing more than a year-to-year deal with "options." The actor is bound for seven years, but the studio has the right to drop him at the end of any twelve-month period or to keep him on at a modest increase of salary agreed upon when he signed his contract. Now, if the public suddenly develops a great fondness for the pictures he appears in, and writes thousands of fan letters a week, it is only natural that he or his agent should begin to feel that the player deserves more money than he is getting and more than the next option calls for. Sometimes, but not always, the studio tears up the old contract and makes a new deal "to keep him happy"—which means avoiding the danger that the player might "take a walk" and wait for the studio to capitulate.

A Pig and Three Players

There is a story of such a revolt where no options and no agents were involved. The owner of a trained pig working in a feature film discovered that the animal was the life of the party. One day in the middle of the picture, the porcine player failed to show up for work. The owner reported that his sensitive pet was "unhappy," and the studio raised his pay rather than close down the picture until it could find an intelligent pig of the very same size.

More typical, perhaps, was the case of Greta Garbo in 1925, as reported by Bosley Crowther in his book *The Lion's Share*. Through two years of triumphs, she had moved, option-wise, from $400 to $500 a week. Some say she demanded $5,000, some say her agent did, and some say that the figure was a bit smaller. At any rate, MGM came back in fighting mood. Garbo sat it out for seven months. The studio gave in only when it discovered that she had been a minor when she signed her contract, and therefore the other companies were free—and undoubtedly eager—to pay the salary she wanted.

Let us now consider a case where there was no agent, no contract, and no spectacular raise. Early in 1921, Metro Pictures Corporation released a film, which, if released a year earlier, might have saved the indigent company from being swallowed up by Loew's, Inc. This was *The Four Horsemen of the Apocalypse*. It spread an uncommon luster over an actor who had worked in minor parts or minor films for some two or three years—Rudolph Valentino. Perhaps agents were not so common in the early twenties as they were when Garbo rebelled, for what happened to this actor suggests that he had no "ten percenter" to protect him. When he and the picture were obviously headed for enormous success, Valentino made the modest suggestion that his salary be raised from $350 to $450 a week. Though Metro had no contract for his further services, it proposed to split the difference, and Valentino—sans agent—walked into the office of Jesse Lasky at Paramount to become the star of *The Sheik* at $500 a week, and to enter on a brief career as the screen's greatest lover.

Another tale of acute optionitis comes from Hampton's book and concerns a foreign actress who was unhappy with a salary of $300 that rose to only $500 her second year. By that time she had learned the kind of money American stars received, and she proposed to go to another studio for better pay. Her employer threatened her with deportation if she broke her contract. So the actress went to work again, but she was too unhappy to understand what the director wanted her to do. The studio found that a larger paycheck improved her knowledge of English and speeded up production.

Unhappiness and Riches Among the Producers

Producers could be unhappy, too. The brilliant Irving Thalberg is an example. He had been getting along pleasantly enough as the studio manager of Universal at $450 a week when Louis B. Mayer, then an independent producer, hired him at $600 in 1923. Nothing disturbed him when he soon went to work for MGM at $50 more, for Mayer, whose company had been merged by Loew's with Goldwyn and Metro, promised Thalberg one-fifth of the 20 percent that the Mayer unit was to get from MGM's profits. Then Thalberg grew restive and, a year and a half before the contract expired—as Bosley Crowther recounts the story —the success of Thalberg, with the backing of Mayer, forced a revision of his pay. More revisions followed. In 1926 his employers guaranteed him an income of $400,000 a year, and later he got the right to buy shares in Loew's, Inc., below the market price. Before his tragic death at the age of thirty-seven, Loew's and MGM had agreed to finance an independent company for Thalberg. In twelve years, he had received an income of $5,000,000 from salary and bonuses, which together with options to buy stock produced an estate of between $8,000,000 and $10,000,000.

Over the long years, Mayer did even better. For a number of years the Treasury Department listed him as the highest paid executive in American industry, and one year his check from Loew's Inc.-cum-MGM came to $1,296,503. Other film executives prospered in the twenties. Marcus Loew was able to buy a $500,000 Long Island estate with a house of thirty-five rooms and a small golf course, and he commuted to New York in a sixty-foot yacht. Jesse Lasky, like DeMille and Goldwyn, had begun in 1913 with a salary of $250 a week, but before the crash of 1929 he was drawing $2,500 and 7½ percent of the profits of Paramount. In New York he had two 10-room apartments knocked into one, and in Santa Monica a beach house with a sun-deck gymnasium, and, to supplement the Pacific Ocean, two swimming pools. In 1927, *Variety* estimated Lasky's fortune at $20,000,000, but it was only the eighth largest in the entertainment world. And the depression all but wiped it out.

Inflation Trickles Down from High Places

As I have said, the success of a film increased the demand for its star, its director, its supporting actors, even its writers, and salaries went up. In a subtler way, the ego of the producer and the director fed inflation. The executive earning two or three thousand a week felt himself a bigger man if he hired an actor for five thousand. Directors were happiest with casts of supporting players who were paid twice what they could earn on Broadway. Elaborate settings and costly details pleased everyone but the treasurer of the studio, and he didn't dare urge economy on a director until the man had a failure as complete as it was costly. Not many directors were financially irresponsible, but the boom days of the nineteen-twenties tempted some into what Thorstein Veblen termed "conspicuous consumption." Of course, economics can force economies—even on Hollywood—if times are hard enough. The depression of the thirties and the "regression" of 1938 curbed temporarily the vagaries of many film makers. But the war-borne boom of the forties released not a few egos. I remember that a Paramount director had a silversmith make two dozen settings of specially designed knives, forks, and spoons for a seventeenth-century dinner scene; if the director took close-ups of the silverware, they never appeared on the screen.

Economy—for a Time

Hollywood suffered two blows as America came out of World War I. In the fall of 1918, the first great influenza epidemic closed a large num-

---

DeMille's Record

The first 27 motion pictures directed and created by this man [1913 to 1917] cost the grand total of $1,200,000. [In] the next 29 pictures, from 1917 to 1932, he invested $13,500,000. . . . Following that period of time—up until 1955—he made 14 pictures and he invested in that the sum of $24,500,000. In the year 1956 . . . he has invested $12,000,000.
    —Y. Frank Freeman, at the Screen Producers Guild dinner of 1956 honoring C. B. DeMille.

---

ber of theaters as well as schools. With the armistice in November, when the theaters were already embarrassed by the "war tax" on admissions, Hollywood found its financial troubles multiplied by a backlog of war pictures that the public refused to go see. For a time the industry seemed interested in economizing, but not for long. It paid all too little attention to a theory that DeMille put into successful practice.

It may seem odd that the first prescription for cutting costs should have come from a man who, within five years, was to be the high priest of Hollywood's cult of spectacular opulence. Moreover, the DeMille remedy came as a kind of prophetic vision, a premonition of things to come—and to pass. Before the influenza struck, he had convinced Lasky and Zukor that there was money in making pictures without expensive stars but with the emphasis on story and direction.

Mary Pickford's films were costing around $175,000, according to Hampton, and they were grossing from $350,000 to $380,000. Now, the so-called gross of a picture is not what the public pays the theater, but what the theater pays the distributor. Furthermore, the difference between the cost of a production and the money it gets from the theaters doesn't give us the net profit. First, distribution must be paid for, which at that time was figured, rather arbitrarily, at 35 percent of the gross. This may seem to be a mere matter of bookkeeping, since the distributor is usually an agency of the producing company, but competitive distribution is wasteful, and it affects costs unfairly. Thus, as you will see in the box below, a Pickford film grossing $380,000 might show no more than a $77,000 profit.

DeMille believed that if a film had story quality, good direction, and good acting—though no star—it could gross as much as a Pickford production. In 1918 he made *Old Wives for New* at a cost of only $66,000, and he remade *The Squaw Man* the same year for $40,000 (somewhat more than the cost of the 1914 production). When these unpretentious pictures grossed about as much as Pickford's, the day of the director dawned again. He had ruled production before the stars rose over the Hollywood horizon. He was to rule again—with or without stars—until sound came along. But he didn't follow the momentarily economical DeMille, and DeMille himself soon turned again to star-studded displays.

And so, after a brief experiment in economy, Hollywood slipped back into its more accustomed ways. By 1921, according to Hampton, modest program pictures were twice as expensive as they had been three years before. "Specials," which had run from $100,000 to $200,000, went as high as $350,000.

Grosses, Costs, and Profits—1918

The following rough figures are drawn from Benjamin B. Hampton's *A History of the Movies.*

A Mary Pickford film:

Gross income from theaters	$380,000
Distribution charge—35% of gross	133,000
Net income	$247,000
Production cost	170,000
Net profit	$ 77,000

Old Wives for New:

Gross income from theaters	$380,000
Distribution charge—35% of gross	133,000
Net income	$247,000
Production cost	66,000
Net profit	$181,000

Big Budgets—and Often Bigger Profits

Early in the nineteen-twenties, the big producing companies began to behave, in some ways, like normal corporations. The New York office told the studio how much it could spend on the year's films. The studio set up individual budgets for each picture, as well as detailed accounting methods for every item of expense. Nevertheless, production costs went steadily upward. Perhaps this was a reflection of the general boom of the first half of the nineteen-twenties. It also sprang from the fact that film-making is unquestionably a gamble, and sometimes high stakes bring high profits. In 1919 DeMille made *Don't Change Your Husband* for $75,000, and it grossed $300,000, but, a little later that year, he spent a hundred thousand more on *Male and Female,* and its gross was a million larger. Because the more elaborate films seemed to bring bigger grosses, the New York offices were inclined to increase budgets. When Hollywood pictures went beyond the figures set for them, as they often did, the results in profits and losses were sometimes most interesting.

In 1923 *The Covered Wagon* was budgeted at $500,000 and cost over a quarter of a million more, but it grossed almost $4,000,000, and after distributing costs had been paid, it brought Paramount a profit of at least $1,500,000. The same year, when DeMille was only half through his first version of *The Ten Commandments,* and was going over his budget of $1,000,000, Paramount's New York office became irascible; further friction led to the director's departure from the studio. Although according to DeMille, *The Ten Commandments* cost $1,475,836.93 it made enough money to justify his spending at least $2,500,000 on *The King of Kings* in 1927.

Ben-Hur (1925) was probably the most extraordinary example of an overshot budget. The Goldwyn company, under the dubious management of F. J. Godsol, acquired the rights to the book and the play and started to produce it in Italy early in 1924, on a budget of $750,000. By the time the Goldwyn company had become part of MGM, it had spent $2,000,000, on the building of a colosseum which was never used, the sea battle that actually appeared in the finished film and a few other scenes. Thalberg brought the troupe back to California, built a second arena for $300,000, and shot the chariot race with 3,300 extras and forty-two cameras. Ultimately *Ben-Hur* cost close to $4,000,000. The picture grossed $9,386,000, according to Bosley Crowther, but 35 percent of this went for distribution. Godsol's deal with the owners of the property cost $3,000,000 in royalties, and so MGM lost $1,000,000 on this enormously "successful" picture.

Another Thalberg production, *The Big Parade* (1925), is in heartening contrast to the story of *Ben-Hur*. Under the able direction of King Vidor, the "rough cut" of this $200,000 picture impressed Thalberg so much that he ordered more money spent on added war scenes. *The Big Parade* made John Gilbert an important star, its ninety-six week run on Broadway held the record for almost a quarter of a century, and it grossed $5,500,000. But such an example of successful frugality didn't stop Hollywood from spending a million and a half to two million dollars on such films as *Old Ironsides* (1926), *Wings* (1927), and *The Trail of '98* (1928). In terms of today, these were actually four- or five-million dollar productions.

Larger Theaters and More of Them

The bigger budgets and the bigger profits of the nineteen-twenties were possible only because of bigger theaters and more of them. Along with this development went higher admission prices—50 cents to $1.65 at the Capitol in New York, for instance. Also, the producing companies built up chains of theaters, and "protected" their product through somewhat dubious sales methods.

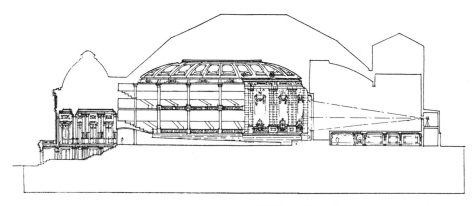

THE FIRST LARGE FILM THEATER. In 1908 a French company tried to convert the Hippodrome in Paris into a moving picture house by placing a translucent screen in the middle of the orchestra floor. The project failed, but after the theater had been devoted to skating for a time, it was opened toward the end of 1910 as the Gaumont-Palace, seating 5,000 people. As this cross section shows, the film was projected from the back of the stage. The theater boasted two projectors for the continuous showing of a picture two reels or more in length. (*From Jean Vivié's* Historique et développement de la technique cinématographique.)

THE "ATMOSPHERIC" THEATER. Most of the large movie houses built in the boom years of the twenties were designed and decorated in some exotic style. The Chinese Theater of Los Angeles, the Egyptian, and the Mayan were only a few examples. Many tried to turn their interiors into out-of-doors foreign climes. The ceiling became a sky with twinkling stars, while along the sides were the roofs and walls of some alien but attractive country. Here is a small example in a theater of Bakersfield, California, designed by S. Charles Lee. (*Courtesy George Schutz and Quigley Publishing Company, Inc.*)

New York's Strand of 1914 wasn't the first huge picture theater in the world. Three or four years earlier the Gaumont-Palace in Paris had begun showing films to twice as many people as the Strand was to hold, but the French theater had been made out of an old entertainment hall, the Hippodrome, while the Strand was the first important house built especially for showing motion pictures. The Strand's success, based on a flood of feature films, resulted in the building of a host of new theaters in America. First-run houses erected in downtown districts to hold 1,000 to 2,000 spectators were matched by neighborhood theaters quite as commodious. Between 1914 and 1922, says Hampton, some 4,000 new houses opened. So many nickelodeons closed down that the total number of theaters shrank from about 30,000 to 18,000. Yet the size of the new ones made it possible in 1922 for more people to see films at the same time than ever before. Still more theaters and ever larger ones appeared between 1922 and 1930. By the time the talkies took over, the boroughs of Manhattan, Brooklyn, and the Bronx had eighty-three theaters seating more than 2,000. Sixteen of these held over 3,000; Chicago, Philadelphia, Boston, Detroit, and Los Angeles added twenty-five more such giant houses.

In New York the tide of big theater-building reached its crest in 1927 after the opening of the 3,600-seater Paramount in the preceding year. The Roxy was to top them all, and top the Gaumont-Palace, too, with 6,200. Such great theaters—and hundreds half as large—were more than just giant auditoriums. In cleanliness, convenience, and sheer luxury they put to shame not only the nickelodeons, but the very best of Broadway theaters. Nothing like them existed outside the opera houses of the world's largest cities.

"Roxy" and the Roxy

Very large theaters were inevitable in America, but there was one man who set his stamp upon them as the home of a very special kind of atmosphere and entertainment. His name was originally Samuel L. Rothapfel. The "p" became a casualty of World War I while he was winning fame as America's outstanding exhibitor. By 1927, fifteen years of devotion to the cult of the picture palace had prepared "Roxy" to be the high priest of "the cathedral of the motion picture," as he called the theater that bore his nickname. Mitchell Mark had had the basic idea for a great theater like the Strand, with comfortable seats, restful anterooms, and no second balcony, but Roxy was responsible for the sumptuous entertainment provided by the Strand and the other houses he managed. It was Roxy who developed a symphony orchestra out of the musicians who accompanied the films. It was Roxy who created the "atmospheric prologue," or "presentation," that introduced the feature, a mélange of song and ballet, vaudeville headliner and spectacle, occupying up to an hour's time. From 1914 to 1927, while he managed the Strand, Triangle's Knickerbocker, the Rialto, the Rivoli, and the Capitol, Rothafel not only provided elaborate stage entertainment. He lavished courteous attentions upon his patrons, and surrounded them with an atmosphere of luxurious elegance.

As with the Strand, Rothafel wasn't responsible for the building of the Roxy Theater. Credit for financing this $12,000,000 picture palace must go to a self-effacing man named Herbert Lubin, no relation to Sigmund, the film maker of Philadelphia. But Roxy saw to it that the largest theater built since the fall of Rome had six box offices, room for 2,000 people to wait for the end of the picture while beguiled by an automatic organ, a hospital with two nurses, and, for Roxy himself, a huge radio studio from which he could broadcast and a private apartment that included a kitchen. An orchestra of 110 musicians came up from the pit on an elevator and enjoyed the services of three conductors and one composer, while five organists commanded three organs.

Backstage, 150 people danced, sang, ran lights, or shifted scenery. Another 150 were busy in the front of the house, at various times, four-fifths of them ushers. In resplendent uniforms, this corps of reputed ex-Marines —Roxy had served a hitch in that service—saluted patrons but were forbidden to salute each other. I wish I had a list of the rooms provided for the relaxation of spectators overcome by the excitement of the stage show. Instead I must quote from Lasky's account of the glories of the Paramount. There the public had its choice of "an Elizabethan Room lounge, a College Room, the Chinoiserie, the Venetian Room, Peacock Alley, the Club Room, the Hunting Room, the Music Room, the Colonial Room, or the Empire Room." It is not true that there was a Sigmundfreudzimmer for patrons suffering from nervous indecision over the choice of rooms.

One of the smaller satisfactions that Roxy must have enjoyed was the thought that he could seat at one time the whole population of Forest City, Pennsylvania, where, twenty years before, he had rented 200 chairs from an undertaker to start his first theater, the Family, with three reels for five cents—behind a saloon. He must have got even more satisfaction from seeing the Roxy take in an average of $100,000 a week, a record in those days, and from serving, however briefly, as consultant to the Rockefellers at the Radio City Music Hall.

The Roxy—Last Flagship House of a Theater Chain

Just before the opening of the Roxy, William Fox bought the theater and made it the New York showcase for his pictures, the "flagship" of his theater chain. This was a climax in the long story of how producers became exhibitors, and exhibitors became producers, and how chains of theaters threatened to breed monopoly.

Fox and Loew had begun as theater owners; Lasky and Zukor, after very early theater experiences, as producers. Fox and Loew went into production to protect their theaters. As Paramount, Zukor and Lasky bought theaters to protect their pictures. The development of chains of theaters was as inevitable as the building of large movie houses. The control of the first-run and the bigger neighborhood houses was essential to the success of producing companies. By 1919, there were also many independent chains of theaters in almost all parts of the country, crushing local competition and making deals with the producers. A few years after Griffith, Pickford, Chaplin, and Fairbanks formed United Artists, the corporation began to acquire houses.

The Government Steps In

In 1923, the Federal Trade Commission began to worry lest the competition for theaters was ending in collusion between the producers. Believing that the major producing companies had secret agreements that penalized independent theaters, large and small, first the Commission and later the Justice Department made investigations that finally forced the divorcement of producers from the ownership of theaters, following a court decision of 1948.

In the process another potent source of profits fell by the board. This was the system of "block-booking." It had begun when the first producers of fifty-two or more pictures a year made the exhibitor buy them all, sight unseen. This changed to selling blocks of five or more films. Stars like Gloria Swanson were worth many thousands a week because to get her pictures, as Lasky explains "exhibitors were compelled to give playing dates to blocks of weak features that we might otherwise have had trouble selling. The government finally broke up the practice of block-booking, but while it existed, Gloria was worth very much more to us than her own pictures brought in." And so we see how the economics of distribution added its mite—a mighty mite—to Hollywood inflation.

Chapter

18

The Twilight of the Silent Stars

IN ALL BUT VITAL achievement, Hollywood ruled the screen world in the ten years that followed the armistice of 1918. Hollywood produced more films than any of its rivals. It spent more money on its pictures and it made more money. The settings of its films were usually high and huge and almost always magnificent. The skills of the cameraman made them as glamorous as the radiant apparel of the stars. When Germany, Sweden, France, and Russia rose Phoenix-like from the ashes of war and developed new directors and new techniques, Hollywood tried to take over the men or use some of their methods.

Full of Silence and Fury, Signifying Nothing?

All this to what end? The content and the significance, the outward emotion and the inner meaning, of Hollywood films—what did they amount to at the climax of the silent era? The stories were mostly shallow or absurdly pretentious; if they came from novels or plays, they suffered a sea change into something that might be rich but was certainly strange. Whether in Westerns or in war films, in spectacular visions of luxury or in daring dalliance with sex, in tough melodramas about not-so-low life, or in excursions to the lands of Araby and Ruritania, the plots of most Hollywood films ran the gamut of emotion, as Dorothy Parker said of an actress, from A to B. And so, of course, did the emotions of their audience.

There were exceptions, I admit. Or perhaps I should say good enter-
tainments. I am thinking of some of the Westerns, certain spectacles from
DeMille and Fairbanks, and particularly the comedies of Chaplin *et al.*
I have to grant that Hollywood gave opportunity and some applause
to men who tried to match the realism of Germany, but the producers
and their audiences preferred to see von Stroheim and von Sternberg
devote their talents to synthetic glamor and cynical posturings. These
realists were not to interrupt the more popular cycles of Hollywood
films, or distract the studios from selecting stories with an eye to the
care and nurture of stars.

The Ten-Year Rhythm of the Silent Screen

1896–1905   From news, filmed or faked, and comic episodes to one-
reel melodramas. Store theaters appear.

1906–1915   From the Nickelodeon to the Strand. The triumph of the
feature film, led by Italy and climaxed by *The Birth of
a Nation.*

1916–1925   Hollywood dominating the world screen. More than 650
films in 1917, almost 850 the next year. Germany and
Russia awakening a bit late. Hundreds of huge theaters.

1926–   Will Hays speaking from the screen, followed by Bernard
Shaw and others. The voice of the talkie is heard in the
land.

New Cycles for Old

Cycles have been a habit with the screen since the days when *The Great
Train Robbery* begat *The Bold Bank Robbery* and many another felonious
film. Other industries are no more innocent of cyclical imitation. *News-
week* follows *Time.* The laconic titles of *Time* and *Life* are aped by
Look, See, Pic, Real, Sir, Male, Stag. Crisp names spread from magazines
to detergents, and we buy Dreft, Tide, Fab, Cheer, Dash, or Sheer,
and brush our teeth with Brisk, Crest, or Gleem. Automobiles sprout
tailfins one year and twin headlights the next. In Hollywood it is the
astute pioneers, of course, who start new cycles by a combination of
daring and intuition. Cecil B. DeMille was one of these. So was Irving
Thalberg, and later, Darryl Zanuck, David Selznick, Dore Schary, and
a few others.

As I have pointed out in the previous chapter, DeMille began in

1918 to make films cheaply, using only prospective stars. He was content to take Gloria Swanson out of a Sennett bathing suit, parade her in satin, and pass her on if some reckless producer wanted to give her ermines. Economy might appeal, for a time, to Lasky and Zukor, but in even the first of these cheaply made pictures there were hints of what was to make them not only highly attractive to post-war audiences, but also more expensive, with or without stars. DeMille began to exploit sex and luxury in tune with what was to be the "jazz age" of the booming nineteen-twenties. Others followed his lead—and quickly.

Sex—Exciting and Glamorized, but Quite "Moral"

DeMille's new type of film, from *Old Wives for New* (1918) to *The Golden Bed* (1925), reflected, distorted, and capitalized upon the changes in the sexual pattern of American life that came out of the war, and the avid pursuit of material ends that seemed likely to continue through untold years of peace and prosperity.

The change in our mores was real enough, but Hollywood jazzed it up. As DeMille said, "The ruined woman is as out of style as the Victorian who used to faint," but film makers sensationalized whatever "new freedom" women had won. Sexual temptations became accomplished facts. According to Hollywood, "affairs" were common practice among the smarter "debs," and infidelities spiced married life. "Orgies" seemed to be almost as common in our high society as in ancient Rome's, and perhaps as spectacular. Yet, and this was another distortion, eccentricities of sex always led to readjustments that even Victorianism could have accepted. The substance of the films was dalliance, but they always had a highly moral ending. The old fidelities, the sacredness of marriage, and the primacy of Home and Mother were exalted in the last reel. Sin made good entertainment, but—and also because—it led inevitably to a properly moral conclusion.

The Delights of Boudoir and Bath

DeMille added to his films of sexual diversions a further spice for the filmgoers of the nineteen-twenties. He introduced audiences to an atmosphere of modern luxury that was as new to them—even to the wealthy— as it was new to the screen. He showed shopgirls feminine wardrobes such as they had never seen before. He pleasured them with dressings and undressings, in and out of lavish bedrooms. "Underclothes," as his brother William C. De Mille observed, "became visions of translucent promise." C. B. called for bathtubs no plumber had ever before installed.

"He made of the bathroom," continued the other De Mille, "a delightful resort . . . a mystic shrine dedicated to Venus, or sometimes to Apollo, and the art of bathing was shown as a lovely ceremony rather than a merely sanitary duty." The purpose of all this was obvious to its creator: "Your poor person wants to see wealth, colorful, interesting, exotic." In 1919, exploiting Gloria Swanson as a glamor girl, he lavished luxury on *Don't Change Your Husband* and turned J. M. Barrie's ironic little comedy *The Admirable Crichton* into a combination of sex and spectacle called *Male and Female.* Around the same time, Erich von Stroheim wrote and directed the sexy and sophisticated *Blind Husbands* for Universal. In *The Marriage Circle* (1924) and *Forbidden Paradise* (1924), Lubitsch, in a wittier way, contributed to the delinquency of the screen. Other directors and other studios followed the primrose path that DeMille had blazed.

Latin Lovers and Easy Ladies

For some the path led to sexual never-never-lands, and to new and strange loves in Araby and the Balkans. After Valentino added *The Sheik* (1921) to *The Four Horsemen of the Apocalypse,* there came a scad of Latin Lovers. Mostly tall, always dark, and inevitably handsome, they promised passion instead of merely love. *L'amour royal* appeared in *The Prisoner of Zenda* (1922) and *Rupert of Hentzau* (1923) as Hollywood discovered that seat of high and sometimes rueful romance, Anthony Hope's mythical kingdom of the eighteen-nineties. Elinor Glyn with her *Three Weeks*—the *Forever Amber* of 1907—came to Hollywood in the early twenties to queen it in the passionate Balkans.

Since men as well as women succumbed to the temptations of the flesh in the films of the twenties, someone on the distaff side had to be tempting. Instead of deep-dyed vamps like Theda Bara, there were actresses— and characters, of course—who could range from the neglected wife to the seductive, and usually repentant, siren. Of such were Pola Negri, Mae Murray, Carmel Myers, Betty Blythe, Nita Naldi, Joan Crawford, and even Gloria Swanson. Myrna Loy had to wait for sound to make her a good woman as well as a delectable comedienne. Often, these actresses were called on to provide such corporeal displays as Miss Blythe's in *The Queen of Sheba* (1921) and Miss Myers' in *The Dancer of the Nile* (1923).

As that decade of delight, the nineteen-twenties, ran its course, Hollywood added to the dalliance of the married the dissipations of jazz-age youth. Here is a small sample of the many films—I won't trouble you with dates—whose titles reflected these two appeals: *Foolish Wives, For-*

bidden Fruit, Don't Tell Everything, Three Week-Ends, Prodigal Daughters, Daughters of Pleasure, Daughters of the Night, Daughters Who Pay, Flames of Desire, Flame of Passion, Flaming Youth. At long last, in 1927, a picture called *It*—the term for sex appeal invented by Miss Glyn—starred the "It Girl," Clara Bow, and marked the climax (if, unfortunately, not quite the end) of Hollywood's own jazz age.

If I seem to have dwelt overlong on the works of DeMille and the films that followed, it is because they did much to create state censorship in the early twenties, and impose the "production code" on the studios ten years later. Other factors, as you will see in a later chapter, brought Will Hays to Hollywood, in 1922, as czar of the screen at a salary first of $100,000, and later, of $150,000.

Hays induced the studios to add "morality clauses" to their contracts, established the Central Casting Agency to weed out most of the foolish young girls who flocked to Hollywood seeking work, and launched a publicity campaign to rehabilitate the industry and kill some of the censorship bills that had been proposed in over thirty states. Hays tried to persuade the producers to clean up their pictures, but their lack of complete cooperation may be judged by a publicity photo that Paramount sent out for its *Prodigal Daughters* (1923). Gloria Swanson posed beside a poster that listed: "THE SEVEN DEADLY WHIMS," "NEW LIPS TO KISS," "NO MORE CHAPERONS," "LIFE WITH A KICK IN IT," "OUR OWN LATCHKEYS." I'm sure that *Prodigal Daughters* had a highly moral ending, but until the last sequence of many a picture, youth continued to flame on our screens.

DeMille's Conversion

DeMille himself did a quick and very helpful about-face. He had brought Paramount more than $9,000,000 in profits from the eleven films that he had made in some four years, but in 1923 he reversed his field and turned to religious spectacle in *The Ten Commandments*. In the first of his Biblical films, however, DeMille included a modern story. It involved a luxurious bed and a Eurasian adventuress, but Cupid and cupidity brought Rod LaRoque to financial as well as moral ruin, and thus the works of Moses triumphed. Four years later, DeMille told with skill and taste the story of Christ in *The King of Kings*. His only deviation from the Bible was to make Mary Magdalene a bejeweled courtesan.

From Sweetness and Light to Horror and Westerns

All was not sex and high society in the Hollywood films of the nineteen-twenties. Mary Pickford went on her pure and popular way from *Pollyanna* (1920) and *Little Lord Fauntleroy* (1921) to *My Best Girl* (1927).

There was earnest sentiment as well as heart throbs—on different levels —in *Humoresque* (1920) and *The Little Shepherd of Kingdom Come* (1928). Charles Ray, made a star in 1915 through *The Coward,* played the boyish rustic for more than ten years. Backwoods virtue triumphed over vicious violence in *Tol'able David* (1921). Lifted into fine excitement by the able direction of Henry King, the film put the name of Richard Barthelmess on marquees. *The Miracle Man* (1919), well handled by George Loane Tucker, a talented director who died too soon, had also been starless until it hit the screen. Then its audiences discovered three new luminaries—Lon Chaney, Thomas Meighan, and Betty Compson. Chaney made a career out of horrific make-up, bizarre contortion, and excellent pantomime in films such as *The Hunchback of Notre Dame* (1923), *The Phantom of the Opera* (1925), and *Laugh, Clown, Laugh* (1928). Hollywood opened up the West as a field for historic spectacle with *The Covered Wagon* (1923), directed by James Cruze, and *The Iron Horse* (1924), an epic of the railroad pioneer that introduced John Ford as a potentially great film-maker.

War Films—Realistic, Humorous, and Aerial

A new cycle in the story of Hollywood's emulations began in 1925 with the discovery that the public was willing to go to see realistic war pictures. In *The Four Horsemen* of 1921 exotic romance had shared the screen with battles and propaganda of 1918 vintage, but now came pictures with more reality and more guts. Also, some had humor and some exploited that new field of conflict, the skies. King Vidor was chiefly responsible for starting the cycle, but a former officer of the Marines and two airplane pilots must be credited with guiding it into humor and dogfights. The Marine was Laurence Stallings, collaborator with Maxwell Anderson in the Broadway success *What Price Glory?* When Vidor persuaded Irving Thalberg to risk a war film, he went to work with the writer Harry Behn, and Stallings, on an original story that MGM had bought from the latter. The result was *The Big Parade* (1925). The next year, in Cruze's *Old Ironsides,* Stallings went back in martial history to the Navy's war with the Barbary pirates. *What Price Glory?* (1926) dwelt—as did its sequels, *Two Arabian Knights* (1927), and the talkie *The Cock-Eyed World* (1929)—on the lusty humors of Captain Flagg and Sergeant Quirt.

With *Wings* (1927) the war film took to the air, piloted by two aviators of World War I, writer John Monk Saunders and director William Wellman. Clara Bow, nominal star of the film, was overshadowed by

Sketches by
GARY COOPER

1870—Coast to Coast—20 Days.

GARY COOPER—ARTIST. Before the actor left his native Montana, he made drawings such as these for a newspaper.

three new actors whom it brought to public attention, Buddy Rogers, Richard Arlen, and Gary Cooper. The power of *Wings*, which won the first Academy Award for the best production of the year, lay not so much in Wellman's aerial dogfights as in the unique dramatic situation of two friends mistakenly battling each other in the skies. Of course a cycle of this new kind of war film was soon airborne.

Past Films of Pain and Pleasure

What makes almost all the films of the nineteen-twenties so hard to enjoy today? I think it is because in most of the pictures, the realism of the photography was thwarted by absurdly unreal stories and characters, which we were supposed to take seriously. The pleasure we still get from the best Westerns, such as *The Covered Wagon*, lies partly in the truth of wide lands and deep skies, and partly in our ability to believe in a pageantry of violent action that has passed away. Yet reality is no test, for with a few exceptions, the films that now seem the most entertaining were never completely or even partially real. We believe—and we believed then—in their unreality because it was so skillfully presented. I am not referring to the silly posturings of Nazimova's *Salome* (1922), which we were supposed to consider art, but rather to the comedies and the romances in which logical absurdities became delightful truths. One group of films that can still entertain us is the broad farces of Chaplin, *et al;* another, the costumed spectacles of Douglas Fairbanks.

The aging though still athletic Fairbanks (he was over thirty when he made his first picture) turned from pseudo-reality to period romance with *The Three Musketeers* (1921) and *Robin Hood* (1922), and then

FAIRBANKS GOES SPECTACULAR IN THE 1920's. Among his romantic films of this era was *Robin Hood,* directed by Allan Dwan. This setting, the interior of a castle, was built out of doors, shadowed by black curtaining, and lit largely by sunlight kicked into the set by reflectors. It was a triumph for cameraman Arthur Edeson and art director Wilfred Buckland.

provided other spectacular and amusing escapes from reality in *The Thief of Bagdad* (1924) and *The Black Pirate* (1926). Some of his films are much too long, but, while the star is on, they are more than good clean fun. They are beguiling. Part of the interest lies, of course, in the ingenuity of his physical gags—sliding down the crease of a forty-foot curtain in *Robin Hood* or somersaulting over a villain in *The Three Musketeers* while he puts a dagger in the man's chest. But, above and beyond such stunts, there was the comic verve of the man, the way he turned his physical vitality into a happy display of grace and power. He stood, he strode, he leapt with a style that mingled the skill of an athlete with something close to the art of a dancer. He triumphed over his opponents and his audience through a joyous perfection of body and spirit that the one couldn't match and the other longed for. Fairbanks had grown up from the Great American Boy into the paladin of high-spirited romance. *Sans peur et sans reproche,* he was a Roland with a sense of humor.

A Little Realism—for the Few

In the last decade of silent pictures, the audience seemed satisfied with the dream that it saw. There were only a few attempts to use the screen as a mirror of life. Some were praised by the critics, some by film-makers, but not one was notably successful at the box office.

William C. De Mille tried for realism via the adaptation of stage plays—Zona Gale's *Miss Lulu Bett* (1921), A. E. Thomas' *Only 38* (1923), and Owen Davis' *Icebound* (1924). He may have made others, but even these three are mentioned in only one history of the screen. Lasky fails to speak of them in his autobiography, commenting instead on the man's impeccable "breeding and background." The elder De Mille lacked C. B.'s flare for the sensational. In *The Rise of the American Film,* Lewis Jacobs dwells on William's early hostility—or blindness—to the possibilities of the screen, and quotes a 1911 letter from De Mille to Belasco in which he coined the phrase "galloping tintypes," and, having tried to save Mary Pickford from a fate worse than Thespian death, conceded regretfully: "So I suppose we'll have to say good-by to little Mary Pickford. She'll never be heard of again and I feel terribly sorry for her." Later, this De Mille tried to play a sincere part in the progress of the motion pictures, but except for his early appearance as the Cassandra of the screen, he is too little remembered.

In *The Crowd* (1928), King Vidor made an earnest and honest picture of the frustrations of modern life, the sorrows and the joys, too, that come to simple middle-class people. Vidor dramatized the regimentation of their working days, and he used the moving camera subjectively to make us see life as his principals saw it. *The Crowd* was acclaimed by the critics but not by the public. At best, it did no harm to Vidor's reputation in Hollywood. Producers could see that he worked imaginatively and within the bounds of a reasonable economy.

American Realism from Central Europeans

Two other men worked differently and with very different results. They were Erich von Stroheim and Josef von Sternberg. They were both from Middle Europe, and for a time, they both tried to picture American life realistically. In 1923–24, von Stroheim spent half a million of MGM's money on *Greed,* a screen version of Frank Norris' novel *McTeague.* In 1924 von Sternberg made *The Salvation Hunters* for buttons.

So far as the studios were concerned von Stroheim remained "the man you love to hate," for after many months of work on *Greed* he gave MGM a print that ran to forty-two reels, then cut it to twenty-four, and refused to look at the picture when the studio boiled it down to ten. Such prodigality was a habit with him. Paramount, blind to his record at Universal and MGM, and recognizing a certain flair in the man, let him make another gargantuan production, which they chopped down to four hours and then split into two unprofitable features, *The Wedding March* and *The Honeymoon.* Von Sternberg, financing his experiment in low budget production *sans* studio and using almost entirely unknown actors, was content to turn out a film of normal length—a *succès d'estime.*

There is another interesting contrast between the two. Von Stroheim began with exposés of Continental luxury, contrasting its glamor with "realistic" portraits of degenerate society that were as exaggerated as they were cynical. After *The Salvation Hunters,* von Sternberg started the gangster cycle with *Underworld* (1927), directed Emil Jannings in *The Last Command* (1928), and then turned away from realism to make an all-too-brief career out of the all-too-easy task of glamorizing Marlene Dietrich.

As pictures, neither *Greed* nor *The Salvation Hunters* seems satisfactory today. In MGM's ten-reel version of *Greed* we aren't seeing the picture that the director conceived and shot. Many scenes are still effective, and many never could have been. Jean Hersholt is particularly good, but Gibson Gowland plays the chief role with a heavy overemphasis that isn't helped by a hairdo like Harpo Marx's. Without benefit of trick photography, von Stroheim provided natural interiors while the life of

San Francisco streets appeared illusively through the windows; his trick was to tear out the walls of a house in that city so as to light the interiors adequately. *The Salvation Hunters* remains a slow and obvious film with too much emphasis on a harbor dredge, on the intercutting of series of single scenes with subtitles, and on a symbolic use of such things as birds. Its theme is thoroughly muddled. Yet, in spite of all its faults, the film seemed startling enough to win the fervent endorsements of Charlie Chaplin and Douglas Fairbanks, who forced their company, United Artists, to try to distribute it.

Inert England—1905 to 1925

The story of film-making in France and in England before, during, and after World War I, is full of interesting contrasts. France had been more active and more creative before the blow fell. After 1914, French directors went to America and the British into some form of war activity. In the nineteen-twenties, however, the French outdistanced the British.

The English story is the simpler. In the two or three years before World War I, England had begun to recover from its slump of 1905. Producers made longer films; *East Lynne* (1913) ran to 6,500 feet. There was no new director, however, to match Cecil Hepworth, and Hepworth was tiring. Too often the screen reproduced in dull fashion worthy successes of the London stage. Of course, lovers of the theater would be happy if they could find the films that recorded Sir Herbert Tree in *Henry VIII* (1911) and Sir Johnston Forbes-Robertson in the somewhat more filmic *Hamlet* (1913), but these pictures contributed nothing to the art of the screen.

American invaders were doing much better. While a British film recorded in 8,000 feet the scenery, costumes, and actors of the stage production of *Ivanhoe* at the Lyceum Theater, Herbert Brenon brought King Baggot from the United States to appear in the same story at Chepstow Castle, in what the English film critic Rachael Low calls "scale and splendour." Four other American directors were working in Great Britain: George Loane Tucker, Frank Powell, Larry Trimble and Sidney Olcott.

Between the end of World War I and the coming of sound, England developed only one director of note, Alfred Hitchcock, and his career belongs far more to the talkie era. In *The Lodger* (1926) he showed a flair for suspense that carried him through *The Man Who Knew Too Much* (1934), *The Thirty-Nine Steps* (1935), *The Lady Vanishes* (1938), and on to Hollywood.

French Directors in America

Just before World War I, the French screen had escaped from the influence of Film d'Art and seemed headed for real creativeness. In 1913, Albert Capellani turned *Les Misérables* into a feature almost three hours long, and made Zola's *Germinal* into an eight-reel picture. Other men of vitality were at work. But with the coming of war, production practically stopped, and many directors went abroad. Léonce Perret and Maurice Tourneur, as well as Capellani, came to America.

Perret accomplished little in Hollywood, but Capellani directed Alla Nazimova in a number of successful films, and Tourneur enjoyed still greater success. Tourneur made some popular American melodramas, and he also directed *Trilby* (1915), *Barbary Sheep* (1917) with Elsie Ferguson, and *The Poor Little Rich Girl* (1917) with Mary Pickford. His chief distinction was his pictorial imagination and the use of stylized settings against a neutral or even black background in *The Blue Bird* (1918) and *Prunella* (1918), a type of decor that Charles Bryant ruined through exaggeration in Nazimova's *Salome*.

France After the War

André Antoine, father of stage naturalism in the nineteenth century, left the theater to direct films just before the war began. He returned to his new field in 1917. Working outdoors in realistic settings, he might have accomplished much if he had known how to develop good scripts. Antoine was forced into the background by a number of new directors of whom the most astonishing—and the least successful—was Abel Gance. French critics call his talents disorderly but undeniable, and his work gigantic and incredible. His *La Roue* (1922), absorbed with modern machinery, was so long that it was only shown in a curtailed version. His *Napoleon* (1926)—conceived to cover the whole life of the emperor, but never getting beyond his first Italian campaign—I shall describe in a later chapter. It was projected on a triptych of three screens, outdoing CinemaScope and rivaling Cinerama.

The brilliant former critic, Louis Delluc, sought true filmic qualities in *Fièvre* (1921) and other films. Jacques Feyder distinguished himself with a sensitive rendering of Anatole France's *Crainquebille* (1923), *Carmen* (1926) with the Spanish dancer Raquel Meller, and Zola's *Thérèse Raquin* (1928). In Hollywood he made *The Kiss* (1929) with Greta Garbo; it had no dialogue, only synchronized sound effects. He returned to France, and later created the brilliant comedy *Carnival in Flanders* (1935). Finally, there were Alberto Cavalcanti, who became a distinguished maker of documentary films, and René Clair and Jean Renoir, whose best films were made in the days of sound. Clair, always a master of comedy, began in 1923 with *Paris Qui Dort* (*The Crazy Ray*) to use trick effects against well-observed reality, and went on to the fantastic wit of *The Italian Straw Hat* (1927). Renoir's silent films ranged from Zola's *Nana* (1926) to the fairy tale *La Petite Marchande d'Allumettes* (1928).

Vitagraph—R. I. P.

The death of Ince at forty-two and the end of Vitagraph are two of the sadder events of the nineteen-twenties. I have said enough about the producer-director to suggest that he might have been a considerable force in the time of talkies. I have not said enough about Vitagraph, the company that took shape in the nineties, and was bought in 1925 by Warner Brothers, when that company coveted its system of exchanges.

As a member of the Patents Company, Vitagraph suffered from the restrictions that the film trust imposed upon it, but it was the first of the group to rebel. Despite the antagonism of the Patents Company to anything but shorts, Vitagraph made the five-reel picture *The Life of Moses* in 1909 and worked up to an eight-reel film, *The Christian*, in 1914. Also, it was the first producing company to lease a Broadway theater to show a number of its feature films. Vitagraph might have developed and retained more stars if the trust had allowed the company to advertise their names in the early days. Nevertheless, it had important players ranging from Maurice Costello and Sidney Drew to Anita Stewart and Clara Kimball Young.

Found or Starred by Vitagraph

John Bunny	Antonio Moreno	Constance Talmadge
Maurice Costello	Mabel Normand	Norma Talmadge
Sidney Drew	Wallace Reid	Florence Turner
Flora Finch	Larry Semon	Rudolph Valentino
Alice Joyce	Anita Stewart	Earle Williams
Victor McLaglen		Clara Kimball Young

The chief of Vitagraph's three partners was J. Stuart Blackton. Director, cameraman, actor, and promoter in the eighteen-nineties, he made one of the earliest American trick film effects, and legend says that he was the first to use dialogue in subtitles. The second partner was the aforementioned Albert E. Smith. The third, "Pop" Rock, opened the first American movie house on record, Vitascope Hall in New Orleans.

Hail, MGM!

Except for sound, the most important development of the twenties was the founding of MGM under the suzerainty of Louis B. Mayer and the creative supervision of Irving Thalberg. If Ince had lived, I doubt that he could have rivaled Thalberg as a producer of films and as an organizer of a studio. Thalberg had the happy faculty of growth; the ability to learn from such associates as Albert Lewin, Bernard Hyman, and Paul Bern, and also from his rivals and their pictures. Thalberg talked less than Mayer about MGM's "family of stars," but it was the younger man who had to use as best he could acting talents that varied from those of Ramon Novarro, Renée Adorée, and Marion Davies to those of Buster Keaton, Greta Garbo, and Norma Shearer. He was readier than the head of any other studio to move forward into the sound era with complete effectiveness, to build a far stronger group of the all-necessary stars, and to make "prestige pictures" that were profitable at the box office.

Eminent Authors—Pioneers of Progress?

The great problem of the nineteen-twenties, at least in America, was the story and the writer. Directing and acting were effective. Camera-work was excellent, scene design picturesque if sometimes extravagant, and editing skillful. But, as we see most silent films today, they seem to lack some basic appeal in plot and characterization. Was this because the very nature of the silent film put a premium on the broad and the obvious, on stereotypes and swift violence, on chases and spectacles?

From the beginning of the feature film, the screen had made pictures based on well-known novels and plays. Almost always, however, the stories appeared less significant on the screen. The movement of the films seemed stiff and the action static. And—most important—characterization suffered. Some blamed this on the adapters and tried to get novelists and playwrights to work directly for the screen.

The pioneer in this effort was Goldwyn. In 1919, after hiring painters and illustrators to design sets and even codirect, he began to engage popular novelists. Already, through his partnership with the Selwyns of Broadway, he had acquired more than the second syllable of his name, for they had brought him a number of their most successful playwrights. Not satisfied with these, Goldwyn hired half a dozen well-known novelists, including Rupert Hughes, Rex Beach, Mary Roberts Rinehart, and

ANNOUNCING EMINENT
AUTHORS' PICTURES

EMINENT Authors' Pictures, Inc., organized by Rex Beach and Samuel Goldwyn, unites in one producing organization the greatest American novelists of today. It insures the exclusive presentation of their stories on the screen and each author's cooperation in production. These authors are:—

Rex Beach	Gertrude Atherton	Mary Roberts Rinehart
Rupert Hughes	Gouverneur Morris	Basil King
	Leroy Scott	

The creation of Eminent Authors' Pictures, Inc., is the natural outgrowth of the association of Mr. Beach and Mr. Goldwyn in the making of such successes as "The Crimson Gardenia," "The Brand," "The Auction Block."

Editors and magazines vie with one another to secure the manuscripts of these writers. They pay large sums for the exclusive rights to their works. Every word of these men and women is contracted for, both for serial and book publication, months in advance.

Every picture will be as popular an achievement for the motion picture world as the story has been in literature. It will not be offered for release until the author has given his personal approval to it. The picture must first pass the severest critic that it will ever meet—the author of the story.

During the year each author of the corporation will be represented by at least two stories. These splendid productions will be sold *only in the projection rooms* of the Goldwyn exchanges one at a time—on merit.

GOLDWYN TRIES TO MAKE THE WRITER KING. A double-page spread in a 36-page insert in the trade magazines announced that Goldwyn had enlisted seven of the most popular novelists of 1919. More than that, each writer was to have the unheard-of right to approve the picture before release. Also, no block-booking, no blind sales. The ad failed to mention the fact that Goldwyn would send the writers to Hollywood to study production before they began to write for the screen.

Gouverneur Morris. Goldwyn advertised them as his "Eminent Authors," and—because he wanted better stories that were better fitted to the screen—he sent these novelists to Hollywood to study film production in his studio before they began to write for the screen. Except in the case of Hughes, the producer drew a blank. Whether or not Paramount followed the Goldwyn pattern by having novelists actually writing at its studio, in 1921 it boasted that Sir James M. Barrie, Joseph Conrad, Arnold Bennett, and Somerset Maugham, among others, "were now working with Paramount." Unfortunately, the results were no better than when journeymen screen-writers adapted the works of other men and women.

Some of these adapters were highly skilled. I have already mentioned Anita Loos and Ince's writers. Now I must add two women of the nineteen-twenties: Jeanie Macpherson, who is said to have whispered the words "sex" and "luxury" into the receptive ear of her employer, DeMille; and June Mathis, who acted also as a producer when she put together *The Four Horsemen of the Apocalypse*, the youthful director Rex Ingram, and the almost unknown Valentino. In the silent days when there was no spoken dialogue to worry about, directors worked closely with screenwriters and sometimes with novelists who had been induced to aid in the adaptation of their own work.

The Way to Better Films from Novels and Plays

I rather suspect that the great success of *Tol'able David* was due not only to Henry King's able direction, but also to the fact that the book provided the kind of rugged action that could be made effective without the aid of either stars or sound. Many of the novels that won such success on the silent screen were those which could stagger the audience with spectacular action or seduce it with exotic romance—for example, Lew Wallace's *Ben-Hur*, Emerson Hough's *The Covered Wagon*, Blasco Ibañez's *The Four Horsemen of the Apocalypse*, P. C. Wren's *Beau Geste* (1926), Elinor Glyn's *Three Weeks* (1924).

Now, I am not trying to say that the less spectacular or gusty stories borrowed from the bookshelf or the stage didn't make successful films. They did, but only because their success was ensured by their stars. Mary Pickford carried *Pollyanna*, Valentino *Blood and Sand* (1922), John Barrymore *Beau Brummel* (1924), Norma Talmadge *Smiling Through* (1922), Geraldine Farrar *Carmen* (1915), and so on back to Sarah Bernhardt and *Queen Elizabeth* (1912). The success of such films wasn't due to the writer of the original story or to the peculiar powers of the silent screen. To make most novels and plays into films that could be effective with or without stars, writers, producers, and directors needed spoken dialogue and a more mature audience. By the end of the nineteen-twenties, both of these were to be possible. A new screen was to be born.

Chapter
19

The Inventive Struggle—1906-1926

WHEN LEE DE FOREST invented the audion amplifier in 1906, he fathered other things beside the radio. A few of these were the public-address system and radar, computers and automation equipment, hi-fi and TV transmission. Also—the talkies. Edison stumbled on the basic idea but didn't realize what it could do for his phonograph and therefore for the talking pictures he was to try to develop.

De Forest's vacuum tube provided the means for making an actor's voice loud enough to reach the last row of a 3,000-seat theater; indeed, it has now increased the intensity of a sound more than a thousand times.

Circa 1890

In a crude form, the talking picture is as old as the silent. It is said that as early as 1890, Edison began work on wedding the motion picture to the mechanical phonograph. In 1894 and for a short time afterward, some of his Kinetoscopes had earphones to give peep-show patrons sounds as well as pictures. Two years later, Charles Pathé and Oskar Messter tried fruitlessly to combine motion pictures with a German talking machine. Between 1896 and 1900, half a dozen French inventors and showmen succeeded somewhat better in linking phonograph records with movies, and gave private and public showings. The talking pictures of three of these men—Berthon, Dussaud, and Jaubert—attracted the attention of a French steamship company, and were made a feature of

TALKIES WITHOUT SOUND. Georges Demeny, an assistant to Marey, developed in 1891 a device that projected very rapidly a series of pictures mounted on the edge of a disk. Demeny called it a Phonoscope and used it to show in close-ups the lip movements of a man saying a short phrase. The deaf who had been trained in lip-reading could "hear" *Vive la France!* when the pictures above were projected on a screen. (*Drawing from* Le Cinéma: des origines à nos jours.)

its display at the Paris Exposition of 1900. At the same time Clément Maurice opened the Phono-Cinéma-Théâtre, a movie house devoted entirely to talkies. There, the distinguished players Coquelin and Réjane acted dialogue scenes from famous plays. The English comedian Little Tich sang and danced, and there were many vocal numbers. Sarah Bernhardt appeared in the duel at the end of *Hamlet*, but the audience may have heard only footfalls and the clash of rapiers provided by noise-makers behind the screen. The Paris fair had yet a third show of talkies, this one at the Théâtre de la Grande Roue. Here Henri Joly presented an original comedy *Lolotte*. Instead of confining his films entirely to songs, music-hall turns, and scenes from plays, this inventor became the first screen-writer for talking pictures.

A SOUND FILM OF THE NINETIES? While the early talkies were supposed to hide musical instruments off screen or prerecord sound, in this film the camera photographed the violinist—supposed to be Dickson himself—playing into a phonograph horn while two workmen danced. (*Courtesy Edison National Historic Site.*)

The Failings of the Phonograph

From French accounts, these shows were none too popular. Yet for fifteen years, inventors in Europe and America went on trying to link the screen image with dialogue from a crude form of phonograph. Léon Gaumont showed quite a number of films in Paris as well as a few in New York in 1913.

The failure of all these attempts was due to several things. The recording mechanism was too insensitive. Except in a close shot, it couldn't be placed near enough to the actors to get a good volume without being in the view of the camera. So, sometimes the voices were recorded first; and then the acting was photographed to a "playback" from a phonograph—a method now used for all musical numbers. Even when the image and the voices were correctly recorded on film and record, it was extremely difficult to keep the two synchronized—"in sync," as the trade says—at a showing. Ropes and pulleys and electrical connections, as well as ingenious signals to the projectionist to speed up his hand-driven machine, didn't solve the problem satisfactorily. Worse still, the early phonographs behind the screen couldn't get enough volume out of the mechanical vibrations of needle and diaphragm.

B. F. Keith's New York Theatres

CONCERTS TO-DAY, 2:15 and 8:15.   Week of FEB. 17.   MAT. DAILY, 25c.

UNION SQ

B'WAY & 14TH ST. 'Phone, 3400—Stuyvesant.

Grand Vaudeville Carnival

THOS. A. EDISON presents his latest & greatest invention
Talking Motion Pictures
"THE KINETOPHONE."

Afternoon.	Time Table.	Evening.
2:10	....Lewis Sisters	8:10
2:20	....Jerry & Delaney	8:20
2:30	....D'Arcy & Williams	8:30
2:42	....Edna Phillips & Co.	8:42
3.00	....Darrell & Conway	9:00
3:15	....Rube Dickinson	9:15
3:27	...Sam Watson's Farmyard	9:27
3:47	{ Edison's "Kinetophone," Talking Motion Pictures, }	.9:47
4:03	....Ray Elinore Ball	10:03
4:13	.."The Fighter and the Boss"	10:13
4:33	..Billy Gould & Belle Ashlyn	10:33
4:51	....The Camille Trio	10:51
5:00	....Curtain	11:00

COLONIAL

B'WAY & 62D ST. 'Phone, 4457—Columbus.

BESSIE WYNN
"THE LADY DAINTY OF VAUDEVILLE."

"IN THE Jesse Lasky's Production.
BARRACKS"
with MYLES McCAR-THY & company of 18.

THOMAS A. EDISON
presents his latest and greatest invention,
Talking Pictures   "The Kinetophone."

JULIUS TANNEN	MRS. GENE HUGHES & Co.

COURTNEY SISTERS

ASHLEY & LEE	BEN DEELY & CO.

SEVEN BRACKS

SAMUEL ASH	ASAKI

ALHAMBRA

7TH AV. & 126TH ST. 'PHONE, 5000—Morning.

BELLE STORY	FRANK FOGARTY
The Tetrazzini of Vaudeville.	The Dublin Minstrel.

THOMAS A. EDISON
presents his latest and greatest invention,
Talking Pictures   "The Kinetophone"

ELSA RUEGGER	S. MILLER KENT & CO.
World's Greatest Cellist	in "The Real Q."
ED. GALLAGHER & JOE FIELDS	AL & FANNIE STEADMAN
4 FLORIMONDS	BERT MELROSE

Melody Lane Girls: 3 Leightons

BRONX

3D AV. AND 149TH ST. 'Phone, 5017—Melrose.

MIDWINTER CARNIVAL

1:45	Overture	7:45
1:50	Chalk Saunders	7:50
2:02	Reidy & Currier	8:02
2:17	Charles Drew & Co.	8:17
2:28	"The Apple of Paris"	8:28
2:44	Cadets de Gascogne	8:44
3:13	Murphy & Nichols	9:13
3:41	Geo. Drumm's Harmonists.	9:41
3:45	Hart's Six Steppers	9:45
4:01	Joe Jackson	10:01
4:11	Truly Shattuck	10:11
4:29	"Detective Keen"	10:29
4:48	Dooley & Sayles	10:48
5:08	Kluting's Animals	11:08
5:22	News of the World	11:22

SOUND PICTURES FROM EDISON. Three of Keith's vaudeville houses present the Kinetophone, while the Bronx shows only "News of the World." (*Courtesy Louis Sheaffer.*)

Other crude efforts were made to supply dialogue and the sounds of nature. Enterprising exhibitors put actors behind the screen to speak the lines of the characters. Some installed machines from which an operator could draw as many as fifty different sounds, which ranged from the cry of a baby and the bark of a dog to the noise of escaping steam and the wind and thunder of a storm.

COQUELIN TALKS, BERNHARDT ONLY FENCES. Yet this was the first important demonstration of the linking of the motion picture and the phonograph. (*Courtesy University of California Press.*)

Talkies via the Phonograph Again—Briefly

When sound at last came from Hollywood in 1926, it came on a phonograph record. Just as Edison mistakenly concentrated on the cylinder instead of the disc for his talking machine, the first producers of modern talkies began by using the disc instead of a photographic sound track.

Since sound on film was available—indeed, it was soon to replace the phonograph record—it may seem extraordinary that the first studio to adopt sound used the older method. This was partly because projectors were no longer hand-driven, and they could now be synchronized more accurately with the turntable of the phonograph. Then, too, through electronic means, records were better than they had been; thanks to de Forest, their sounds could be greatly amplified. Finally, we must remmember that sound on film was slow in developing. It was hardly achieved by 1920. And up till 1925 or 1926, a voice on a phonograph record was far clearer than a voice on film. In 1922, a technician who heard one of de Forest's film recordings found it "barely understandable"; and de Forest himself wrote, "I well remember the grim satisfaction I felt when, for the first time in reproducing a photographic record of my voice, I was able to clearly determine whether or not it was being run backwards!" A year later he said of another recording—in accents of triumph— "one can understand every word first time through."

Pioneers of Sound on Film

The story of the recording and the reproducing of sound on film involves very difficult concepts and the development of very intricate scientific processes. It is, in fact, even more complicated than the history of the invention of the silent motion picture. The chief problem was the turning of sound into pulsating light, and of light into sound again. Along the way, sound became electricity, and electricity became sound.

The first experiments go back to 1878. Only a year after Edison had

---

The Pioneers of Sound on Film

The team of A. G. Bell, C. A. Bell, and S. Tainter, who recorded light from sound through a fine slit (1886).

C. J. Hohenstein, who put sound on film by a method similar to one used later by General Electric (1887).

J. Poliakoff, who used positive film images with a photoelectric cell (1900).

Ernst Ruhmer, whose Photographophon is described as "something like the sound camera of today" (1901).

Eugene A. Lauste—formerly with Edison, the Lathams, Rector— one of whose contributions was later developed by RCA (1906).

E. E. Ries, whose patent proved almost basic but took ten years to get through the Patent Office (1913).

perfected his talking machine, Professor E. W. Blake of Brown University described how he attached a mirror to the diaphragm of a phonograph and then recorded photographically the vibrations of a beam of light reflected from the mirror. By 1880, Alexander Bell was sending his voice on light and using the sensitive metal selenium to turn it into electric impulses. At the same time, another American, Charles E. Fritts, used selenium to reproduce sound patterns photographed on a band of paper. More than two dozen inventors, here and in Europe, worked on the numerous problems of sound via light before the recording and reproducing of sound on film began to take definite shape in 1918. For the most important men and the dates see the box on page 280.

After de Forest's invention of the audion amplifier in 1906, more than ten years passed before he and his fellow technicians began to close in on the problem of sound on film. It was another ten years before Hollywood began to think of making talking pictures.

The end of World War I set some scientists free to work in the area of entertainment. Three Germans, three Americans, and a number of men employed by the big manufacturers of radio and electrical equipment in the United States led the field. The Germans worked together as Tri-Ergon. Of the three Americans, de Forest sometimes worked by himself and sometimes in loose association with Theodore W. Case and his associate Earl I. Sponable. The chief manufacturing companies that developed sound on film were General Electric, the Bell Telephone Laboratories, Western Electric, and Westinghouse. Bell and Western Electric cautiously produced both films and records.

De Forest Brings Talkies to Broadway in 1923

The association between de Forest and Case-Sponable was a curious one. They exchanged information freely while developing their own sound cameras. Between 1923 and 1925, they had an agreement by which de Forest used certain devices of the other two in his Phonofilm system. I am not belittling the work of de Forest when I say that he gave a great deal of attention to production and exhibition while Case and Sponable made the greatest technical advances.

De Forest showed a program of his short films at the Rivoli Theater in New York on April 15, 1923. The program started off with a picture in which a man explained the making of movies with sound. (This, remember, was the year when de Forest boasted that he could "understand every word first time through.") During 1923, de Forest exhibited some twenty-five short subjects. The next year, he recorded speeches by

President Coolidge, Senator Robert La Follette, and other notables. More important than films of monologues by comedians like Eddie Cantor, George Jessel, and DeWolf Hopper, he produced in 1924 a two-reel comedy, *Love's Old Sweet Song*, with Una Merkel. Surprisingly, this early talkie attracted little attention.

In 1925, in the first theater built especially for talkies, de Forest showed his films at the British Empire Exhibition in London. By the end of the year, he saw Phonofilm equipment installed in a number of American movie houses. But de Forest couldn't gain the ear of Hollywood, while William Fox—who was later to adopt the Case-Sponable system as Movietone—ordered the de Forest projectors out of the six Fox theaters where they had been installed.

The Work of the Radio Manufacturers

Besides de Forest, Case, and Sponable, scientists working for the makers of radio and electrical equipment played an important part in exploring the mysteries of sound for the screen. From the work of all these men came refinements in the use of the oscillating mirror, the photoelectric cell, and the vacuum tube, and also notable developments such as the light-valve, the microphone, and the loudspeaker. As early as 1920, Charles A. Hoxie of General Electric demonstrated sound on film in one of its laboratories, and the next year recorded speeches by President Coolidge and other public figures. In 1923, Western Electric made an animated sound film on the workings of the audion tube, while it was developing the electronic recording of sound on disc. Bell as well as Western Electric achieved good synchronization through an electric motor that drove both projector and phonograph. Electronic recordings and powerful amplifiers made this system reasonably satisfactory, though not so good as sound on film.

Thus, by 1925, the work of de Forest, Case, Sponable, and the manufacturers made the talkies a reality—outside Hollywood. The mute movie and the blind radio had brought forth a child that could talk and be seen.

Sound for Money's Sake

Up till 1926, the film studios felt too prosperous to waste time and money on the gestation and accouchement of this prattling baby. When the Hollywood talkie was born at last, it was under the sign of the dollar— or, perhaps I should say, under the sign of the missing dollar.

The silent screen didn't die of old age. By 1926, its artistic potentialities were far from exhausted, as Russia was beginning to demonstrate.

But the commercial film, made to please as many people as possible, began to repeat itself and grow dull. To hold the audience, America's first-run exhibitors added symphony orchestras and vaudeville; and they fused these into what they called "presentations" or "prologs." For an hour, film audiences watched revues with singers, comics, vaudeville acts, elaborate scenery, and a teeming chorus of dancing girls whose mechanical perfection would put a millepede to shame. In spite of all this, the size of audiences shrank. And, although audiences shrank, all the Hollywood producers turned a deaf ear to the sounds that ingenious inventors were offering them—all the Hollywood producers, that is, except the one that was in the worst shape financially. This was Warner Brothers. It was on the edge of bankruptcy, so it had nothing to lose. As things turned out, Warners, and the film producers of both hemispheres, had a world to gain.

At first, Warner Brothers seems to have thought mainly of bringing orchestral scores, musical stars, and short turns, not only to the first-run theaters but also to the smaller houses that couldn't afford to hire performers. (As early as 1924, de Forest had recorded Hugo Riesenfeld's musical accompaniment to *The Covered Wagon* and projected it at the Rivoli during the "supper shows" when the regular orchestra was resting.) On August 6, 1926, adopting the Western Electric process under the name of Vitaphone, Warner Brothers presented its first program with electrically recorded sound on discs. The feature was the silent picture *Don Juan*, with John Barrymore, accompanied by a score recorded with the New York Philharmonic Orchestra. There were short films in which Mischa Elman played the violin and Martinelli and Marion Talley sang solos. The only talking voice came from a motion picture of Will Hays, czar of the industry, who—with more vision than most Hollywood men enjoyed—introduced Vitaphone as something that would revolutionize the screen.

Fox Steps in with Case and Sponable

Before William Fox ripped out the de Forest equipment that had somehow wormed its way into a few Fox theaters by 1924, the magnate had refused to talk to the inventor on a transatlantic crossing. But, a couple of years later, when the film man heard that Warner Brothers had made a contract for Vitaphone, he was willing to listen to a Case-Sponable demonstration. The realistic twitterings of a canary decided him. Before the rival studio showed *Don Juan*, Fox had agreed to accept the Case-Sponable brand of sound on film and to exploit it under the name of

Fox Movietone. This was in the summer of 1926. By the end of October, the Fox-Case Corporation was making tests on a new sound-stage in New York. Sponable has amusingly noted that Harry Lauder stopped in the middle of a song, and to make sure the film couldn't be used commercially announced quite clearly, "This is a test."

A Leisurely Race between Two Studios

Fox was a late starter compared with the Warners. They had broken the barrier in August, 1926, with a synchronized score, musicians, and Hay's speech. It was the following January before Fox put his silks on a singing short with the Spanish Raquel Meller. In May, Movietone showed its heels with the first Hollywood short with dialogue—*They're Coming to Get Me*, starring the comedian Chic Sale. After that, it was a dingdong race for position. But it was a slow race all the same.

The Warner brothers were sluggish pioneers. After the debut of Hays, they waited more than a year to put songs and a little dialogue into a long film. Then nine months of gestation went by before they brought forth the first "all-talking" feature. Fox, too, found it slow going in the fiction field. It took him two years to move from the Chic Sale short to his first feature-length talkie.

Fox moved faster, however, in the field of the newsreel. Case-Sponable's sound on film proved more mobile than Vitaphone's phonograph recording. In the summer of 1927, camera crews recorded the departure of Lindbergh and his welcome back in Washington; they went abroad and interviewed Mussolini. By the autumn, the first weekly issue of Movietone News appeared. In little more than a year, the output trebled; and in July 1929, Fox delivered four newsreels a week.

The Jazz Singer—"You Ain't Heard Nothin' Yet"

In spite of earlier demonstrations, it was Warner Brothers that first amazed and staggered moviegoers with the possibilities of spoken dialogue on the screen eighteen months after Edison had said that there was "no field for talking pictures." For some reason, the sensational success that de Forest couldn't win with his Phonofilm in 1925, or Fox with the Chic Sale film on May 25, 1927, Warners achieved when it presented *The Jazz Singer* on October 6 of that year. Al Jolson's six songs were arresting, of course, but the public had already heard singing in one-reelers. It had heard dialogue, too. Yet, when Jolson finished his first song in reel two and said to the guests in a café, "Wait a minute, wait a minute. You ain't heard nothin' yet. . ." the theater audience was elec-

A MODEST REVOLUTION. Perhaps Warner Brothers was too broke to spend much money on advertising the introduction of sound. At any rate, an announcement of *Don Juan* in the New York *Times* of August 7, 1926, immediately following its opening, did not mention the synchronization of sound for Will Hays's speech—only "Vitaphone."

trified. There was a kind of prophecy in this favorite line of his, which he had carried over from many a musical show on Broadway. *The Jazz Singer* had only a few more lines of dialogue, but the success of the film told other producers that they must turn to sound. Even so they were surprisingly slow to react.

The First All-Dialogue Films

After the success of *The Jazz Singer*—it made a handsome profit even though there were only about a hundred theaters equipped with sound projectors—Warner Brothers, Fox, and others hurriedly added talkie sequences to films that were all but finished. The first completely dialogued full-length film, *The Lights of New York*, didn't come from Warner Brothers till July, 1928. Paramount joined the all-talkie procession five months later with *Interference*. The otherwise enterprising Fox didn't come through until January, 1929, but *In Old Arizona* had the distinction of being the first talking feature shot out of doors. Griffith, who had made a failure with songs recorded on phonograph discs for *Dream Street* in 1921, let Lupe Velez sing and dance in *Lady of the Pavements* (1929) before he made his first all-talkie, *Abraham Lincoln.*

In 1928 there had been musical numbers and night-club scenes in *The Singing Fool* and *The Lights of New York;* and early the next year, with MGM's *Broadway Melody,* Hollywood discovered that sound made a new kind of film possible and very profitable—the musical show. MGM cautiously made a silent version as well as a talkie, a feat accomplished by cutting out a third of the picture. RKO was more confident, toward the end of 1929, when it concentrated solely on an "all-talkie" reproduction of the Broadway hit *Rio Rita.*

In 1930 the Silent Fades Away

For Hollywood, 1929 was the year of decision. In March, Fox gave up producing silent pictures. The others slowly followed. According to listings in the *Film Daily Year Book,* in twelve months Hollywood companies made 335 features with complete dialogue. They turned out only 175 silent films. In between lay 75 with musical scores and sound effects, and 95 with a mixture of a little dialogue and a lot of subtitles. The number of theaters wired for sound increased more than fifty times between December 31, 1927, and December 31, 1929. Sponable has said that at the end of 1927, there were only 157 houses equipped for sound and not more than 55 of these could handle sound on film. Two years later, he counted 8,741, and most of them could use both disc and film. There remained some 10,000 theaters, mostly on the small side, that had no sound equipment of any kind. That was why 175 of the 335 all-talking features of 1929 went out in silent versions, too, replete with subtitles. All told, however, there were 505 features with some kind of sound against 175 that could be seen but not heard.

Sound spoke long and loudly in comedy and drama, the Western, the musical show, and the operetta. Even Britain listened. Under some strange misapprehension, the otherwise astute Alfred Hitchcock had shot *Blackmail* silent; when he heard the belated news from Hollywood, he remade most of it in sound for release in 1929. Germany saw Tri-Ergon films as early as 1922, but her producers didn't go in seriously for talkies until 1929.

By the end of 1930, the screen of America and Europe was full of sound and fury, signifying—what?

Chapter

20

"*Garbo Talks!*"

Hollywood resisted sound for a number of good reasons besides general inertia. Most of its actors and many of its stars were pantomimists with untrained voices and questionable ability to convey emotion through words. Hollywood stages weren't soundproofed. The theaters as well as the studios had to buy a great deal of expensive equipment. The companies had a large backlog of silent films. And there was the foreign market where few houses were ready for sound, while Hollywood's sound would be English.

Sound Saves Hollywood

It was doubly fortunate for the Hollywood studios that they had all taken to sound before the depression that began in the fall of 1929. The Wall Street boom and the quick success of the talkies enabled exhibitors to borrow and then pay back the money needed for new sound equipment; the cost ran from $8,500 to $20,000. If the producers had waited till late October, 1929—as they might well have done except for the daring of Warner Brothers and Fox—sound would have been impossible for ten more years, and receiverships would have come quite some time before 1932.

The reverberating boom of sound may be measured by a few of the gaudy operations of the expanding film companies. In 1928 Fox built a wholly new studio, five miles west of its old one, investing $4,000,000 in buildings alone, and within a year it bought for $50,000,000 temporary control of Loew's, Inc., which owned MGM. The Rockefellers thought so well of picture-making and exhibiting that they built the Radio City

Music Hall and had their Radio Corporation of America (which made sound-on-film equipment) buy FBO, a film-producing company, and the Keith-Albee-Orpheum vaudeville theater corporation, and set up RKO; until 1932, the film business had withstood the depression so well that RCA added the Pathé studio to its interests. Warner Brothers was prosperous enough to bid against Fox for Loew's, and to buy the Stanley chain of theaters, along with First National, the producing company that had been set up by a group of exhibitors. Warner Brothers now controlled about 500 theaters, and other companies bought up other chains of houses. Guesses at the weekly attendance are unreliable, but one source says that 57,000,000 went to movie theaters in 1927 and 90,000,000 in 1930; the proportion of increase is probably correct. The fact that the depression didn't hit the film business until about 1932 is proved by the increase of sound-equipped theaters from almost 9,000 at the end of 1929 to 13,000 two years later. When Warner Brothers gave up the use of discs in 1930, exhibitors were able to meet the expense of scrapping Vitaphone equipment and putting in sound-on-film projectors.

New Players for Old

Sound—that reluctant revolution—upset the personnel as well as the techniques of Hollywood. Almost anyone could be made reasonably effective in silent pantomime. Acting with the voice was another matter. Then, too, the recording mechanism was crude to start with. It couldn't handle the croaking voice of Andy Devine. Sibilants were so exaggerated and distorted that "success" sounded something like "shucshesh." Sound cut off the careers of some good actors as well as of many incompetents. The imperfect vocal cords of that excellent comedian Ray Griffith produced something like a husky whisper. John Gilbert's voice was too high. Silent actors with stage experience had nothing to fear—men and women like Ronald Colman, Claudette Colbert, William Powell, John and Lionel Barrymore, George Bancroft, Marie Dressler, and Clive Brook. Millions of playgoers however, held their breaths when they read in the advertisements of Anna Christie (1930), "GARBO TALKS!"

The studios hired, with varying success, Broadway stars and actors of less experience, such as George Arliss, Helen Hayes, Alfred Lunt, Lynn Fontanne, Fredric March, Leslie Howard, Clark Gable, Frank Morgan, Sylvia Sidney, Fred Astaire, Paul Muni, Spencer Tracy, and Katharine Hepburn. The screen gained much from character actors who had learned to speak in the theater: Boris Karloff, Jean Hersholt, May Robson, Nigel Bruce, James Gleason, Charles Laughton and others.

Voice specialists and teachers of acting flocked to Hollywood. With or without the aid of coaches, a number of silent stars who had had little or no experience behind the footlights kept their hold on the public— for instance, Janet Gaynor, Norma Shearer, Charles Farrell, and Gary Cooper.

Playwrights and Directors from Broadway

The greatest sufferers when sound came in were the screen writers. A very few, like John Emerson, had had practice in the theater, and they could handle dialogue. Some makers of silent plots learned to do so. But, for a few years after 1929, Hollywood hired playwright after playwright from Broadway. It didn't much matter whether their plays had been successes or flops. They knew how to write lines.

There was some turnover among the directors, though not so much. Most of them had to have what were called "dialogue directors" in Hollywood and "directors of elocution" in London. Some of these dialogue directors—George Cukor, for example—were soon placed in complete charge of a movie stage. Hollywood hired experienced stage directors like Richard Boleslavsky and Rouben Mamoulian, and started them at the top. Many of the silent directors adapted themselves quickly and effectively to sound. Among those who made a definite contribution to the talkies were Frank Lloyd, King Vidor, John Ford, Lewis Milestone, Josef von Sternberg, Clarence Brown, Woodbridge Van Dyke, Frank Capra.

The Frozen Camera

During the first three years of the talkies, from 1928 through 1930, Hollywood all but took the motion out of motion pictures. This was partly due to the studio's turning to plays because they had ready-made dialogue, but mostly to a problem in recording sound. The camera made a noise. To keep this noise off the sound track or the disc, they put the camera in a soundproof cubicle with glass walls. This "ice box," as it was soon called, might be a cube as much as eight feet wide. The ice box froze the camera. This cumbersome structure could be shifted about, but only with considerable delay. Two cameras, with different lenses, in one ice box, and another camera in another ice box, could give a director three angles, but the lighting was often unsatisfactory in one shot, and the cameras couldn't pan or follow the actors. In general, the first talkies weren't so very different from the static films made by Film d'Art in Paris twenty years before.

Problems of Sound Recording

Also, there was trouble with the microphones. As yet Hollywood had no "boom," or pole, to hold the mike over the heads of the players. Sound receivers had to be hidden in different parts of the set where an actor might stand. Andy Devine was wide enough to hide a mike strapped to his chest or back, and thus he began to work again, in nonspeaking roles, as a human "boom." The editing of sound developed very slowly. So did the mixing of speech and natural sounds or music—technically called rerecording or dubbing. Songs were recorded directly on the set through their whole length; after a time, they were recorded without a camera and played back to the singer, altogether or bit by bit, while he mouthed the words.

The films slowly escaped from the strait jacket of the immovable camera and mike. Somebody put the camera into a padded cloth "blimp," and it could ride on the wheels of the "dolly." It was still awkward to handle, but smaller, boxlike blimps came in, and then these gave way to cameras with noiseless gears. The mike acquired a "boom" that could be lengthened or shortened, and moved about just out of the picture.

Disc-recording of dialogue made it difficult to shoot exterior scenes. With sound-on-film it was much easier. Fox's production of *In Old Arizona* during 1928, and its release early in 1929, brought the Western back to the screen—a kind of film that had been peculiarly fitted to the swift and wide-ranging mobility of the silent camera.

Another development is worth mentioning. Silent film had run through camera and projector at sixteen frames, or one foot, a second, which meant 60 feet a minute. A reel of 1,000 feet lasted for about sixteen minutes on the screen. To improve the quality of sound recording and reproduction, the film was speeded up to twenty-four frames a second, or 90 feet a minute; thus a reel ran for only about eleven minutes. A five-reel feature of the nineteen-twenties occupied an hour and twenty minutes of playing time, while a five-reel sound film occupied only fifty-five minutes. Take this into consideration in judging the length of modern pictures as against silent features.

Putting Movement Back on the Screen

In 1929, two directors began to show their fellow-workers and the public that the talkie could have much of the freedom of movement of the silent film, and that sound could add greatly to the effectiveness of a story. One of the directors had worked for some time in Hollywood; the other came from opera and the stage.

In the silent days, King Vidor had created the exciting superficialities of *The Big Parade* and he had shown fine skill with camera and editing in his middle-class tragedy *The Crowd*. When he turned to sound in *Hallelujah* (1929), with an all-Negro cast, he used dialogue as little as possible and introduced imaginatively the sounds of the wind and water, birds and insects, and the off-screen sound of running feet, as well as Negro spirituals.

Rouben Mamoulian had directed productions of the American Opera Company and staged a number of Broadway productions brilliantly, including *Porgy*. In his first Hollywood film, *Applause* (1929), in which the singer Helen Morgan played an aging queen of burlesque, he blended music and camera movement deftly, developed lyrical love scenes in contrast to the tragedy of the woman played by Miss Morgan, and came close to the skills of today's films.

In 1930, the silent directors Lewis Milestone and Josef von Sternberg used both camera and sound freely and imaginatively. After Milestone's silent and swiftly moving gangster film the *The Racket* (1928), his first important picture was *All Quiet on the Western Front*—Erich Remarque's tragic and mordant story of World War I, told from the point of view of young German soldiers—and he gave it great pictorial power. He intercut most skillfully the sweep and din of battle with intimate scenes of dialogue. Audiences long remembered the scene in the shell hole between the dying French soldier (played beautifully in silence by Raymond Griffith) and Lew Ayres' young German who was soon to die. Von Sternberg, brought to Berlin by Erich Pommer to direct Emil Jannings and Marlene Dietrich in English and German versions of *The Blue Angel*, used all his skill with camera and background action, as well as a new sense of the possibilities of dialogue and music, to make a highly effective film. In the newcomer Marlene Dietrich he found a *femme fatale*. Back in Hollywood, he exploited her rare personality in *Morocco* (1930), along with Gary Cooper and Adolphe Menjou, and then led Miss Dietrich through a descending scale of pictorially glamorous films that had only one high spot, the melodrama *Shanghai Express* (1932).

These directors brought back camera movement and blended it adroitly with varying amounts of dialogue. In *The Front Page* (1931), Milestone showed how a play that depended very greatly on speech could be filmed with swift effectiveness. By the next year, the skills of sound editing had reached the point where the thoughts of the characters in Eugene O'Neill's *Strange Interlude* (1932), which had been spoken soliloquies on the stage, could be heard from the screen while the lips of the actors were still.

The Opponents of Sound

On the whole, motion picture directors readily accepted sound. So did the big public. Only the intelligentsia, including many film critics and a few actors resisted. It was natural that men and women who saw the silent screen reaching a new perfection with the Russians, the Germans, and a few American imitators, should sorrow over its untimely extinction. (They now look aghast at most of the silent movies that they had so admired.) In 1929 Gilbert Seldes wrote in his book *An Hour with the Movies and the Talkies,* "it is the great popular art and the aesthetes are weeping over its demise." More than one writer recalled that "silence is golden." Aldous Huxley, in his Utopia of *Brave New World,* envisioned the perfection of screen art in the "feelies"—stereoscopic, of course. One film critic spoke contemptuously of "Mr. de Forest and his deadly little audion." Mary Pickford said of sound: "It's like lip rouge on the Venus de Milo," completely forgetting, by the way, that the Greeks painted the lips as well as the bodies of their statues.

Some of the opponents of the talkies went in for arguments of a fuzzily scientific nature. The eye was quicker then the ear. Man could understand pictures better than sounds. Yet hearing interfered with visual comprehension. The two faculties were at war with one another.

The German Rudolf Arnheim in *Film*—written as the talkies were just taking shape—said that "light gives a more complete and therefore more accurate picture of the universe than sound. Light gives us the 'being' of the things, while sound generally only gives us incidental 'doing.'" Writing in 1930, the English film-maker and critic Paul Rotha said in the first edition of his book *The Film Till Now:*

> . . . No power of speech is comparable to the descriptive value of photographs. The attempted combination of speech and pictures is the direct opposition of two separate mediums, which appeal in two utterly different ways. . . . a silent visual film is capable of achieving a more dramatic, lasting, and powerful effect on an audience by its singleness of appeal than a dialogue film. . . . Immediately a voice begins to speak in a cinema, the sound apparatus takes precedence over the camera, thereby doing violence to natural instincts.

When Rotha revised *The Film Till Now* for republication in the late forties, he gracefully admitted that "prophecies about the dialogue film" had been "largely disproved."

Belief in the silent film died hard. In 1928, Jesse Lasky saw that the talkie had "its definite place in the film scheme." He continued, "this does not mean that the silent picture is doomed. On the contrary, it will remain the backbone of the industry's commercial security." The next year, Seldes, too, asserted that silent films would continue to be made, but he recognized that picture and sound might be merged in "an entirely new form—cinephonics, perhaps—in which the principles of the movie will not be abandoned." Seldes was wrong about the future of the silent film. He was right, in all but name, about "Cinephonics".

Sound Eliminates Subtitles

Few defenders of the silent film recognized the very obvious fact that sound eliminated a major blemish on all but a few of the films made before 1930. This was the use of subtitles to convey information. Obviously they were at odds with the flowing nature of silent film, and yet it was extremely difficult to do without them. Arnheim saw that "a simple phrase like 'She lived absolutely alone in her cottage' is extraordinarily hard to express on the [silent] screen." Directors tried to reduce these "literary" interruptions to a minimum, and some got as low as a dozen an hour.

One way of escape from the lettered subtitle was the "insert." Inserts—letters, clocks, or newspaper items—were, after all, visual objects. They were less offensive than "Came the dawn" or "All the tears of the ages gushed over his heart" or "I'm going back to the country I like and where I belong. Will you come with me?" Present-day directors and screen writers strive to eliminate inserts. They try to supply information through dialogue or camera work; if it has to be in a letter, they may sometimes have the over-screen "thought voice" of the one who wrote the note repeat the words as the recipient reads it.

Spoken dialogue speeded up action. If you study almost any silent film that is not overloaded with subtitles, you will note how long it took characters to convey by action and pantomime what could be told through dialogue in a much shorter time.

Dialogue Makes the Film More Significant

Much more important, of course, was the power of dialogue to characterize people. For centuries good plays had demonstrated this. In silent films a man or a woman tended to be a stereotype—unless a subtitle provided an essay on his character. Working only with the camera, a director had to fall back on visual clichés. A man who stroked a cat was a good man; a man who kicked a dog was a bad man. Through spoken dialogue, on the other hand, a film could present well-rounded characters. Its men and women could have the breadth and depth of true humanity.

Out of this and out of much of the talk in a film, the screen at its best could give us content ranging from emotion to ideas. The moving picture was able at last to take on the high values that lie in the dialogue of a good play.

At first the problem of the talkie was to retain as much as possible of the unique pictorial meaning of moving pictures while adding the values of the spoken word. This was a most difficult problem and, even today, only the exceptional director succeeds in solving it. But when he does succeed, he demonstrates the vital superiority of the talking picture to the silent movie. As Roger Manvell has put it:

> The most delicate of all instruments, the human voice, and the most highly patterned and artificial of all sounds, musical composition, add their powers to the flow of mobile pictures. The beauties of the silent film seem elementary and oversimplified in comparison with the multi-dimensional experience the interplay of sound and pictures is able to create.

Sounds That Silent Films Needed

Of course there are other uses of sounds besides dialogue. These are not so important in terms of character and story content, but they may add greatly to the excitement of a scene, and they may help to make the emotions of a character clearer and more compelling. These sounds include the noise of machines, animals, and nature, and off-screen speech.

The early writers on the talkies were bothered a good deal over sound that was not synchronized dialogue. They pointed out some of the methods that silent producers had used to visualize sounds, and they debated whether such sounds should be heard while we looked at their source. There were deep doubts that an audience should see and hear a clock at the same time; this would mean a double and wasteful emphasis. Yet it was obvious that a clock couldn't go on ticking all through a scene, and it couldn't start ticking at a particular moment unless the camera brought us so close to it that we had to hear it. One writer said that *seeing* a dog bark was sufficient; to *hear* him, too, "adds nothing to the expressive qualities of the image," except "a gain in realism." (I don't think anyone explained that if we saw a watchdog asleep and then a man nervously attempting to enter a house, it would be much more effective to hear an off-screen bark than to cut to a silent shot of a dog barking.) In von Sternberg's silent film *The Docks of New York* (1928), a man fired a gun, and the director cut to a rising flock of startled birds. Arnheim claimed that this was not merely "a contrivance on the part of a director to deal with the evil of silence"; it was, "on the contrary, a positive artistic effect."

In silent comedies like Harold Lloyd's *The Freshman* (1925), a sound would often have been far more effective than a visualization of its source. For instance, during football practice Lloyd looked distressed over something and his legs seemed to be giving him trouble. A cut to a man splitting wood told us that the comedian thought he heard his bones cracking. If we had seen Lloyd's anguish and heard the noise, we would have thought, as he did, that it came from his bones; then, a cut to the real source of the noise would have made the gag more amusing than it was on the silent screen.

Obviously, off-screen sound could do many other things more effectively than visual images. Take the subjective reactions of characters under some tension like fear. Griffith used the material of Poe's *The Tell-Tale Heart* in the best of his early films, *The Avenging Conscience*. In the short story, the mind of the terror-stricken murderer, who has buried his victim beneath the floor, magnifies the imagined ticking of a watch into the fearsome beating of a human heart. If Griffith had been able to use sound, he could have swelled the ticking of the watch into throbbing and reverberant heartbeats. Instead, he introduced a subtitle approximating "Like the beating of a dead man's heart," and cut to the pendulum of a clock.

Alfred Hitchcock's first talkie, *Blackmail*, showed us the power of off-screen speech to dramatize subjective fear. In a silent film, if a woman committed murder and the director wanted to emphasize her fear of discovery without resorting to a subtitle, he would double-print over her closeup some newspaper headlines, accusing faces, great lips that seemed to shout her guilt. Through sound, Alfred Hitchcock got a more exciting effect. His heroine had stabbed a man who attempted to seduce her. At breakfast, she heard a neighbor discussing the murder and when she reached for a breadknife, the neighbor's conversation became indistinct except the word "knife," which echoed on the sound track over her tortured face.

Contrapuntal Sound That Is Realistic

Some early theorists on sound vs. silence often thought the off-screen speeches were "contrapuntal" when they were largely realistic. In Fritz

Lang's first talkie, *M* (1931), the unseen mother of a missing child—whom the audience knew had been murdered—called her name again and again over the empty stairs, the girl's empty plate on the table, her ball in the grass, and the balloon that her murderer had given her, which was now entangled in some telephone wires. Then there was the menace of the tune from Grieg that the killer whistled off-screen; heard by a blind beggar, it led at last to the murder's doom. Lang used with equal skill and enormous effectiveness other off-screen but natural sounds.

Pudovkin thought he was using contrapuntal sound in *Deserter* (1933) during a scene in the fog:

> For the symphony of siren calls with which *Deserter* opens I had six steamers playing in a space of a mile and a half in the Port of Leningrad. They sounded their calls to a prescribed plan and we worked at night in order that we should have quiet.

In 1954, without such a complicated operation, Elia Kazan mixed sound tracks of harbor noises in *On the Waterfront*, and used them with far greater imagination. They drowned out the attempt of a young tough, played by Marlon Brando, to justify himself to the heroine.

Eisenstein's "Monologue" Becomes Narration

Another use of the sound track was foreshadowed—and with rather absurd emphasis—by Eisenstein when he stated in 1932: "the true material of the sound film is, of course, the monologue." Now, there are monologues and monologues. When the chief of police in *M* told a higher official about what his detectives were doing, Lang cut to their activities, while the chief went on talking. Film-makers began to find in the off-screen voice of a character a useful way of conveying information and saving production costs. Thus, in *Stanley and Livingstone* (1939), Stanley's voice told the story of his search for Livingstone, while we watched silent shots made in Africa with "doubles." Next, the monologue became an envelope for the story and a subjective guide through its action; it was used effectively in *How Green Was My Valley* (1941), *Brief Encounter* (1945), and on through many more pictures. What Eisenstein called a "monologue" we now find in the narration of all but a very few of the nonfiction films that we speak of as documentaries. *Night Mail* (1936) from Basil Wright and Harry Watt, and Pare Lorentz's *The River* (1937) were early and notable examples.

Making the Talkies Filmic

While critics worried over the problems that sound created, workaday directors went on experimenting in its use. They recognized that the public wanted this novelty and wanted it badly. Arnheim had said that in a silent film, if people were walking across the screen no one missed the sound of their feet, but I remember with what excitement an audience recognized the crunch of the gravel as George Bernard Shaw strode down the garden path to make his first speech on film. Arnheim said that "one of the chief tasks of sound film is to avoid sounds." There was something in that. Talkies should not be merely stage plays photographed and recorded. But, on the other hand, it was foolish to avoid the use of dialogue to draw out character and increase excitement and pleasure. Directors like Lang and Pabst in Germany; René Clair, Feyder, Renoir, and Duvivier in France; Hitchcock and Alexander Korda in England; Vidor, Milestone, Lubitsch, Ford, Mamoulian, Frank Lloyd, Frank Capra, and many others sought more and more successfully to make a motion picture that would be filmic as well as audible. The Americans found an easy and an old form in the Western, and a new and lively vehicle in the gangster film. And directors of many nations learned how to make screen drama and comedy rich in content as well as kinetic in movement. The talkie became the movie at its best.

Chapter

21

How a
Major Studio Works

B<small>Y</small> 1930, <small>SOUND HAD</small> made the motion picture the most complex of the arts and also the most collaborative. Now television, whether live or shot on film or tape, has added the electronics of the broadcasting studio and the receiving set. As Eric Larrabee has said, "No more elaborate equipment exists than that by which Americans communicate with themselves."

Once upon a time—which, in the wonderland of the movies, means around 1900—film-making was rather simple. And it was not an art. One man with a motion picture camera and a couple of friends could turn out a few feet of comedy like *Watering the Gardener*. Most of the product lacked the modest artistry of still photography of the period. There was little composition and there were scant light values.

Making Silent Films Grows Complex

By 1905, film-making becomes a more elaborate business. Stories take the place of comic incidents. The length of the pictures increases as the camera is forced to record more than one scene. Plots begin to call for parlors and kitchens instead of just roads and gardens. So interior settings have to be built; out of doors at first, but soon in glass-walled studios. By 1910, directors discover that a scene can be more interesting and effective if it is shot from more than one angle. Out of this develops the art of editing, which is to reach its perfection in the silent "montage" of the Russians. When the feature film and the picture palace arrive, movie sets grow larger and fancier. For indoor scenes, electric light begins to replace the sun that had come through the walls of studios built like towering greenhouses. Out of doors, cameramen use reflectors to light faces that would otherwise be too much in shadow. Soon the camera starts to move in and out and round about on wheeled platforms.

The technical advances of twenty years produce division of labor. Gone are the days when actors like Maurice Costello protested at having to build scenery. Hundreds of men—carpenters, painters, electricians, property men, costume-makers, projectionists, members of camera crews, cutters—work only at their specialty. Smaller groups of specialists appear. There are technical experts and well-staffed research libraries to see that the habits and habitats of various peoples are not too absurdly distorted on the screen. "Script girls" make sure that the position of the pocket handkerchief of the hero matches perfectly in set-ups of the same scene taken on different days, and that a man doesn't go into a phone booth in a light suit and come out in black. Out of sight of the camera, men with violins play "side-line" music to put the actors "in the mood." To the complexities of making any single film, studios that are organized to turn out forty or fifty features a year add more complications and new kinds of collaboration. Executives grow in number. Story editors have staffs to read novels, plays, and "originals" written for the screen. Studio managers keep production moving. Producers, with the help of "supervisors," direct the directors when they can, and watch "rushes," the previous day's work, and budgets with equal interest. By 1925, an active studio employs a thousand or two thousand men and women every day.

Sound Called for Even More Collaboration

Sound altered and added much. It created still more complexities. Also, it increased the amount of creative collaboration that had to go on.

The writing and speaking of dialogue was, of course, the prime new factor. This curbed the powers of the director in certain areas, increased them in others, and changed some of his ways of work. Sound gave the screenplay and its author an importance that—in spite of Goldwyn—they had never known before. The director was forced into a new kind of collaboration with the writer. The actor, linked inescapably with the words of the script, became a more creative factor in production. The character that he played could no longer be manipulated or almost completely changed through subtitles. Finally, dialogue had a considerable effect on camerawork and the technique of cutting.

With sound came other new and complicated technical operations besides just getting dialogue on film. Songs, musical scores, and natural sounds had to be recorded. Then some or all of these had to be mixed with the dialogue track. This rerecording involved the use of new and very sensitive equipment. It meant adding more men to the studio staff—to some extent, more creators.

For a short time, the use of "ice boxes" brought down the cost of production. There were fewer set-ups and longer "takes," and this meant shorter shooting schedules. But as soon as directors like Mamoulian and Milestone, Vidor and von Sternberg, turned the camera into a free agent again, the making of a talkie became even more elaborate and costly than the making of a silent film. This—and the chill breath of the depression, which Hollywood at last began to feel in the early nineteen-thirties—called for a tighter, though more complex, form of studio organization.

Studio vs. Factory

In twenty years, through recovery, war boom, and recession, past television competition and wide-screen processes, Hollywood worked out a scheme of studio operation that seemed, at the time, if not completely stable, certainly adjustable. It wasn't as efficient and economical as a Detroit production line, but motion pictures can't be as uniform as a single make of automobile. As a matter of fact, they shouldn't be. We complained—and, in spite of the increase in independent producers, we still complain—about a certain sameness in Hollywood films, yet in the very way they have to be made there is a creative potential that breaks out, every now and then, in freshness and experimentation. Under the shiny bodywork of Hollywood's cars there may be new engines and new transmissions, or there may be old spark plugs and gas lines that have never worked together in quite the same way. Even in the old-line studios a happy combination of these things may turn out an entertainment vehicle of a fresh or even significant sort. This depends on the imagination and tact, the discernment and courage, the drive and sheer luck, of the man who dominates the film. Sometimes he is the producer, sometimes the director, usually a combination of both. Often he is a writer who has turned producer or director.

What Is a Producer?

In Hollywood mythology, a producer used to be "a man who asks a studio employee a question, gives him the answer, and tells him he's

wrong." Until the Screen Producers Guild emerged in 1950, hardly anyone tried to replace this portrait of egotistical incompetence with a
more realistic picture of a man who might be contributing creatively
to the screen.

At his worst, the producer may be a frightened fellow who keeps
his eye on the past and tries to turn out the sort of films that made
money last year. This kind of man lives in a world of cycles. He follows the patterns that others set. If some daring gambler puts his
money—or, rather the money of his studio or his backer—on number
13, and 13 comes up, then the producer I am talking about will play
that same number until his luck runs out. That is why we have had
cycle after cycle of films dealing with gangsters, back-stage life, the
Negro problem, anti-Semitism, Biblical characters, dope addiction,
comic GI's, juvenile delinquency, mythological heroes, Americans in
Japan, prostitutes with hearts of gold, adultery, and sexual deviates.
Fortunately, in the natural course of events—even Hollywood events
—producers who follow cycles and old patterns too closely sooner or
later eliminate themselves.

At his best, the producer has real creative power. He can recognize
a good story that doesn't follow a cyclic pattern or any current formula.
He can see how such a story must be handled to make an effective
contribution to the progress of the screen and the profits of the business. He can bring to it the writer and the director who will be sympathetic to the material and capable of getting the most out of it. The
creative producer will add to these elements good casting and even
good ideas about how to exploit the film, how to sell it to the theaters
and the public. The result will be successes like David O. Selznick's
Gone With the Wind (1939), Jesse L. Lasky's and Hal Wallis's *Sergeant York* (1941), Samuel Goldwyn's *The Best Years of Our Lives*
(1946), Darryl Zanuck's *The Snake Pit* (1948), Stanley Kramer's
Champion (1949), Dore Schary's *Battleground* (1949), Buddy Adler's
From Here to Eternity (1953), Mike Todd's *Around the World in
80 Days* (1956), Sam Spiegel's *The Bridge on the River Kwai* (1957)
and *Lawrence of Arabia* (1962), and Samuel Bronston's *El Cid* (1961).

What schooling need a producer have outside the studios of Hollywood and their New York offices? Higher education was not exactly
at a premium in the days of Lasky and Goldwyn, Fox and Laemmle.
Since then producers have varied widely in education and sophistication as well as ability. Charles Brackett, Arthur Hornblow, Jr., and
Harry Joe Brown studied law. David Selznick, Buddy Adler, William

Perlberg, Julian Blaustein, Walter Wanger, David Susskind, and Sol Siegel were Ivy Leaguers. Others went to state and city colleges. Sam Spiegel attended the University of Vienna, and likes to impress new colleagues with his Latin. On the other hand, lack of book learning never stopped Samuel Goldwyn from adding distinction to the screen as well as novelty to the English language. As an innocent bystander at a story conference I heard the very successful head of a studio (not Goldwyn), a man with one of the best story minds in Hollywood, give a writer this rough idea of a certain character: "That son of a bitch will go to no lengths to make the accusation stick."

The Old Order and the New

So far as the producer is concerned, the various Hollywood studios have seldom operated in quite the same way. There has been a general pattern, but with many variations. This has always made for a certain amount of healthy diversity and therefore, creativeness.

In each of the major studios there is one man, usually called Vice President in Charge of Production, who is responsible for its output. Up through the nineteen-forties, he kept a firm control, from the purchase of the story to the "sneak preview," on all pictures produced, except for some of the low-budget "B" pictures designed for double bills. He supervised some of these if they were of an unusual nature or presented opportunities to develop new stars or directors. Under him he had anywhere from a half-dozen to twenty-five men called producers or associate producers. Their work ranged from the herd-riding function of the old supervisor to something only a little below the importance and power of the head of the studio. Superior status depended on the success of the films that such men saw through production.

Between 1950 and 1955 the picture changed radically—and, I think, for the better. There was still a Vice President in Charge of Production, but he became more a manager than a producer. The studios curtailed the number of features, began to make TV films, to finance independent producers, and to lease their stages to these outsiders and to companies making films for television. But this is another story, for another chapter.

After the Screenplay—the Cast

What are the mechanics of film production, from finding a story to the sneak preview of the finished product? They vary, of course, with the size of the operation. Producing a program of feature films at a studio like Twentieth Century-Fox is more complicated than making an independent production. Yet a number of operations are common to both.

First of all comes the story; then the writer. How is the story chosen? What are the problems of the writer? These are crucial questions. They, too, are worth a chapter apiece. Here, in describing how a Hollywood studio works, I will presume that the screenplay has been finished to the satisfaction of the producer, the director, and in some cases the star. It is from this point that the complexities of production grow and grow until they make the screen the most collaborative of the arts.

Casting may be easy or difficult, but it always involves cooperation. Sometimes the story has been chosen and the script written to fit a star who has agreed to appear in the picture. Sometimes a star has to be found, sometimes two or three stars. If a vitally important actor falls ill, or if he is in another film that has lagged behind schedule, the producer may have to delay the starting date—which costs money— or search desperately for another star. In the sixties the huge salary demands of some dozen players made casting a long and difficult business.

The director and often the producer have ideas about actors for supporting roles. To help them, each major studio has a casting director and staff. Every four months the Academy of Motion Picture Arts and Sciences provides them with a *Players Directory* in two volumes totaling over 1,000 pages and carrying pictures and credits of at least 5,600 actors and actresses. The Association of Motion Picture Producers, Inc., founded by the majors, maintains Central Casting, which registers about 3,600 other men and women and calls them for work when studios need "walk-ons", mobs, or "dress extras." Dress extras who own enough modish clothes get $33.54 a day (circa 1962). With a simpler wardrobe, or wearing costumes supplied by the studio, other extras get $25.47. In 1962 the total wages of the extras came to more than $3,300,000.

Designing the Production

The planning of settings and wardrobe begins as soon as a shooting date is set. The art department in a major studio is run much like an architectural firm. The head sets the general tone of the production and supervises the work of a staff member assigned to the particular picture. Both confer with the producer and the director, and both usually get screen credit. The head of wardrobe works in somewhat the same way.

Plans, drawings, and sometimes models of sets, as well as costume sketches, have to be approved before production begins. The independent producer who works outside a major studio usually hires his designers for each film, though a very few keep an art director on salary. A "production designer" sometimes works out sketches of each set-up, as well as settings, in close collaboration with the director. William Cameron Menzies was one of the pioneers in this field, long before his outstanding job on *Gone With the Wind*. Architect William L. Pereira also worked in this way for Selznick, and Rudolph Sternad for Stanley Kramer.

One of the problems of the art director is when to be extravagant and when to be economical. The public all over the world has learned to expect from Hollywood—and, save the mark, to enjoy—something more than fidelity to life, something beyond reality, something glamorous and extravagant. Often this means something oversize. The ballroom of Versailles in *Marie Antoinette* (1938) was somewhat larger than the one that satisfied Sun King Louis XIV. The brigantine that MGM built for *Mutiny on the Bounty* (1962) outclassed the ship it had used twenty-five years before. The art department, on the other hand, tries to save time and money where penny pinching won't be obvious. It makes over "standing sets" such as restaurants and swank or not so swank apartments that have served earlier productions and have not been "struck," or dismantled. The same sort of adaptation goes for the shells of exteriors on the back lot or the ranch in the San Fernando Valley. The day of these architectural museums seemed to be passing when Hollywood began to make more and more productions abroad, when many majors sold their ranches, and when Twentieth Century-Fox disposed of its acres of black lot and watched bulldozers raze the Southern mansion where Shirley Temple once played, the Middle-Western farm of Will Rogers, the buildings that the Chicago Fire never really burned, the railroad station where many a star had boarded genuine Pullmans, the New England street where the sweetheart of Alexander Graham Bell once lived.

The Hollywood Paradox

Its trade, which is in dreams at so many dollars a thousand feet, is managed by business men pretending to be artists and by artists pretending to be business men. In this queer atmosphere, nobody stays as he was; the artist begins to lose his art, and the business man becomes temperamental and unbalanced.

—J. B. Priestley in *Midnight on the Desert*.

TWENTIETH CENTURY-FOX FILM CORPORATION

SHOOTING SCHEDULE FEBRUARY 18, 1939

Director___HENRY KING___ No._A-108_ Picture Title "STANLEY AND LIVINGSTONE"

Asst. Dir. - Robert Webb

DAY AND DATE	NO. DAYS	NAME OF SET & SCENE NUMBERS	CAST AND COSTUME NOS.		EXTRAS AND BITS	LOCATION
MON. 2/20	1	EXT. LONDON DOCK SEQ. L - DAY - SCS. 318-319- 320-321-322-324 325-326-327-328 329 5 P.	STANLEY JEFF GARETH EVE	#8 #8 #4 #5	X Men X Women X Children 2 Bit Reporters X Messenger Boys X Officers X Stevedores X English Boat Officials	STAGE 6
TUES. 2/21	1	EXT. DOCK AND PACKET STEAMER SEQ. N - DAY SCS. 398-399- 400 1 1/4 P.	STANLEY JEFF EVE GARETH	#10 #10 #7 #6	X Ship's Officers X Stevedores X Spectators X Passengers X Bit Boy	STAGE 6
WED. 2/22	1	INT. GEOGRAPH- ICAL SOCIETY HALLWAY AND ROOM - SEQ. L - DAY - SCS. 330- 331-332 3 3/4 P.	GARETH STANLEY LORD TYCE VANE FRENCH	#4 #8 #4 #1 #1	X Young Explorers X Smug-looking Gentleman	STAGE 14
THURS. 2/23 FRI. 2/24 SAT. 2/25	3	INT. PAVILLION SEQ. M - DAY - SCS. 337 to 397 Incl. 18 1/4 P.	STANLEY JEFF LORD TYCE GARETH EVE KINGSLEY CRANSTON FRENCH HOLCOMB SIR JOHN GRESHAM	#9 #9 #5 #5 #6 #4 #1 #2 #1 #1	"Sir Henry Forrester" 1 Bit Messenger X Men on Committee X Audience	PROCESS
NOTE:		- - - - - - - - Should Richard Greene be needed for Lanfield Company, #A-187, for one day, King Company will do Fort at Bagomayo and then continue as scheduled. - - - - - - - -			- - - - - - - -	- - - - - - - -
	1	EXT. FORT AT BAGOMAYO AND COURTYARD - SEQ. J - DAY - SCS. 124-125- 126-127-128-129 130-131-132 3 1/4 P.	JEFF STANLEY MOMBAY HASSAN	#7 #7 #1 #1	1 Bit "Webb" #1 X Natives in Safari	PROCESS STAGE 14
						WM. KOENIG

PART OF A SHOOTING SCHEDULE. Day by day the unit manager and the assistant director of a film issue a schedule of work for the next four or five days. It lists the sets, the cast and costumes required, and where the company will be.

The "location" department which catalogs exterior backgrounds isn't so busy as it once was, but it still has an elaborate file of photographs taken here and abroad. It can still show a director the deep front lawns of Topeka, conveniently at hand in a town of upper California, or a bit of the Sahara near Yuma, Arizona.

Other Studio Services

A surprising number of other services are at the disposal of the producer and the director working in a major studio. The special-effects department will provide all manner of trick shots, from painted backgrounds to "process" work and "traveling mattes," of which you will hear more later. Next to the carpentry and paint shops there may be an arsenal of a couple of thousand various weapons. For miniatures, a specialist in "greens" will supply dwarf vegetation to simulate almost any kind of natural growth. Another expert can offer snowflakes in several sizes. And for accidents and emergencies, there is usually a small hospital as well as a fire station located on each lot.

The research department usually has 20,000 to 40,000 bound books and periodicals—some quite rare in Southern California—files of clippings, and indexes of material that may be especially useful. For any production with an exotic background or historical content, the staff compiles loose-leaf books of photographs and articles. These serve the screen writer as well as the art and wardrobe departments. Research at Fox supplied over 800 words of "period" advertising and signs that were lettered on the windows and fronts of stores *In Old Chicago* (1938), for example, "Ladies' Dept. No Men Clerks."

In spite of all the efforts of the research department, things may go wrong, as when just before shooting, a director orders a sign reading "Paris 50 Kilometers" for a film story taking place a couple of years before the French Revolution spawned the metric system. Perhaps the producer didn't employ a "technical expert," who usually haunts the sets of historical films after he has vetted script, sets, props, and wardrobe.

The legal department is apt to be of more use to the staff producer than to the independent. One of its jobs is to avoid trouble. A common form of this is plagiarism claims. Too often either the higher authorities or the lawyers decide to settle such nuisance suits, which encourages more. Since the early thirties studios have leaned over backward to avoid litigation. Many times they buy biographies, even though (if the author is indeed reporting the truth and not writing fiction) the material is in the public domain. When RKO was producing *King Kong* (1933), it bought Conan Doyle's *The Lost World,* though the only resemblance between the two stories was that a pterodactyl in one case, and a gigantic ape in the other, were brought back to London and New York respectively.

Extreme legal caution probably stems from *Rasputin and the Empress* (1932), in which Ethel Barrymore played the Czarina; brother Lionel, Rasputin; and John a character named Prince Chegodieff. In the film Chegodieff murdered Rasputin after Princess Natasha had been raped by the redoubtable monk. Rasputin's real murderer, Prince Youssoupoff, sued MGM for libeling his wife, and won handsomely after he described how he had done Rasputin in. (Three years after this case, the legal columns of the London *Times* announced that an action against MGM by a Prince and Princess Chegodieff for both libel and slander had been settled out of court.) A less expensive case concerned Fox's *King of the Khyber Rifles.* This was not the film released in 1953, but the popular book by Talbot Mundy that the studio had bought twenty-five years before. When Zanuck took over Fox in 1935, he was intrigued by the title and horrified by the corny plot; consequently he asked me to have some writers develop a new story. After nine months gestation Boris Ingster and Milton Sperling had a script that satisfied Zanuck. The British authorities indicated that the film could not be shown in the United Kingdom, but that was not where the legal department—and the amusement—came in. When Fox had filmed the book in 1929, it had used the absurd plot, but changed the glamorous title to *The Black Watch* (Britain frowned on this, too). After the new script was finished the legal department reread the contract with the author, and discovered that if the studio used the title of the book, it had to use the plot, too. In 1953, after some negotiations with the author's estate, the words *King of the Khyber Rifles* on theater marquees heralded a third story laid in and around the famous pass of northwest India.

Hollywood Ways to Economy

In a major studio or on an independent production there are plenty of men trying to cut the costs of film-making. This is largely in preplanning. After the script is finished, most of the cast signed up, and the set designs and costuming approved, the assistant director works out a shooting schedule that will suit the director and at the same time cut production costs. He organizes the shooting in such a way that scenes involving expensive players who are paid by the week may be filmed as soon as possible on consecutive days. At the same time he tries to avoid the costs of moving from one stage to another and then back again; he tries to bunch together all work on location. This explains why scripts are almost never shot in continuity, why the first scenes are sometimes the last to be photographed or vice versa. When a film involves shooting away from Hollywood, the weather poses a problem; if it rains, the cast can't be brought back to the studio to shoot interiors until the skies clear. In the case of *Shane* (1953), which took the company to Jackson Hole, Wyoming, for weeks of work outdoors, the staff arranged to turn a local hall into a small studio where interiors could be built and shot.

The Financial Watchdogs

Men from the various departments involved in production prepare cost estimates in their fields. These are brought together and listed on a budget sheet covering about forty items. In some studios most of these items are broken down on perhaps twenty separate pages. At what is called a budget meeting, attended by the producer, the director, his staff, and the heads of departments, all the items are examined and revised to fit roughly a previously approved cost. Watching over the preplanning and continuing on until the end of shooting, is the "unit manager," representative of the "production office." He sees that the producer, among others, gets a "daily production report." This includes such items as the number of elapsed days and those remaining, the time when the cast and staff began work and finished, the footage of film used, the script scenes shot, any retakes made, the number of minutes photographed, a list of all the set-ups, or camera positions, along with the lenses used. There is usually a "daily budget reconciliation" that shows how much money has been spent and will be spent, and whether the film is running under or over budget.

The daily cost of shooting varies as much from film to film as the total cost of production and the length of the shooting schedule. At a major studio in the nineteen-sixties, a day's shooting of a film might cost anywhere between $10,000 and $30,000. *One-Eyed Jacks*—which began as a purchased story in the summer of 1957 and reached the screen four years later—is said to have cost close to $50,000 a day on a schedule that grew from sixty days to six months.

The layman may be surprised to hear that even a very economical professional production, in most cases can't be shot with a crew of less than fifty. When he watches shooting on a sound stage, he may feel that too many men seem to be doing nothing. Yet all this staff is essential, for any delay through lack of manpower to meet an emergency will

Release Season	1939-1940			TWENTIETH CENTURY-FOX FILM CORPORATION		Production No.	A 108	Class A
Starting Date	February 2-1939			PRODUCTION BUDGET		Producer	Kenneth MacGowan	
Finishing Date	April 1-1939			STANLEY AND LIVINGSTONE		Director	Henry King	No.18
Production Days	50 & 1 Da. Travel			RELEASE TITLE		Title	STANLEY AND LIVINGSTONE	

Acct. No.	DESCRIPTION	Sheet No.	BUDGET Cost To Jan. 21st	BUDGET To Complete	BUDGET Total	ACTUAL COST	OVER OR (UNDER) BUDGET
101	Story Rights and Expense	6				12,000.00	12,000.00
102	Scenario Cost	6	121,278.91	1,150.00	122,428.91	123,743.83	1,314.92
103	Music Department	17	13.61	13,551.67	13,565.28	33,531.94	19,966.66
104	Direction and Supervision	5	13,863.44	100,000.00	113,863.44	115,703.22	1,839.78
105	Staff Cost	5	70,059.78	10,541.50	80,601.28	81,773.21	1,171.93
110	Cast	2	16,652.31	135,009.09	151,661.40	159,322.60	7,661.20
111	Extras	3	7,233.17	22,478.33	29,711.50	26,860.67	(2,850.83)
112	Singers and Chorus Salaries	7		1,000.00	1,000.00	1,888.45	888.45
114	Art Cost	8	6,464.74	8,057.82	14,522.56	14,507.17	(15.39)
115	Set Cost	4	7,229.96	49,116.54	56,346.50	57,892.56	1,546.06
	Strike Labor	4	186.81	4,500.00	4,686.81	6,680.51	1,993.70
	Transportation	4	32.33	6,310.00	6,342.33	3,937.17	(2,405.16)
116	Operating Labor and Material	8	4,686.54	27,158.50	31,845.04	23,047.54	(8,797.50)
117	Miniature Cost	10		2,355.00	2,355.00	980.86	(1,374.14)
118	Camera Department	9	13,060.22	9,171.00	22,231.22	21,343.13	(888.09)
119	Sound Department	9	38.37	7,274.00	7,312.37	7,129.27	(183.10)
120	Electrical Department	9	153.03	13,621.95	13,774.98	18,430.51	4,655.53
121	Special Effects	10	1,072.74	6,406.00	7,478.74	6,764.32	(714.42)
122	Snow Dressing	14				77.85	77.85
123	Set Dressing Cost	11	2,026.76	18,161.50	20,188.26	16,354.91	(3,833.35)
124	Animals and Action Devices	11	91.07	2,150.00	2,241.07	3,510.80	1,269.73
125	Wardrobe Department	12	3,583.14	18,557.39	22,140.53	17,328.60	(4,811.93)
126	Make-up Department	13	1,120.14	8,708.40	9,828.54	10,166.64	338.10
127	Scenic Art Department	10	2,095.04	6,125.00	8,220.04	6,302.09	(1,917.95)
128	Process Department	10	10,528.79	14,250.00	24,778.79	22,930.07	(1,848.72)
129	Re-Recording Department	14		6,186.40	6,186.40	12,755.25	6,568.85
130	Editorial Department	8	1,916.12	5,420.00	7,336.12	6,597.99	(738.13)
140	Production Film Cost	15	5,365.67	25,649.95	31,015.62	21,263.33	(9,752.29)
141	Still Department	5	1,458.80	2,520.83	3,979.63	4,068.32	88.69
142	Title Department	14		755.00	755.00	788.07	33.07
143	Insert Department	14	35.06	1,535.00	1,570.06	1,106.30	(463.76)
144	Optical Printing Department	14	4.25	1,014.00	1,018.25	909.22	(109.03)
145	Fades and Dissolves	14		317.00	317.00	1,979.28	1,662.28
150	Insurance and Tax	14	11,534.54	20,065.00	31,599.54	30,887.59	(711.95)
160	Location Expense	16	106,181.25	5,415.00	111,596.25	114,657.84	3,061.59
165	Stock Film Library Cost	15	336.77	1,830.00	2,166.77	4,246.03	2,079.26
170	Miscellaneous	13	3,391.77	4,175.00	7,566.77	9,690.34	2,123.57
180	Overhead	17	104,547.02	218,845.44	323,392.46	336,769.21	13,376.75
	TOTALS		516,242.15	779,382.31	1,295,624.46	1,337,926.69	42,302.23

Principal Players	Story Certification

Spencer Tracy, Walter Brennan, Sir Cedric
Hardwicke, Richard Greene, Nancy Kelly,
Henry Travers, Henry Hull, Charles Coburn

Script Dated Jan. 18-1939   Title STANLEY & LIVINGSTONE

Approved for Production
By (Sgd.) Wm. Goetz

Actual Time	Budget Certifications

Date Started Feb. 2-1939 Finished Mar. 31-1939
Date Shipped Jul. 14-1939 Released Aug. 18-1939
Days Production ____49____ Retakes, Added Scenes, etc. 2

Date Compiled: Jan. 25-1939

(Sgd.) A. M. Gameral
Estimator

(Sgd.) F. L. Metzler
Studio Treasurer

(Sgd.) K. MacGowan
Associate Producer

Remarks

Added cost to production on account of
re-scoring and additional scoring in excess
of originally anticipated   34,000.00
2 days added scenes & retakes   8,000.00
Total amount over budget   42,000.00

Correct: (Sgd.) V.J. Christensen
Head of Estimating Dept.

Producer

(Sgd.) Wm. Goetz
Executive Assistant to Vice-President

Approved For $1,296,000.00

(Sgd.) Wm. Koenig
General Production Manager

(Sgd.) D. Zanuck
Vice-President in Charge of Production

PRODUCTION BUDGET—COMPLETED. *Stanley and Livingstone* (1939).
The original budget is in the third column; more than thirty items
were broken down on successive pages. The first column shows
what had been spent in preparation and on the second unit in
Africa before work began on the sound stages; the second column
shows what then remained to be spent. The total actual cost appears in the fourth column, while the fifth shows how much each
item was over (or under) budget. Such careful, detailed cost
accounting has long been the custom in Hollywood.

DAILY PRODUCTION REPORT

DIRECTOR___HENRY KING_____ DATE_____April 6, 1939.

WORKING TITLE___STANLEY AND LIVINGSTONE_____ DATE STARTED___February 1, 1939.

PICTURE NO.___A-108_____ ESTIMATED FINISH DATE___April 1, 1939.

ALLOTTED DAYS___50_____ ELAPSED DAYS___50_____ STATUS___PICTURE CLOSED____
                                                           TONIGHT.

SET. INT._____ SET NO._____

SET. EXT.___UJIJI and AFRICAN JUNGLES_____ SET NO._____

LOCATION:___STAGE 8 AND NORTH LOT, STUDIO_____

TIME		NEGATIVE REPORT			SCRIPT REPORT	
NO. SCENES ESTIMATED DAILY	8	PICTURE NEGATIVE			SCRIPT SCENES	
NO. SCENES TAKEN DAILY		Good	WASTE		SCENES IN SCRIPT	403
COMPANY CALLED	Crew 8:00 AM / Cast 9:00 AM	USED PREV. 198,172	PREV. 18,263		TAKEN PREV.	287
SOUND CALLED	8:30 AM	USED TODAY 1,795	TODAY 205		TAKEN TODAY	
LINING UP & REHEARSING	"	USED TO DATE 199,967	TOTAL 18,468		TOTAL TO DATE	287
1st SHOT	9:40 AM	TOTAL USED TO DATE	218,435	TO BE TAKEN (Credit)		116
LUNCH	12:15 PM	SOUND TRACK NEGATIVE			ADDED SCENES	
SOUND	"	Good	WASTE		TAKEN PREV.	316
LINING UP & REHEARSING	1:00 PM	USED PREV. 112,122	PREV. 20,076		TAKEN TODAY	11
1st SHOT	1:28 PM	USED TODAY 4,270	TODAY 920		TOTAL TO DATE	327
DINNER		USED TO DATE 116,392	TO DATE 20,996		RETAKES	
SOUND		TOTAL USED TO DATE	137,388	TAKEN PREV.		38
LINING UP & REHEARSING		STILLS	PROC. & MISC.		TAKEN TODAY	2
1st SHOT		TAKEN PREV. 544	21,085		TOTAL TO DATE	40
COMPANY FINISHED	6:35 PM	TAKEN TODAY ---	960		TOTAL SCENES TAKEN TODAY	13
SOUND FINISHED	"	TOTAL 544	22,045		TOTAL SCENES TAKEN TO DATE	654

SCENE NO._____

CREDITS_____

ADDED SCENES___91B, 92D, 92E, 142, 142A, 176, 176A, 231, 231A, 244, 263A

RETAKES___R159B, R153C_____EXTRA SOUND TRACKS 1530, 1531, 1532, 1533

TIME CALLED	CAST	TIME DISMISSED	TIME RECALLED	SPEAKING BITS	EXTRAS MUSICIANS—STOCK—CAMERAMEN
9:00AM	Spencer Tracy	2:00PM	See Remarks		22 Extras
"	Hassan Said	3:00PM	Closed		
"	Jack Clisby	"	"		J. Schumacher (Standin)
					PROCESS CREW
					SPECIAL EFFECTS
					WELFARE WORKER
					CAMERA CREW
					G. Barnes 8:30AM-6:35PM
					I. Rosenberg " "
					J. Warren 8:15AM-6:45PM
					P. Garnett 9:00AM "

ADVANCE SCHEDULE

DATE___PICTURE FINISHED_____ TIME CALLED_____

SET_____ SET NO._____ LOCATION_____

SEQUENCES_____

DAILY MINUTES		REMARKS
PREV. TIME	1 Hr. 43' 28"	5 EXTRAS CALLED AT 7:00AM; 8 AT 8:30AM; 9 AT 9:00AM; LUNCH 12:15AM-1:15PM; 12 DISMISSED AT 1:45 PM; OTHERS DISMISSED 2:45PM.
TODAY'S TIME	40"	
TOTAL TIME	1 Hr. 44' 08"	ENTIRE CASE AND CREW CLOSED TONIGHT. JACK CLISBY STARTED AND CLOSED TODAY. SPENCER TRACY WILL RE-RECORD AFRICAN SPEECHES TONIGHT AT 8:30 PM.- THEN WILL BE FINISHED.
DELAYS RESULTING FROM ILLNESS OF CAST REPORT FULL DETAILS AND SHOW TIME LOST		

SIGNED___ROBT. WEBB_____ APPROVED___Tom Loeweg____
           ASST. DIRECTOR   PRODUCTION MANAGER

FORM 454A SM 11-37

WHAT THE COMPANY HAS ACCOMPLISHED. Every day the assistant director fills out a form that shows in great detail the work of the past eight or ten hours. On the back is a list of all set-ups, including the lens used, the length of each take in minutes and seconds, and the takes approved by the director.

mean a greater increase in shooting costs than the salaries of the men who may not seem to be doing anything.

Final Complexities

When the film is "in the can," production is still far from over. The final editing of the picture and its sound tracks, the writing and recording of the musical score, and the laboratory work involved in making a final print don't mean that all the work is over. Finally comes the "sneak preview" and the attempt to evaluate the entire picture and its individual scenes with the assistance of an audience. Sometimes such a preview means very little. Paramount showed *The Lost Weekend* (1945) to an audience in San Francisco that had come to see a musical. The result of this and other previews was so disappointing that Paramount decided to release it merely as one of a group of films (this was when block-booking was still permitted). After the picture created a sensation when shown to an audience that was prepared for this study in alcoholism, the distributor yanked it out of block-booking, and sold it as a "special."

But before a picture can reach this final stage, film-making reaches its highest complexity. When the weeks of script-writing and preparation for production are over, when actors, cameramen, cutters, and crew are at work, then the closest of collaboration is called for. The center of this complexity and collaboration is the director, but there are many other factors, as will be seen in later chapters, that we must consider.

A Rose by Any Other Name

Following the *noms de théâtre* of two distinguished men of the European theater, here are the real names of a number of screen players of the talkie era, and the elegant aliases that they preferred.

Constantine Sergeyvich Alexeyev	Constantine Stanislavsky	Frederick Austerlitz	Fred Astaire
Max Goldmann	Max Reinhardt	Anna Maria Italiano	Anne Bancroft
Eddie Albert Heimberger	Eddie Albert	Marjorie Bitzer	Lynn Bari
John F. Sullivan	Fred Allen	Benny Kubelsky	Jack Benny
Eunice Quedens	Eve Arden	Milton Berlinger	Milton Berle
Guenther Schneider	Edward Arnold	Israel Baline	Irving Berlin
		Vivian S. Stapleton	Vivian Blaine

Martha Janet Lafferty	Janet Blair	James Stewart	Stewart Granger
Thelma Ford	Shirley Booth	Archibald Alexander Leach	Cary Grant
Nathan Birnbaum	George Burns	Zelma Hedrick	Kathryn Grayson
Richard Jenkins	Richard Burton	Harlean Carpentier	Jean Harlow
Aaron Schwatt	Red Buttons	Edythe Marrener	Susan Hayward
Mario Moreno	Cantinflas	Margarita Cansino	Rita Hayworth
Ira Grossel	Jeff Chandler		
Tula Ellice Finklea	Cyd Charisse	Audrey Hepburn-Ruston	Audrey Hepburn
Blanca Rosa Welter	Linda Christian	William Franklin Beedle	William Holden
Louis Francis Cristillo	Lou Costello	Judith Tuvim	Judy Holliday
Bernard Schwartz	Tony Curtis	Leslie Stainer	Leslie Howard
Walden Robert Cassotto	Bobby Darin	Roy Fitzgerald	Rock Hudson
Doris von Kappelhoff	Doris Day	Henry H. McKinnies	Jeffrey Hunter
Peggy Middleton	Yvonne de Carlo	Martin Fuss	Ross Hunter
Diana Fluck	Diana Dors	Art Gelien	Tab Hunter
Isur Danielovitch	Kirk Douglas	Phyllis Isley	Jennifer Jones
Melvyn Hesselberg	Melvyn Douglas	William Henry Pratt	Boris Karloff
Fabian Forte Bonaparte	Fabian	Elia Kazanjoglous	Elia Kazan
Grace Stansfield	Gracie Fields	Constance Keane	Veronica Lake
William Joseph Shields	Barry Fitzgerald	Hedy Kiesler	Hedy Lamarr
Marilyn Louis	Rhonda Fleming	Alfredo Arnold Cocozza	Mario Lanza
Frances Gumm	Judy Garland	Rosetta Jacobs	Piper Laurie
James Baumgarner	James Garner	Rose Louise Hovick	Gypsy Rose Lee
		Jeanette Helen Morrison	Janet Leigh

A Rose by Any Other Name (Cont'd)

Viven Mary Hartley	Vivien Leigh	Maureen Fitzsimmons	Maureen O'Hara
Joseph Levitch	Jerry Lewis	Edward Flanagan	Dennis O'Keefe
Jane Peters	Carole Lombard	Suzanne Burce	Jane Powell
Sophia Scicolone	Sophia Loren	Robert Preston Meservey	Robert Preston
Dolly Loehr	Diana Lynn	George Ranft	George Raft
Robert Moseley	Guy Madison	Helen Beck	Sally Rand
Mary Tomlinson Krebs	Marjorie Main	Donna Mullenger	Donna Reed
Malden Sekulovich	Karl Malden	Emanuel Goldenberg	Edward G. Robinson
Jayne Palmer	Jayne Mansfield	Virginia Katherine McMath	Ginger Rogers
Frederick McIntyre Bickel	Fredric March	Leonard Slye	Roy Rogers
Dino Crocetti	Dean Martin	Luis Antonio Damasco De Alonso	Gilbert Roland
Ilona Hajmassy	Ilona Massey	Joe Yule, Jr.	Mickey Rooney
Ethel Zimmerman	Ethel Merman	Harriette Lake	Ann Sothern
		Kim Reid	Kim Stanley
Reginald Truscott-Jones	Ray Milland	Ruby Stevens	Barbara Stanwyck
Norma Jean Mortenson	Marilyn Monroe	Patrick Barry	Barry Sullivan
Muni Weisenfreund	Paul Muni	Spangler Arlington Brough	Robert Taylor
Marjorie Robertson	Anna Neagle	Marion Michael Morrison	John Wayne
Lewis D. Offield	Jack Oakie	Shirley Schrift	Shelley Winters
Estelle Merle O'Brien Thompson	Merle Oberon	Natasha Gurdin	Natalie Wood
		Sarah Jane Fulks	Jane Wyman

Chapter

22

The Old Order Changeth

As stars began to set up their own producing companies in the nineteen-fifties, some Hollywood executives echoed the famous quip of thirty years before when Charlie Chaplin, Mary Pickford, Douglas Fairbanks, and D. W. Griffith formed United Artists: "The lunatics have taken over the asylum." Somehow the new crop of lunatics managed pretty well. By 1960 they were riding high. "Sinatra," read a headline in *Daily Variety,* "Sets $15 Mil UA Deal. Will Star in Program of Pics Under His Essex Banner." This somewhat temperamental actor had already proved his good sense as a producer. "Who do you think came in under budget?" asked an executive of the corporation that had financed him. "Frank Sinatra."

The Czar Becomes Negotiator

Producers and directors, as well as stars, set up their own companies. As independent producers they made over the face of Hollywood; they clipped the wings on which the Vice President in Charge of Production had soared for more than a generation. Darryl Zanuck summed up the new status of the head of a studio when he called him merely "a negotiator, an executive, a peacemaker. Everyone," he complained, "was becoming a corporation, with their own managers, their own agents, their own lawyers. You can't deal with individuals any longer."

So far as a studio's own productions were concerned, its head still approved the stars and the subject matter of the pictures, and usually the scripts. He set the budgets. He had the final say on editing. But the producers under him enjoyed power and responsibility they had never known before, and they had a share in the problematical profits. Beyond this modification of the old routine, something radically new developed. Making deals to finance films for other producers, for directors, and even for stars, became a major task of the head of the studio. How different from the old days when a Thalberg, a Mayer, a Lasky, a Zanuck, or a Wallis was called "the Czar of all the rushes"! However, studio executives still enjoyed six-figure salaries, just like the men who ran General Motors or U. S. Steel. But in the nineteen-sixties it became clear that studio heads had better wake up to the fact that the future was not so rosy as it used to seem. Indeed, the present, in terms of the Hollywood they had known, was unbelievably drab. Others were making more money. Worse still, beset by the independents, the men who ran the studios had much less power. Their egos suffered. They had been used to dealing as equals with Alfred Hitchcock and John Ford. And now to defer to Gregory Peck or Rock Hudson—! Small wonder that the far-sighted Hal Wallis left Warner Brothers in 1944 to set up his own company, and that Jerry Wald, Darryl Zanuck, and Don Hartman later stepped down—or was it up?—to become independent producers.

By 1960 it was hard to find a creative producer willing to run a major studio; Sol Siegel at MGM was the only exception and within two years he resigned. A screen writer summed up the matter when he said of the film called *The Incredible Shrinking Man*, "It is not the story of a Hollywood studio head, though it might be." And *Variety* wryly remarked that a studio would soon have to advertise:

> Wanted: Top production executive: young and energetic with strong administrative qualities and a creative bent; must be able to get along with independent producers on the Coast and home office executives in New York. Salary: Tops plus percentage. Applications will be kept confidential —*as long as possible*.

Independents of Earlier Days

Independent producers are not a new phenomenon, nor are stars and directors with a share in the profits. But we have to go back to the silent days to find as many, perhaps, as we have now. In 1914 W. W. Hodkinson set up Paramount Pictures to finance Zukor, Lasky, and others. A few years later First National and United Artists followed somewhat the same pattern. At one time or another, D. W. Griffith, Charlie Chap-

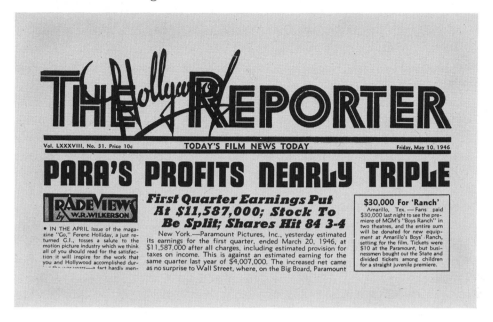

THE TOP OF THE BOOM. Here in a headline of *The Hollywood Reporter,* one of the trade dailies of the industry, we have evidence of moving picture prosperity at its peak in 1946, before war prosperity ended and the blight of television had come.

lin, and Harold Lloyd had their own companies. Paramount set one up for Mary Pickford. C. B. DeMille and Gloria Swanson left that studio to be—somewhat disastrously—their own producers. Just before Irving Thalberg died, MGM had agreed to a deal much like the one that Zanuck made with Fox when he gave up studio management and $5,000 a week in exchange for a free hand with his own productions and a reputed 50 percent of their profits. When silence was still golden, stars like Anita Stewart, Clara Kimball Young, and Louise Glaum had their own companies and a cut in the profits. Erich von Stroheim and Victor Seastrom often had a percentage; King Vidor's contract called for 20 percent of *The Big Parade* (1925) until the wily L. B. Mayer sweet-talked him into settling for less. Directors like Frank Lloyd, Hobart Henley, and Victor Schertzinger provided many a major with films that were advertised as "A So-and-so Production." But the productions of these independents were a drop in the bucket. In 1928 the head of a studio was still a busy fellow and a powerful one.

Independents Born of TV Panic

After sound came in, there were only a very few men—Samuel Goldwyn, Walt Disney, David Selznick for a time—who could establish or success-fully maintain their own producing companies truly free of control by studios or banks. It was terror of television in the fifties that created a spate of lesser independents both outside the studios and within them. Panicked by the box office slump, the majors tried to cut costs by dropping their leading contract players and directors when option time came round. United Artists, a releasing company without a studio, woke up from years of sleep, and began to finance stars as well as directors; soon new corpora-tions, like the Mirisch Company and Seven Arts Productions, Ltd., owning neither studios nor distributing subsidiaries, arose to back independents. Thus Burt Lancaster (with his partner and former agent, Harold Hecht), Kirk Douglas, Gregory Peck, Marlon Brando, Bob Hope, John Wayne, Cary Grant, and a number of other stars found ready backing. Some of the new independents were directors—for example, George Stevens, Wil-liam Wyler, Alfred Hitchcock, Elia Kazan, Otto Preminger. Some had been writers as well—John Huston, Richard Brooks, Billy Wilder, Delmer Daves, Robert Rossen, Joseph Mankiewicz, George Seaton in partnership with William Perlberg. A few, like Sam Spiegel and Arthur Hornblow, had been salaried producers. When the screen writers went on strike in 1960, they had to blacklist no less than fifty-six independent companies; some independents, of course, had more than one corporation. The studios kept many of their producing staff in line—Sam Engel, Pandro Berman, Arthur Freed, for instance—by giving them a share in the profits of their pictures in exchange for a modest cut in salary.

Creators Under Contract—1940 to 1960

	1940	1945	1950	1955	1960
Actors	458	804	474	209	139
Writers	375	490	147	67	48
Directors	117	152	99	79	24

These figures from five issues of *The Film Daily Year Book* estimate the number of actors, writers, and directors under contract to the majors during the previous year. They show how drastically the Holly-wood studios economized—in the wrong areas—when television began to make inroads on box office receipts.

Does Independence Insure Quality?

Through all this, Hollywood has been approaching England's free-and-easy mixture of independent film-makers and of producing and distributing companies, a system that nurtured a certain amount of distinction. As yet America has not fully met the early challenge of *The Stars Look Down* (1939), *Brief Encounter* (1945), *Henry V* (1944), *Tight Little Island* (1949), or *Kind Hearts and Coronets* (1949). Nevertheless, the Hollywood independents have added much to the quality of our films. From 1954 through 1962, they produced seven of the nine films that won Oscars as the best picture of the year: *On the Waterfront* (1954), *Marty* (1955), *Around the World in 80 Days* (1956), *The Bridge on the River Kwai* (1957), *The Apartment* (1960), *West Side Story* (1961) (when all five nominees came from independents) and *Lawrence of Arabia* (1962). The complications of financing, production, and distribution reached a climax in *West Side Story*, billed by *Variety* as "United Artists release of the Robert Wise production presented by Mirisch Pictures in association with Seven Arts."

There were other independent films of unusual merit: *All the King's Men* (1949), *The African Queen* (1951), *A Streetcar Named Desire* (1951), *High Noon* (1952), *Roman Holiday* (1953), *Baby Doll* (1956), *Paths of Glory* (1957), *Twelve Angry Men* (1957), *God's Little Acre* (1958), *Separate Tables* (1958), *The Defiant Ones* (1958), *Odds Against Tomorrow* (1959), *The Diary of Anne Frank* (1959), *The Sundowners* (1960), *The Hustler* (1961), *Judgment at Nuremberg* (1961), *Advise and Consent* (1962) and *Lilies of the Field* (1963).

Yet independent producers don't necessarily make better pictures. They have turned out plenty of trash—obvious horror films, absurd science fiction, blatant exploitations of sex, violent gangster yarns, all of them cheaply made "quickies." On the other hand, some of the most ambitious and expensive "block-busters"—*John Paul Jones* (1959) and *Alexander the Great* (1956), for example—fell on their empty faces. Gregory Peck botched the editing of *Pork Chop Hill* (1959). A star isn't always the best judge of the parts that fit him.

Independent producers are seldom as truly independent as they would like to be. Unless they have the unusual stature of Goldwyn or Disney, they must get their stories, as well as their stars, okayed by a distributor or a bank or both before they are given a release or the money for production. The distributor or the bank will be looking for the same story values as the head of a studio. Will these make a film that hundreds of millions of people will enjoy? The independent must think of financial success in big terms, if he hopes to make another film. He is under pressure to seek the lowest common denominator of that huge audience, and unfortunately, the surest and easiest way of finding this is to cater to majority opinion and majority interests. If the producer wants more freedom and less risk he must find some way of holding down production costs without sacrificing quality or box office draw.

"Deferment" Becomes "Participation"

One way to hold down costs is to persuade a star, a director, and sometimes a writer, too, to take less than his regular salary in exchange for a share of the profits. Twenty years ago small-time producers used this "deferment," as it was then called, to help finance minor films. Stanley Kramer set the pattern for his successful career as an independent by applying it to significant material and producing in partnership with Carl Foreman and Mark Robson *Champion* (Kirk Douglas took part of the risk) and *Home of the Brave* (1949). Working in much the same fashion, Kramer made *High Noon* (1952) for only $750,000 because Gary Cooper took a cut in salary and got, in compensation, what is now called a "participation."

In the second half of the nineteen-fifties participation took a new turn. Gone were thoughts of economy. After the success of *High Noon*, Gary Cooper and other stars participated with great enthusiasm, but they insisted on getting their regular salaries as well as a share of the film's profits or even of its gross income. And the salaries grew larger and larger as their agents realized how essential these actors were to the financing of productions. By 1960 the economics of the independent producer were tied in with the economics of some fifteen stars, six of whom were over fifty and looked it. Unless he had one, or more often two, of them committed to a picture, he couldn't get substantial backing and a release. The banks and the distributors ignored the fact that though a star's name could help a good picture, no star could save a story that the public didn't like. Gary Cooper couldn't salvage *The Court-Martial of Billy Mitchell* (1955), Tony Curtis and Burt Lancaster *Sweet Smell of Success* (1957), John Wayne *The Barbarian and the Geisha* (1958), Clark Gable and Lancaster *Run Silent, Run Deep* (1958), or Lancaster, Kirk Douglas, and Laurence Olivier *The Devil's Disciple* (1959). There are many more examples.

Huge Salaries As Well As Participations

With or without a cut of gross or net, the salaries of fifteen to twenty Hollywood players became fantastic at the end of the nineteen-fifties. In the pages of *Variety* these stars glittered in magnitudes of $500,000 to $1,000,000 per film. Ten years before, the majors had paid no such sums for yearly contracts, with twelve-week lay-offs. One-sided participation became the rule. An actor like Clark Gable—not so popular as of yore—could rival Elizabeth Taylor by getting $500,000 and 10 percent of the gross; then Miss Taylor's guarantee would double. Other actors who have taken such participations are Kirk Douglas, Cary Grant, Marlon Brando, Gary Cooper, Jimmy Stewart, Tony Curtis, Burt Lancaster, Gregory Peck, William Holden, John Wayne, Frank Sinatra, Audrey Hepburn, and Marilyn Monroe. The most fantastic deal was probably the one set up by two writers turned producers, John Lee Mahin and Martin Lee Rackin, for *The Horse Soldiers* (1959). John Wayne and William Holden were said to have received $750,000 each, as well as 20 percent of the profits; John Ford rated only $200,000 plus 10 percent of the producers' share after it reached twice the negative cost (the total expenditure on the film before prints and advertising costs are added).

Of course a cut of the gross is a lot safer than a share of the problematical profits; the ratio is, generally speaking, 10 percent of the first or 50 percent of the latter. Harry Belafonte is said to have gotten a salary of $350,000 for *The World, the Flesh, and the Devil* (1959), and not a cent from his half of the nonexistent profits. Jimmy Stewart had confidence enough to go for broke in much the same manner. Paramount is said to have split 70 percent of the net of *White Christmas* (1954) among Bing Crosby, Danny Kaye, and Irving Berlin. Naturally, studios like to see a star take the bigger risk; he may work harder, and faster. Also, the 30 percent of the gross charged for distribution leaves a tidy profit for the producing corporation.

The Tax Dilemma of the Star

Taxwise, the way of the star is dolorous. So is the way of the prosperous director. Before the star reaches box office maturity, he pays the government no more than does the average head of a small business. When he clicks, Uncle Sam puts the bite on. If a married actor earns $300,000 a year, taxes eat up all but about $75,000. If he earns $100,000 more, he gets only about $9,000 of this. If he is lucky he has fifteen or twenty years of big income—and huge taxes. Then his popularity is over and his earnings, as well as his taxes, shrink. Thus it is a matter of feast or famine. Unlike the owner of an oil well, he gets no tax relief of 27½ percent to take care of the years of depletion to come.

I doubt whether stars like Kirk Douglas or John Wayne knew a few years ago that the maximum tax on the income of a corporation is only 52 percent, and the tax on capital gains (profit on the sale of goods or stocks) is a mere 25 percent. But when his agent explained this to a star, and began to talk to him about setting up his own producing company, he listened intently. This looked like a way to minimize his taxes as well as maximize his ego. (To the director more control of the film was an added lure.)

Alas, the vision of vast savings through personal incorporation soon began to fade. The eye of the tax man was alert. At best, the star had to watch the government take 52 percent of the corporation's income and, if the company was very successful, he had to pay a big tax on what was left—when he got it. Unless his corporation had made quite a number of bona fide productions, he couldn't "collapse" the company by selling its assets and paying a capital gains tax of 25 percent. It was only an exceptional star that wanted to get involved in such a long-term operation. Producers and directors, like William Perlberg, George Seaton, Hal Wallis, Stanley Kramer, and Alfred Hitchcock, felt better qualified.

If the personal corporation was not too practicable there were other ways of beating the 75 to 92 percent bite above a $100,000 income. One of these was to "spread" a salary or a participation. John Wayne made a contract with Fox for at least three pictures at $666,000 apiece. He was to have no share of the gross or the net, but his $2,000,000 was to spread over 30 years—an annuity that took care of depletion. In addition to salary, William Holden gambled on 10 percent of the gross of *The Bridge on the River Kwai*. His cut was to be paid him at the rate of $50,000 a year. Since the film seems likely to gross $20,000,000, he, like Wayne, will have to be over eighty years old before he can bank all the money. Elizabeth Taylor was content to take a million-dollar salary, sans participation, paid over a period of years. Later she advanced to $1,725,000 plus 10 percent of the gross over $7,500,000 for her labors in *Cleopatra* (1963).

Another and a very odd financial dodge was for a star to be given all rights to the negative of his picture after a certain number of years. He could then reissue the film or sell it to television. Aside from salaries or participations, Cary Grant got such a bonus for starring in *Operation*

Petticoat (1959), as did Marlon Brando in the case of *One-Eyed Jacks*. Here was a different kind of spread.

Taxwise, Europe Lures the Star

Another way of reducing taxes—the best and safest way around 1960—involved migration. This meant the migration of either the star or his corporation or both. Many a company was set up in Switzerland, Spain, or Liechtenstein. Many a star left his home in Beverly Hills to live in the shade of the Alps. In these countries corporate and personal taxes rarely go over 12 percent. A star or a director could not escape paying taxes on his income from investments in the United States, unless he became a permanent expatriate. But as late as 1962 a pamphlet of the Treasury Department assured him that it wouldn't tap any money earned through "personal services" abroad so long as he, together with his family, was a "bona fide resident of a foreign country . . . for an entire tax year." Of course "bona fide resident" was open to interpretation. Moreover, if a star living in Europe wanted to earn tax-free money, he could appear only in pictures made outside the United States. The fact that this escape hatch was open to anyone who produced, directed, or wrote for the screen resulted in a curious reversal of an old Hollywood habit. Nunnally Johnson—a triple-threat-man who combined all those activities—went to England to make a film version of *The Visit,* by the Swiss playwright Friedrich Duerrenmatt. Johnson planned to change the setting from what he called "the *Lederhosen* country" of Central Europe to Virginia City, Nevada, and then shoot it in Europe. Casting trouble balked the project, but Fox coproduced a Western in Spain, *The Sheriff of Fractured Jaw* (1958), and Leo McCarey found the Chinese backgrounds for *Satan Never Sleeps* (1962) in England. However, under new tax regulations introduced in January 1963, U.S. citizens living abroad were no longer totally exempt from taxation on money earned overseas; only a maximum of $35,000 was tax free.

Oddly enough, neither Nunnally Johnson nor a star like William Holden had to persuade American studios to cooperate in easing their tax loads. Hollywood had already discovered the attractiveness of producing films abroad.

At Home Abroad and Vice Versa

As early as 1910 enterprising producers began to send companies to faraway places. In Ireland, Kalem's director, Sidney Olcott, made 17 pictures in 18 weeks, including a three-reel version of Dion Boucicault's fifty-year-old drama *The Colleen Bawn* (1911). Then he shot other films in at least a dozen countries. In Palestine, free from "home office" control, he made the first American overseas feature, *From the Manger to the Cross* (1912). Kalem was horrified at the cost and the subject matter of the film, and then as much delighted at its success.

No one can say that Olcott's daring launched a flood of what we now call "runaway" productions, but in the next dozen years a number of American companies made ambitious productions abroad. Edwin S. Porter and Hugh Ford went to Europe to direct *The Eternal City* (1915). Henry King shot *The White Sister* (1923) and *Romola* (1924) in Italy. Just before MGM acquired its middle initial, the old Goldwyn company started to make *Ben-Hur* abroad, but supervision seems to have broken down, and after about a year of almost fruitless work on location, Thalberg and Mayer decided they could finish the picture better and more cheaply in Hollywood. When Kirk Douglas' company produced *The Vikings* (1958) he felt that he had to go to northern Europe to find fiords and a tenth-century castle, but in the case of *Spartacus* (1960) he knew that the Roman villas of the Old World were a bit ruinous, whereas the Hearst estate at San Simeon in California offered a fine specimen complete with pool.

Even before 1929, Hollywood studios had built all manner of foreign exteriors on their "back lots" or on "ranches" in the San Fernando Valley. In the days of the depression, when budgets were at their tightest, location trips were few and far between. A minor producer told his director: "A rock is a rock and a tree is a tree. Shoot it in Griffith Park." By this time, fortunately, film technicians had developed new and better trick shots to bring foreign locations to the screen as cheaply as possible.

I was involved in an interesting example of such economy when Twentieth Century-Fox made *Stanley and Livingstone* (1939). We sent a camera crew and a "second unit" director to Africa along with three "doubles," including one for Tyrone Power, who was to play Stanley. When the company returned with its film, the editor cut into the picture long shots of the doubles, crowds of charging warriors, wild animals, and the veldt in flames. For close shots of the principals, director Henry King used process photography to pose them against the backgrounds shot in Africa. The only difficulty was that the director had picked a double who resembled Power in height, and he had trained him to walk like that actor, whereas while the expedition was in Africa, Zanuck had succeeded in borrowing Spencer Tracy from MGM to replace Power. The result was that many shots had to be cut off before the double got too near the camera.

As the film boom of World War II eased the economic problem, Hollywood companies began to go to more and more distant locations. For instance, in the case of *Pride of the Marines* (1945) the exteriors, complete with principals, were shot in the East in order to give the film the authentic flavor of West Philadelphia. A company under Elia Kazan shot almost all of *Panic in the Streets* (1950) in New Orleans, using real rooms as well as the streets and the levee.

"Runaway" Productions Overseas

Postwar economics lured Hollywood overseas once more. When foreign governments held much of America's profits in blocked currency, the studios sent directors and actors abroad to make pictures with impounded funds. *Prince of Foxes* (1949) took its players to Italy, *The Big Lift* (1950) to Berlin, *King Solomon's Mines* (1950) to the Dark Continent.

Through the nineteen-fifties the habit of making films abroad grew on Hollywood. Neither the lack of well-preserved Roman hippodromes in Europe nor MGM's bitter experience with its first *Ben-Hur* deterred that studio from making a new version in Italy. Even when blocked currency ceased to be much of a problem, other things made the American producer work more and more in foreign locales. At first, labor was cheaper, though less efficient. (Then, except for armies of extras, costs advanced and, always, the weather was more capricious than in southern California and the work went more slowly.) Another factor, however, sometimes made production in certain countries more profitable. England had created subsidies for the production of "British films," and Hollywood found out how to produce them. To qualify for a subsidy, films had to be made by English corporations; so Hollywood set up such companies. Most actors, and all technicians and labor had to be British, but any film could use an American director and an American star, or a British director and two American stars. "Co-production," or partnership, with a European producer brought financial advantages. Then Italy and France joined Great Britain in the offering of subsidies. An added reason for making more and more films abroad was the aforementioned fact that some of our most popular stars couldn't work in the United States if they wanted to save taxes by living on the Continent.

The end result of all this was a terrific increase in the proportion of American films made in Europe. Count only the majors—forgetting the independents—and you find that in 1940 less than 5 percent of their releases were shot abroad, in 1950 about 10 percent, and by 1960 almost 30 percent. Despite the increased production in Hollywood of films for television, this meant serious unemployment in the old screen capital and guilds and unions cried out against "runaway" productions.

Hollywood Fades as a Producing Center

In 1960, the Hollywood majors were not only making almost a third of their films outside the walls of their vast array of sound stages; they were making fewer pictures, both here and abroad, than ever before.

Hollywood, the Ghost Town

The truth is that Hollywood has become in the most literal sense a ghost town. The major studios, once hives of activity, are all but deserted, and the corporal's guard that remains is more than likely working on TV films. Warner Brothers, with twenty-two huge stages, currently has only two films shooting on the lot. The vast commissaries at Twentieth Century-Fox and Paramount have dozens of empty tables each noontime. On the third floor of the Irving Thalberg Building, the powerhouse of M-G-M, almost half the offices stand empty. Other studios reflect the same degree of inactivity.
—Arthur Knight, *Saturday Review*, August 13, 1960.

. . . only one of the 1959 pictures [nominated by the Academy for the best production of the year] was made in Hollywood. One was filmed in Rome, another in Britain. A third split its locations between Belgium, Africa and Italy. A fourth was made in Michigan, of all places. Only *The Diary of Anne Frank* is a contender from the former "capital" of motion pictures.
—Editorial, Los Angeles *Mirror News*, March 30, 1960.

In 1927 the majors released 510 features, only 9 of them made abroad. By 1940 the total had dropped to 363, by 1950 to 263, while the number made abroad rose to 15 and then 21. In 1961 the majors produced only 102 and imported 60—all this while American industry was vastly increasing its domestic output.

On the other hand, the films of the nineteen-fifties and early sixties were much longer and much, much more expensive. This was the era of the "blockbusters." The single year of 1956 saw them reach what then looked like the peak of extravagance. If we may believe the figures trumpeted in the trade papers, *The Ten Commandments* cost $13,500,000, *War and Peace* some $6,000,000, *The King and I* $6,500,000, *Around the World in 80 Days* nearly $6,000,000, *Moby Dick* more than $5,000,000. The spending spree continued. *Ben-Hur* (1959) may have cost $15,000,-000 and *Spartacus* is said to have cost $12,000,000. *Mutiny on the Bounty* (1962) and *Cleopatra* (1963), both beset by production delays, cost around $18,000,000 and $31,000,000, respectively. Of course there were highly successful films with much smaller budgets—*The Bridge on the River Kwai, Peyton Place* (1957), *The Shaggy Dog* (1959), *Pillow Talk* (1959), *Happy Anniversary* (1959), *To Kill a Mockingbird* (1962), and *Hud* (1963) for example—but Hollywood had to spend well over a million on films with top-flight stars.

Inflation at the Box Office

Hollywood made blockbusters and star-studded features to stem the box office slump. These films and even their more modest rivals played longer engagements at higher prices in first-run and many neighborhood houses. The rather dramatic results appear in *Variety's* list of "All-Time Top Film Grossers" that appears each January. These are films that have taken in, according to the editor's estimates, $4,000,000 or more in gross rental in the United States and Canada, and new films that seem headed for such prosperity. (Remember that in addition, most if not all of the older films probably earned 30 to 45 percent more in Europe and Latin America.) The list for 1955 included 124. By 1964 it had more than doubled—291.

The decades in which these films were made is highly interesting. How many, do you think, were produced in the silence of the nineteen-twenties? Only 3—*The Big Parade, The Four Horsemen of the Apocalypse,* and MGM's early *Ben-Hur.* Of course, *The Birth of a Nation* would have ranked high, perhaps at the top, if any figures had been available, but it was sold for lump sums to independent distributors after the road shows ended. It is significant that 124 films out-grossed *The Big Parade,* that *The Four Horsemen* was down in the second half, and that the silent *Ben-Hur* was an also-ran in the last 25 that barely got in under the $4,000,000 wire. As for talkies, they showed how inflated our box office became with the war boom, particularly after the blockbusters raised the price of seats. Only 4 top films were released before 1940, and only 67 in the next decade. Of the 45 top films from *Gone With the Wind* (1939) at $41,200,000 down to *That Touch of Mink* (1962) at $8,500,000, all but 5 were products of the blockbusting era. Out of the 291, 219 were released after 1949.

High Salaries and Costs Even in the Depression

Inflation—but not always at the box office—has ever been the chronic disease of Hollywood. Even the depression of 1929 couldn't curb it, as my own experience will show.

In January, 1932, on the basis of a moderately successful Broadway production, I came to RKO at $600 a week, first as story editor and soon as an associate producer. During that year, the studio and its distributing organization lost a little more than $3,000,000, and three times as much the next year. RKO was then in receivership, while Paramount had been adjudged bankrupt. In the persons of Shirley Temple and Will Rogers, "a little girl and an old man saved Fox," as *Variety* put it. In lonely contrast, MGM was going strong. With the depression still hanging over Hollywood, and with neighborhood theaters giving away sets of dishes, it seems rather absurd that by 1937 my weekly salary should have risen to $2,000, even though I was then at Twentieth Century-Fox, where Zanuck's management was sound and profitable.

At RKO, by 1935, I had handled eighteen films, that cost a little more than $5,000,000, an average of about $280,000 apiece; at that time MGM and Paramount made features at an average of some $500,000 each. In ten years under Zanuck, I was responsible for thirty productions costing about $24,000,000. My first, *King of Burlesque* (1935) came close to $600,000. Later, my budgets edged toward the million mark, while four went over it. *Lifeboat* (1944) cost more than $1,500,000. Within another ten years that was to be the minimum investment for a class A film with stars.

More Inflation in the Nineteen-fifties

After the first setback of World War II, which closed most of the Continent to American films, Hollywood began to prosper. From 1941 to 1947 it boomed. So did the cost of production. Even the blow that television dealt the box office around 1950 didn't halt Hollywood inflation.

I have explained how the panicking studios dropped the big stars off their contract lists and had to buy them back at fantastically high salaries and a share in the gross or the net. Some of the majors claimed that the bigger returns from the theaters meant bigger profits for the distribution arm of their corporations. This might have been a good argument in the case of the biggest grossers, but costs increased for all types of pictures. When the studios went to the five-day working week in 1956, they added about 15 percent to the shooting schedules of all films and almost as much to total costs. Strikes and threats of strikes upped the pay of supporting players, of technicians and craftsmen. The actors' walkout of 1960 raised the minimum pay of various performers 11 to 81 percent. It forced the studios to contribute a few millions to pension, health, and welfare funds, and to share some of the TV profits on future films. The writers' strike boosted costs in a somewhat different way. For six months no scripts were written. So, in order to get production rolling again, the studios paid fancy prices to the most competent writers—in some cases $75,000 and $100,000 per script. Statistics published by the State of California for 1945 and 1962 show that, although the number of employees, including those in television, dropped by almost a third in seventeen years, payrolls increased by almost a third.

In light of all this, some of the more sober minds in the film industry grew apprehensive. Hollywood seemed—if I may borrow a phrase from Will Rogers—to be going to the poorhouse in a Rolls-Royce.

From Deferment to Diversification

The high cost of film production hit the independents as well as the majors, but the majors were burdened with expensive studios that turned out less and less product. The first answer for them was to rent stage space to the independents and to the companies making television shows on film, and then, at last, to go into TV production on their own.

There were other answers, too—sometimes curious ones.

One of these was what big business calls "diversification." In the past the studios had financed Broadway productions to secure the film rights. Some had taken to music publishing. Some had gone into the record business. Some had bought broadcasting stations. Fox and MGM had found oil on their back lots. Then came ventures into even newer fields. Paramount expanded into electronics, bought into a company developing a color tube for television, acquired Dot Records and stock in the Ampex Corporation and in International Telemeter, a pay-TV project. Walt Disney placed far more emphasis on live features, went into television, and diversified spectacularly with Disneyland. The theater chains that had been divorced from the producer-distributor companies acquired all manner of sidelines. Stanley-Warner bought out International Latex, a girdle company that was also in the pharmaceutical business. Loew's, separated from MGM, took to real estate and hotels. Paramount's old chain united with the American Broadcasting Company. RKO theaters, controlled by List Industries, became involved in real estate, restaurant services, electronics, and textiles. National Theaters, once the Fox chain, began to talk of going into film production, then produced *Windjammer* (1958) in Cinemiracle.

Sometimes diversification worked in reverse. The General Tire & Rubber Company bought RKO, stopped production, and sold the studio to Desilu for television use. Decca Records bought control of Universal and sold the studio (but not the producing and distributing arms) to Revue, the TV subsidiary of MCA, the biggest talent agency. Subsequently, after giving up its talent agency, MCA absorbed Decca and all of Universal Pictures Company, Inc.

"Worth More Dead Than Alive"

The most curious maneuver by which the producers kept out of the red has been the "sell off."

The first move looked profitable on the books, but it gave aid and comfort to the movies' great competitor. This was turning over to television the backlog of pre-1948 feature films. A gesture of financial desperation, it brought in something between $250,000,000 and $350,000,000. In the sixties Hollywood leased many post-1948 films that should bring far more.

Then came the discovery by the big producing companies and by various men of Wall Street that the majors had a number of assets equally marketable. The San Fernando Valley, hardly ten miles from Hollywood, had been little more than a desert when some of the studios bought land there for outdoor sets. Now it is a sea of real-estate developments. So Warners, Paramount and RKO sold their ranches at enormous profit. In the nineteen-thirties Twentieth Century-Fox, on the edge of Beverly Hills, had bought a golf course to add a huge back lot of exterior sets to its adjoining property. What could be more natural than to sell the combined 286 acres to a building firm for some $43,000,000? The firm will create Century City to house 12,000 families and provide various public buildings, while Fox will lease back its 75 acres of studios at $1,500,000 a year for ninety-nine years. (Universal paid MCA a million a year to use part of its old plant.)

Besides valuable real estate and the backlog of post-1948 films, dollar-sharp eyes in Wall Street discovered many other assets that producing companies hadn't thought much about. There were overseas holdings of many sorts: a TV station bought for about $225,000 and now worth $6,000,000; a diversification that had grown in value from $1,000,000 to $21,000,000; real estate up the Coast that was purchased for $212,000 and should subdivide some day to the tune of $50,000,000; and so on and so on. Canny speculators wanted to sell off the majors and pocket many millions as stockholders. They nearly did it to Loew's-MGM. Not yet divorced from all its fifty first-run theaters, the corporation looked like a juicy $200,000,000 plum.

Hollywood—Today and Tomorrow

So, at the beginning of the nineteen-sixties, we had:

Hollywood's tight old system of production disrupted. Six majors instead of seven, only two headed by true producers, Jack L. Warner and Darryl F. Zanuck.

Fifty or more independent producing companies. Some financed by the majors, the rest by banks and distributors.

"Hollywood productions" shot all over the world. The sound stages of Los Angeles devoted more to films for television then to films for theaters.

Stars paid three and four times their normal salaries and made part owners of their pictures.

Inflated production costs matched by inflated income from the box office.

The majors selling parts or all of their real estate, two of them leasing back their stages.

Producing and distributing companies taking over other kinds of businesses or merging with them. Theater chains doing it, too.

Hollywood cutting its own throat by turning over its past productions to television.

The major companies—never too sound financially—discovering that they may be worth more dead than alive.

Will Hollywood sell the films of the future to theaters or to "free" or pay-TV? If the theaters continue to shrink in number or almost disappear, what kind of films will Hollywood make for the tiny home screen?

Chapter

23

The Search
for Story Material

"IT'S MORE DIFFICULT to find a great
story," Sam Goldwyn once said, "than a great star." He might have said
just a *good* story. Many a producer who aimed no higher than that has
ended up with white hair, ulcers, or a heart attack.

Feature films start with a story or a reasonable facsimile thereof. Where
does it come from? How is it found? Why is it considered good enough
to produce?

The Story Department

In the twenties, when most of the Hollywood studios were making fifty
to a hundred pictures apiece each year, they had to create "story departments" in both Hollywood and New York to find and recommend
material. In the sixties, though the majors were releasing less than half
that number—many made by independents—the story editors were still
busy. Each had a small staff of well educated and skillful writers, called
"readers," within the studio walls. All told, they numbered about forty
and belonged to a union known as Story Analysts, Local 854 (IATSE).
Under that honorific yet appropriate moniker, they earned from $111.60
a week to $168 after fifty-four months of service.

Their job is to read novels, plays, and "originals" (stories expressly written to sell to Hollywood), to make synopses of varying length, and to venture opinions on whether the stories might make successful pictures, as well as sometimes to suggest changes. The story analyst must work fast because the same material is usually covered by a number of studios, and yet, as Mervyn LeRoy has said, he must write "a synopsis that conveys the story in condensed form and also the style of the author and of the story itself. The story shouldn't lose anything by being synopsized." When Dore Schary was the head of MGM he wrote: "Often our reader's synopsis, particularly of a long novel, is better than the original for our purposes; crisper, the story line cleaner, and the characters standing out in sharper relief."

"The towering structure of Hollywood," says William Fadiman, long an able executive in charge of the search for stories, "rests its massive weight upon a fragile foundation of paper—the paper that pours forth unceasingly from printing presses, typewriters, and mimeographing machines, to be shaped in the end into film stories."

The number of stories that the readers cover in a year is all but staggering—10,000 to 15,000. The late Kenneth MacKenna, a most knowledgeable story executive at MGM before he resumed his acting career, watched 25,000 pieces of material go through his department annually at a time when, in addition to novels and plays, it dealt with short stories, live TV scripts, and many nonfiction articles. Largely as the result of the activities of the story departments, Hollywood spends about $5,000,000 a year, according to Fadiman, on literary "properties."

"Oddly," writes Dore Schary in *Case History of a Movie*, "the Story Department does not so much buy stories as 'sell' them—that is, bring them to the attention of the studio's producers." The head of the department and an assistant or two weed the synoptic seedlings, and send the more promising to the head of the studio and/or staff producers. In the past the final decision was usually based on synopses, though film-makers have been known to read books, especially after studying an intriguing outline. Louis B. Mayer seldom or never read a synopsis of a best seller or a promising original; instead he had a Scheherazade or two on whose story-telling abilities rested the future of a property as well as their own survival at MGM.

In the sixties there were not quite so many readers on studio staffs and fewer in New York. The Hollywood readers, in the main, were busy covering originals, synopsizing old books that some producer might be interested in, or seeking material for TV series. Some independents have readers. The more important film-makers become their own story editors by reading the manuscripts or proofs of new books and plays that literary agents, publishers, and Broadway managers send them. Agents often interest a star and a director in a book or play, and then present a "package deal" to a studio or an independent.

"Pre-Sold Properties" vs. "Originals"

For many years Hollywood has leaned heavily on the best-selling novel or the Broadway hit as the firmest foundation for an important production. The producer's explanation is that these properties have been

---

What is a "Property"?

When a fabled young woman like Audrey Hepburn expresses an interest in anything filmable . . . it has the instant effect of lifting a work of literature to the status of a "property."
—S. N. Behrman in *The New Yorker*.

"pre-sold" to the public. This rash assumption that the movie audience reads novels, has a nodding acquaintance with best-seller lists, sees plays in New York, or follows critics sometimes hides the producer's lack of confidence in his own unsupported judgment. There is a sounder reason, however, for buying and producing the best seller and hit play. As MacKenna saw it, the success of a popular story is almost sure to be duplicated on the screen.

> For a book or play to become a truly top seller it must have demonstrated an almost universal quality of "narrative pull"—an intrinsic and compelling force that makes its audience desperately eager to see what happens next to characters which have become emotionally identified with the reader. This is a rare quality, but one that if it exists in any given piece, translates itself easily from one medium to another. It is basic. For instance, it is not spectacle, but the powerful narrative pull that made *Ben-Hur* a tremendous success as a book, a play, and twice as a film.

The pre-sold play pays off handsomely when a producer wants to hire a big star, for an important property is a potent magnet. And yet, so far as the box office is concerned, a star is *more* pre-sold than any novel.

Originals are another breed of pups, and usually a lowly breed. At times a few directors have raised that breed's status. Leo McCarey wrote the stories for both his *Going My Way* (1944) and *The Bells of St. Mary's* (1945). Preston Sturges did the same for almost all his films; Billy Wilder for *Sunset Boulevard* (1950) and *The Apartment* (1960); Nicholas Ray for *Rebel Without a Cause* (1955). Although producers actually prefer to pay large story costs when they expect to spend two or three million dollars on a production, they buy more originals than best sellers for their relatively low-budget and their run-of-the-mill pictures. At the top of the more modest films, we have had *Miracle on 34th Street* (1947), *Bad Day at Black Rock* (1954), *On the Waterfront* (1954), and *The Defiant Ones* (1958) and, at the bottom, "exploitation" films like *High School Confidential!* (1958), *I Was a Teenage Frankenstein* (1957), *Attack of the 50 Foot Woman* (1958), *Vice Raid* (1959), and *Sex Kittens Go to College* (1960).

Trial by Facts and Figures?

Two sets of statistics show how much Hollywood concentrates on the "pre-sold" story and how much on the original. Neither test is too exact. One deals with all the films released by the major companies, the other with those that drew the biggest public.

The Motion Picture Association of America, embracing the chief producers, has analyzed the source material of the features approved by its Production Code Administration each year. By this over-all test, 60 percent of Hollywood's films from 1942 onward were based on originals; about a quarter came from novels and short stories, and about 6 percent from plays. The high point for originals was 73.4 percent in 1942, when the Code Administration passed more than 500 features. With only 108 films in 1960, originals were close to their low point, at 48 percent. Against these figures, Fadiman claims that out of all the properties *purchased*, not just those produced, 85 percent are novels—which should leave a lot of books on the studios' shelves.

Another set of facts, or near-facts, can be drawn from *Variety's* list of "All-Time Top Film Grossers." Let us take the top twenty-nine on the January 1964 list, which begin at a modest $10,000,000. Of these we can leave out two Cinerama shows; they were not fictional. Of the twenty-seven remaining, twenty-three were based on printed stories, ranging from *Samson and Delilah* (1949) and *The Ten Commandments* (1956) to best sellers; the not-so-best seller *The Bridge on the River Kwai* (1957); and successful plays and musical shows. By the widest stretch of the imagination only four could be considered originals—*The Best Years of Our Lives* (1946), *The Greatest Show on Earth* (1952), *White*

Christmas (1954), and *How the West Was Won* (1962). Goldwyn's film (*The Best Years of Our Lives*) creeps in only because it grew from an idea that he gave to MacKinlay Kantor, who turned it into a novel in blank verse that formed the basis of Robert Sherwood's screenplay.

When a producer buys a famous novel or a Broadway hit, he may think he has bought an annuity or staked a claim on a mother lode. But even though he sees to it that the plot and the characters are well handled on the screen, the result may be a financial failure or nothing more than a *succès d'estime*. Recall *Our Town* (1940), *The Ox-Bow Incident* (1942), *Intruder in the Dust* (1949), *The Four Poster* (1952), *The Member of the Wedding* (1952), *The Brothers Karamazov* (1958), *The Old Man and the Sea* (1958). The producers of some of these films will be lucky if showings on television bail them out.

From News Stories to Past History

The basis of a film story may be an idea or a topic, rather than a novel or a play. Sometimes it crops up in an original. Often a producer or a staff writer finds it in a news story or in past history. When Zanuck was running Warner Brothers in the early thirties he announced that "as far as possible" the studio's productions would be based on "spot news." Thus many gangster films came out of the daily press and the magazines. So did *Boys Town* (1938), *Wake Island* (1942), *Stage Door Canteen* (1943), *The Story of Dr. Wassell* (1944), *The House on 92nd Street* (1945), *The Best Years of Our Lives*, *Lost Boundaries* (1949), *The Big Lift* (1950), *Mister 880* (1950), and *The Well* (1951). In the blockbuster period there have been a few topical films of merit—for instance, *The Wild One* (1953) with Marlon Brando, and *Strategic Air Command* (1955) with Jimmy Stewart, and Billy Wilder's *One, Two, Three* (1961).

A serious difficulty about basing a film on topical material is the fact that if a picture is made with any degree of care, at least twelve months and often a year and a half to two years must pass between the inception of the project and the film's appearance in a theater. Hence the topic must be of some lasting interest. "Spot news" pictures, in the narrow sense, are apt to be quickies on the level of *Dragstrip Riot* (1958), *The Atomic Submarine* (1959), and the "Twist" pictures of 1962.

Past history and its institutions sometimes spur the mind of the producer. Zanuck suggested that I turn my attention to the great Chicago Fire of 1871, and Stanley's search for Livingstone, and I aroused his interest in the invention of the telephone, and the Mormon pioneer

Brigham Young. In the nineteen-thirties Zanuck made so many films with stories laid in a period twenty-five to a hundred years before he was born that someone dubbed his studio Nineteenth Century-Fox.

Stories of the past may be peopled with fictitious men and women; that was true of *San Francisco* (1936), *Lloyd's of London* (1936), *In Old Chicago* (1938). Or they may be straight—or more or less straight —biographies as in *The Story of Louis Pasteur* (1935), *The Life of Emile Zola* (1937), *Wilson* (1944), *The Court-Martial of Billy Mitchell* (1955), *Beau James* (1957)—which turned Jimmy Walker into Bob Hope—*I Aim at the Stars* (1960), and *Lawrence of Arabia* (1962). As an antidote to Capone and Dillinger, Hollywood adapted from book and magazine the life of Rocky Graziano in *Somebody Up There Likes Me* (1956). The baseball diamond contributed Lou Gehrig, Monty Stratton, and Jim Piersall. When John Wayne turned producer-director, he found real-life parts for other stars besides himself in *The Alamo* (1960). For a number of years there has been quite a run on the life stories of entertainers like Al Jolson, Florenz Ziegfeld, Helen Morgan, Jeanne Eagels, Lon Chaney, Buster Keaton, Glenn Miller, and Gene Krupa.

Can—and Must—Stories Fit Stars?

When a producer or a reader is trying to decide which novels or plays, ideas or topics, may make successful films, he is faced with a dozen different problems. Some are very difficult indeed. Some have nothing to do with the merit of the material.

The easiest is: Will the story fit some very popular star or stars? A harder one: Can the producer get the cast he needs? Once upon a happy time, films like *Crossfire* (1947), *Miracle on 34th Street, Home of the Brave* (1949), *All the King's Men* (1949), and *Mr. 880* needed no true luminaries of the day. A few years later, even with the salaries of stars skyrocketing, the casts of the big successes were apt to look like the Milky Way.

Will the General Eat Caviar?

When we come to the quality of the stories—their integrity, their importance, their distinction, their significance—the producer has to face the problem of mass appeal. He never worries that the acting may be too perfect for audiences in a New England town, the camerawork too fine for Duluth, the sound too well recorded for Natchez, the cutting too subtle for Oshkosh, but he is very apt to fear that the story is too good for Tallahassee—or New York. Perfection is all very well in the crafts of movie-making, but beware of too much quality in the story! The Hollywood producer may take heart from Basil Wright, one of the founders of the documentary movement in England, who wrote in 1948: ". . . the film industry is faced with the challenge . . . of improving the quality of its product. . . . This does not mean taking up a high-brow attitude and demanding that every film shall be a masterpiece; one might as well expect a Picasso on every chocolate box."

Just how mature, how sophisticated, how "highbrow," can a film dare to be? Though the producer may like to have his pictures tagged "artis-tic," he is still conscious of his audience. He considers their age, and their education or lack thereof. Pollsters have told him that 50 percent of moviegoers are under twenty years of age. He wonders how much the education of the young has improved since the silent days.

It was back in 1919, when Lasky and DeMille were releasing *The Admirable Crichton,* that the sales department of Paramount thought the public would confuse the word "admirable" with "admiral" and stay away because "sea pictures weren't very popular." So Barrie's comedy became *Male and Female.*

Twenty years ago a studio mailman brought me a letter from which I quote hardly a tenth:

> Dear Sir,
> I have been reading hundreds of books of actress. That is my wish to be an actress. Mr. please make me an actress. I don't care what I have to do . . . I am 17 years old. I am in the 7 grade. I don't like school very much . .

World War II was well over when a Marine, private first class, with a Scottish name, sent me a story with a typewritten letter.

> I have WRITE and pictory to my way i think a lot of it i like for you read it over . . . sure I no it as well as i know my face but the way people look at it dont no my face very well . . .
> Close here turly your MR. Macgowan

Of course such letters speak for the very bottom of the film audience. The thousands upon thousands of young men and women who provide Hollywood with fan mail every week must be considerably more intelligent, although five years after the death of James Dean, his admirers were still writing to him. If the producer keeps his sights reasonably high, it is because he remembers that the mass audience of the movies left their television sets to see many a film of fine quality, from *The Snake Pit* of 1948 to *To Kill a Mockingbird* of 1962.

Story Costs and Foreign Profits

Then there is the matter of the costs involved, the cost of the story itself and the cost of its production. Once upon a time the price for an original was $15. Anita Loos got that from Griffith for her first story, which was made into *The New York Hat* (1912). With the coming of features the price of novels went up. In 1919 Ibañez got $20,000 plus 10 percent of the gross for *The Four Horsemen of the Apocalypse*. In the early years of the depression RKO paid only $22,500 for Charles Morgan's best seller *The Fountain* (1934). The price of plays advanced. In 1932 RKO bought Philip Barry's *Animal Kingdom* for $50,000. By the fifties studios were acquiring plays before they had gone into rehearsal, paying as much as $150,000 with more to come if they proved hits. By 1960 Hollywood was buying popular novels and Broadway hits for $250,000 to $500,000, sometimes against 10 percent of the gross rentals, and it soon paid $5,500,000 for *My Fair Lady*. Such prices seem justified only if the property is enormously popular or if production costs look reasonable. But with the boom in the foreign market the ultimate investment was often forgotten.

With 50 percent of gross rentals coming to Hollywood from overseas and Latin America, what kind of stories get the quickest nod? Obviously stories that can be turned into blockbusters well laced with stars. Often this means tales with picturesque backgrounds, or historic epics that can exploit sex, a bit of sadism, and lots of spectacle. (The producer now disregards the small-town exhibitor who wrote: "Don't send me any more pictures in which the hero signs his name with a feather.") At times studios shy away from expensive musicals loaded with songs that defy translation; but in the sixties Hollywood produced *West Side Story, The Music Man, Flower Drum Song, Babes in Toyland, Gypsy,* and *My Fair Lady*.

Unfortunately, shooting for the foreign market and its big grosses has narrowed the producer's interest in many American subjects, and in the kind of modest-cost production that gave us *Boomerang* (1947), *Champion, The Well, Marty,* and *12 Angry Men*. The producer and his readers are no longer looking for the kind of stories that served Jackie Coogan, Jackie Cooper, and Shirley Temple. The old-line studios make few "family pictures." Independents and English producers gave us *The Little Kidnappers* (1953), *A Dog of Flanders* (1959), *Misty* (1961), *Whistle Down the Wind* (1961), *Flipper* (1963), and *Island of the Blue Dolphins* (1964). Disney remains the only important producer, either here or in England, who concentrates on the family appeal.

In most cases he does this by exploiting some gimmick—canine or human —in such moderate-cost films as *Old Yeller* (1957), *The Shaggy Dog* (1959), *Toby Tyler* (1959), *Pollyanna* (1960), *The Absent-Minded Professor* (1961), *Nikki, Wild Dog of the North* (1961), *Greyfriar's Bobby* (1961), *The Parent Trap* (1961), *Moon Pilot* (1962), *The Incredible Journey* (1963), and *The Moon-Spinners* (1964).

Tragedies and Films Without Love

In contrast to the family films aglow with good cheer, and also to escapist fare, the Hollywood producer sometimes tolerates stories with unhappy endings, stories that don't rely on women in love, stories that try to say something about our life and its new problems.

"What the American public always wants," William Dean Howells told Edith Wharton many, many years ago, "is a tragedy with a happy ending." Just such a story, Somerset Maugham's *Of Human Bondage*, made Bette Davis a star when John Cromwell directed it so well in 1934. Howells would have thought that *Johnny Belinda* (1948) came close to the mark.

Contrary to what most people think, Hollywood hasn't always shied away from tragic stories. As far back as 1930, von Sternberg deliberately added an unhappy ending to a German novel when he made *The Blue Angel*. Spurred perhaps by this foreign success, the next year Paramount produced Dreiser's *An American Tragedy*, an unfortunate failure. Producer Pandro Berman added no happy ending when he made Edith Wharton's *The Age of Innocence* (1934) and Maxwell Anderson's *Winterset* (1936). The same producer risked and lost on Dostoyevsky's *The Brothers Karamazov* (1958). In 1939 Bette Davis had quite a run of stories that were not exactly cheerful—Wharton's *The Old Maid; Dark Victory;* and *The Private Lives of Elizabeth and Essex*. There was *Mary of Scotland*, with Katharine Hepburn and Fredric March in 1936. In the forties came *The Ox-Bow Incident, The Treasure of the Sierra Madre* (1948), and *The Heiress* (1949). Stage success led producers to risk —not too successfully—*The Glass Menagerie* (1950), *A Streetcar Named Desire* (1951), *Death of a Salesman* (1951), and *Desire Under the Elms* (1958). In 1951 George Stevens made Dreiser's *An American Tragedy* into a successful picture as *A Place in the Sun*. Elizabeth Taylor and the sensationalism of Tennessee Williams made *Cat on a Hot Tin Roof* (1958) and *Suddenly, Last Summer* (1959) profitable. There was little but tragedy in *The Big Knife* (1955), *Paths of Glory* (1957), *I Want to Live* (1958), or *The Hoodlum Priest* (1961). The love—intense though blighted—of men and women helped a number of these films. Happier subplots came to the aid of some, as in *The Alamo* and *Spartacus*.

Before World War II there were very few American talkies with all-male casts; I remember only *Journey's End* (1930), *Men Without Women* (1930), and *The Lost Patrol* (1934), all war films. It is, I think, a sign of the greater maturity of the American screen that under the stimulus of World War II features without a shred of love interest—or with hardly any—could be made and shown successfully. American theaters booked a number of documentaries such as Ford's *Battle of Midway* (1942), Wyler's *Memphis Belle* (1944), and Huston's *San Pietro* (1944), all made while these directors were in the armed forces. Hollywood got into the act. It made eight or ten war films without women or love stories; among them were *Wake Island* (1942), *Guadalcanal Diary* (1943), and *Bataan* (1943). There were others, such as *The Moon Is Down* (1943), *Destination Tokyo* (1943), and *Thirty Seconds Over Tokyo* (1944) that gave hardly more than a nod to absent loved ones. Since the war, several films have excluded women from their plots: *Command Decision* (1948), *Twelve O'Clock High* (1949), *Steel Helmet* (1951), *Moby Dick* (1956), *12 Angry Men* (1957), *War Hunt* (1962), and *The Hook* (1963).

Beyond Escapism

Ideas, themes, propaganda, meaning, point of view, social significance —whatever you prefer to call an awareness of problems in our common life—were popular in the early days of the film, though delivered in a rather obvious and shallow fashion. But as Hollywood became "big business" it also became more careful. Aiming to please everyone, it tried to offend no one—except "Huns," gangsters, and lynching parties. The screen reflected the depression of the early thirties in the comedy-melodrama of Capra's *Lady for a Day* (1933) and the naiveté of King Vidor's *Our Daily Bread* (1934). Until America felt the impact of World War II, Hollywood showed scant concern over the many and acute problems of our times. "When I want to deliver a message," Goldwyn once declared, "I'll send for a Western Union boy." By 1946, however, when Goldwyn had made *The Best Years of Our Lives*, his point of view was a bit different: "What the American people want is not pure escapism in their pictures, but some reflections on their own emotional turmoil." How far was he right? Was Hollywood to escape escapism, at least to some extent?

For a few years after the war films of the early nineteen-forties, it looked as if Hollywood would continue to be interested in stories that tried to say something besides "Boy meets girl, boy loses girl, boy gets girl." Of course boy continued to meet girl, but once in a while he also met an idea. Some of the problems of the post-war world got an airing, along with some that had been with us a long time. *All My Sons* (1948) took a swing at war profiteering, and *Boomerang* and *State of the Union* (1948) at political corruption. In 1947 *Crossfire* and *Gentleman's Agreement* attacked anti-Semitism. The Negro problem won attention in 1949 through *Pinky, Home of the Brave* and *Intruder in the Dust*, and the next year through *No Way Out*. After making *Crossfire*, Dore Schary tried other "message" pictures, not too successfully, with *The Boy with Green Hair* (1948) and *The Next Voice You Hear* (1950). There were a few other films of "social significance" such as *Paths of Glory, Compulsion* (1959), *Odds Against Tomorrow* (1959), *A Raisin in the Sun* (1961), and *Lilies of the Field* (1963). But by the sixties the only major producer steadily interested in off-beat significance was Stanley Kramer with his record of *The Caine Mutiny* (1954), *The Defiant Ones, On the Beach* (1959), *Inherit the Wind* (1960), *Judgment at Nuremberg* (1961), *Pressure Point* (1962), and *A Child Is Waiting* (1963).

I like to believe that the stresses of war awakened the public and therefore the producers to the possibility that the screen could come closer to literature and the more serious magazines in commenting on life. There is some evidence, but there might well be more. We must not lay too much weight on the pictures that dealt with anti-Semitism and with the Negro. When you note that the first group appeared mainly in 1947 and the second in 1949–50 you may suspect that Hollywood was playing its old game of "cycles."

Cycles, Series and Remakes

The Frankenstein-Dracula-werewolf type of film has had a long though fitful career. Of all the cycles that have continued steadily, year after year, the longest-lived seems likely to be the science-cum-terror variety. In the many years since Hiroshima, the wonders of nuclear power and rocketry, jet planes and supersonic speed, electronic computers and solar energy that replenishes sputnik batteries have fired stage after stage of this newest cinematic missile. By the early sixties the novels of Jules Verne had become the biggest source of screen stories next to the Bible and the books about Charlie Chan and Tarzan in previous years.

Hollywood knows that in the end cycles wear themselves out, and it has found a safer way of cashing in on what might be called the residuals

of a successful picture. This is to make a series with the same characters. I am not thinking of *Father of the Bride* (1950) and *Father's
Little Dividend* (1951), for unfortunately there were no more of those
delectable comedies by Albert Hackett and Frances Goodrich. It was
at a lower level that the studios discovered how to capitalize on popular
favor. Sometimes a series has been based on a family or a part thereof
—the Hardys, the Joneses, the Aldriches, Ma and Pa Kettle, Nick and
Nora Charles of the Thin Man films, Dr. Kildare, Maisie. More often
and more successfully, it has been built around a striking character,
from Frankenstein to Francis, the talking mule. Since 1918 there have
been more than thirty films about Tarzan. Aside from shorts—Sherlock
Holmes has appeared in thirty-four features. Someone has counted forty-
eight Charlie Chans, made by four studios, with six different character
men, none of them Chinese and two of them Japanese. Hopalong Cassidy
rode the dusty trails in more than sixty features.

Remakes, under their old names or new ones, aren't quite so safe a
bet, but many of them have done very well. The most successful—
Rebecca of Sunnybrook Farm (1917, 1932, and 1938); *Little Women*
(1919, 1933 and 1949); *A Tale of Two Cities* (1917, 1935); *Quo Vadis?*
(made three times before 1951); *Mutiny on the Bounty* (1935 and 1962);
State Fair (1933, 1945, and 1962); *Back Street* (1932, 1941, and 1961);
The Prisoner of Zenda (1922, 1937 and 1952); *The Three Musketeers*
(1921, 1935, 1939, and 1948)—were popular novels and retained their
famous titles. I doubt, however, that *A Farewell to Arms* of 1957 and
Cimarron of 1960 made as much money as the original films; *The Blue
Angel* of 1959 and the new *Four Horsemen* (1962) certainly didn't.
Instead of reissuing the highly successful *It Happened One Night* (1934)
with Clark Gable and Claudette Colbert, Columbia changed the title
as well as the cast, added some songs to the old story, and came a
cropper with *You Can't Run Away from It* (1956). On the other hand,
producer Bryan Foy boasts that he used the plot of *Tiger Shark* (1932)
successfully in ten other films by changing the title, the locale of the
story, and the names of the characters.

Screen Fashions Come and Go

The opposite tack from following cycles or remaking old successes is
to gamble on something new—or, rather, on some kind of film that is
supposed to be passé. In the early thirties theater marquees were lit up
with such titles as *One Mad Kiss, Wild Company, Children of Pleasure,
The Lady of Scandal, A Lady's Morals, Roadhouse Nights, Anybody's*

Woman, Her Wedding Night, and *The Matrimonial Bed.* In spite of this, Fox decided to risk a remake of *Rebecca of Sunnybrook Farm,* hoping that Janet Gaynor would carry it. By 1932 the script was written, the sets built, and Alfred Santell hired to direct the picture. For some reason, Miss Gaynor refused to play the rather saccharine lead. Santell persuaded the studio to try to salvage its considerable investment by casting a minor but charming actress, Marian Nixon, as Rebecca. The result was a neat little success, an order from my boss at RKO to find a "sweetness and light" story, and—*Little Women* (1933).

Avoiding cycles and trying to follow new patterns have their dangers. At what was almost my first meeting with the head of RKO, he told me not to bother him with suggestions for comedies, costume pictures, or fantasies; their day was done. Yet among the successes of 1933 were comedies called *Tugboat Annie* with Marie Dressler and Wallace Beery, Capra's *Lady for a Day, Mama Loves Papa* with Mary Boland and Charles Ruggles, and *Three-Cornered Moon;* a costume film named *Berkeley Square;* and two that combined comedy and costume, *She Done Him Wrong* with Mae West and *The Bowery* with Wallace Beery; there was only one fantasy, but a very successful one, *The Invisible Man.*

"Have You Heard Any Good Stories Lately?"

Since the end of the war in Korea and the beginning of the battle of the big screens, the American producer may not seem quite so daring as before. Yet he has given us one or more significant films each year— not always to his profit. There were *From Here to Eternity, Julius Caesar,* and *Martin Luther* in 1953; *The Caine Mutiny, Executive Suite,* and *On the Waterfront* in 1954; *Marty* and *Blackboard Jungle* in 1955; *War and Peace* and *Lust for Life* in 1956; *12 Angry Men, Paths of Glory,* and *A Face in the Crowd* in 1957; *The Defiant Ones* and *Separate Tables* in 1958; *The Diary of Anne Frank, The Nun's Story,* and *On the Beach* in 1959; *Sons and Lovers* and *Sunrise at Campobello* in 1960; *Judgment at Nuremberg* and *A Raisin in the Sun* in 1961; *The Miracle Worker* and *Freud* in 1962; *Hud* and *Lilies of the Field* in 1963. There were vivid or amusing films such as *Shane* and *Roman Holiday* in 1953; *The Country Girl* and *The Glenn Miller Story* in 1954; *Picnic* and *Mister Roberts* in 1955; *Friendly Persuasion* and *Around the World in 80 Days* in 1956; *The Bridge on the River Kwai* in 1957; *Cat on a Hot Tin Roof* and *The Inn of the Sixth Happiness* in 1958; *Some Like it Hot, Middle of the Night,* and *Ben-Hur* in 1959; *The Sundowners* and *Exodus* in 1960; *West Side Story, Breakfast at Tiffany's* and *The Guns of Navarone* in 1961; *Bird Man of Alcatraz* and *Requiem for a Heavyweight* in 1962; *The Great Escape* and *It's a Mad, Mad, Mad, Mad World* in 1963. On the other hand, the wide screen and the growing European market lured producers too often into empty spectacle. Far worse, only a few of the pictures I have mentioned were made from original screenplays. And the original screenplay, I believe, should be the prime and rightful objective of the Hollywood writer as well as his producer.

Chapter

24

To See

or Not to See?

THERE WAS A TIME when producers and their story analysts had to consider very seriously what censorship might do to a story. There was the censorship practiced in half a dozen states and numerous cities in America, as well as in many foreign countries. Also there was the self-censorship of the producers' association. This could obstruct, too, but it could show the studios how to get around local censors.

Why Pick on the Movies?

Why should there be censorship of the movies but not of books, plays, magazines, and television? Of course youth can learn things about life from other than their parents and teachers—and learn them ill. But how is it that the screen can corrupt more quickly and effectively than the other media?

The common explanation is partly psychological and partly economic. The Production Code of the Motion Picture Association of America that has watched over the morals of the Hollywood screen for thirty years put it this way: "Most arts appeal to the mature. This art appeals at once to every class, mature, immature, developed, undeveloped, law abiding, criminal. . . . This art of the motion picture, combining as it does the two fundamental appeals of looking at a picture and listening to a story, at once reaches every class of society." So far as youth is concerned—and youth is what censorship is worrying about today—

action and emotion are far more vivid and effective on the screen than they are on the printed page.

The Case for Censorship

There are many people, people of some knowledge and distinction, who have worried over what they believe may be the corrupting effects of the movies on children and adolescents. These men and women—some of them psychiatrists, criminologists, or sociologists—believe that children, teenagers, and even others a bit older may be hurt by what they see and hear. When adolescents have to deal with the awakening of sexual interest, then glamorous distortions and excitations may make it difficult or even impossible for them to make a wholesome adjustment

---

Gorky Views With Alarm

Without fear of exaggeration, a wide use can be predicted for this invention, because of its tremendous novelty. But how great are its results, compared with the expenditure of nervous energy that it requires? Is it possible for it to be applied usefully enough to compensate for the nervous strain it produces in the spectator? A yet more important problem is that our nerves are getting weaker and less reliable, we are reacting less to natural sensations of our daily life, and thirst more eagerly for new strong sensations. The cinematograph gives you all these—cultivating the nerves on the one hand and dulling them on the other! The thirst for such strange, fantastic sensations as it gives will grow ever greater, and we will be increasingly less able and less willing to grasp the everyday impressions of ordinary life. This thirst for the strange and the new can lead us far, very far, and *The Salon of Death* may be brought from Paris of the end of the nineteenth century to Moscow at the beginning of the twentieth.

—From a newspaper review by Maxim Gorky in 1896, *reprinted from Jay Leyda's* Kino.

---

to the realities of life. Some believe that the violence shown on both movie and television screens—in television more often, perhaps, than in the movies—may contribute to juvenile delinquency in teenagers and may cause psychological injury to children. Louis M. Pesce, formerly a social worker and later in charge of the motion picture division of the New York State Department of Education, recognizes that movies of violence, brutality, crime, and sex do not produce delinquency, but they can have a profoundly bad influence on an adolescent exposed to a disturbed home life, a social environment in a state of flux, and many other of the least productive aspects of human nature. On a broader issue there are sociologists who would agree with the following statement by Margaret Mead:

> In small societies, children learn by imitating their parents, relatives and neighbors. In our huge society we use our mass entertainments to instruct our children on how they should express their emotions and what values they should have. . . . We are showing our youngsters exactly the opposite of what we want them to imitate. We are showing them men who brutally attack others when angry. We show people who murder because of hatred or expediency. We show that love is expressed only by hunger for another's body. And we show them little else!

Whatever the justice or the injustice of attacking the movies on moral grounds, the attack has been going on a long, long time. The issue has merely been sharpened by the increase in films of violence, horror, and sex. It was sharpened also by what seemed to many a slackening of moral standards in literature and non-literature, as four-letter words crept into best sellers, "nudie" magazines flooded the newsstands, and records of pornographic songs appeared in stores on Broadway and other hick Main Streets.

From Nickelodeons to Censor Boards

Films had barely opened their first store-theaters when the wrath descended. In *The Rise of the American Film,* Lewis Jacobs quotes from an editorial in the Chicago *Tribune* of 1907 attacking the "five cent theater" as "ministering to the lowest passions of children. . . . They cannot be defended. They are hopelessly bad." He quotes from a judge's letter: "Those nickelodeons indirectly or directly caused more juvenile crimes coming into this court than all other causes combined." When the editor of *The Christian Leader* declared: "A set of revolutionists

---

Shaw on Censorship

. . . the danger of the cinema is not the danger of immorality, but of morality.—1914

. . . the movie play . . . is reeking with morality, but dares not touch virtue. And virtue, which is defiant and contemptuous of morality, even when it has no practical quarrel with it, is the lifeblood of high drama.—1924

training for the overthrow of the government could find no surer means than these exhibitions," he anticipated by forty years the claim by "one of the most important club-women in the United States" that the violence of moving pictures is a "dirty and deliberate plot by Reds to condition America to the gross brutality practiced under the Soviets." In the days of the nickelodeons, there were few who joined Jane Addams, founder of Hull House in Chicago, in their defense; this wise woman knew that "rightly conducted [they] are a benefit and not a menace, especially to the poorer classes." No, the movies had to be curbed.

Chicago set up the first municipal censorship board in 1907; Pennsylvania, the first state board in 1911. Ohio, Kansas, Maryland, New York, and Virginia had acted by 1922, along with still more cities; and over thirty restrictive bills had been introduced in state legislatures. In 1922 the voters of Massachusetts rejected censorship by almost three to one, but within a few years there was a total of more than twenty states where municipal or statewide censorship was enforced. Threats to the liberties of Hollywood continued, and laymen, as well as film makers, tried to meet them.

The first move had come from laymen as early as 1909, and it had been endorsed and, indeed, supported by the producers. The People's Institute of New York formed the National Board of Censorship of Motion Pictures. Its procedure was to review films and provide a seal of approval for those without sin. Its hope was that the seal would protect a film from being banned or cut by state and local censors. The Motion Picture Patents Company, then all-powerful, shared this hope. Later, so did the makers of features in and out of Hollywood. For this kind of protection, the producers were willing to pay the National Board of Review—a new name for the Board of Censorship, that continues to this day—a fee for each reel reviewed. Its review committees have been sane and constructive.

The Case Against the Censor Boards

Fighting film censorship should have been easy. There are so many grounds on which to assail it besides the fact that it picks out one form of expression, and one form only, for attack. The first is freedom of speech and press, prime article in our Bill of Rights. From obscenity to libel, restraint or punishment cannot be had until *after* publication. Against censorship there is also the argument as to who can be allowed such dangerous power. As Jefferson put it: "Whose foot is to be the measure to which ours are to be cut or stretched?"

Then there is the natural and the inevitable inconsistency of censor boards. A film may be passed by one and banned by another; cuts may be different in different states and in different nations. In *The Film Till Now* Paul Rotha documents the varying cuts in Pabst's *The Joyless Street* (1925):

> France accepted the film, deleting two thousand feet and every shot of the "street" itself. Vienna extracted all sequences in which Werner Krauss appeared as the butcher. Russia turned the American lieutenant into a doctor and made the butcher the murderer instead of the girl.

The Hollywood Production Code never forbade double beds, but it warned the producers that they were frowned on by the British Board of Film Censors. When we were producing *Little Women* in 1933, we were cautioned, much to our surprise, to shoot the wedding scene so that the words of the marriage service could be cut in England without ruining the scene. Britain soon recovered its common sense, and proved it could be more liberal than Hollywood about profanity. Noel Coward's fine, grave picture of World War II, *In Which We Serve* (1942), had ten "damns," two "hells," two "Gods," two "bastards," and one "lousy" —all of them honest and natural words of men under stress. When United Artists proposed to release it in the United States, the self-censorship of Hollywood said that all those words must go. It compromised when it found that some could not be cut without wrecking whole scenes.

Rotha writes that the British censors in banning Germaine Dulac's *La Coquille et le Clergyman* (1928) gave this Gilbertian reason: "[The film] is so cryptic as to be almost meaningless. If there is a meaning, it is doubtless objectionable."

As a movie critic in Philadelphia, I encountered many of the absurdities of censorship. Often the cuts in films were so obvious that audiences knew something had been removed, and many must have imagined far worse episodes than those that had actually been cut. On the laughable side, the censor banned violence even in Mack Sennett's slapstick shorts. Chester Conklin raised a threatening bung starter above the head of Mack Swain. Before it could descend we saw Swain on the floor. Theaters circumvented censorship in ingenious ways. If the censor cut a certain vital subtitle, the management stopped the film and lowered a lettered sign into a spotlight in front of the screen. When the censor cut a whole scene in *The Battle Cry of Peace* (1915), the theater raised the screen and had the episode played in pantomime by actors in a stage set.

Trouble in the Twenties—and a White Knight

Hollywood, described a few years ago as "not only the most timorous of industries, but the most inconstant, slothful, and supine," has twice been forced to look to its morals as well as its laurels. The first time was in the early twenties, the other ten years later. Now it is facing new attacks that may lead to a new kind of self-censorship.

In 1922–23, the producers not only had to fight a flame-up of censorship. They also had to light a backfire against the charges of immorality in Hollywood that fed the flames. Those charges centered on the unsolved murder of William Desmond Taylor, the relations of Mary Miles Minter and Mabel Normand with that director, the Fatty Arbuckle trial, and the death from drug addiction of the young star Wallace Reid.

While the Arbuckle case (he was indicted for the death of a minor actress) was being tried by numerous women's clubs, twelve representatives of the companies that ruled Hollywood invited Postmaster General Will Hays to become head of an organization composed of all the major producers and distributors. This organization, The Motion Picture Producers and Distributors of America (MPPDA, the Association, or the Hays Office), was founded in March 1922. Hays was an astute choice; he had many qualifications. He knew his way around Washington and other important places. Shortly after his reign began, a resounding victory over censorship was won in Massachusetts. In 1923 his influence meant much in defeating a Congressional bill to license films in interstate trade. Also, as one man described Hays, "He is one of us. He is folks." He had the common touch, or at least he knew how to use a reasonable facsimile thereof. At Christmas, 1921, when he was debating the producers' offer, he heard his little boy and two playmates arguing about which one should play Bill Hart. There went through his mind, he said later, the words: "Out of the mouths of babes and sucklings hast thou ordained strength." "It wasn't just a job that had been offered to him," wrote Raymond Moley in his eulogy, *The Hays Office*. "It was a challenge, a duty. And the tears still come to his eyes when he tells that he stood up, then, in the shadow of the Christmas tree, and silently repeated the vow of St. Paul: 'And this I do.' "

General Hays—as his associates often called him in dubious honor of his one year as postmaster general under President Harding—knew that his biggest headache lay in the films that were exploiting the public's postwar interest in speakeasies, joy riding, necking. As Frederick L. Allen wrote in *Only Yesterday*, the movies "played incessantly upon the same lucrative theme. The producers of one picture advertised 'brilliant men, beautiful jazz babies, champagne baths, midnight revels, petting parties in the purple dawn, all ending in one terrific smashing climax that makes you gasp'; the vendors of another promised 'neckers, petters, white kisses, red kisses, pleasure-mad daughters, sensation-craving mothers . . . the truth—bold, naked, sensational.'" Moley lists thirty-five such films, mostly made from 1920 to 1922, with luridly alluring titles that ran from *A Shocking Night* to *Virgin Paradise*.

Hollywood Slaps Its Own Wrist

Under Hays the producers were to create "self-regulation" in order to prevent more drastic action by the federal government, as well as by states and cities. The first move now looks like a combination of Alcoholics Anonymous, Moral Re-Armament, and the Roman Catholic *Index Librorum Prohibitorum*. The studios, by sharing their guilty impulses, would strengthen their determination to go straight. Tempted to indulge in the heady wine of sexual sensation, the studios agreed to have their story editors send the Hays office synopses of "questionable" books, plays, and originals that they might be tempted to buy and produce. The Hays office, in turn, would warn the studios of any salacious material it came across. This "Formula," as the Czar of Hollywood called it, would aid the studios "in their continuing effort 'to establish and maintain the highest possible moral and artistic standards.'" For, as everyone knew, the fault lay with literature and the stage, not with the film-makers. The Formula would "prevent the prevalent type of book and play from becoming the prevalent type of picture." Finally, to make sure that no studio had a relapse from virtue, Hays drew up an index of prohibited books and plays, and added to it from year to year. As late as 1929, the list included about a hundred and twenty-five titles. Fifteen were Broadway hits.

Thus Hays freed the producers from the twin horns of a peculiar dilemma. They would no longer have to compete for expensive properties that couldn't be produced without a thorough job of bowdlerization—which would lay them open "to a charge of deception." And they were to "prevent misleading, salacious or dishonest advertising" and suggestive titles to pep up less sensational material than the banned plays.

Such was the high moral intent of the Formula of 1924 and its Index. It came too late to stop the filming of *Three Weeks*, Elinor Glyn's incandescent book about a lusty Balkan queen. It didn't prevent the release between 1924 and 1929 of pictures with such gaudy titles as

Husbands and Lovers, The Golden Bed, Paid to Love, What Price Beauty?, The Godless Girl, Mad Hour, The Secret Hour, A Woman of Affairs, Charming Sinners.

Hollywood Sterilizes Broadway

Three years after the Producers' Association asked the studios to put the finger on questionable plays and books, and Hays began his Index, Hollywood indulged in a moral maneuver of a highly amusing kind. In the early twenties burgeoning Broadway had at last developed a crop of worthwhile American playwrights. Many of their plays were as innocuous as all Hollywood scripts were supposed to be. In some of them Portias faced life a bit more squarely than did the film producers. I am thinking of Eugene O'Neill's *Desire Under the Elms*, for example, and Sidney Howard's *They Knew What They Wanted*. Other playwrights, some from abroad, gave Broadway plays that Hollywood would have to consider "questionable." (The question, of course, was could Hollywood produce them and get away with it?) Among the latter group were *The Green Hat*, about Michael Arlen's sensationally promiscuous woman; *Rain*, a dramatization of Somerset Maugham's short story of the affair of the missionary and the tart; *The Constant Wife*, Maugham's own comedy of the wife who thought sauce for the philandering gander was sauce for the goose; and *The Command to Love*, a Continental delicacy. Each was a success and even, in the opinion of many bluenoses, a *succès de scandale*. Hollywood sniffed pleasurably. Conscious, however, of the Formula and the Index, the producers held aloof from purchase. But wasn't there some way that they could eat their cake and have it too? Or, rather, how could they eat their cake and pretend not to have it? Hays found a way.

It took some time, for the studios were in a ticklish position. They wanted to film such "sensational" stories, but they had agreed not to. They wanted to exploit "sensational" titles, but they had agreed not to. They could change the plots enough to satisfy Hays, but if they dared to use the notorious titles, that would be deception, and they had promised not to be deceitful. In the end the solution was easy and absurd. The maneuvers, however, that brought it about are mysterious, and they are locked away in the files of the Producers' Association.

When the playwrights discovered that they couldn't sell certain plays to Hollywood, they were naturally unhappy. When they discovered that the Producers' Association was responsible, I suspect that they talked a bit about conspiracy in restraint of trade. At any rate, Hays got out of the mess by describing "an agreement" with the Authors' League, which the League denies. Nonetheless, Hays decided that if a writer would cut out the questionable elements and supply whatever was needed in the way of a new plot, then Hollywood could buy the property, and add some more plot if it wanted to. But the studios were not to use the celebrated title or to advertise the fact that the film was based on a banned play. Thus at one blow Hays seemed to have avoided sensationalism and deception—and any danger from the Sherman Act. I am not at all sure that Hollywood's publicity men and the reviewers kept the secret. I know that the new titles were suggestive in the good old Hollywood tradition. If the new materials were as "wholesome" as required, then the titles must have been deceptive. *The Green Hat* became *A Woman of Affairs; They Knew What They Wanted, The Secret Hour; The Command to Love, The Boudoir Diplomat; The Constant Wife, Charming Sinners.* (Again, let us forget the individual dates, which ranged from 1928 to 1930.) *Rain*—a pallid title—got nothing more vivid than *Sadie Thompson,* the name of the heroine of Maugham's short story *Miss Thompson,* from which the play came. Perhaps the producer believed that the devotees of the silent screen read the shorter works of English authors. Or he may have realized that reviews of *Rain* and the publicity and photographs involved contained the name of Sadie Thompson.

Thus the Presbyterian pope of Hollywood added an *Index Expurgatorius* of wicked works that could be produced and seen by the public after certain rites of purification. But so far as original screenplays were concerned, there were still no real teeth in the jaws of censorship, though the jaws had been very busy.

"Don'ts and Be Carefuls"

While this charade was going on in 1927, Hays persuaded the producers to adopt a list of what were called "Don'ts and Be Carefuls." There were eleven "Don'ts." They listed things that could not be shown on the screen. Among them were "pointed profanity—by either title or lip," "any licentious or suggestive nudity," "the illegal traffic in drugs," "any inference of sex perversion," "miscegenation (sex relationships between the white and black races)," "ridicule of the clergy." Twenty-five "Be Carefuls" dealt with subjects that might be treated, but that must be treated with "special care." Among these were "international relations," "the use of firearms," "theft, robbery, etc.," "brutality and possible gruesomeness," "technique of committing murder by whatever method," "the sale of women, or of a woman selling her virtue," "first night scenes" (of marriage, not Broadway), "men and women in bed together," "the institution of marriage," "the use of drugs," "excessive or lustful kissing, particularly when one character or the other is a 'heavy.'"

The producers' resolution establishing these "Don'ts and Be Carefuls" declared that living up to them was "a fair trade practice." Still no teeth.

The Production Code Takes Shape

This lack of dentition had serious consequences in the next two years. Early in 1929 Jason S. Joy, whom Hays had appointed to oversee self-regulation, reported that he was able to deal with only about 20 percent of the feature films. Some producers played ball, some did not. Others sent in only parts of their scripts, and paid little or no attention to Joy's criticisms. Attacks from high places were numerous. *The Churchman*, for example, said that Hays and his assistants were "men whose occupation it is to shield, for enormous salaries, the panderers who have made their millions selling vice, crime and sexual suggestion to a public that is in the main composed of the immature." *The Literary Digest*, then a power in the land, attacked "the cheap, the nasty and the suggestive . . . the vulgarities and obscenities" in films.

Among others particularly distressed was a Catholic layman of some distinction in the industry, Martin Quigley, publisher of *The Motion Picture Herald* and other trade papers. With the consent of Hays, he enlisted the aid of Father Daniel A. Lord, a teacher of dramatics at St. Louis University, in drawing up what they called a Production Code, which the producers adopted in March, 1930. It was more elaborate than the "Don'ts and Be Carefuls," more carefully developed, and more thorough. In some 4,000 words it set down the reasons for self-regulation and the particular matters that needed attention. The Code covered more than the "don'ts" and "be carefuls." It declared that "dancing costumes intended to permit undue exposure or indecent movements in the dance are forbidden." So were dances "suggesting or representing sexual actions or indecent passion." "Ministers of religion in their character as ministers of religion should not be used as comic characters or as villains." (The adulterous missionary of *Rain* had been turned into a "reformer.")

The Woes of Joy

Still, the Production Code had no real teeth. The producers merely agreed to follow its injunctions, and submit scripts to the Hays office.

They were not compelled to do so. Some milk teeth began to appear at the end of 1931, when the submission of scripts was made compulsory. Joy was allowed to appeal on questionable material to the board of directors of the Association, over the heads of the rotating panels of three studio executives that had invariably ruled against him. However, for some unknown reason, Joy never used the right of appeal, and "pictures whose doubtful moral integrity," says Moley, "is now almost universally recognized," were passed over Joy's disapproval.

As the depression deepened, producers grew more and more reckless in their pursuit of the fast buck. During 1930–31, in films like *Millie*, *Common Clay, Born to Love,* and *The Easiest Way* heroines lost their virtue before they won a wedding ring. The next year, in *Faithless*, *Call Her Savage,* and *Blonde Venus,* wives sold their bodies to get food or medicine for their loved ones. In the face of this, the producers blandly "reaffirmed," twice in one month, their devotion to self-censorship.

Catholic Pressure Puts Teeth in the Code

A book and an actress of 1933 did much to crystallize public opinion against Hollywood. The book was Henry J. Forman's *Our Movie Made Children.* The actress was Mae West. Forman's summary of studies made by the Payne Fund on the effect of films lit new fires of criticism. Mae West in *She Done Him Wrong* furnished a splendid example of what could get by the Code. If you are over forty you may remember her catch line "Come up and see me some time," and her song "I Like a Man Who Takes His Time."

In the end it was the Catholic Church that forced the producers to put teeth in the Code. In the spring of 1934 a committee of its bishops launched the National Legion of Decency. Its purpose was to warn Catholics against what it considered immoral films, and to exert pressure on film-makers. Since 1936 it has reviewed all available features, and issued moral ratings. These place a film in one of six categories. The first four include those "morally unobjectionable" (A–I) for all, (A–II) for adults and adolescents, (A–III) for adults only, and (A–IV) for adults, with reservations. A fifth rating, (B), is for films "morally objectionable in part for all;" the Legion lists its "objections," which are mostly based on "a light view of marriage," "acceptance of divorce," or "suggestive elements." The rating (C) is for films wholly condemned "because of theme or treatment . . . described by the Holy Father as 'positively bad.'" The (A–IV) rating is given to those films which "while not morally offensive in themselves, require caution and some analysis and explanation as a protection to the uninformed against wrong interpretations and false conclusions." (Interestingly enough, *Suddenly, Last Summer, Anatomy of a Murder* (1959), *Lolita* (1962), and *Freud* have been so rated.) Occasionally the Legion urges laymen to attend a particular film; for instance, *Ben-Hur, The Last Angry Man* (1959), and *To Kill a Mockingbird.*

Before the Legion had had a chance to test the value of its rating system, the action of a Catholic bishop in Philadelphia exerted a pro-

---

Form E-3—20M—K-I-J Co. 2-33

R K O STUDIOS, INC.
Inter-Department Communication

To..... PRODUCERS AND WRITERS ....   Date.... JULY 12, 1933 ....

From.. M. G. Whitman ....   Subject.................................

Below is a list of words and phrases which are unacceptable to Censors in several states.

Mr. Cooper asks that you kindly delete all such from your scripts, present or future:

Alley-cat	Madam
Bag	Mistress
Bat	Moll
Broad	Nigger
Chippies	Nude
Cocotte	Nursery
Courtesan	Nuts
Dago	On the make
Dame	Pansy
Eunuch	Punk
Fanny	Rump
Filthy	Scut
Floozy	Sex
Guts	Sexual
Harlot	She's nothing more than a--
Hell cat	Slut
Hellion	Son-of-a
Hellish	Trade (sense of prostitution)
Hot Mama	Traveling salesman) When Farmer's daughter) reference is to joke
House broken	Trollop
Huzzy	Virtuous
In your hat -	Want you
Jeez	Wench
Jew (when used derisively)	Whore
Kike	"Yid"
Lousy	

NAUGHTY WORDS—1933. Upon instructions from the Production Code Administration, this list went to all RKO's associate producers with directions from the head of the studio not to allow these words or phrases to appear in screenplays.

found effect on Hollywood. A boycott of certain theaters hit the film industry in its pocketbook. At last the Code seemed important. Strong-minded Joseph I. Breen was made director of a Production Code Administration. In June 1934, the Association adopted a "Resolution for Uniform Interpretation" that required all producers either to abide by the rulings of the Production Code Administration, or else to appeal to the board of directors of the Association. The next month the Association required a seal of approval on all films distributed by its members, and set up a $25,000 fine for any infraction. This fine—a paltry sum compared to the income from any picture—was levied only once, and never collected. A much more important action of the producing companies was to agree that they would bar from their theaters any film that had not won the seal of approval of the Production Code Administration. This brought the smaller producers into line. Since the majors owned or controlled large chains of theaters all over the country, any film was doomed to failure that couldn't play these vitally important first-run and neighborhood houses. By 1940 Hays could boast that 95 percent of America's theaters showed only films that had a seal. "Self-regulation" had become monopoly censorship. At last the Code had a fine set of teeth.

The 1930 Production Code lasted twenty-six years. Enforced by Breen and his successor, Geoffrey Shurlock, it washed Hollywood's dirtier linen in private, but got a good deal of public criticism for doing so. After all, self-censorship was also pre-censorship. It left no work for the police or the magistrates, and very little for the censor boards of states and cities. There was criticism of the Code from liberal Catholics. The weekly *Commonweal* said of it: "Some of the provisions are good; some are indifferent; some are anachronistic; some are stupid; and some are practically vicious." Dore Schary said in 1961: "It is possible to make a completely salacious picture under the motion picture Code." Some attacked this girdle of chastity as barring film-makers from handling many mature, adult subjects of true merit.

Chapter

25

Classification— "For Adults Only"

I<small>N</small> 1956 <small>THE PRODUCTION CODE WAS</small> revised—downward. Also, from then on it was interpreted with great liberality. Oddly enough, the Legion of Decency has to take the credit (or the blame). At least that is what the Production Code Administration says.

In 1955, Otto Preminger's film *The Man With the Golden Arm* was refused a seal because it dealt with drug addiction. Since the Legion didn't put the film in its list of "condemned" pictures, the producers began to think that the Code itself might be a bit too strict. (Though the Code was liberalized the next year, *The Man With the Golden Arm* wasn't given a seal until 1961.) I cannot help believing—and the representative of the Legion in Hollywood agrees—that altering the Code was based on something more. After all, the Legion didn't whitewash Preminger's picture. Though it failed to condemn it, the Legion put it on its list of films "morally objectionable in part for all," and criticized it for "morbid sensationalism" and "suggestive costuming, dialogue, and situations." Were the changes in the Code due, perhaps, to changes in the economies of the film business?

TV and Divorcement Cripple the Code

The end of the forties saw two momentous shifts in the entertainment world that Hollywood had so long shaped and so easily dominated. First, television mushroomed when the war was over. Second, the government forced the major companies to sell their chains of theaters. The competition of TV cut into box office returns and gross rentals so heavily that Hollywood became desperate; it turned to wide screen and blockbusters and all-star casts and encouraged higher ticket prices. Divorcement of the theaters hurt income, too, but it was to hurt the Code far more. It eroded the teeth that had forced the seal of good conduct on film-makers. For some time, the theaters avoided films not approved by the Code Administration. Except for foreign pictures, there weren't too many of these. Then came the independent producers who released through United Artists and elsewhere. UA offered *The Moon Is Blue* in 1953 without the seal of the Code, and the film prospered. Two years later the same happened with *The Man With the Golden Arm*.

Meantime, more and more of Europe's "adult" films were doing excellent business in the "art" theaters and some were playing in a few first-run and many neighborhood houses. Among these were: *Rififi* (1955), *Companions of the Night* (1953), *Illicit Interlude* (1950), *Le Plaisir* (1952), *The Earrings of Madame de* (1953), *The Man Who Loved Redheads* (1955), *Diabolique* (1954), *I Am a Camera* (1955), *The Bed* (1954), *Game of Love* (1953), *Adorable Creatures* (1952).

In the face of all this it was only natural that Hollywood—still worrying about television competition and envious of the rocketing success of United Artists—looked with a longing eye at the growing market for films without the seal of purity. Hollywood thought: How about liberalizing the Code? Why not meet—with profit—the pleas of most critics and many film-makers for greater freedom in dealing with more mature materials?

Letting Down the Bars a Bit

What were the changes in the Code in 1956? It is worth noting that one of the subjects the Code eased up on was drug addiction. Hedged around with provisos, the subject was thrown open to film-makers. Similarly guarded against abuse, stories involving kidnapping, prostitution, and abortion were admitted to the screen; but "brothels in any clear identification as such may not be shown." "Vulgar expressions" such as "chippie," "fairy," "nuts," and "son-of-a" were still banned. Though profanity was forbidden, "hell" and "damn" had recently been permitted provided they were used with moderation. A step forward —"No picture shall be produced that tends to incite bigotry or hatred among peoples of differing races, religions, or national origins." The old Code merely required that "The history, institutions, prominent people and citizenry of other nations shall be represented fairly."

The changes in the Code may have seemed slight, but its interpretation has been another matter. *Monkey on My Back* (1957) and *The Pusher* (1959), dealing with drug addiction, were entitled to seals, and got them. But so did *Butterfield 8* (1960), *Girl of the Night* (1960), and *Go Naked in the World* (1961), all involving prostitution and seeming to some critics to go beyond the cautious limitations of the Code, while *The World of Suzie Wong* (1960) had a rather merry time with the light ladies of a Hong Kong "hotel." Rape, which the Code said "should never be more than suggested," became the heart of Preminger's *Anatomy of a Murder* (1959); the act was never shown but it was thoroughly discussed and the court scene included words like "slut" and "contraceptive" and frank statements such as "He tore my panties off and did what he wanted." On perversion the Code held the line up through 1960, when it refused seals to two British films on Oscar Wilde. During the next two years it gave way to *The Children's Hour, Advise and Consent*, and *Walk on the Wild Side*. Films could now deal with "sex aberration, provided any references are treated with care, discretion and restraint."

Even after the Code had been softened up and very loosely interpreted, many a foreign film and some that were made in America never asked for seals, because they felt sure that they would be refused or that too many changes might be required. There were *Rosemary* (1959) and *Never On Sunday* (1959) with prostitutes for heroines; some Brigitte Bardot films including *And God Created Woman* (1956); *Private Property* (1960); *The Savage Eye* (1960); *Expresso Bongo* (1959); *Shadows* (1959); *A Cold Wind in August* (1961); *The Connection* (1961); *Breathless* (1959); *L'Avventura* (1960); *Rocco and His Brothers* (1960). In recent years, according to the New York State Censor Board, over 90 percent of foreign films reviewed lacked a Code seal.

Sex in the Good Old Days and the New Ones

You must not think that the screen was innocent of seductions before the Code was liberalized. Films were merely less literal than *The Lovers* (1958), or some recent American pictures that have won seals. In the old days, after a couple kissed in the grass, the eye of the camera discreetly wandered away to the treetops or a handy moon. The audience knew what happened before the camera returned—perhaps through a dissolve—to the loving couple.

The preliminaries were never so passionate as they are today. The deep kisses that Breen sometimes cut out of release prints were tame indeed compared with the osculatory maneuvers of the French "new wave" and the Italian riptide.

No seduction in the Hays era ever began with the girl's saying, "Be gentle with me," or ended with the boy's assurance, "It'll be easier next time." The first remark was in *Room at the Top* (1958), the second in *Shadows*, neither of which got seals. As for language in general, one may expect such a foreign film as *Never On Sunday* (1960) to assail our ears with "whore" and "I've been dying to sleep with you." The lack of a seal might seem to account for "whore" and "knocked up" in the American-made film *A Cold Wind in August*, and "belly against belly, tongue against tongue" in another native product, *The Savage Eye*. But what must have been Breen's thoughts when in the Code-approved *The Apartment* (1960) a man who was interrupted in his love nest said, "We were having a ringadingding"? That deft film of Billy Wilder's which won the Academy Award for the best production of 1960 would have shocked Hays and Breen to the core. They would never have passed a story whose aspiring hero lent his flat to his bosses and their sweeties. They would hardly have approved of starting *Psycho* (1960), and *The Dark at the Top of the Stairs* (1960) with bedroom scenes. Nor would they have smiled at the line from *Hud* (1963), "I've done my time with one cold-blooded bastard." Indeed they would have agreed with *Time's* list of "the varieties of erotica and sexual aberrations explored by today's film makers: fornication, adultery, incest, prostitution, pimping, nymphomania, voyeurism, frigidity, rape, homosexuality, cannibalism and necrophilia. . . . Examples, in order: *From the Terrace, Portrait in Black, The Last Sunset, Let No Man Write My Epitaph, Girl of the Night, The Fugitive Kind, The Bramble Bush, Two Loves, Sanctuary, Tea and Sympathy, Suddenly, Last Summer* and *Psycho*."

More worldly critics than the priests who review films for the Legion of Decency were shocked by pictures shown in the early sixties with the seal of the Code. In the New York *Times* Bosley Crowther wrote of "the tendency of producers, made evident in any number of recent films, to go for licentious stories and/or inject extreme and gross sex details in their works." He named four celebrated films that he thought "betrayed a concentrated predilection on the part of major producers with the abnormal and crass aspects of sex." *Variety* called *A Cold Wind in August:* "another example of the modern screen's almost morbid preoccupation with distorted sex." Critic John Crosby attacked *Walk On the Wild Side* as being "perfectly dreadful, rampantly sexual, a really dirty movie" and described *Cape Fear* (1962) as "the most sordid, vicious and utterly depraved movie I have ever seen."

When such films are shown on a Saturday afternoon before an audi-. ence of kids from six to sixteen, the effect is rather frightening. Giggles and gasps, snickers and hoots, over words like "harlot," "half-virgin," and "call house." Whoops at "a cruise to the Virgin Islands" and "She says I bounce when I walk." The plot of *Happy Anniversary* (1959) hinged on the fact that the hero and heroine had lived happily in sin for a year before they got married. The Production Code insisted that the man should express regret. He did so in a soliloquy that ran: "I was wrong. I never should have taken Alice to that hotel room before we were married. What could I have been thinking of?" The audience of little ones knew, and told him by their gales of laughter.

Advertising—Questionable and Deceptive

Motion picture advertising has always been more unbridled and sensational, more offensive and salacious than the films themselves. And therefore it has been deceptive. Hays saw the grave danger to the industry that lay in such advertising. Suggestive words and sexy art work would be seen by millions who never saw the picture; therefore the film would be damned in the eyes of many as even more objectionable than it actually was. The Production Code of 1930 was quickly followed by an Advertising Code, equally ineffective over the long haul. Under the direction of J. J. McCarthy—who had helped to make *The Birth of a Nation* a two-dollar roadshow attraction in 1915—the Advertising Code was fairly well enforced between 1933 and 1937. After McCarthy's death it languished, and ten years later the divorcement of the theater chains made it all but a dead letter.

Deceptive advertising is not always sensational. Sometimes it is merely an attempt to sell unmarketable onions as Chanel #5. This policy goes much further back than 1944, when Warner Brothers found moviegoers cold to the first-runs of *The Adventures of Mark Twain* and dreamed up a new advertising campaign that turned the honest biography into a glorified Western. Sometimes when Hollywood makes a film about war, the "New York Office," where advertising is prepared, grows panicky over the lack of love interest. So MGM put out ads for *Battleground* (1949) in which Elizabeth Taylor declared. "Here is a picture, if ever there was one, that every girl and woman will love." The same company promoted *The Red Badge of Courage* (1951) with a lobby display in which Audie Murphy stood beside a girl who wasn't in the picture.

RECORDS SHOW that MOVIES are Schools for CRIME: Corrupting to MORALS and Producing MULTIPLIED THOUSANDS of YOUNG CRIMINALS!

THIS AND OTHER ANTI-VICE POSTERS MAY BE OBTAINED FROM THE PILGRIM TRACT SOCIETY, Randleman, N. C. THIS WORK SUPPORTED ON THE FREE-WILL OFFERING PLAN.

THE ATTACK GOES ON. This thirteen-by-ten-inch poster comes from the Pilgrim Tract Society of Randleman, North Carolina. Besides such displays, the society offers many 600 and 1,000 word leaflets. It is now turning its attention to television: "the greatest menace of modern times," "HELL'S PIPELINE INTO THE HOME."

Usually, the ways of deception are sexy. Sometimes there is no justification and then the financial results are disappointing. An injection of testosterone into the ads for that innocent English satire *The Life and Death of Colonel Blimp* (1943) had no more effect than the monkey gland treatment of Doctor Voronoff. Perhaps the most remarkable case was *Androcles and the Lion* (1952). After Shaw's gentle little comedy had failed to draw a sizable public, RKO began to promote it with ads showing dancing girls in brass bras, and such words as: "Barbaric Revelry to fire the senses of the world . . . in the story of history's most sin-swept era!" The ads for *The Millionairess* (1960) turned the most puritan of playwrights into "That wicked—worldly—George Bernard Shaw," and his comedy into "The sultry story of a beautiful babe who pants for romance."

To "sex up" Renoir's somber drama of sharecroppers, *The Southerner*, in 1945 theaters had a lobby display of a young woman lying on her back in black lace undies; of course there was nothing of the kind in the picture. "Movie advertising," Preminger once told TV audiences, "is the most dishonest in the world." (Perhaps he had never joined his viewers in watching commercials.)

"Glad to Be Bad—for a Price"

Around 1960, when the tide of sex was at its height in literature as well as on the screen, film advertising was not untouched by the carnal.

It is easy to say that the producers of quickie pictures were the worst offenders. Their exploitation of the sensational began with the very titles of their films. These ran to sex, violence, and pseudo-science shock. *Love by Appointment* shared a double bill with *Unmarried Mothers*, *Sin Alley* with *Vice Dolls*, *The Incredible Petrified World* with *Teenage Zombies*. A resourceful producer combined sex, horror, and science-fiction in *I Married a Monster from Outer Space*. (Only three of these preceding titles are listed and dated in *The Film Daily Year Book* or *International Motion Picture Almanac*, but it is worth noting that, although few films from the major studios had such inflammatory titles, *I Married a Monster from Outer Space* (1958) was a Paramount production.)

As for advertising, "B" pictures, with a natural affinity for "B" girls, shrieked: BEAUTIES WITH A PRICE TAG—CHOOSING THE EASY WAY! MARRIED OR NOT, YOU'RE MINE! A FRANK EXPOSÉ OF A BIG CITY VICE THAT SCORCHES THE SCREEN! NEVER HAS THE SCREEN HAD SO MUCH FUN WITH A STUDENT BODY! SEE BEAUTIES TORTURED BEFORE YOUR VERY EYES! YOUNG PAWNS

THRUST INTO PULSATING CAGES OF HORROR IN A SADISTIC EXPERIMENT! The lobbies of the theaters in which such quickies were shown had displays to match their ads: "Real! Raw! Racy!" "Glad to be bad—for a price." "*Reckless Girls*—beautiful, misguided, love-hungry BABES." John Crosby recorded in the New York *Herald Tribune* that *Love by Appointment* had this caption under the picture of a half-dressed girl: "Call me anything but call me often." A theater where Warner's *Girl of the Night* was shown called the attention of pedestrians to telephones by the sidewalk: "Use these phones and listen to her *sizzling* conversation."

It is not difficult to understand why certain of these [producers] might be desirous of going back to sinister themes which pandered to base desires. . . . it is often relatively easy to attract a certain type of person and certain classes of people to theatres which present picture plays calculated to inflame passions and arouse lower instincts latent in human hearts . . .
—Pope Pius XI in an encyclical letter on motion pictures, July 2, 1936

What they heard was: "I'm Bobbie Williams, your girl of the night. I've been waiting for *your* call." MGM advertised the call girl of *Butterfield 8* with a series of catch lines like these: "Some women never give a name . . . just a phone number" and "The most desirable woman in town and the easiest to find . . . just call . . . Butterfield 8." Other majors were almost as bold. "She was born to be bad." "Defiant young moderns! Eager for experience . . . hungry for each other." "Ingrid Bergman, Yves Montand, and Anthony Perkins shock the screen in a shameless affair!" Having prefaced Inge's play *The Dark at the Top of the Stairs* with a bed scene, the producing corporation ran this line in many of the ads: ". . . as if you suddenly opened a door and found two people in the most unguarded moment of their lives!" Following an art-house opening, John Huston's *Freud* (1962) was withdrawn for a time and eventually reappeared as *The Secret Passion* with ads reading, "Out of her nightmares came the clues to a sexual fantasy that only he dared explore!"

Responsible producers like John Houseman have criticized the promotion of their films. Of *All Fall Down* (1962), Houseman has said, "I believe there *is* an audience for that picture, but the way it was released and promoted I'm not sure *that* audience ever saw it. In fact I haven't the faintest idea who saw it, but I suspect that three-quarters of the people who did see it expected to see something quite different."

Much Talk of Classification

We first had "classification" from the National Board of Review and then from the Legion of Decency. By the early sixties a number of other organizations were reviewing films and rating their fitness for various audiences. Much of this action was prompted by the increasing number of pleas for some kind of censorship.

Of course there was fevered argument inside and outside the film industry. In general the producing companies and the theater owners preferred the status quo of the emasculated Code. The less biased and more socially minded favored classification as a way of keeping children and adolescents from seeing horror and brutality on the screen, and from meeting sexual problems before they were able to understand and handle them properly. Most of the public that worried about "adult" films agreed with the various rating groups that classification should be voluntary. Parents should be guided, and they should guide their youngsters. On the other hand, many began to believe that classification should be forced by law on the producers and the men who run the theaters. They pointed to the example of the United Kingdom.

The British Muddle Through

With the characteristic compromise of the English, their system is technically voluntary. The state plays no part in censorship. The British Board of Film Censors was created by the film industry in 1912. Its president—usually a man who has had wide experience in public life and administration—is chosen by a committee representing all branches of production and distribution. The president appoints a very active secretary and a staff of reviewers. They must have no connection with the industry. Each film approved by the Board is classified in one of three categories, and given a certificate. Certificate "U" (for "universal") means that the film is suitable for "general exhibition." Films stamped "A" (for "adult") are "more suitable . . . for adult audiences," and no adolescent can see them without a parent or guardian. Certificate "X" classifies a picture as "suitable for adults only." Cuts may be made, by the distributor, to make the film suitable for a particular category. The Board may refuse a license, and sometimes does so, mostly for an excess of horror or brutality.

But how is such self-regulation by the film industry enforced? This is done through the more than 700 local authorities that were authorized by Parliament in 1909 to license cinema theaters. They accept the censor's classifications, though they may reverse the Board's ban on any picture. When this happens, theaters use the additional "come on" of "BY PERMISSION OF THE LOCAL MAGISTRATES" in their advertising. Fortunately, this situation is not widespread. The teeth in classification lie in the fact that any theater will ultimately lose its license if it shows an "X" film to anyone under sixteen, or an "A" film to an adolescent who can't persuade a parent to come along. The Board has no code of rules. It "prefers to judge each film on its merits and to consider each incident and line of dialogue in relation to the tone of the film as a whole." Thus when *La Ronde* (1950)—that amatory daisy chain—came

---

If America Had Britain's Censor Board

The following feature films were passed by the Production Code Administration and widely exhibited to young and old in the United States. In Great Britain, however, they were classified by the Board of Film Censors and given certificates as suitable for only certain classes of moviegoers, and not for general showing.

Certificate X—Adults Only

Cat on a Hot Tin Roof	Experiment in Terror
Suddenly, Last Summer	Lolita
The Fugitive Kind	Advise and Consent
Psycho	The Children's Hour
From the Terrace	Boys' Night Out
Butterfield 8	All Fall Down
Sanctuary	Sweet Bird of Youth
Return to Peyton Place	Splendor in the Grass
The Hustler	The Chapman Report

What Ever Happened to Baby Jane?

Certificate A—Adolescents With Parents

A Summer Place	The Misfits
Ben-Hur	Fanny
Happy Anniversary	Five Finger Exercise
Sons and Lovers	Barabbas
The Apartment	Lonely are the Brave
Spartacus	The Four Horsemen of the Apocalypse
The World of Suzie Wong	West Side Story
Exodus	Tender is the Night
Parrish	The Manchurian Candidate

A Girl Named Tamiko

up for judgment, the Board gave it an "X" for adults because "we found it charming and gay." The Board "can treat one film that is made, say, with integrity more generously than a film that seems to us to be made for exploitation purposes."

The Board was not always so broad-minded, so urbane. In its early days it was often as silly as an American censor and as politically minded as the French. In 1931 it banned *Outward Bound,* in 1932 Eisenstein's *Ten Days That Shook the World,* in 1933 *Extase,* in 1934 *An American Tragedy,* and so on and so on. During the forties the Board seems to have made other unfortunate decisions, and some rather absurd cuts. But since 1951, when the Board began giving "X" certificates, there has been less criticism of its decisions, and they have not so often been upset by the London County Council or other local authorities.

Britain's censorship system is fifty years old. Our press and public learned about it only recently and only because of the breakdown of our Production Code. They do not know that the principle of classification is practically worldwide. One survey of forty-eight countries with official censorship has indicated that thirty-four classify the films they pass. An interesting sidelight falls on the figure of Brigitte Bardot. Except in perhaps a couple of her films, her vivid charms have been veiled from the eyes of the adolescents of her native land. Largely however, France, along with Egypt, Spain, and the USSR, is even more concerned with political censorship.

Some boards read scripts or synopses before production, and venture an opinion as to whether the finished picture will be passed or rejected. Our own Production Code Administration requires such submission.

Will Classification Be Bad for Business?

Most of our film-makers and distributors fear a serious drop in box office receipts if classification is established in America. Eric Johnston, head of the producers' organization, said in 1961: "In every place where a classification of pictures has been used, the sale of tickets has been retarded." In the same year an unrevealed executive of the same organization said that "80 to 90 percent of American films are prohibited to children under sixteen or seventeen overseas." Though foreign censors are particularly tough on films of horror and brutality, these figures may be somewhat exaggerated. Yet in 1963, only 273 out of 531 feature films—many American—got "U" certificates in Britain, 164 were barred to adolescents unless accompanied by a proper adult, and 94 were marked "X."

On the other hand, far-sighted theater owners have worried over the danger that sexy films are alienating the "mom-dad-and-the-kids clientele," and also over the danger of more and stricter old-fashioned censorship. Certain makers of "adult" films have begun to look with favor on classification. Richard Brooks, for example, said, "if we are to have adult films we must have classification." Preminger who had shown *The Moon Is Blue* and *The Man With the Golden Arm* without Code seals, came out for classification "done voluntarily by the producers." Fred Zinnemann, Billy Wilder, and William Wyler take much the same position.

The Motion Picture Association of America has been carrying water on both shoulders. The Code has long declared, "A careful distinction can be made between films intended for general distribution, and films intended for use in theatres restricted to a limited audience." Whatever the codifiers were thinking of when they wrote that, Eric Johnston argued against classification: "Some people complain about too many 'adult' films. The number would zoom under classification. Adult films would really become 'adult,' if not 'adulterous.'" Yet meantime the Association was backing financially *The Green Sheet*, a monthly publication that reviews and rates feature films including those without Code Seals. To a mailing list of about 60,000 monthly, it presents "the composite opinion" of ten national organizations, nine of which are women's groups. Its parent, the Film Estimate Board of National Organizations, is housed in the same building as the New York offices of the producers' association. A number of other organizations and some national periodicals have joined the classification parade.

It is important to note that all these American efforts at classification are voluntary and merely advisory. Most of the people concerned cry down enforced ratings as just another form of censorship. They don't have quite the fervor, however, of the representatives of the industry. Johnston argued: "Could an 'Adults only' system really work? Who could decree what is suitable for an adult . . . at 14? . . . at 16? . . . or at 18? . . . . or at 21?" *The Film Daily* editorialized: "Any such control is based on a fallacious premise—that the moral impact of a film is changed at a patron's 16th or 18th birthday anniversary."

Of course, many exhibitors would try to exploit classification. I once saw a sign outside a London theater that read: "The X-iest Picture in Town." But it is surely better to know that children cannot see such a film than to read an American ad that says, "BROADMINDED ADULTS PLEASE!" or "Definitely NOT FOR JUNIOR!," and then to watch the box office sell tickets to any youngster with cash in hand.

Chapter

26

The Screen Writer and His Problems

T̲he screenplay from which the feature film is drawn has a unique form. It is not the form of the novel, the short story, or even the play. It has been with us for many, many years, and yet we have no name for it. I mean a name—a noun—that might suggest its peculiar form: the mixture of narrative and drama, of wide-sweeping movement and the intimacy of the close-up; and the fusion of what we see and what we hear, which gains fresh meaning through the psychological spell of editing. In trying to describe the special quality of these elements at their best, most critics get no further than the awkward adjective "cinematic." Some of us prefer the simpler word "filmic."

Without the screenplay there can be no fiction film of the sort we know. The prevision that lies in the script is basic. Its marshaling of scenes and sequences, quite as much as its dialogue, establishes the unique form of this newest art. To some degree it does not matter whether the script is an original screenplay or an adaptation from another form of fiction. The essential point is that it must be filmic; it must provide the basis for collaboration between director, editor, and cameraman.

The Case for the Original Screenplay
Unlike plays, screenplays are rarely written by a private entrepreneur, risking his time and hoping to make an eventual profit out of his invest-

ment. Nearly always the screenplay is the work of a writer to whom the studio pays a weekly salary or a lump sum to make a screenplay from material which the studio owns.

When the writer ventures to create a screenplay that is wholly his own in material and in writing, and for which he is paid nothing unless a studio buys it, the work is customarily called "an original screenplay."

Personally, I am for the original screenplay. Plot and all, it should be conceived and written for the screen just as a play is conceived and written for the stage. That is, it should be written on speculation in any handy garret. If it is sold for production, then, like a play, it should be made with only such changes as the producer and director can persuade the writer to accept.

Naturally enough, most Hollywood writers also favor the original screenplay—at least in theory. As far back as 1952, Robert Buckner advised his fellows that a writer "ought to be like a farmer—raise his own crop and bring it to market." A contract writer, said Buckner, is "a sharecropper and can never have the full sense of integrity and freedom with which to express himself. A free-lancer may have less security but the only security worth the name is pride and self-respect."

Sam Goldwyn agrees. Speaking at an annual awards banquet of the Screen Writers Guild, he attacked those writers "who can't even think about a story unless they are on someone's payroll." He urged the writers to become independent creators of screenplays, assuring them that they would "wind up not only feeling better, but with a much healthier bank balance." But Goldwyn did not promise that their scripts would be as inviolable as a play. Nor did he cite any original screenplays that he had bought after they were finished. However, his interest in original work is clear from his record. Among the more than sixty pictures that Goldwyn has produced since the coming of sound, more than a third have been made from original screenplays or have been based on stories written for the screen, which should remind us that he brought Broadway playwrights into his studio in 1917, and popular novelists a little later.

Old Patterns Hinder Progress

The paucity of original screenplays is in the largest sense the result of Hollywood's reluctance to reshape its patterns of operation.

Unlike the playwright, who has a long tradition of royalty payments, the screen writer has almost always been hired to work on a weekly basis, though sometimes induced to accept a lump sum for the entire job. Writers are paid salaries that range from $400 to $4,000 a week, or they may get a handsome fee for piece work. Such a financial pattern seems more attractive to the screen writer than the gamble of writing an original screenplay on his own time.

It is attractive to the studios, too, and not merely because the pattern is hallowed by age. So long as it exists, the screen writer can never have the control over his material that the playwright enjoys. Obviously, if the screen writer is content to be paid—and paid well—for turning out what the studio wants, he cannot expect to gain also the creative status that the speculating playwright commands in the theater.

All this might long since have been changed if some of our distinguished playwrights and novelists had led the way. Because their ma-

---

Tolstoy: "I Rather Like It."

You will see that this little clicking contraption with the revolving handle will make a revolution in our life—in the life of writers. It is a direct attack on the old methods of literary art. We shall have to adapt ourselves to the shadowy screen and to the cold machine. A new form of writing will be necessary. I have thought of that and I can feel what is coming.

But I rather like it. This swift change of scene, this blending of emotion and experience—it is much better than the heavy, long-drawn-out kind of writing to which we are accustomed. It is closer to life. In life, too, changes and transitions flash by before our eyes, and emotions of the soul are like a hurricane. The cinema has divined the mystery of motion. And that is greatness.

When I was writing *The Living Corpse* [a film version, *Redemption*, was produced with John Gilbert in 1930], I tore my hair and chewed my fingers because I could not give enough scenes, enough pictures, because I could not pass rapidly enough from one event to another. The accursed stage was like a halter choking the throat of the dramatist; and I had to cut the life and swing of the work according to the dimensions and requirements of the stage. . . .

But the films! They are wonderful! Drr! and a scene is ready! Drr! and we have another! We have the sea, the coast, the city, the palace —and in the palace there is tragedy (there is always tragedy in palaces, as we see in Shakespeare).

I am seriously thinking of writing a play for the screen. . . .

—From an interview
supposed to have occurred on Tolstoy's 80th birthday in 1908.
(*From Jay Leyda's* Kino, *as translated by David Bernstein.*)

terial was in such demand, they could have stipulated that their work should not be substantially altered. Instead, through indifference or through contempt for the screen, they took the cash and let the credits go.

Another studio pattern works against the original screenplay. This is the habit—unfortunately on the increase—of buying the presold novel or play that has already gained a substantial audience. This the screen writer knows all too well. And he knows that if he is going to speculate with his time, he will find a readier motion picture market, and a more lucrative one, if he can first turn his material into a published novel or a produced play. If his work is successful, the market will be even more lucrative.

"Story and Screenplay"

A great many Hollywood writers make a living of sorts by writing stories aimed directly for the screen. Almost always these stories are submitted in a kind of outline written in the present tense. (Another instance of Hollywood patterns, since this bastard form—prose in the present tense —probably continues from the silent days when such a film story was the scanty blueprint from which the director shot his picture.)

When a present-day writer is able to sell an original story he can often make a deal by which he is hired to work on the screenplay. Thus he may earn a credit of "Story and Screenplay by John Doe." The most impressive title, usually understood only by screen writers, is "Written by John Doe," which means that Doe has done the entire story and screenplay by himself, with no material from anyone else. A Swedish writer-director has used—quite legitimately—the words "A Film by Ingmar Bergman" ahead of the title of the picture. When director (but nonwriter) Otto Preminger tried to do this with his *The Man With the Golden Arm* (1955), the Screen Writers Guild successfully objected.

Quite often, the only true begetter has to split a screenplay credit when the studio decides he needs a collaborator, or when the studio fires him and hires someone else to change and "polish" what he has written.

Although very, very few writers ever risk the time involved in developing a full screenplay on speculation, there have been some interesting recent exceptions. Arthur Miller developed *The Misfits* (1961) as a screenplay that in its printed form looks rather like a cross between a screenplay and a novelette. William Inge wrote and sold *Splendor in the Grass* (1961) as an original screenplay.

Originality Without Speculation

Earlier in this chapter I have defined an "original screenplay" as something written on speculation and sold for production. In an effort to simplify and clarify writing credits, the Screen Writers Guild has eliminated the credit "Original Screenplay by John Doe." We must recognize, however, an *ersatz* variety. It is not written on speculation, yet it can stand on its own feet as an original contribution to screen writing. This kind of screenplay develops when a writer or a writer-director interests a studio in a story outline or an idea, and then, with or without a collaborator, turns out the shooting script. Whether or not this was the full history of the following pictures, they are examples of notably successful films created in much this way: *The Great McGinty* (1940), *Citizen Kane* (1941), *Woman of the Year* (1942), *Princess O'Rourke* (1943), *The Bachelor and the Bobby-Soxer* (1947), *Battleground* (1949), *Sunset Boulevard* (1950), *On the Waterfront* (1954), and *The Defiant Ones* (1958). All won Academy Awards. Another type of original screenplay is the historical biography such as *The Story of Louis Pasteur* (1935), *The Life of Emile Zola* (1937), *Young Mr. Lincoln* (1939), *Dr. Ehrlich's Magic Bullet* (1940), and *Freud* (1962).

The innate desire to write original screenplays—on salary, however —sometimes takes odd forms. I knew a man who always spent weeks of wasted effort trying to change the plot of whatever material he was working on. A classic case of a sea-change into something rich and strange was *The Cisco Kid* (1931). In O. Henry's short story, the central figure was an American, not a Mexican; a villain, not a hero. "It has been one of the Kid's pastimes to shoot Mexicans 'to see them kick.'" I have never discovered how this degenerate sadist was turned into the caballero that Warner Baxter played, but the Kid lived on into radio and TV. Sometimes the task of the writer is to manufacture a plot for a nonfiction best seller. It took James Hilton, two other men, and one woman to do this for *Mrs. Miniver* (1942). Curtis Kenyon dreamed up the plot idea for *Wake Up and Live* (1937), but others wrote the screenplay.

Adaptations Began with the Greeks

Although we may hope that the original screenplay will dominate the screen as the original play dominates the theater, something can be said—and warmly—for the screen writer who does the very difficult job of adapting a novel or a play. He can be more than the mere craftsman we sometimes call him. And perhaps we should be patient with film-makers in their slow progress toward the exclusive cultivation of thoroughly original material.

The stage itself was slow. The tragedies of the great Greeks were almost all adaptations of the myths of gods and heroes. One of the few "originals" we know about is Aeschylus' *The Persians*, based on Athens' victory over the invaders. The plots of all but two of Shakespeare's plays have been traced to romances or histories from other pens. All the Elizabethans were practiced adapters, and Corneille and Racine stuck more or less to history and myth. Perhaps it was the self-reliant Spanish playwrights of the "Golden Age" who spurred Molière into devising new plots. It took two centuries more to make originality the hallmark of genius in the theater.

Of course the modern playwright sometimes adapts a novel or goes to history for his material. In a single season Broadway saw *Ethan Frome*, a dramatization by Owen Davis and his son Donald Davis of Edith Wharton's novelette; Helen Jerome's version of *Pride and Prejudice;* and the play that Sidney Howard made from Humphrey Cobb's *Paths of Glory.* Maxwell Anderson went to history for *Elizabeth the Queen, Mary of Scotland,* and *Valley Forge.* In the field of prose fiction, originality is more highly valued. Novels are seldom adapted from short stories or long poems, and a novelist of today wins little critical respect when he turns famous figures into heroes, and poses as being privy to what they said to their valets.

The Dubious Status of the Screen Writer

Though some writers are hired to make their original stories into screenplays, the great majority are assigned to turning novels, plays, ideas, and other people's originals into motion picture scripts. They have no more control over their work than has the author of the material they are working on, who sells a piece of fiction to a studio under a contract that allows the purchaser to "freely adapt, change, transpose, revise, rearrange, add to and subtract from" his work. The writer working for a studio writes nothing solely to please himself, and when he is done, he owns nothing except his salary.

A typical contract makes clear that all he writes belongs to the "partnership, firm, or corporation" employing him. It provides that his "employment shall include (but not be limited to) the writing, composing, and preparation of original stories, treatments, adaptations, continuities,

The Passionate Screenwriter to His Love

Oh, come, my love, and join with me
The oldest infant industry.
Come seek the bourne of palm and pearl,
The lovely land of Boy-Meets-Girl.
Come grace this lotus-laden shore,
This Isle of Do-What's-Done-Before.
Come, curb the new, and watch the old win,
Out where the streets are paved with Goldwyn.
Here let me guide your sedulous pen
To trace the proven lines again;
Here ply your quill, in glory dipt,
And see what happens to your script;
Hear how your phrases—metered, guarded,—
With actors' jokes are interlarded.
Oh, come, my love, nor fret the while
The mighty disregard your smile,
For Cohens, in this haughty small berg,
Bow but to God [Who's cut by Thalberg].
Oh, cast your scruples to the winds
And join us Pegasus' behinds!
Come, learn along with me, my sweet,
How charming thrice a day to eat,
How good to bend the stubborn neck
And hail the rhythmic weekly cheque!
But when, my love, you have been here
A little less than half a year,
You start to talk, who once were dumb,
Of "what a wondrous medium,"
And "why, they haven't scratched the surface,"
[While grieved Mnemosyne hides her face]
And "here's the writer's noblest art"—
That day, my perjured love, we part!

— Dorothy Parker in *The Screen Writer.*

screenplays, polishing jobs, gags, and/or incidental dialogue for and in connection with (but not limited to) the picture tentatively entitled _____." After a couple of pages of legalisms, the contract tells the writer that all his work "shall automatically become our property, and for this purpose, we shall be deemed to be the author thereof." Thus the studio creates a sort of "corporate author," who owns not only the work of the writer, but also the copyright of anything that may arise from his activities. Obviously the studio values his abilities most highly. If he has any doubts, he should consider two other provisions in his contract. His employer insists on the right to use his "name, voice, likeness, and photograph in such manner and to such an extent as may be desired." Further, it is prepared to assert against all the world that the writer's services are of a "special, unique, unusual, extraordinary, and intellectual character which gives them a peculiar value." What more could a noncorporate author—he is also known as a "natural person"—possibly desire?

Multiple Authorship

The man writing the screenplay may be hired by the week, by the month, or—now very rarely—by the year. Within those limits he may be fired or he may have to tolerate a collaborator. (He is always subject to "suggestions" from his producer.) Sometimes he is paid a lump sum for delivering a script within a certain period, but the script may be rewritten by others. By the early sixties there was less collaboration than before. When Kenneth MacKenna came to MGM in 1938, writers averaged seven per script; that had been Thalberg's way of working. When he left, about twenty years later, the figure was down to one and one-half. There was a time, however, and not so long ago, when if a Broadway producer had followed the Hollywood pattern, a playbill might have read:

Musical Chairs

A New Play by Arthur Miller and Tennessee Williams
Adapted by Moss Hart & William Inge
from an original idea by Eugene O'Neill

I say "might have read" because although credits were pretty elaborate, some Hollywood writers never took a bow. Even today a man who works for a while on some screenplay may not see his name on the screen. This may be fair enough, for the writers have an excellent arbitration system to settle any disputes. But working in either collaboration or shifts makes for frustration. And frustration is the occupational hazard of writing for the screen.

Television and Other Frustrations and Irritants

When television began to loom on the Hollywood horizon the Screen Writers Guild, now known as the Writers Guild of America, West, appointed a committee to explore the possibilities that the new medium might hold. Its spokesman, Francis Faragoh, wryly reported: "For the writer, television promises to open up vast new realms of frustration." Of course many things besides the indignity of a writer's having to do his work under the direction of the producer, and seeing his dialogue, his scenes, and even his plot changed by others, have given rise to the Hollywood crack that "writers are usually splitting their fees with a psychiatrist."

One of the irritants is feast and famine. A large proportion of the writers work only a few weeks and only for the minimum scale set by the Guild. The highly paid fear that they may lose out. They are haunted by the specter of having to grind away at scripts for television, for gone are the days when the home screen offered a fine opportunity to men like Paddy Chayefsky, Reginald Rose, Horton Foote, Tad Mosel, Sumner Locke Elliott, Robert Alan Aurthur, J. P. Miller and Gore Vidal. Among the productions still remembered are *Marty, Days of Wine and Roses, The Rabbit Trap, Requiem for a Heavyweight, Patterns, 12 Angry Men, Visit to a Small Planet, A Man Is Ten Feet Tall*.

There can be no question about the caliber of most of this work. Over all, the stories were original, and they often carried significant themes. Their characters were usually sharp and recognizable. The best of them, particularly the plays of Chayefsky, had dialogue that seemed to come straight out of life.

All the aforementioned plays eventually appeared as motion pictures and it was an added thorn in the sensitive flesh of the screen writer that men like Chayefsky and Rose were better known to the public and more respected in the studios than even the best of the professionals who had been turning out good motion picture scripts for many years.

Whatever screen credit a writer may get seems lost on the critics. It

SLAVE OF TIME. The airwaves author, as conceived by Robert Osborn for *Television News Writing* by CBS News Staff. Copyright © 1958 by Columbia Broadcasting System, Inc. All rights reserved.

is no pleasure to read in the New York *World-Telegram:* "Miss Sothern's unceasing flow of witty sayings redeems a dull script." The writer has to bear the slings of novelists and playwrights who might have used their reputations to insist that their material was never distorted. Instead the screen writer, whose work is dictated by the producer, has to read these words from Evelyn Waugh: "Each book purchased for motion pictures has some individual quality, good or bad, that has made it remarkable. It is the work of a great array of highly paid and incompatible writers to distinguish this quality, separate it, and obliterate it."

For This Relief Much Thanks

Although, as you may have gathered, the lot of the screen writer is not a happy one, it has improved since the late forties. In the thirties and forties each of the major studios kept a stable of writers under contract. (MGM once had seventy on its payroll.) This may have pleasured these men and women financially, but it often resulted in someone's having to work on an unsympathetic story. Because a studio was paying $1,500 a week to a writer of high-powered drama who had just finished his script, the vice president in charge of production might assign him to a broad comedy or a sentimental story. The studios' agonizing reappraisal that followed the slump at the box office in the early fifties saw the lists of contract writers cut almost to the vanishing point.

Another extravagance had been the putting of writers—singly, in double harness, or troika-style—on story ideas or originals of dubious promise. While I was producing thirty features at Twentieth Century-Fox between 1935 and 1943, I supervised the writing on fifty-two stories that were never produced. At least ninety writers worked on these abortive assignments. Some of the plots got no further than a preliminary treatment. Very few reached screenplay form. Of the thirty features actually produced, two-thirds had more than two collaborators. On a quarter of them, six to eleven writers were involved between the first outline and the final shooting script. Only two could be credited to a single writer—*Young Mr. Lincoln* (1939) to Lamar Trotti and *The Return of Frank James* (1940) to Sam Hellman. The days of reckless gambling with hazardous material now seem to be over. Both the majors and the independents are playing it safe—in a new and better way.

Collaborating with a Director

There is one kind of collaboration that has always seemed to cause the fewest frustrations. This is collaboration with a director rather than apother writer. Most critics and many authors of screenplays believe that the best films come from such teamwork. In the silent days this was common practice. Later some producers like Zanuck had scripts prepared without any directorial advice. The director liked the screenplay or else he didn't shoot it; there might be some small changes, but no more. Nowadays most directors get into the picture much earlier and have more to do with shaping the script. Alfred Hitchock, George Stevens, William Wyler, and most other director-producers are in from the start.

For most writers, working with men of such talent is more than satisfactory. However much they may contribute to the screenplay, they never seek collaborative credit as some lesser directors—and many major directors in France and Italy—sometimes do. They contribute greatly, and the success of the film adds to the reputation of the writer. There is one disadvantage, however. The critics and the public are apt to credit the director rather than the writer with an effective piece of business, an ingenious way of bridging time, or even a dialogued scene. Now it is quite possible that in such close collaboration the director *was* responsible, but how are we to know?

Who Should Take the Bows?

Here are a few examples of values that may have been written into the script by either of the two men, or improvised by the director on the set. In the first, from *The Wild One*, the cutter might have been responsible. While the citizens of a small town are trying to subdue the marauding motorcyclists, there is a scene in which the policeman's daughter urges her father to intervene. He refuses, and slams his gun into a drawer. The film cuts sharply to a movement in the same direction. It is a fist crashing into Brando's jaw. In *Rebel Without a Cause* (1955) James Dean, panicked and breathless, grabs a bottle of milk from an icebox and gulps down a few great swallows, and then, as he sinks back, he rubs the cold bottle across his sweating forehead. Was this last expressive bit of business invented by screen writer Stewart Stern or by director Nicholas Ray, who also wrote the original story?

In *Cavalcade* (1932), made from Noel Coward's play, two newlyweds stand on the deck of an ocean liner, dreaming of the many years they are to spend together. As they go inside, the girl lifts her shawl from the rail, disclosing a life buoy that had been hidden behind it, and we read: "S. S. Titanic." If movie critics had credited this staggering *coup d'oeil* either to director Frank Lloyd or the screen writers Reginald

WRITER OR DIRECTOR? This powerful scene in *Pork Chop Hill* (1959) may have been taken directly from the book by S. L. A. Marshall, created by the screenwriter, James R. Webb, or suggested by the director, Lewis Milestone. As indicated in these sketches made before shooting began, there is first a tremendous explosion. As the screen clears we see the big boot of a wounded soldier in the foreground. Then, as he cries, "I'm hit! I'm hit!" another soldier drags the man backward and upward into a sitting position, and we see that his boot fails to move. The soldier screams, "My foot! My foot!" Then all we see is the boot as the scene fades out. (*Courtesy Mr. Milestone.*)

Berkeley and Sonya Levien, they would have been equally wrong. It had been conceived by the author of the play, who was also a stage director.

When George Seaton shared in the writing of the screenplay for *This Thing Called Love* (1941), he wanted to establish as quickly as possible in the first scene that a married couple were forever quarreling. He showed the end of a squabble, and as the husband stormed out of the room, the wife threw a shoe after him. As it hit the closed door, the camera moved in to show us the scars of other heels. Seaton was a bit distressed when critics praised the director, Alexander Hall, for "a Lubitsch touch."

Sometimes, perhaps, we may rightly blame the director, rather than the writer, for a blemish in the script. But was it Mamoulian, who guided the first script of *Porgy and Bess* (1959), or Preminger, who replaced Mamoulian, that kept the film much too close to the play? I feel that it must have been George Stevens and not Frances Goodrich and Albert Hackett—authors of the play based on the diary of Anne Frank and also of the screenplay of the film produced in 1959—who injected into the *comédie humaine* confined to the attic, the sinister shots of Nazi trucks taking away other Jews to concentration camps.

Creative collaboration between writer and director occurs in play production. Men like Elia Kazan and Joshua Logan contribute in various ways before and during rehearsals. Designer Jo Mielziner made *Death of a Salesman* into a one-set show that was more effective than the many separate scenes that Arthur Miller's original script called for could have been. Yet, as in the movies, the audience can know little or nothing of what the director has contributed. A rare exception is *Cat on a Hot Tin Roof*. Kazan persuaded Tennessee Williams to write a new last act, and the playwright published both versions.

The Prescription of Dr. G.B.S.

Thirty years ago George Bernard Shaw suggested other and better forms of collaboration for the screen writer. Going through some correspondence with him, over an abortive attempt of mine to make a film version of *The Devil's Disciple* with John Barrymore as Dick Dudgeon in 1934, I found him suggesting—ahead of his time as usual —not only that a playwright should prepare the screenplay of his own drama, but that he should turn director and put it on celluloid: ". . . there is nothing for it but to assume that the author knows his job, and stand or fall by it. This is, of course, unless the author can stand by and produce [the English stage uses the word 'produce' as we use 'direct'] his work himself, which is the ideal plan."

Following and even extending Shaw's idea, some Hollywood writers have found a tranquilizer that ends or allays frustration. This is to become a producer or a director or both. Dore Schary, Samuel Engel, Jerry Wald, and Zanuck were writers to begin with. There are many others who have given up the typewriter for executive posts. An increasing number have become writer-directors or writer-producers. Sometimes the man continues to write screenplays. Sometimes he hires and works with another writer in close, intelligent collaboration. I shall name only a few of the "hyphenates," as Hollywood calls them. Charles Brackett, Milton Sperling, and Norman Krasna have written scripts as well as produced films. George Seaton, Philip Dunne, Richard Brooks, Valentine Davies, and Frank Tashlin have directed their own screenplays. Nunnally Johnson, Joseph L. Mankiewicz, Robert Rossen, Delmer Daves, John Huston, and Billy Wilder usually produce as well as write and direct. For a time the most successful of director-writers was Preston Sturges. He deserves special and separate mention for the original screenplays of his cynical *Sullivan's Travels* (1941) and his hilarious *Miracle of Morgan's Creek* (1943) and *Hail the Conquering Hero* (1944).

Writers turn into directors and/or producers. Directors and producers seldom become writers. This is what industrial engineers might call the pattern of work-flow in the factories of Hollywood. Irving Pichel, an actor and a brilliant critic who became a director, used to say that it was easier for a writer to become a director than for a director to become a writer. George Seaton has said that when he was still a writer but looking forward to his first job of directing, he thought that directing might be easier than writing, and after he had taken the plunge, he *knew* it was. Ben Hecht once said: "A writer who can't direct or a director who can't write is almost as big an amateur as the producer who can do neither."

For most writers, Hollywood was, by the sixties, a place of remarkable skills and deep frustrations. In commenting on the creators of Elizabethan drama a writer in the *Encyclopaedia Britannica* might be describing the ways of Hollywood screen writers:

> Writing for the stage only, . . . they acquired an instinctive insight into the laws of dramatic cause and effect, and infused a warm vitality into the dramatic literature which they produced, so to speak, for immediate consumption.

On the other hand, the same cause made rapidity of work-manship indispensable to a successful playwright. *How* a play was produced, how many hands had been at work upon it, what loans and what spoliations had been made in the process, were considerations of less moment than the question *whether* it was produced, and whether it succeeded.

This period of the English drama could not therefore yet be one of full consummation.

Chapter

27

The Director —
Prime Partner in Film-Making

Iт TAKES FIVE MEN to make a movie. They are the producer, the writer, the director, the cutter, and the cameraman. Yes, I am leaving out the actor and many a necessary technician, but that is because I am using "make" in the special sense of giving a movie its unique form. Three of these five—the director, the cutter, and the cameraman—are hard to isolate. Their work overlaps so much. The director must provide hundreds of shots for the cutter to edit. The cutter must, or should, try to get more out of them than the director quite imagined. The man with the camera not only makes these shots possible, but gives them meaning and beauty. As I write about the three who labor together, I find it impossible to seal off their work in the neat, literary pigeonholes called chapters. In this chapter and the next two you will find a mingling of the three activities—with the director's always to the fore.

For Some Directors, Supreme Kudos

The dominance of the director on the sound stage and in the cutting room is reflected—and perhaps exaggerated—in the public credit he receives. At worst, his name stands in lonely and climactic splendor on the last card of the film's main title. For some there is even greater *kudos*. The moviegoer doesn't have to read the contracts of certain outstanding directors to realize how high these happy few have risen in esteem. Newspaper and magazine advertisements spell it out; so do the marquees of theaters.

Even the critics, free of any contractual obligations, write of "Billy Wilder's *One, Two, Three* and Kazan's *Splendor in the Grass.*" This is an old habit, acknowledging the primacy of the director. In the silent days it was Griffith's *The Birth of a Nation* and DeMille's *The King of Kings.* When sound came in, we read of Hitchcock's *The Thirty-Nine Steps* and Ford's *The Informer.*

You may think that something new has been added when you see such an ad as this:

> 20th Century-Fox Presents
> George Stevens' Production of
> *The Diary of Anne Frank*
> Produced and Directed by George Stevens

This is no new kick. In 1947, I remember how surprised I was to see on a preview screen:

> A Paramount Picture
> A John Farrow Production
> *Easy Come, Easy Go*
> Produced by Kenneth Macgowan
> Directed by John Farrow

I had forgotten how the film version of Frank Norris' novel *McTeague* was billed way back in 1924:

> Louis B. Mayer Presents
> Erich von Stroheim's Production
> *Greed*
> Produced by Metro-Goldwyn Corp.
> Personally Directed by Erich von Stroheim

The fact that we now see more of this sort of thing merely means that studios and distributors have been forced to admit how decisive a hand our more accomplished directors can and do have in production—especially if they are independents.

Of course we still have producers who don't direct, and some of them get top billing. But when an advertisement begins with the words "A Samuel Goldwyn Production" or "Walt Disney's Production" we are dealing with a Titan, one of those primordial deities of Hollywood who, like Selznick, Zanuck, or Wallis, have controlled a studio or had a long career as an independent. When a writer gets such high and lonely credit, it is only because, like Billy Wilder, he has become an outstanding director.

from
METRO·GOLDWYN·MAYER
WILLIAM WYLER'S
PRESENTATION OF

BEN-HUR

A TALE OF THE CHRIST
TECHNICOLOR® — FILMED IN CAMERA 65

INTO THE EMPYREAN WITH WYLER. Once it might have been "MGM Presents *Ben-Hur.* . . . Produced by Sam Zimbalist, Directed by William Wyler" or, later, "MGM Presents William Wyler's *Ben-Hur.* . . . Produced and Directed by William Wyler." The emergence of independent producers and new companies financing and/or distributing their films resulted in some fantastically complicated billing. For example, in 1962: *"The Day the Earth Caught Fire.* Produced and Directed by Val Guest. A Val Guest Production. A British Lion-Pax Picture. A Universal-International Release."

The Dominance of the Director

Even though a director may not rate the accolade of "A So-and-So Production," he is usually the most important factor in the shooting of a picture. Such supremacy is the result of the complexity of production that I have described earlier. A dynamic and creative producer may dominate a pliant director, but this is mainly in the preliminary work on script and casting, the design of sets and costumes. Once shooting has begun, the director has to control and guide the actors, the cutter, and the cameraman. He must pull together the work of the others if there is to be a successful film, let alone an outstanding one. The film must be a synthesis, yet it must never seem synthetic.

The director has both lost and gained through the coming of sound. Unless he has the special abilities of a writer, he has lost the power to shape—even create—the story and its characters. He has gained the power to dramatize the story more fully and to interpret its characters more vividly through the dialogue.

Linkéd Credits Long Drawn Out

What do you do while that dreary, dull line of technical credits flashes on the screen at the beginning of every new movie following the main title? Daydream, talk to your neighbor, twiddle your thumbs or eat popcorn? If you're like myself you rarely bother to read them.

Who cares if the sound was mixed by Joe Zilch and the gentlemen's hairpieces were designed by Effie Yogurt, except Joe and Effie and their close associates?

What we want is for the picture to get started. Instead we have to squirm through this deadening delay to the opening of every film.

If the same principle were followed in the presentation of this and every column in The Mirror, the opening credits would go something like this:

"TODAY'S COLUMN"

A Los Angeles Mirror Production

Norman Chandler, president, The Times-Mirror Co.

Arthur Laro, Editor and Publisher

Jack Donahue, Managing Editor

Written by Dick Williams.	Page makeup by Don Stone.
Edited by Fred W. Fox.	Stereotyping by Edwin Waugh.
Copycutting by Don Baltzell.	Printing by Gene Bell.
Linotyping by John Stewart.	Delivery by Jesse Moody.
Proofreading by Arthur Berg.	Wholesale dealer: Ted R. Branson.

—Dick Williams in the *Los Angeles Mirror.*

From Silence to Sound

Forty and fifty years ago, the director was usually the complete dictator and often the sole creative force. The story might be merely a smile on the face of D. W. Griffith. At best, it was hardly more than a plot outline. The man who first called a script a "scenario" may or may not have known about the bare plots on which the players of the *commedia dell'arte* improvised, but the comparison was apt. Shooting "off the cuff," the director could ornament and alter the plot and the characters. Even those stray bits of dialogue and description that flashed onto the screen could be rewritten or improvised in the course of the editing. The director could reshape the picture as he pleased, unless—and this happened rarely—the studio took over and put a cutter on the job of "saving" a sick film.

I wonder if some of the opposition to sound came from directors who saw the writing on the wall—or, rather, the writing in the dialogue script.

At any rate they soon discovered that altering characters and changing the plot was impossible while a talkie was shooting, and afterward it meant costly retakes. Improving the dialogue was another matter, if the director had some talent along that line. In the thirties Gregory La Cava, of *My Man Godfrey* (1936), was the only one I knew who was so happily endowed. There are few today, unless they are writer-producers. Besides, independents as well as the major studios fear the costly delays involved in script changes. La Cava had the happy knack of shooting fast after he had spent the first hour or so of each day teaching his cast new dialogue. But when Marlon Brando urged his actors to "improvise" in *One-Eyed Jacks* (1961), the Western took six months to shoot.

New Power Through Dialogue

Between 1928 and 1930, the silent director discovered that in the beginning was the word, and the word was God—the written word that became the spoken word. Yet there was a ray of hope. He also discovered that though the word was "with God"—as it had been in the Bible—God was only the producer, and the producer was usually too busy to be able to tell all his writers what to write. Since few of the men who wrote the silent scenarios could handle dialogue, the studios had to import Broadway playwrights. These men needed guidance, and they welcomed it as much from the directors as from the writers of silent scripts. Thus many directors continued to work with the screen writers for some weeks before shooting began. Today more and more of them play a considerable part in preparing screenplays—some quite brilliantly. Before Alfred Hitchcock became his own producer, I remember how much of the basic plot, as well as individual lines, he contributed to *Lifeboat* (1944). However, the sad fact remains that it is easier for a writer to become a director than for a director to write a screenplay.

Because of the potency of the spoken word, the director of a talkie can make a far solider contribution to the character and quality of a film than his silent predecessor. Beyond the shaping of the "continuity" —the current six-bit word that replaced "scenario"—he and he alone has the power to evoke and shade and vitalize the emotions, the characterizations, and the ideas that may be conveyed by the words the actors speak. What the director does about the camera and the editing is of great significance, and I shall spend much of this chapter and most of the next two on such matters; but what he does with the actors and the dialogue may be far more important to the artistic as well as commercial success of a picture. In this area the tasks of a film director and the director of a play are much the same; in others far different. Perhaps the easiest way to explain what a film director does is to compare him to a director who works with a stage play.

Direction for the Screen vs. the Stage

First among their common problems is casting. In Marlon Brando and Jessica Tandy, Elia Kazan found exactly the right players for Stanley and Blanche in the stage version of *A Streetcar Named Desire*. He chose as wisely when he used Carroll Baker, Karl Malden, and Eli Wallach in *Baby Doll* (1956). The need for a star name sometimes forces miscasting, as, for instance, the same Miss Baker in *But Not For Me* (1959).

Beyond casting lie all the subtlety and the violence of emotion—or of comedy—that the script may call for, and that the director must bring out of the actors. Pace is as important on the screen as it is on the stage. It may mean swift speech and the pounding interchange of lines, or a long pause and a slow emphasis on certain words. All the basic skills of acting, and therefore of direction, are common to stage and screen, except one. This is voice projection. The intimacy of the camera and the power of the amplifier have eliminated the kind of actor who, as a critic once said, can put three o's in Roman.

On the sound stage there are many tasks and many problems unknown to the theater. These involve the interlocked skills of camera and editing. Most of them arise from the fact that an average reel contains from 70 to 80 separate pieces of film, which means between 400 and more than 1,000 in a feature film, depending on length and tempo. In a single reel of *The Charge of the Light Brigade* (1936), cutter George Amy used 295 cuts. All these bits of film—even though some may have come out of one single scene—call for many different set-ups of cameras and lights. They involve the magic intricacies of sound recording. Through a few weeks to many months, shooting is seldom done in strict continuity. To bring order out of all this, the film director must have the omniscience of a Monday morning quarterback.

The Matter of Rehearsal

The job of the stage director is far, far simpler. He works slowly and by a kind of trial and error. Rehearsing for three or four weeks, he and his actors can develop a sense of emotional continuity as they read the script together, then concentrate on each act, and finally run through the whole play time after time. The director watches the thing grow under his hand. Though he can't alter or add lines without the permission of the author, he can change the acting emphasis at any time if he thinks he can thus improve the flow and impact of the drama. Even after the first night, usually on the road, he can still reshape the performance. All this is impossible for the film director.

Griffith relied heavily on rehearsals; according to Seymour Stern, there were six weeks of such work before the cameras rolled on *The Birth of a Nation*. But by the time dialogue made rehearsals most useful, the studios had almost forgotten about them. A stage star, George Arliss, introduced rehearsals again when Warner Brothers brought him to Hollywood in 1929. Nowadays it is only the exceptional director (usually his own producer) who can assemble a few of his actors for what is little more than the line readings of the first days of rehearsal in the theater. The film-maker cannot watch and guide the development of a production, as the stage director can, through three or four weeks. Worse still, he can't do this with a sequence or even, in most cases, with a single complex scene. He must break down the action into smaller fragments, and complete one shot at a time. Barring later retakes, this shot is set, frozen, finished. In fifteen minutes to an hour or more—depending on the length and difficulty of any shot—the film director must go through all the steps in the development of the action that the stage director has weeks to perfect. First the cameraman and the "gaffer" (chief electrician) work out the lighting for the shot, with "stand-ins" taking the place of the chief actors. Next, the director rehearses his players in their lines and movements, while lights may be added or readjusted. Then, at last, the scene is played while the camera rolls; or, rather, one single shot is taken out of however many may make up a scene. There may be one take or there may be ten or more. But in a fraction of a working day, this single shot has passed from a run-through, in stage terms, and four weeks of rehearsals into a dress rehearsal and finally a first night.

E Pluribus Unum *the Hard Way*

To make the work of the director still more difficult, scenes have to be shot in higgledy-piggledy order. This is a matter of economy. A shooting schedule that groups together the days when expensive players work can save a good deal of money. It is much cheaper to finish all the scenes laid in a certain set than to take only some of them and then move to another set or sound stage. Days on location must be grouped together for the same reason. Thus a director may have to start toward the end of a picture, and then switch to the beginning. Working on one stage for a week or more, he may be forced to shoot scenes that leap forward over gaps of weeks, months, or even years. All this means that the film director has to have so firm, so complete, a conception of the whole film that he can make any scene at any time, and give it just the emotional quality that will make it fit into the pattern of other scenes that he may have completed ten days earlier or may not shoot for two more weeks. The film director has the enormously difficult and enormously important task of keeping in his head the entire development of the action and the characters and of shaping the performances of the actors in each shot so that, when some hundreds of separate shots are put together, the characterizations and the story will flow on consistently and effectively. Jumping back and forth from scene to scene, he must be able to see each one as part of a previsioned whole. Until he watches the picture at a sneak preview he must be, as John Cromwell has put it, his own audience.

The Actor—Super-Marionette

What does this mean for the actor? By and large, he is more completely in the hands of the director than in a stage play. Only the more important players have complete scripts. The others must depend on the director for any real idea of what their scenes are about. No actor can benefit, as he does in the theater, from the gradual development of the significance of a character through long rehearsals. Yet players often gain from the methods of film production. They may give better performances than they could on the stage. This is not alone because of the emotional power of the close-up. The director, concentrating on a single scene at a time—indeed, on a single shot or even a single line of dialogue—and going through it a dozen times, can cajole, cozen, or browbeat a player into giving him just the reading he wants. In this, and the elimination of voice projection in favor of intimacy, lies the secret of the admirable performances of actors who have been "hams" on the stage, and the astonishing work of children on the screen.

An actor may not only give a better performance on the screen than on the stage; his playing can never deteriorate through the exaggeration or the slovenliness that may develop during a Broadway run. But he loses, and the spectator loses, that wonderful sense of immediacy, of personal contact, and of the triumph over fallibility that takes place each night in the living theater. To compensate for this, the screen actor—super-marionette in the director's bag of tricks—has only the uncertain chance of greater security and wider fame.

Play vs. *Film Script*

Shakespeare and romantic playwrights wrote in many scenes. A modern play is much more compact. Ibsen, in his maturity, and most of those who followed him, were content with three or four acts, and often with only one set. Plays of today—*Death of a Salesman,* for example—may be told in quite a number of scenes, but these scenes are played in different areas of a kind of multiple setting; there is a certain compactness even here.

The script of a film is much more complex. Its action is much more dispersed. It may tell its story in scores of scenes laid in almost as many different locales. Furthermore, because of the very nature of the motion picture, the director must break down these scenes into many individual shots. Further he must foresee how these shots will react on one another, and move the story forward.

To grasp the complexities and the possibilities of both directing and editing, let us begin with something that was as peculiar to silent films as it is to talkies, and as alien to plays. It may seem only a matter of technical trickery. Sometimes it serves no better end than saving time and money. Yet often it can heighten the power of speech and action, deepen and quicken characterization. When you understand it, you have a clue to the editing process that makes the directing of a picture so different from the directing of a play.

Film Tricks with Time, Space, and Emotion

This unique factor in film-making is the influence of one shot upon another. Or perhaps I should say the influence of two successive shots upon an audience. The whole becomes greater than the sum of its parts, and something quite different. Shots that are physically unrelated take on continuity. They may merely deceive an audience, but they may also move it.

In the chapter on Russian technique, I have mentioned the classic demonstration by Kuleshov of how an audience can read different emotions into the same close-up of an actor when it is intercut with a bowl of soup, a woman in a coffin, or a child at play. The Russian director, Pudovkin, gave another example: if a cutter follows a close-up of a smiling man with an insert of a revolver, and then the same man terror-stricken, the spectator decides he's a coward. Transposing the two close-ups makes him a hero.

The psychological effect of one shot upon another was more important in many ways in the silent film than it is in the talkie. Today character is slowly built up through dialogue. The emotion of most scenes can't be drastically altered by cutting, though it may be heightened by "reaction shots." Yet, in another way, the relation of two or more shots has the same impact in a talkie that it has always had. This is a matter of juggling geography and consolidating space. Besides saving time and money, it sometimes achieves an effect that would otherwise be impossible.

A scene in a room of an Italian villa, shot on a Hollywood sound stage, ends as the hero exits through an impressive door. Then the film cuts to a long shot of the actor or a double walking out through the same-shaped door onto the terrace of a house actually overlooking Lake Como. Then will come a close shot of the actor against the wall of the Hollywood villa. The spectator accepts the idea that the room and the terrace are both in Italy.

Similarly, a scene may include a newsreel shot of marching soldiers, a close-up of the tear-stained face of Ethel Barrymore, and then a shot of Van Johnson in battle helmet jogging along on an invisible treadmill, and we know that a sorrowing grandmother is watching a boy march off to war.

Older and more obvious, yet still potent, is a cutting trick used by Griffith in *Intolerance*, for example, and by many others later on. An actor on top of a high wall falls off in a medium shot, landing safely in a net out of sight of the camera. In the next cut, the same man hits the ground, having leaped from a low-out-of-shot platform.

The Syntax of the Film

H. W. Fowler, author of the wise and often witty book *A Dictionary of Modern English Usage,* defined syntax as how words are arranged in sentences. Film has its syntax, too, which is how shots are arranged in scenes, and scenes in sequences. Here lies the special and peculiar art of the motion picture. It is practiced by both the director, who must supply the various shots, and the cutter, who, collaborating with the director, arranges these "words" into sentences.

It was in the silent days that Terry Ramsaye first linked the word "syntax" with the movies. Since 1930 the talkies have vastly enriched and perfected the editing process—so much indeed, that you can get a good deal of interest out of quite mediocre pictures if you understand some of the basic things about the "sentence structure" of film-making.

THE SIMPLEST EDITING TRICK. When Chaplin first worked for Sennett, he was much disturbed over making an exit from a park and then entering and playing the next scene in front of a store actually three blocks away. In the first two frames above, a man leaves such a park, and in the next frame he walks into another locale. As he turns and shakes his stick to our left, we believe he is threatening the woman. This is the same illusion of remote locales being close together that Kuleshov showed his film students. (*Sketched by Raymond Kitchener.*)

I learned them first early in the thirties by watching the daily rushes of uncut takes as they were shown to the executives of RKO, and then by seeing how they were combined in the rough cuts, preview prints, and finished films. Of course when an audience sees a finished film in a theater, only someone involved in the production can know what shots were left on the cutting room floor before the release print went into distribution, but as a layman you can watch the artistry—or lack of it—with which scenes are put together.

Shots Make Scenes as Words Make Sentences

Of course no two scenes in any film are shot and put together in quite the same way. Some may be very simple indeed. Many are built up out of a number of different shots taken from different spots and different angles. Each camera "set up" alters the size of the actors on the screen or shows them from a new point of view, as you will see from the illustration on page 401.

Sometimes a scene is made in a single shot as the camera follows an actor through a room or out a door and down a street. Often a director needs only two or three shots to cover a scene. The simplest way, however, to explain the synatax of film-making is to analyze a very elaborate scene made up of many shots. Here the director may make a long shot, or establishing shot, of an exterior or a room, with two or more characters in the background. He may then shoot a medium shot, a closer view of actors. Next he may photograph a couple in a two-shot, and

---

The Film's Building Blocks

Take—a series of successive frames taken by a single camera from one set-up.

Shot—a complete take, or a part of a take used in an edited scene.

Scene—a single shot or series of shots that covers a single and continuous dramatic action.

Sequence—a series of closely related scenes.

To complicate matters, there is another term—*cut. Cut* may be used instead of *shot* for any part of a take used in editing a scene; a director may say, "Take out that shot of her face," or, "Add a cut of her hands." "To cut" may mean to add one shot to another: "Cut from her face to her hands." Also, a "rough cut" or a "fine cut" are different stages of the assembled picture.

after that the close-ups of individuals and also over-shoulder shots which concentrate first on one speaker, then on another. (See the illustration below.)

The director may shoot all the action, including the dialogue, in a medium shot—a "master scene"—or he may cover only the beginning and the end and perhaps some broad movement such as an exit during the action. He will then break down the scene into closer shots that repeat the action and dialogue from more intimate angles.

FIVE BASIC SHOTS. Here are the shots most commonly used to build up a scene without panning or dollying the camera. Top left, a long shot, or establishing shot. Top right, a medium shot. Then follow: a two-shot, which might cut the figures at the waist, a close-up, and two over-shoulder shots. In the last type the camera must be kept on one side of an axis line from one head to the other; then the man will always be on the same side of the frame in different shots and will not seem to jump across the screen in the next cut. Sometimes the over-shoulder shot favors the character speaking a line; sometimes it plays on the other to register an important reaction. (*Sketches by Phil Babet.*)

ESTABLISHING SHOT

② (REVELATIONAL SHOT — DINING ROOM)

① (LOBBY) D.

BOOM AND PAN DONNA
SHOT 35 m.m.

MASTER HI-L SHOT THRU EXIT M & J 35mim.
SHOT

MASTER SHOT AFTER J & M EXIT SHOT
40 mm.

OVER·SHOULDER 50 M.M.
PAST SYLVIA TO KEN
SHOT

ALSO INDIVIDUAL KEN 3"
SHOT

OVER·SHOULDER
PAST KEN TO SYLVIA 50 M.M.
SHOT

ALSO
INDIVIDUAL 3"
SYLVIA SHOT

BREAKING DOWN A COMPLEX SCENE. In these sketches made by Delmer Daves for an episode in *A Summer Place* (1959), the establishing shot begins on Donna as she comes downstairs, and pans until we see the dining room. Then comes a master shot of the six principals, and a closer shot as two leave the table. At the bottom are over-shoulder shots. Within both, Daves shows the frame of a close-up taken with a different lens. Daves indicates the lenses used as 35mm, 40mm, 50mm, and 3-inch. The last, which he used for the close-up, takes a larger image than the 50mm from the same position. In shooting this scene the director covered twenty-five speeches in twenty set-ups. Because of some intercutting, the edited version included twenty-three pieces of film. (*Courtesy Mr. Daves.*)

Different Set-ups for Different Scenes

There is no fixed pattern, however, even for long and elaborate scenes. The director is guided by what has gone before and by how he feels a scene can be made most effective. If he has already shot an earlier scene in the same locale, he can skip an establishing shot and open on a medium or even a two-shot. He may combine two types of shots by having the camera move from a two-shot to a close-up. Or he may have an actor walk up to the camera. The script itself affects the director's use of varied set-ups. A very short scene may call for only one shot. If the story has worked up suspense over the passing of time or the signing of a document, the director may open the scene with an "insert," a close shot of a desk clock or a signature and then pull the camera back to take in one or more of the actors. There can be much more elaborate camera movement, which I will discuss in a later chapter.

The Unique Close-up

Sooner or later a director is bound to use a close-up. But how often? Also, the close-up, like most other shots, can vary in size. Usually it includes the head and shoulders of an actor. Often it is just the face. The camera may move in so close that a sweating forehead, a screaming mouth, or even a single eye fills the screen. The close-up is one of the most powerful tools of film-making. Hence it must be used most carefully. Head-and-shoulder shots and over-shoulder close-ups are safe enough in speech and reaction. Anatomical details—the eyes, the mouth —are good only at rare high-points of intense emotion; you see them seldom on the screen. Griffith was the first director who used the close-up significantly. He went to a full-screen face only for a climax; for example, Lillian Gish's terror-stricken close-ups toward the end of *Broken Blossoms*. It was only at the climax of Elizabeth Taylor's tortured self-revelation in *Suddenly, Last Summer* that director Joseph L. Mankiewicz concentrated on her face from chin to eyebrows.

Ingmar Bergman—the most effective yet subtle of the new directors who appeared in the fifties—has said: "Our work in films begins with the human face. We can certainly become completely absorbed in the esthetics of montage, we can bring together objects and still life into magnificent rhythms, we can make nature studies of astounding beauty, but the approach to the human face is without doubt the hallmark and distinguishing quality of the film." Mark Robson may well have been thinking of his own *Home of the Brave* when he said: "The close-up is the cornerstone of greatness in films. . . . It is here that film is unique as a medium of entertainment."

The Cutter—First Aid to the Director

Film-making is so complex that, as I have said, it is impossible to pigeonhole the work of the director, the cutter, and the cameraman. I am trying to treat the chief tasks of each of them in three separate chapters, but again and again they overlap. This is particularly true of the work of the director and the cutter. You have already seen something of how their activities intermesh. Let me give you another example.

Many a director who has come from Broadway to Hollywood owes his training in screen techniques to a cutter. This man, or sometimes a cameraman, has told the tyro where to place the camera, when to

ACTION AND REACTION. Lewis Milestone fills his script with drawings made to guide him in shooting. Here are some for a scene in *Pork Chop Hill*. Three soldiers jump into a shell hole as an explosion catches two others. The director makes a shot of two men turning around and looking back, and intercuts this with what they see as the smoke clears. At the end of the second cut of their reaction, Clemons says: "This flank is yours. Put your men to work." (*Courtesy Mr. Milestone.*)

FIVE CAMERA ANGLES IN ONE SCENE. Before Stanley Kramer began shooting *Judgment at Nuremberg*, the director and his designer, Rudy Sternad, as always worked out the composition of all the scenes. Here are set-ups that gave variety to a very talky scene between the three American judges. In most of the picture there was much camera movement. (*Courtesy Mr. Sternad.*)

move it, how to get all the different shots that will be needed to make a scene effective. Yet I have read an article by such a director in which he mentions every worker, from producer to script girl, except the cutter.

Even a veteran director relies on his cutter—who usually works with him through picture after picture—to make a creative contribution to the finished film. For example, it was cutter Elmo Williams who suggested using the expressive *High Noon* ballad throughout the film and not just over the credit titles as was originally intended. Moreover, before shooting begins, a cutter may suggest the shortening of dialogue or the dropping or rearrangement of scenes to tighten up the script. He will stay on the set as much as he can in order to get the feel of the picture as an aid to editing. Here and there he may suggest an added close-up as a "protection shot"—a means of shortening a scene by cutting dialogue if that should prove necessary. When the director and the cutter

CUTTING IN A COMIC STRIP. You can see good directing and cutting, by film standards, in the top strip from *Gasoline Alley*. The characters stay on the same side of the frame, as in over-shoulder shots. Below, the characters jump from one side to the other. This is partly due to the fact that there isn't room for the character at the right to complete a speech in a single panel, but the creators of comic strips often violate the film rule for sake of variety. (*Courtesy Frank King and Chicago-Tribune–New York News Syndicate, Inc.*)

look at the "rushes," there may be suggestions from both of them as to what shots should be used where. But, whoever makes suggestions, it is the task of the cutter to build up the picture, scene by scene, from hundreds of separate shots. Again and again he has to decide just how long any shot can run. Day after day through the weeks of shooting and cutting, he must choose exactly the right moment to go from shot to shot—say from medium shot to two-shot, from two-shot to close-up. He must sense whether a scene calls for swift cutting from speech to speech or whether it must have its slow moments. He must try to guess which shots will bring laughter, and not follow them too closely with a line of dialogue. All this is work that calls for dramatic instinct based on much experience. The man who does it must have seasoned sensibility.

The director—not the cutter—is, of course, in top authority. When an important long scene or a sequence of shorter ones has been assembled,

THE MOVIOLA. The machine with which the cutter can see and hear a scene or sequence while he is editing it. The sound track runs off the bottom lefthand reel, to be reproduced above; the picture track runs up from the lower righthand reel and the frames are synchronized and the image seen on the small screen. The film can be run forward and backward and stopped for close inspection and the correction of synchronization.

the cutter will show it to the director. He may approve or he may suggest changes. This goes on until a rough cut of the whole picture is ready for final polishing. Today we have no all-embracing Griffith, but a man like George Stevens spends many hours over the moviola (a sort of miniature projector that can run the picture forward or backward and stop it where the director or the cutter wants to alter a scene). Yet Stevens would never deny that his cutter had contributed notably to the finished picture.

Chapter
28

The Cutter—
Right Arm of the Director

IN THE BEGINNING was the camera. And the cameraman was also the director and the writer. But, for some time, he was not a cutter. So long as he told his story in a single shot, he had no scenes to cut apart and no scenes to splice together. When he began to carry his camera from one setting to another—from a garden, perhaps, to a bridge—in the course of telling a story, he had to do a crude form of cutting. Finally, he moved his camera from place to place in the same setting, and a new skill began to appear. At first this looked like a very simple task, as simple as splicing a garden scene to a bridge scene. But it was to grow intricate, exacting, and creative—the very heart of film-making. When the man with the camera became a cutter the motion picture was on its way to becoming an art.

As, in the course of time, the director-cameraman-writer-cutter split into four specialists, one of them had to dominate and direct—note that last word—the functions of the others. Yet however much the director has become responsible for the character and the quality of a film, for half a century he has owed a very great deal to the dramatic sense and the ingenuity and industry of the man who puts the physical film together.

This man has two names. At first he was called a "cutter" because all he had to do was shear off the waste ends of a shot and splice on a main title or another shot. When it slowly became clear that the intricate

409

organization of a great many pieces of film made the motion picture an art, some began to call him an "editor." Both names still stick. In the studio he is a cutter; in the screen credits he becomes an editor.

Cutting Becomes the Art of Editing

A director who was his own cutter alerted the movie world to the prime importance of editing. Around 1910 D. W. Griffith began to build scenes out of a number of different shots, and then organize such scenes into long sequences. He later did this most notably in *The Birth of a Nation.*

In analyzing such a film, it is better to speak of "cuts" rather than "shots," for like later directors, Griffith often used two to a dozen different *parts* of a lengthy shot. These cuts were often very short and, as Griffith organized them, they gave his scenes a swift and highly dramatic tempo. His reenactment of Lincoln's assassination probably lasted only some five minutes, yet in it he used about 55 separate cuts. In the climax of the picture, which involved a Negro's attempt to force the heroine into an interracial marriage, the Negro militia in the streets, the attack on the cabin, and the ride of the Clansmen to the rescue, Griffith used nearly 255 cuts in about twenty minutes of screen time. We don't know the exact length of the cuts in the original print, but in an analysis that the film historian Theodore Huff made in 1939, the cuts in the assassination and the climax averaged about five seconds each. They added up to the first great feat in film-editing.

When sound came in at the end of the thirties, it set back editing, but by 1930 fast cutting was possible again.

Four Planes of Progress from Porter to Sound

Lumping together the contributions of directors and cutters—writers and cameramen, too—we can see four plateaus in the art of editing:

First, the basic contribution of Porter, Hepworth, and Griffith, worked over and added to by Ince, DeMille, Tucker, King, and others between 1915 and 1922.

Next, in the mid-twenties, the moving camera of Murnau, Mayer, and Freund.

At about the same time, the "montage" of the Russians.

Finally, all the refinements and amplifications that sound developed.

In the twenties, Hollywood made no important contribution of her own to the art of editing. And before sound came in, her directors, cutters, and cameramen had scant time to profit by the work of the Germans and the Russians. *The Last Laugh* was produced in 1924,

Potemkin in 1925, *Mother* in 1926—and 1927 was the year that *The Jazz Singer* upset the applecart. The moving camera froze in the "ice boxes" of the first talkies. The swift and ideological "montage" of the Russians would have bogged down in the quicksands of dialogue.

The Cutter Would Be King—and Could Be, Long Ago

In an odd sense, the high time of the cutter, the time when he did indeed become an editor, was the last ten years or so of the silent film. Then he was the man who sometimes saved the studio from the mistakes of the director. A preview would show that something was very, very wrong. Two or three scenes would have to be "fixed" or a whole picture "saved." If the director was working at another studio or if, like von Stroheim, he refused to have anything to do with "slaughtering" his film, the cutter got the salvage job. Today it is different. The presence of dialogue makes almost any important change impossible without retakes, and retakes bring back the old director or a new one. In the silent days, however, radical changes could be made in the cutting room. The man with the splicing machine could effect a miracle by moving scenes around and adding new subtitles. He could drop characters or whole incidents. Through words lettered on title cards, he could change motivations, or even great stretches of plot.

Editorial Legerdemain

Thirty years before Arthur Ripley became a professor of film studies at UCLA he turned his cutting room at Universal into a surgery for a very sick film indeed. When the first preview audience saw this 1922 production by young Irving Thalberg they were barely able to tell the hero from the villain, and they certainly had no liking for the man who got the girl. He was cloyingly sentimental, sweet, and weak, while his opponent had humor and dash. Far along in the fourth reel, Ripley detected a bit of color in the hero. While playing cards at a bridge party, he got angry, tipped over the table, rushed out of the room, tripped and fell. Ripley grafted this scene onto the beginning of the film, and at the next preview the audience accepted the leading man as a reasonable facsimile of a hero.

I remember from about the same time bits of legerdemain that director George Loane Tucker displayed when he was running Samuel Goldwyn's studio in Fort Lee, and I was his assistant. Some tricks were simple enough. He used plastic surgery on Mary Garden's wrinkles in *The Splendid Sinner* (1918) by dropping all her close-ups, and he cured the hero's alcoholism—which he considered superfluous—by cutting to another shot every time the man sidled up to a liquor cabinet. The same year, Tucker saved the life of another film, this time by addition instead of subtraction. The director of *The Beloved Traitor*, starring Mae Marsh, had left several gaps in the story that had to be bridged. The deepest chasm came after the end of one sequence, in which a young fisherman with a talent for sculpture left his home to go to the city as the pet and protégé of the daughter of a rich man, and before the beginning of another, in which we found him famous but dissolute. The release date was so close that Tucker had no time to shoot new scenes. Instead he fell back on a kind of illustrated subtitle. Here is the first part as he wrote it down for the technicians who would make a pair of complex titles:

> Iris into left-half of empty frame the title: "Two years, much money, and new friends make many changes." Soft iris opens at upper right corner (leave words on) circling in the boy's southwester hat without showing his face. Dissolve this out into a stylish silk hat. Another iris opens below this, circling in the rough hand of a fisherman with the heads of a string of fish showing. This dissolves into a gloved hand holding a silver-topped walking-stick. Finally, an iris at the bottom right circles in an old rubber boot; this dissolves into a stockinged foot which slips into a patent leather pump held in the hand of a valet.

All this faded out and then came a similar treatment of the hero's fall from grace.

Sound Ends Trick Editing

The repair jobs I have cited were only a few out of hundreds. To them you can add Herculean tasks of cutting down three- and four-hour films like von Stroheim's and others' to salable length. Such *ex post facto* operations are a sign of how careless, irresponsible, or plain pig-headed some directors could be in the days when they thought a money-loaded public would tolerate almost any picture that moved. Producers were not much better; too often they relied on cutters to salvage badly made films. One of the virtues of sound was that it forced the film-makers to accept their proper responsibilities. It also forced the director and the editor to refine the cutting process and to discover new ways of guiding the audience through time and space.

Punctuating the Film

Besides its syntax, the film has its punctuation marks—semicolons, exclamation points, and periods. Sometimes indicated in the script, sometimes inserted by the cutter, they are:

The dissolve, or lap dissolve. One shot begins to fade out as the next fades in. For a few seconds they are superimposed. Then the first disappears and the second has the screen to itself. (See illustration on page 414). With the coming of sound, and the resultant loss of titles, filmmakers seized upon the dissolve as the best way of indicating a short gap of time or a change of place within a series of closely related scenes that form what is called a "sequence." It may be thought of as a semicolon.

The swish-pan. This is a blur of highlights and racing shadows as the camera seems to pan very swiftly out of one setting and into another. This substitute for a dissolve is used occasionally to add excitement during violent action. If the dissolve is a semicolon, the swish-pan may be called an exclamation point—in the middle of a sentence.

The fade. A shot grows darker and darker, and out of blackness a new shot slowly appears. (See the illustration on page 414.) This fading-out and fading-in is used as a signal that a sequence of scenes is finished, that a more or less major development in the plot has come to an end, and a new one is to begin. The fade-out is the period to a filmic sentence.

The talkies developed some visual devices of dubious value. One is the "wipe." While a shot is held steady and bright on the screen, the next one, just as steady and bright, appears at one edge and takes the place of the first as a faintly visible line runs across the screen. (See the illustration on page 414.) This harshly artificial device replaced the dissolve in some instances. The soft wipe, with a blurred edge between the two cuts, seemed more natural, but neither is used much today. Similar optical tricks, such as diagonal wipes or one shot spiralling out over another or exploding through it, have gone to their grave in TV commercials.

Making Dissolves in the Early Days

When you see old films of the silent days you will note very few dissolves. The reason is simple enough. All dissolves had to be made in the camera. Through the last three or four feet of a shot the shutter was slowly closed. Then the film was rewound to the exact frame where the shutter had begun to close. Finally, when the next shot was made, the

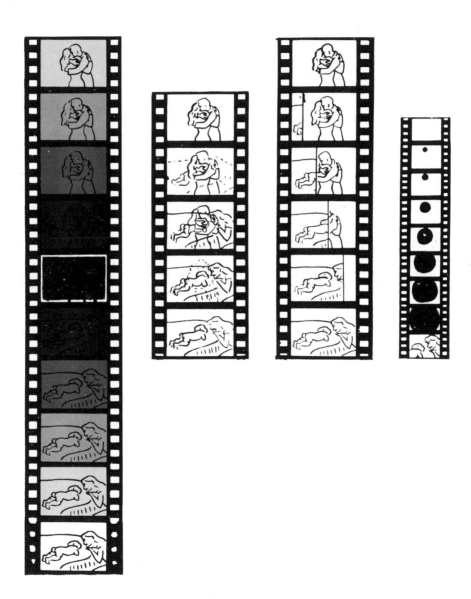

FILMIC PUNCTUATION MARKS. At the left, a fade-out and a fade-in from lovers to a mother and child. Next, a dissolve and then a wipe made with the same shots. Last, the iris once used instead of a fade-out or fade-in. (*Drawings by Phil Babet.*)

shutter was opened at the same speed as it had been closed, thus super-
imposing the fading-out of one shot and the fading-in of the next. This
took time and pains; an error could ruin two shots and require expensive retakes. Worse still, it could hinder the recutting of certain
scenes or the elimination of some shots. Therefore the director—forced
to risk the danger of freezing dissolves into the finished picture—used
them sparingly. He seldom employed them, as he does now, to show
short lapses of time or to smooth out jumps from one locale to another.
Sometimes the dissolve in silent pictures was rather like a visual ornament; it might blend a medium shot of a dancer into an overhead angle.
It was most useful in trick shots such as materializing a ghost. Sometimes, though very rarely, a director made the dissolves the very heart
of a short scene. In visualising Gray's "Elegy," Allan Dwan used some
35 dissolves in about 200 feet—a little over three minutes—of film.

Imitating Shakespeare's Technique

Early in the history of the feature film, directors and cutters found two
ways to dodge the knotty problem of deciding on dissolves long before
editing began. Both ways were truly filmic.

When I noticed them first in the feature films of about 1915, it struck
me that movie-makers were borrowing something from Shakespeare.
Though the Elizabethan stage lacked scenery, in one respect it was
rather like the screen. It had no curtain. Scene after scene had to flow
across the empty stage in smooth continuity. Sometimes, as in the last
eight scenes of *Macbeth*, it was merely a matter of "cutting" from one
imaginary locale to another when a group of characters left the stage
and another entered. Thus the action passed from Dunsinane to Birnam
Wood or to a plain outside the castle, and from Macbeth and his followers to Macduff and his, until both sides met at the end. Griffith did
much the same thing in the climax of *The Birth of a Nation* when he
cut back and forth between the miscegenetic perils of Lillian Gish, the
rioting Negroes, the ride of the Clansmen, and the beleaguered cabin.
The distinguished French director, Robert Bresson, has said, "Shakespeare's cutting is like a door through which poetry enters."

In other cases the Elizabethans used a technique that was to have
its parallel on the screen three centuries later. You may see an example
in the early scenes of *Richard III*. At the opening Richard enters on a
street, talks with characters who come and go, and then exits. It would
have been absurd if he had reentered immediately to start the next scene
in "another street." Instead, a funeral procession enters. When Richard

appears, after about thirty lines, the audience feels that he has had time to walk some distance. The silent movies sometimes did much the same thing to avoid dissolves. For example Mr. and Mrs. Van Rensselaer told their son Whitney that he must end his affair with Anita Latour, the musical comedy star. Whitney delivered a few impassioned words on the virtue of Anita, and then dashed angrily out of the room. His parents talked for a minute or so about his infatuation. Then the film cut to Anita's dressing room. After a short scene between the star and her manager, came a knock on the door. Whitney entered, and the audience took it for granted that enough time had passed for him to come by taxi from Park Avenue to Broadway.

Many of the silent films used a more obvious method of avoiding dissolves. When a scene was over and a passage of time or a change of place had to be allowed for, the director or editor would cut, or sometimes fade, to a subtitle, such as "Meantime Prince Charlie amused himself with a few friends." Then came a scene of revelry in another place.

The "Chemical Fade"

When fades, as well as dissolves, had to be made in the camera the director used them charily. For, as the editing process went on, he might find it more effective to end a sequence on some other shot than the one that had been faded out in the camera. There was the same problem, of course, about using fade-ins. It vanished, however, when some laboratory technician discovered how to make a "chemical fade." This was done by applying to the end of a piece of developed negative a liquid that ate away more and more of the emulsion as the amount of the chemical was increased. Of course the negative that had thus become lighter and finally transparent produced a positive print in which the images grew gradually opaque. The process was not only quicker and cheaper than camera work. With its aid a film-maker could put a fade-out or fade-in on any shot in a picture. The chemical fade was not so smooth, however, as a fade made in the camera.

The "Optical Printer" Comes to the Aid of Editing

It was shortly before the coming of the talkies that another technician found a way to make dissolves after the shooting was over, and also better fades. "Known but to God," this innovator devised the optical printer now used in every film laboratory. Though mechanically complex it is really nothing more than a camera and a projector facing each other. The camera carries unexposed film. The projector, which holds a positive print of the shot to be doctored, has no lens. When the two machines are run at the same speed, the camera takes a picture of each frame as it moves through the projector. Thus, by altering the camera's aperture, the optical printer can fade shots out or in or lap them over one another much as in the regular camera. Additionally, it can super-impose a number of images, produce all sorts of wipes, enlarge a part of the original image, and make "zoom shots" in which the camera seems to be moving closer to the action. It can also slow down an old silent-speed film by printing every other frame twice; thus some of Chaplin's silent films have been made to look acceptable today.

One of the mysteries of film-making is why the optical printer was such a Johnny-come-lately. By the time of *The Birth of a Nation*, tech-nicians, both here and abroad, had developed excellent cameras and projectors, and intricate equipment for printing as well as developing. It is a small tragedy as well as a mystery; for, if the optical printer had been invented ten years earlier, the films of the twenties might have been using the filmic punctuation marks as skillfully and effectively as the talkies of today. By so much, the silent art would have achieved more stature before sound destroyed it. Also, its film-makers might have worked out by trial and error the problem of when to use the dissolve, or some substitute—a problem that bedeviled the first talkies.

Learning to Use Dissolves

Learning how to make talking pictures involved learning how to use the optical printer. Good fades could be inserted anywhere in a picture. The spoken word replaced the lettered subtitles. But what to do instead of flashing on the screen: "And so Courtenay had to appeal to his banker," after the star left a drawing room and before he appeared in an office?

It took two or three years for the makers of talkies to discover the value of the dissolve as a bridge over small gaps of time or space in a sequence of scenes. Instead they used it at random and often illogically. Take, for instance, the first episode in *Alibi* (1929). The director, Roland West—or perhaps his cutter—inflated what should have been a simple scene into shots of a policeman's club, a gong ringing, the running feet of guards, a club striking the ground, cells, an insert of the prisoner's number and name, the convict recovering his possessions, and the man leaving the reception room—all strung together by dissolves. In *Black-mail* (1929) Alfred Hitchcock, or his cutter, Emile de Ruelle, wasn't content to cut from a woman, outside a door, to her entrance into the other room; instead he dissolved her in. Mervyn LeRoy used the optical printer to doll up two restaurant scenes in *Little Caesar* (1930) where continuous action called for straight cuts. I have cited only three pictures out of the many in which editors and/or cutters got swacked on the new brew of the optical printer.

Out-of-Focus for Visions

Through the first twenty years of the talkies, the dissolve seemed settling into place. For a while cutters played with the wipe from one scene to another, but this was obviously an optical trick that shattered illusion. The swish-pan seemed more cinematic, but only for the violence of melodrama or for hallucination. About 1950, film makers began to examine certain problems of the conventional dissolve, and to seek for possible substitutes.

One of these was a kind of wavering, out-of-focus effect between scenes. When it appeared in Orson Welles' *Macbeth* (1948), I thought he had borrowed it from television—which, like the early talkies, was beginning to toy with all the miracles that its multiple cameras could make. I learned later that cutter Louis Lindsay, bothered by the contrast of Welles' realistic chieftain and the weird sisters, used, without benefit of TV, the eerie, out-of-focus effect to make the witches' scene seem a vision in the mind of the earth-bound Macbeth. Thus this too too solid flesh could melt, thaw, and dissolve itself into another world.

How to Indicate Memories?

In many a feature film the dissolve is used to move the story backward as well as forward. This can be confusing unless a voice gives us a clue by saying, "I remember Mama." Sometimes a double exposure—all too painfully familiar to the amateur photographer—when imposed over the close-up of an actor means that he is thinking or talking of a remote event. Without benefit of double exposure or a voice, *Happy Anniversary* (1959) took us briefly into the past by vignetting some retrospective shots against a pale background; this was probably not the first example, but I can't recall an earlier one. The Charles Brackett-Billy Wilder *Sunset Boulevard* (1950) added the out-of-focus dissolve to the reminiscent speech. Over the opening shots, which showed cars and motorcycles carrying police, reporters, and photographers to the house of a former star, came the well-known voice of William Holden telling us that a murdered man (Holden) had been found in a swimming pool. In the fifth shot we saw the body floating face down in the pool. The next shot was a reverse angle, purportedly taken from the bottom of the pool, showing the underside of the body and the crowd gathered on the edge of the pool. Then an out-of-focus dissolve carried us back some months to the exterior of Holden's Hollywood apartment. Toward the end of the film another out-of-focus dissolve took us back to the shot from the bottom of the pool and on to the climax.

New Editorial Experiments

In the nineteen-fifties there came attempts to drop the dissolve as an introduction to the past. Faced with the many flashbacks of *The Snows of Kilimanjaro* (1952), Henry King and his cutter, Barbara McLean, cut sharply, again and again, from the face of Gregory Peck to the past that he reviewed.

Two Swedish directors have made bold excursions into the past without benefit of the dissolve. In Alf Sjöberg's fine version of Strindberg's *Miss Julie* (1950) the director looked backward in two ways. His camera moved upward and away from Miss Julie to come to rest on an old portrait of her mother, then moved away again and downward in the same room, resting at last on the mother herself as a young woman. At another time, Sjöberg united past and present by bringing into the same shot Julie in her mother's arms and grown-up Julie thinking of her childhood. Ingmar Bergman was equally ingenious—and successful—in *Wild Strawberries* (1957). In one instance, he showed a two-shot of father and daughter-in-law in an automobile, cut to a closer shot of the woman as she spoke of a ride with her husband some time ago, then to the son sitting where the father had sat, and finally to a two-shot of husband and wife, both in the past. In another sequence we saw the old man walking in the woods and watching, in separate cuts, scenes of his youth. Finally, in a single shot, Bergman showed a fresh young girl, whom the man had loved and lost, beside him in the shadowed patch of strawberries. It was, of course, Sjöberg's and Bergman's sensitive and sure direction of the actors that made these daring departures successful.

After the dissolve came under fire as a signal that a film is about to set the clock back a month, a year, or a generation, some of our newer directors in Hollywood—or, perhaps, our more enterprising cutters—started to experiment in another direction. They took pot shots at the dissolve that moves a story forward. They didn't throw it out the window, but in certain special cases they substituted straight cuts. Sometimes, as in the chase that makes up the bulk of Stanley Kramer's *The Defiant Ones*, they dropped dissolves to gain a sense of speed. Kramer did somewhat the same thing in *On the Beach*, and Robert Wise in *Odds Against Tomorrow* (1959). Wise added a further excitement in cutting across time and space by keying the moves to a startling line. Here is an example: A criminal is explaining to a new acquaintance a plan for a bank robbery in which they will have a partner. The first man doesn't realize (as the audience does) that the other has a violent, almost maniacal, obsession with white supremacy. When the planner of the robbery casually remarks that the third partner is colored, the racist shouts, "You didn't tell me he was a nigger!" and the film cuts immediately to the man they are talking about, a man the audience has come to like.

France's *nouvelle vague* produced a number of interesting experiments. In *Breathless* (1959), Jean-Luc Godard showed little regard for cinematic conventions when he cut from characters and locations without attempting to retain any normal degree of continuity. However, the peremptory, staccato cutting did, in a way, help to underscore the rather erratic behavior of Godard's "hero."

Before American directors and cutters began moving the story forward by trading dissolves for cuts, Bergman did the opposite. In *Smiles of a Summer Night* (1955) he had a dinner scene in which his six principals were to drink a fabulous wine supposed to release certain very important inhibitions. Instead of cutting to each player in turn as he emptied a glass—apprehensively, eagerly, or with bravado—the director threw in dissolves. The effect was to add significance and a growing suspense as the scene progressed.

Odds and Ends of Editing

In putting together a picture puzzle that is a mile and a half to two miles long and an inch and a quarter wide, the cutter and his assistants have many problems and responsibilities besides those I have mentioned.

Initially, the cutter faces the rather awe-inspiring task of reducing a considerable length of disjointed footage to the compact final cut you see in the theaters. The jousting sequence in *El Cid*, for example, ran to 34,000 feet when presented to cutter Robert Lawrence. By the time the film was released, Lawrence had reduced this to a dramatic sequence running 1,080 feet.

When the editor goes from one shot, in which an actor gets up out of a chair, to another angle that overlaps this movement, he must "match" the action within a fraction of a second. On the other hand, he may speed up movement by cutting away to another object. Thus he can shorten a horse race by intercutting shots of the spectators.

When the script calls for a long shot of London, the Matterhorn, the Atlantic City boardwalk, a jet airliner in flight, a tropical jungle, or the Pyramids, the cutter has to find this "stock shot" in the studio's film library. To introduce a scene in a New York office in *To Mary—With Love* (1936), cutter Ralph Dietrich found a shot that panned down from the top of the Empire State building to the street; by printing it in reverse, he carried the eyes of the audience up to the top, where the film dissolved into the office scene.

The editor and his assistants must cut apart and index every shot, and keep a record of the "trims," or portions not used. More important, they must have a list of every frame in the finished picture. I first realized this is 1935 while the music was being recorded for *Becky Sharp*. A reel, including the ballroom scene and the panic created by the news from Waterloo, caught fire while it was being projected over the heads of the musicians on a sound stage. The film, which had taken a couple of weeks to edit, was burned to a cinder. But the cutter's record of the scores of shots, frame by frame, enabled them to come up with a new print in a very few days.

The Wedding of Sound and Picture

While the editor is assembling his rough cut, he works with two ever-lengthening pieces of film. One carries the camera shots, the other the dialogue. The editing of the sound track—which is finally printed next to the sprocket holes at one side of the finished film—is a bit more complicated than the cutting and splicing of what might be called the picture track.

While the camera photographs a shot, sound technicians are recording the dialogue and incidental noises on a separate piece of film. When the editor uses any part of any shot in his rough cut, he must see that the two tracks match perfectly, that they are "in sync." This is a more mechanical job than editing the picture track, but before the cutter has finished his work, sound adds complications that call for ingenuity and creative judgment. Other sound tracks must be made or found. These may include off-screen noises such as shots, explosions, rushing water, whistles, sirens, thunder, a distant voice, traffic noises, or, for bucolic scenes, what is known as "the birds and the bees." Some shots, such as a railroad train, Times Square, a harbor, marching men, a chase, or pounding surf, may be taken silent; then sound has to be added. Sometimes the noises can be found in the "libraries" that studios maintain. Sometimes they have to be made. In any case they must be introduced at the right moment; the sound of footsteps must match moving feet, the whistle of the tugboat must come when we see a spurt of steam. In addition the studio orchestra records the background music for the picture. After the cutter has got together all the separate bits of sound track that he needs, they must be re-recorded, or "mixed," with the dialogue and music tracks. In the process the volume of each track may be raised or lowered. All this is time-consuming, and sometimes it must be done at top speed. In 1933, when the old Fox studio was counting on the first version of *State Fair* to ward off bankruptcy, Henry King spent thirty-six consecutive hours in a recording session, interspersed with cat naps while the technicians labored.

More Credit to the Cutter!

Whatever a director may contribute to the editing of a film, the cutter never gets the credit he deserves. Even in Hollywood his status and repute are lower than they should be. In the order of precedence—attested by the protocol of screen credits—he ranks below the cameraman and the composer of the music score, as well as the producer, the star, and the director. Outside the film capital, moviegoers know the names of many directors, a few cameramen, but probably no cutters. Yet editing holds a unique place in the development of the motion picture as an art. Writing and directing, acting and photography, set design and sound recording, all existed before the birth of the film. These skills were merely adopted and adapted. Editing was born in and *of* the movies. Without it, the motion picture would never have become the art it is today.

Chapter
29

The Cameraman's Contribution

Inventor . . . cameraman . . . director . . . cutter. Can we call this the metamorphosis of the first filmmakers? Yes and no. The jobs developed in that order, but most of the pioneers had to do at least three of them. Dickson and the Lathams, Lumière and Paul passed from invention to photography and then, as directors, they had to devise little plots and finally do some elementary cutting. At the turn of the century men like Méliès, Porter, and Hepworth, using cameras invented by others, became directors and cutters, as well as writers and even exhibitors. Then, rather suddenly, the filmmaking machine went into reverse and extruded the specialists that we know today.

Among the specialists, the cutter has the unique distinction of being born in and of the motion picture, and nowhere else. He and his skills made it an art—and it is the only art in which these skills have a place. On the other hand, the director and the writer may come from the theater and return to it. Somewhere in between lies the cameraman. Many a portrait photographer turned to the screen, but as a cinematographer he became something quite different and new.

The work of the third member of the film-making team is vitally important. Charles G. Clarke, in his book *Professional Cinematography*, has set down the requisite qualifications for a top cameraman. He "has to have a sense of composition, a complete knowledge of optic and film materials—what they can do and how far he can extend them, and a full

Technicians vs. Actors

After the writer and the director, the movie technicians are, I think, the most important artists in moviemaking. I never cease to be impressed by them. Actors are important, too, of course, but their importance has been so exaggerated by the old star system that one cannot help wanting to belittle them. For actors have been allowed to take rather a cheap advantage of their face value, being the only members of the huge company of people who make a movie who are seen by the public and so represent to the public all the work that has been painstakingly done for them.

—William Inge in *The New York Times.*

understanding of the art of lighting. He must be an expert in color and color psychology, a craftsman in cinema staging methods, and among still other things, have an ability to get along with, and utilize, the potentials of his fellow workers." Yet, like the cutter, he must take orders from the man whose rod of office used to be a megaphone.

The Beauty That Was Silent

In certain ways the early cameramen were inventors, too, not so much of the machine itself as of how to use it.

The camera of today is surprisingly like the camera of 1900. The film and the lenses are faster, of course, and they can work miracles with artificial light. Yet I have seen a beautiful shot by Lumière in which reflected sunlight from the river Seine shimmers entrancingly on the richly shadowed walls of old buildings. This sharply perfect scene had been reproduced almost fifty years later, from a reel of paper on which it had been printed for copyright purposes. It should remind us that we cannot judge the photographic quality of silent films from the worn and faded prints that come to us today after many dupings from positive prints. Griffith's cameraman Billy Bitzer, Eisenstein's Eduard Tisse, Alvin Wyckoff in *The Warrens of Virginia* (1915) and *The Cheat* (1915), Arthur Edeson in *Robin Hood* (1922), Karl Freund in *The Last Laugh* (1924), John Arnold in *The Big Parade* (1925), both Charles Rosher and Karl Struss in *Sunrise* (1927), Rudolph Maté in *The Passion of Joan of Arc* (1928) did finer camerawork in the silent days than most of today's prints would indicate.

Making the Camera More Versatile

Besides the beauties of light and shade and composition that the early cameramen achieved, they found ways to make their cameras do more than record reality. We call many of these effects "trick shots" today. Some we have thrown away, but most of them are still basic to film-making. At this distance in time we cannot always be sure who first found his way to this or that new technique. Also, we can't be certain of whether a director described an effect he wanted and his cameraman worked it out, or whether a cameraman invented it himself. Sometimes it may have been a matter of accidental discovery, sometimes an adaptation from still photography.

Bitzer—Pioneer in Lighting

The greatest inventor among cameramen was perhaps Billy Bitzer. In the old Biograph studio at 11 East 14th Street, New York, where Griffith began his career, Bitzer was the first to use artificial light with dramatic skill. Some four hundred arcs had been employed to photograph the Jeffries-Sharkey fight in 1899, but it was from Bitzer's later experiments, not only with arcs, but with the softer illumination of Cooper-Hewitt mercury lights, that Hollywood lighting developed to the point where another cameraman, Lee Garmes, could rely almost wholly on incandescent bulbs in 1927.

Bitzer's camera was the first to record what we call "lighting effects." It may have been Griffith who asked for the illusion of candlelight, firelight, the morning sun coming through a window, but Bitzer produced them, and as early as 1909. We know that he worked out backlighting by himself, and that he discovered how a tablecloth could throw sunlight into shadowed faces. From this developed the reflectors coated with silver foil that can create clarity and beauty, but when used without discretion, can also spoil the realism in many Hollywood pictures.

Two other pictorial effects may be credited to Bitzer. In one, the use of a diffusion screen in front of the lens to produce soft focus, he may have had the aid of a former professor of physics, the Dutchman Hendrik Sartov. At any rate, the two carried the thing too far in *Broken Blossoms* (1919). Much used in the twenties to beautify an aging actress, diffusion in one shot contrasted absurdly with sharp photography in the next. It is used much more discreetly today. The other effect, the "iris," is as dead as the cameraman and the director of *The Birth of a Nation*. This was a technique by which all of a shot could be blacked out except for a circular area, usually in one corner of the picture. Sometimes, the shot opened on a vignette and then the iris expanded to reveal the whole frame. Sometimes we saw the whole frame and then the camera irised in to a circle in order to emphasize a face or a figure. It is rather odd that Griffith used this technique so much in *The Birth of a Nation* and other films. After all, he was the man who had taught film-makers to cut to or from a close-up.

"Process Shots" and Montage

Cameramen contributed heavily to the trick photography now centered in the "special effects" departments of Hollywood studios. Edwin S. Porter, who photographed as well as directed *The Great Train Robbery* (1903), used a matte shot to show a moving train outside the window of a railroad office. In 1911–13, Norman O. Dawn made many experiments with mattes and background plates which place the hero in a Paris taxi or the heroine against the Taj Mahal. In time other technicians perfected the "traveling matte," a more intricate and more flexible process than any that had come before. I recall that shortly after I came to RKO in 1932 the studio showed its producers a film demonstrating how MGM had made an early Tarzan picture in Hollywood by introducing African backgrounds through mattes and process shots.

Another contribution of the cameraman was the so-called "montage." This, as I have explained in chapter 16, was not the swift cutting to which the Russians applied the French word for editing, but instead a number of shots that dissolved rapidly over one another. Karl Freund shot montages in his camera to express the emotions of characters in *Variety* (1925) and *Metropolis* (1926). Exhilarated by the new freedom of the optical printer, the film makers of some thirty years ago used it rather recklessly to substitute montages for the subtitles that had covered passages of time and action in silent films. When screen writers became more skillful, this device fell into disuse. It still crops up here and there—effectively and amusingly in the "typewriter montage" of *But Not for Me* (1959).

Camera Illusions

No one can say whether the cameraman or the director was responsible for some pictorial effects that may or may not involve tricks. Was it a cameraman or a director who discovered that moving the camera in certain ways can suggest that the set is moving? Rocking a camera dur-

THE MIRACLES OF THE PROCESS SHOT. Before Hollywood got the habit of sending companies as far away as Africa to shoot block-busters, the process shot saved producers untold millions. The studios still use it to show street traffic through the rear window of a taxi or to provide foreign background for a scene in a film largely confined to America. The trick is also called "rear pro-jection" because, as you will see above, a moving picture of some background or other is projected from the rear of the stage onto a translucent screen. While the actors play a scene in front of this screen, which is masked off at the sides by portions of a set, the camera records both the action and the moving background. The shutters of the projector and the camera must be accurately inter-locked, so that each frame of the projected background is still when the camera's lens is open. (If the background is a landscape at a great distance, a photographic slide may be projected instead of a moving picture.) In 80 percent of *Captains Courageous* (1937), the scenes at sea were made with rear projection, and all but a few shots in *Lifeboat* (1944). (*Sketch by Raymond Kitchener.*)

ing a scene in the cabin of a ship creates the illusion that the ship itself is rocking. Jarring a camera sharply suggests the tremor of an earth-quake or the shock of an exploding shell. A train or a ship will seem to move if a camera trucks alongside while panning at the same time. Was it Eisenstein or Tisse who knew how to make the battleship Potem-kim ride the seas when it actually lay at anchor? Who discovered that

AN OLD PROCESS STILL IN USE. Norman Dawn was one of the first people to use the "glass-shot" process. This is a shot in which part of the scenery is actually painted on a glass plate situated between the camera and the set. In this photograph, taken in Tasmania in 1908, you can see how Dawn replaced the roof of a building. The canvas cover prevented reflection of the camera by the glass. (*From the Journal of the Society of Motion Picture and Television Engineers.*)

shooting up at an actor makes him seem imposing, while shooting down helps to make him seem weak or pitiful? Was it Fritz Lang or camera-man Fritz Arno Wagner who posed the arresting shot in *M* (1931) that showed us the murderer looking through a shop window which reflected the knives that obsessed him?

Setting the camera aslant, so that horizontal lines become diagonal

COMPLEX TRICK PHOTOGRAPHY. Most of the great fire of *In Old Chicago* (1938) was the product of filters, mattes, and multiple printing. Filters turned daylight photography into night shots, as in the two illustrations top left. Mattes cut off everyhing above the one-and-a-half-story sets; they also hid two areas of the lake front where the mob in the third picture moved to be photographed again. Into the matted space above the sets, Fred Sersen, responsible for special photographic effects at Twentieth Century-Fox, double-printed the flaming buildings shown above. Between these and other elements eleven separate negatives were involved in this one scene. (*Courtesy Mr. Sersen.*)

and walls and doors lean in or out, can be highly effective. There must be a reason behind this use of the camera, or it will destroy illusion. In the schizophrenic episode of *Un Carnet de Bal* (1937), directed by Julien Duvivier, the slanting rooms suited the mood. This device was most successful—and hardly noticed—at the moment in David Lean's *Brief Encounter* (1945) when the heroine almost threw herself under the wheels of a train.

MAKING A STRANDED SHIP MOVE. The naval vessel, The Twelve Apostles, which Eisenstein used for the Potemkin, was actually filled with old mines and chained to the shore near Odessa. The director had the ship swung out at a ninety-degree angle, and a platform built alongside. Then by trucking the camera backward parallel to the ship, while panning toward the prow, Eisenstein achieved the illusion that the Potemkin was leaving port. The same method is frequently used for the departure of a train. (*Sketches by Raymond Kitchener.*)

Composition on the Stage and on the Screen

The director who comes from the stage to the screen has some problems that the cameraman can help him solve. They involve moving the actors smoothly and effectively in their settings, bringing them into significant relationships, and maintaining compositions that are always pleasing and often dramatic. Some of these things are easier to do on the screen than on the stage; some are not.

On stage or screen, a director must see that no actor "covers" another during important lines or action. Here the film director has certain advantages. He can move his camera instead of his actors. He can cut to another angle. Further, he doesn't have to arrange his action for the varying viewpoints of an audience sitting right, left, and center.

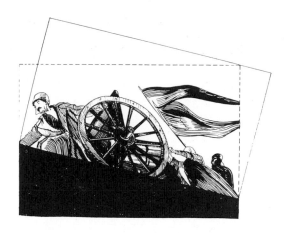

SLANTING THE CAMERA FOR DRAMATIC EFFECT. In *Ten Days That Shook the World,* Eisenstein and his cameraman, Tisse, wanted to increase the sense of strain in a scene showing revolutionists dragging a cannon. The group moved up a slanting platform, which would have normally been photographed within the frame outlined by dashes. Tisse tipped his camera to the right in order to exaggerate the sense of movement. (*From Nilsen's* The Cinema as a Graphic Art.)

He has only one spectator to consider. This man will sit where the camera stood, or perhaps I could say directly behind it. The result is that the director can place his actors wherever he pleases. They can confront one another or turn their backs while talking. They can have all the natural movements and relationships of life itself, exaggerated and heightened within the limits of the plausible.

On the other hand, in the matter of pictorial composition the film director has a problem that the stage director doesn't face. Composition on the stage is like composition in a painting, plus movement; it is almost two-dimensional. The film director, however, must compose like a sculptor. For whenever the camera moves or the picture cuts from one angle to another, he must see that his actors and their surroundings still form an effective composition. In a sense, the film director works in three dimensions. Here the cameraman collaborates.

The Geography of the Screen

The first thing the cameraman has to teach the new director—if the man hasn't noticed it while watching movies—is the geography of the screen. This takes two forms. If there is a series of shots of a character walking or riding or driving from one place to another, then he must always be moving from left to right in all the shots, or from right to left. Another kind of screen geography is based on the maps we use. For instance, a ship leaving San Francisco for the Orient must always move from right to left. Inside its hull, the same rule applies. When Delmer Daves was making a war film about a submarine bound for the South Pacific, he had to use the interior of a submarine that had been built for a picture in which it had sailed from our Atlantic Coast toward France. Since the ship's equipment betrayed the fact that it was bound east, or right, Daves had to shoot a number of scenes with a mirror in order to reverse the set and make the audience feel that the submarine was moving right to left and therefore westward.

The Moving Camera Writes—Sometimes Too Much

The camera can move in a number of ways. It can "pan" right or left across a setting or tilt up or down; both movements can be combined in a panning shot. If the camera is mounted on wheels, it can "truck" in or out along a straight line; it can travel abreast of a moving figure, or ahead of or behind it. Placed on what is called a "crane" or "boom," it can mount or descend, move in or out, while at the same time it can pan or tilt. Such movements can be good or bad. They can feed the drama or they can destroy it. When certain movements are combined the result may be grotesquely disastrous. At the beginning of David Lean's *Great Expectations* (1946), a swift pan with the boy Pip as he ran into the menacing figure of the convict was enormously effective. But, a little later, when the camera trucked and panned at the same time across Miss Havisham's room, the tops of tables and bed posts slid by as if they, instead of the camera, were on wheels. In Griffith's second version of *The Battle of the Sexes* (1928), he committed the same kind of sin.

Who First Moved the Camera?

Through *The Last Laugh* and *Variety* the Germans took credit for discovering the moving camera in 1924 and 1925. They exploited it vigorously and imaginatively, yet the record of its first use goes much further back. In the eighteen-nineties, one of Lumière's cameramen took a moving shot of Venice by mounting his machine on a gondola. About 1901 a producer's catalogue bragged that one of his films panned across New York in a snowstorm. About 1912 Griffith and Bitzer mounted a camera on an auto. I vaguely remember a trucking shot near the beginning of *Cabiria* (1913), but I can't recall whether the camera moved in or out.

MACHINES TO MOVE THE CAMERA. Hollywood has developed several pieces of equipment that allow the camera to indulge in more complicated movements than panning or tilting on a fixed tripod. They all roll on tracks laid across a setting. The smallest and simplest is the "dolly." This has an arm that can swing the camera from one side to another while it pans or tilts; the arm can raise or lower the camera a few feet. A much larger contrivance is the "crane," or "camera boom." Paul Fejos, with the aid of cameraman Hal Mohr, developed the first of these when he was directing *Broadway* in 1929. Maneuvered by electric motors, this crane could move in or out while its great arm, carrying cameramen as well as camera, could project over the set some 30 feet, drop to floor level and swing right or left. This simplified sketch of a small crane shows at one end the camera platform, and at the other counterbalancing weights. (*Sketch by Raymond Kitchener.*)

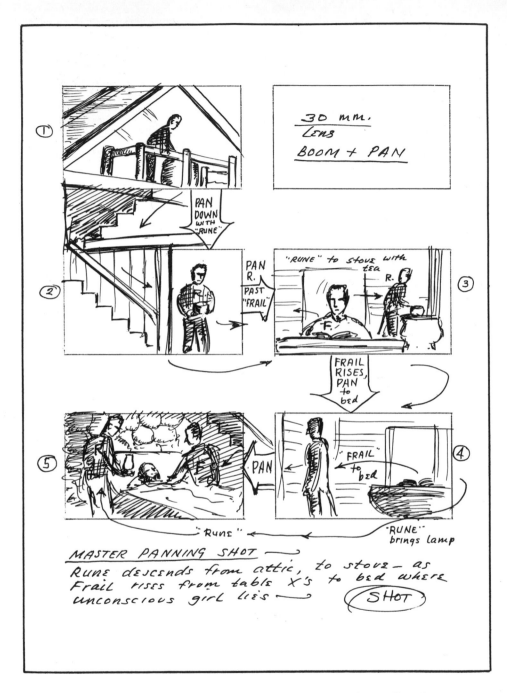

MOVING DOWNWARD AND SIDEWAYS. In one scene from *The Hanging Tree* (1959), Delmer Daves used a boom, or crane, to follow the character of Rune downstairs and then pan across the room. (*Courtesy Mr. Daves.*)

CAMERA MOVEMENT ON LEVEL GROUND. Here Daves shows how the camera, mounted on a "dolly," moves to the right and pans at the same time until it covers the close shot at bottom right. The entrance of "Society Red" is a separate shot to be cut in. (*Courtesy Mr. Daves.*)

Lately I have seen an American film of 1915, *The Second in Command*, in which the camera moved as skillfully as in any picture of today. It rolled in smoothly and unobtrusively from a group shot to the two principals, from a medium shot to a close-up. The camera caught a man outside a door, then cut to the room inside, showed his face as the door opened, pulled back as he entered, and finally gave us a full shot when he joined the group within. More remarkable, perhaps, the camera followed the hero and heroine as they moved about in a dance scene. Discovered by James Card of the George Eastman House of Rochester, this picture seems a mysterious sort of relic—a small masterpiece of movement forgotten for more than forty years. A trade paper of 1915 stated that the film's cameraman, William F. Alder, was "a deep student of photography, and the owner of perhaps the most elaborate laboratory in America." No one seems to have rivaled his innovations till much later.

Movement Pro and Con

By and large, the moving camera is a dangerous weapon. It can so easily destroy illusion. The lens is, after all, the eye of the spectator. It must follow the action. If it seems to be wandering off for no obvious reason, the spectator will be puzzled; he will lose his bearings. In *The Second in Command*—as in almost all films today—the camera was careful to follow the figure at the center of the action. Mark Robson exaggerated a bit when he said: "If the scene is well directed from the point of view of its feelings, the camera can be set down, forgotten, and allowed to record." Billy Wilder remarked, "You will not find in my pictures any phony camera moves or fancy set-ups." John Ford once said: "Nail down your camera and depend on cutting." He uses the pan shot very rarely, mainly to study the reactions of a crowd or to follow a man as he mounts his horse and gallops away. Like almost all directors, Ford will sometimes truck in to a close-up to create more emphasis. Obviously there must be a very good reason for trucking or panning or using a crane shot. Besides puzzling an audience, the moving camera may slow down tempo; direct cuts are quicker. On the other hand, movement is essential in following a dancing couple or covering a racing stagecoach. It is highly effective when it carries the eye of the spectator across the dead on a battlefield.

A moving shot is safe enough at the beginning of a scene or a sequence. As the camera moved through the luxurious lobby of the hotel in *The Last Laugh* it established the atmosphere of the place as it guided the eye of the spectator to the doorman outside. In *Laura* (1944) Otto Preminger and his cameraman, Joseph La Shelle, moved the camera for many minutes before using a cut. Henry King and Leon Shamroy used a six-minute moving shot in *Twelve O'Clock High* (1949) without making the audience too conscious of camera movement.

Occasionally the director, or perhaps the writer, gets the notion of framing a film within two camera movements. In *The Clock* (1945) Vincente Minnelli began the picture with a close view of the huge time-piece under the roof of the Pennsylvania Station in New York, pulled the camera back to cover the concourse, and then moved it down and in to pick up the hero and heroine. In ending the film he reversed the camera movement, and faded out on the clock.

The Camera Sins of Welles and Olivier

In using too much camera movement, directors from the stage are the worst offenders. Like Orson Welles—who said when he first saw a sound stage, "This is the biggest toy train set any boy ever had to play with" —the newcomer is fascinated with the fluidity of the camera. Welles contributed greatly to the screen in *Citizen Kane,* but it was tough on his audience to have to ride with his camera toward a flashing night club sign, through it, and down through a skylight to a table inside. Laurence Olivier went mad over trucking in *Henry V* (1944). In the two big speeches "Once more unto the breach, dear friends" and "We few, we happy few, we band of brothers," Olivier began on a close shot of King Henry, and then, as each speech rose to its climax and demanded the close-up, he pulled his camera farther and farther away. In *Hamlet* (1948) Olivier sinned in the same fashion, but with different means, when he had the Dane run far away from the camera and deliver "The play's the the thing" with his back to the audience. In the same film he set his camera madly racing down corridors and up stairways. By the time of *The Prince and the Showgirl* (1957) Olivier seemed to have learned his lesson.

There are rare cases where a director can pan away from action and be effective. One of these occurred in the early talkie *The Public Enemy* (1931). With something like Greek reticence at showing violence on the stage, William Wellman turned his camera aside as James Cagney was about to shoot a fellow gangster seated at a piano. The suspense held perfectly through the moment when the camera found a henchman by the door and he reacted to the sounds of the revolver shot and the body falling forward onto the piano keys.

The camera picks up a soldier
and pans with him as he crawls.
Toward the end of the pan
he sees an enemy bunker.
As he approaches, there
is a burst of fire.
The angle is wrong for his rifle.
So he throws a grenade.

AS MILESTONE PANS, TRUCKS, AND CUTS. These drawings foreshadowed the movements of his camera in *Pork Chop Hill*. (*Courtesy Mr. Milestone.*)

It hits the side of the
bunker, rebounds,
and explodes,
wounding his right arm.
The camera moves closer
as he throws another
grenade left-handed.
The rifle in the bunker
tilts crazily as the
camera moves back, and
the soldier joins his squad.

7

10

8

11

9

12

The Camera as an Actor

Occasionally directors become obsessed with what is called the "subjective camera." They make the lens into the eye of a character instead of the eye of the spectator. For the first few scenes of *Dr. Jekyll and Mr. Hyde* (1931) Rouben Mamoulian showed everything from the point of view of the physician, and then had to give it up. For the first half-hour of *Dark Passage* (1947), Delmer Daves used the subjective camera to present the experiences of an escapee from San Quentin. Only after the convict has undergone plastic surgery to change his appearance is he revealed with the distinctive features of Humphrey Bogart. Turning director in *Lady in the Lake* (1946), Robert Montgomery shot almost all of that whodunit—ineffectively—from the point of view of the detective whom he played. Although in *Rope* (1948) Alfred Hitchcock didn't toy with the subjective camera, he came as complete a cropper as Montgomery, for he eliminated practically all cuts and moved his camera in continuous and drearily drawn-out shots. The subjective camera has often been used to increase the impact of boxing sequences—the opening of *Requiem for a Heavyweight* (1962) is an excellent example.

Which Lens to Use—and Where?

There is one thing that no stage director can learn by watching movies in a theater. This is the work that different lenses do. He may know something about this if he has a well-equipped still camera. Other-

A LESSON IN LENSES. The cinematographer faces the same problems as the amateur with a Leica. A layman can't cover a building 115 feet high with a 50 mm lens even though he is 270 feet away. If he uses a wide-angle lens of 35mm, then the vertical lines lean inward if he is at ground level. (*Sketches by Raymond Kitchener.*)

wise, a cameraman must initiate him into the mysteries of the lenses most commonly used. From the same set-up they will cover different-sized areas. On the other hand, the same area can be covered by different lenses if the camera is set up at different distances. A short-focus lens makes it possible to work in cramped quarters. A long-focus lens acts like a telescope. With each lens can come disadvantages and distortions.

WHAT DIFFERENT LENSES SEE. From a single set-up, a camera may cover four dancers in a line, or three, two, or one. This depends on which lenses are used. A "wide-angle" lens will cover all four; a "telephoto" or "long focus" lens will take a close shot of one of them. (*Sketches by Phil Babet.*)

A CLOSE SHOT WITH DIFFERENT LENSES. A camera can take the head and arms of a dancer from different set-ups, close to her or far away. At the left, a wide-angle lens includes many folds of the curtain behind her. At the right, a telephoto lens shows only a few. Most close shots are taken with one of the intermediate lenses. (*Sketches by Phil Babet.*)

When a shot is finished and the camera must be moved for the next set-up, a director may use a view finder that shows him what areas will be covered by any particular lens. Some directors tell the cameraman what they want. Alfred Hitchcock will often do this with a quick pencil sketch. Sometimes a specialist is hired—a "production designer." William Cameron Menzies was such a man. Though Lyle Wheeler designed the settings for *Gone With the Wind* (1939), Menzies made for director Victor Fleming an elaborate series of drawings covering every set-up. Before Lewis Milestone goes into production he explains to his art di-

rector just how the camera will be placed and moved, and he has a
small drawing made for every shot. Delmer Daves makes such sketches
himself in his shooting script.

Camera Crew and Set-up Problems

Like the cutter, the cameraman has a special, six-bit title on the screen.
There he becomes Director of Photography. This is more than a matter
of vanity. He presides over a highly complex operation. It involves a
crew of four cameramen besides the "gaffer," or chief electrician. On
the set, the director of photography is called the first cameraman. He is
responsible for the mood of the lighting and for the angle and movement of the camera, but most of the time he sits in his chair and watches
the second cameraman, or camera operator, "riding the camera" and
monitoring the shot. The first assistant cameraman "follows focus" as
camera or actors move, and the second assistant does such odd jobs

SET-UPS SKETCHED FOR *Lifeboat*. Alfred Hitchcock, who was once
an art director, gave Glen MacWilliams, the cameraman, quick
sketches like these for each new shot that was to be worked out
with the stand-ins while the director rehearsed the players. (*Courtesy Mr. Hitchcock.*)

as "slating" each take by holding in front of the camera a "clapper board" that identifies the scene to be taken and provides a noise for "syncing" the sound and picture tracks. Some cameras have a slate and a sync noise within the mechanism.

Changing from one set-up to another may take from a few minutes to a couple of hours. Lights have to be changed or adjusted. Panning or trucking may have to be rehearsed. Perhaps the whole company has to be moved to another stage. In the case of an average film, the crew may get six to eight set-ups a day, which may mean two to four minutes of screen time. Cheaply made pictures will use fewer set-ups and work faster. Blockbusters and productions made by certain meticulous directors involve long schedules and many, many set-ups.

Using two or more cameras at the same time may cut the cost of shooting, but only on big sets that call for no change of lighting. According to legend, MGM's *Ben-Hur* of 1925 had forty-two cameras trained on the chariot race. Later, single cameras got closer shots of the actors. For a battle scene in *Pride of the Marines* (1945), Delmer Daves got close shots at the same time as longer ones. By using six cameras and hiding most of them behind parts of the setting, he covered in one complicated set-up nine and a half minutes of script. Of course setting up cameras and lights and rehearsing the extras took quite a long time.

Kudos to the Cameraman

I have always felt that no cameraman receives the screen credit his work deserves. Almost always, like the cutter, he has to share a title card on the screen while the name of the man who composed the score stands out in lonely glory. Of course, many cameramen are no more than routineers. They use a great deal of overall light and try to get some variety through the glow of cross-lighting and top-lighting here and there. The effect may be either blah or charming, but it lacks both realism and vivid drama. "Low key" lighting—casting more shadows and giving a harsher illusion—came into general favor with the first World War. It calls for more skill and imagination in the cameraman and it rewards him. In between lies a rather atmospheric realism, as in Arthur Miller's photography of *How Green Was My Valley* (1941).

Among the cameramen who have achieved dramatic realism in black-and-white there is space to mention only a few: Lee Garmes for *Shanghai Express* (1932), Karl Freund for *The Good Earth* (1937), Bert Glennon for *Stagecoach* (1939), Charles G. Clarke for *Moontide* (1942), Glen

MacWilliams for *Lifeboat* (1944), the Englishman Guy Green for *Great Expectations* (1946), William Daniels for *The Naked City* (1948), Boris Kaufman for *On the Waterfront* (1954), Hal Mohr for *The Wild One* (1954), Sam Leavitt for *The Defiant Ones* (1958), Eugene Shuftan for *The Hustler* (1961), and Burnett Guffey for *Bird Man of Alcatraz* (1962).

The men who shoot in color have had some trouble in getting away from the postcard look of overall lighting. When the noted designer for the theater, Robert Edmond Jones, codirected with Lloyd Corrigan the first three-color dramatic film, *La Cucaracha* (1934), the Technicolor technicians tried to impose flat white lighting. Jones insisted, however, on adding areas of colored illumination that achieved a rich and almost three-dimensional quality. Among the finest pictures in color have been Charles G. Clarke's *Captain from Castile* (1947); Oswald Morris's *Moulin Rouge* (1953); Leon Shamroy's *The Snows of Kilimanjaro* (1952), and his *The King and I* (1956); Joseph Ruttenberg's *Green Mansions* (1959); Jack Cardiff's *Black Narcissus* (1947) and his *War and Peace* (1956) with its duel scene on a snowy dawn, shot magnificently on a sound stage; Robert Krasker's *Henry V* (1944) and *El Cid* (1961); and Fred A. Young's *Lawrence of Arabia* (1962).

Gregg Toland—before his death, greatest of cameramen—demonstrated in all his work how the cinematographer can and should suit his style to the feel of the script. He caught the mood of "Gothic romance" in *Wuthering Heights* (1939), the beauty of California against the seamy reality of the Okies in *The Grapes of Wrath* (1940), and the mixture of prestige and cheapness in *Citizen Kane* (1941), and he harmonized the contrast of past and present in *Enchantment* (1948). His perceptiveness and his adaptability—as important to his success as his mastery of composition and lighting—were obvious when he said to me in 1937: "I'm going to shoot *Dead End* like a newsreel."

The Cameraman's Unique Status

The cameraman has one great advantage over the director and the cutter. There can never be any doubt about what he contributed. While nobody may be quite sure how much of the editing of a film should be credited to the cutter and how much to the director, everybody knows just what Toland or Cardiff gave to a picture. Furthermore, he doesn't suffer as the director may from the activities of a fourth collaborator —the producer. Only a few directors, independent by contract, can bring a film to the public just as they conceived it. The director is permitted

to show the head of the studio or the releasing corporation his version
of the edited film; that is a concession won by the Screen Directors
Guild. In most cases, however, the director cannot decide just what the
public wants and how a picture should be shortened or recut. The
work of the cameraman rarely suffers from what the producer may do
to a picture.

Chapter
30

The Screen's "New Look"—
Wider and Deeper

T ALKIES WEREN'T ENOUGH for Paris in 1900, even with great stars like Bernhardt and Coquelin. Nor was Lumière's giant screen, which was high as well as wide (about 70 by 53 feet), and which entertained 20,000 to 25,000 people at a time. No, L'Exposition Universelle also had to have movies with the depth of Cinerama. So there was a theater—called, interestingly enough, Cinéorama—where the spectators were completely surrounded by a hand-colored motion picture thrown on a circular screen by ten projectors. Later on, at a Paris exhibition in 1937, the inventor of CinemaScope set up the widest screen the world has ever seen. It was about 200 feet long and 33 feet high.

Here we see, long ago and far away, a forecast of what was to be Hollywood's first positive answer to "TV or not TV, that is the question." For five years, from 1947 through 1952, the answer had been absurdly negative. Then the film producers began adopting or adapting some of the French processes, as well as an American one that was almost thirty-five years old, in a desperate attempt to fight back at the tiny television screen with pictures that were wide and deep.

Hollywood Turns Its Back on TV—for a While

The first idea was to ignore the whole business. Or so it seemed. On the surface Hollywood behaved as if it saw no rival in those tiny little screens. Obviously they couldn't pay the costs of million-dollar productions. Soon, however, you could see that the studios were just a little worried. They refused to make a velvet profit on their twenty-year backlog by leasing old films to TV. They forbade their contract players to appear on television programs. They even ignored the chance of advertising "coming attractions" over the air, and luring back some of their rival's audience.

Then, in 1952, Hollywood discovered that business was bad and growing worse by leaps and bounds. The figures were alarming. According to one of the trade papers, theater attendance had dropped from 76,000,000 a week to 50,000,000. Maybe neither figure was accurate, but Hollywood recognized that box office receipts had dropped at least 20 percent and perhaps 30 percent. And Hollywood was just smart enough to blame this on television.

Between the fall of 1952 and the summer of 1955, Hollywood's negative attitude toward television got a thorough shaking up. How it went into TV production I shall cover later on. This chapter and the next will deal with Hollywood's attempts to give the theaters a different kind of screen—wider and deeper—to compete with the small screen of the television sets.

Box Office Troubles At Last Force Action

The first positive move was characteristic of the film industry. It followed a familiar pattern. Screen history repeated itself as economic pressure at last forced a change in production and exhibition, and Hollywood fell back on processes it had long ignored. Edison had set the pattern when he held out against using a screen. A few years passed, and the movies were dying as chasers in vaudeville before they began to tell stories and open their own theaters. The film "Trust" went broke because its members wouldn't make features or distribute them. Hollywood ignored sound until a tottering studio took a chance. So, of course, film producers did nothing to meet the competition of television till the box office told them that millions of moviegoers were staying home to watch free shows on their TV sets. And even then it wasn't the major studios that discovered the anodyne for migraine in the box office.

Two groups of independent producers gave Hollywood the bright idea of making theater screens look different from television screens, and doing tricks with sound. On September 30, 1952, New York saw *This Is Cinerama*. In Hollywood on November 27, a new company presented *Bwana Devil* in 3-D, or what it called Natural Vision. The first picture had no story, and the other had a very bad one, but both were sensationally successful. The majors recognized the band wagon rolling down Prosperity Boulevard, and they climbed aboard. Hollywood believed it could outflank TV through various kinds of stereoscopic pictures and stereophonic sound, linked with big screens and wide screens and curved screens. Some day, of course, TV might go three-dimensional in picture and sound, but that would be a long way off.

Many New Names for Three Old Methods.

A number of studios started making films in 3-D, and even reshot parts of films that had already gone into normal production. Twentieth Century-Fox took a bolder step. Just as the old Fox studio had been the first to go all-talkie early in 1929, the new one stopped making films of the conventional shape and announced in February, 1953, that all future productions would be made in wide-ranging CinemaScope. Some studios adopted CinemaScope, while some toyed with other ways of making pictures wider than they had been. And so, on top of Cinerama, Natural Vision, and CinemaScope, came a swarm of new names for basically old processes. The motion picture industry was going back fifteen, twenty-five, and even fifty years to processes that had been either ignored or used and then discarded.

In spite of a lot of fancy names, there are three basic processes that have been responsible for the new look of the movie screens. These are Cinerama, 3-D, and wide-screen projection via CinemaScope, Technirama, Panavision, and Todd-AO. Backed by three-dimensional sound, they can do a couple of things beyond the reach of present-day television. In varying degrees, they give an illusion of depth. They all can—and most of them do—provide a screen radically different in shape from TV's screen. Cinerama and 3-D achieved truly illusive depth. The wide screen, aided by stereophonic sound, does this for seats in the middle and toward the front of the theater.

Two Ways to Three Dimensions

There is always more illusion of depth in a motion picture than in a still photograph. This is due primarily to the movements of figures and objects on the screen, and it becomes much stronger when the camera also moves. Cinerama and 3-D achieve a far greater illusion, however, and they do it by two entirely different methods.

The 3-D process is truly stereoscopic. It is based on the fact that each of our eyes sees a slightly different picture. The left eye sees a little more around the left side of an object—unless it is at quite a distance

—and the right eye around the right side. To record these two different views, 3-D takes two shots of each scene at the same moment. The lens of one camera photographs what the right eye would see. The other, about two and a half inches to the left, takes the scene from the point of view of the other eye. The two pictures are projected on top of each other. The spectator wears a pair of glasses that unscramble the two views. His right eye sees one shot, his left eye the other, and his brain fuses them into a single image in depth.

Stereoscopy is older than the camera. We have 3-D drawings made by Giovanni Battista della Porta about 1600, but we don't know how —or whether—he fused these pictures. We do know that in 1838, before there were proper cameras or special glasses, the British physicist Charles Wheatstone achieved the illusion of 3-D through two drawings and two mirrors. Around the middle of the century another English physicist, David Brewster, and the American writer and physician Oliver Wendell Holmes substituted photos for drawings, and lenses for mirrors. Thus grandma was able to enjoy that Victorian novelty, the parlor stereoscope.

With Cinerama, special spectacles are out. Both eyes see the same picture. In its original format it was made up of three separate shots joined side by side to cover a screen 90 feet wide, but the heart of the illusion lies less in the wide expanse of the screen than in its shape. The third dimension that Cinerama gives us is due to something called "peripheral vision," and this depends almost entirely on the deep curvature of the 90-foot screen.

Cinerama and the "Corners" of Our Eyes

When we look at something in real life, our two eyes focus sharply on the central part of what we see. They also take in things far to the side, one eye seeing more to the right and the other to the left; together they cover 145° to 160°, but only about 130° can be seen by both. These things that we see out of the "corners" of our eyes—and out of the "tops" and "bottoms" too—may be vague and hardly noticed, yet they are enormously important in giving us a sense of depth. The inventor of Cinerama, the late Fred Waller, proved the importance of peripheral vision by a very simple experiment. He put on a mask with peepholes that let him look only straight ahead. Then he walked across a room and tried to place his outstretched finger on some object. He found that he missed his goal by inches or even by a foot.

Now an ordinary screen makes no use of peripheral vision. Out of the corners of our eyes, we see only parts of the darkened theater and some of the audience. With a very wide screen, we get a certain amount of peripheral vision if we are sitting in the middle of the house and fairly near the screen. We don't get all of it, even then, because our eyes take in almost half a circle, and therefore off-screen things right and left. Cinerama's screen provides more peripheral vision than Cinema-Scope's. It is so deeply curved that the eyes of a person seated in the center between the ends of the screen see an image that includes more than the 145° to 160° of his arc of sight. For this well-placed spectator, the Cinerama screen covers all but a small part of his peripheral vision. And so, when he looks at the middle of the screen, a good part of the picture comes to him through peripheral vision.

The Illusion of 3-D vs. Cinerama

There is something slightly unnatural about the depth of 3-D, both in terms of the movie houses and in terms of reality. I remember that about 1936, when I was first invited to see a demonstration of 3-D in color, I wondered rather naively what a picture in three dimensions would look like on a screen. To my surprise when I saw the film, I had the illusion that I wasn't looking at a screen. Instead, I was looking out through a window. Some years later, I discovered that something could come in through the window, and look at *me*—a lion, for instance, in *Bwana Devil*. Another odd and disturbing thing about 3-D was that, unless I sat in the front rows of a theater with a very large screen, I saw everything in 3-D with equal sharpness. All that I looked at was clearly in front of me. There was nothing to the side, as in real life.

Spectators at Cinerama, unless they are too far to the side or too far back, get a more natural illusion. They are, so to speak, "in the middle of depth." They seem to see solid objects moving before them. When Cinerama adds another kind of movement by, for example, placing its cameras—and therefore its audience—on a roller coaster or a boat or a plane, the sense of depth is extraordinary.

3-D Begins to Use Photography

Attempts to make motion pictures in three dimensions go back a hundred years. As I have explained earlier, in 1861 Coleman Sellers took still photographs of successive movements of his children at play, using two stereoscopic lenses, and viewed the shots on a kind of paddlewheel behind a parlor stereoscope. Using film, Friese-Greene took twin frames in 1889, and he may have viewed them with the aid of mirrors. In the next thirty years, there were a few experiments with 3-D, all fruitless.

Stereoscopes and Views.

PHOTOGRAPHY IN THREE DIMENSIONS. With the aid of photography the stereoscope became a popular parlor toy in the last half of the nineteenth century. "The stereoscope," said Oliver Wendell Holmes, Sr., in 1859, "is to be the card of introduction to make all mankind acquainted." Some pioneers working on motion pictures complicated the task by using two lenses to achieve three dimensions. Here is an acrostic advertisement of 1872.

One process, shown briefly in New York in 1922 under the name of Teleview, made the spectator look through a special viewer; a moving shutter allowed him to see alternate pictures on the screen, one for the left eye and one for the right. Another process, developed in Russia, does away with spectacles; but the viewer must keep his head in a fixed position in order to see three dimensions on a ribbed screen.

Of late years only two processes have been demonstrated successfully in America. They both had to put spectacles on the audience.

3-D Through Two Kinds of Glasses

The first and cruder process involved "anaglyphs." These are two stereo-scopic pictures in complementary colors—approximately red and green—and they are viewed through spectacles with filters of the same hues. The idea is said to go back to 1717, and seems to have been used in some fashion about 1841. It was certainly suggested for the parlor stereoscope in 1853 by a German named W. Rollmann. In the early 1890's, Ducos du Hauron proposed to superimpose the two pictures on a single surface. Applying superimposed anaglyphs to the movies, J. F. Leventhal made and sold to Paramount between 1921 and 1924 3-D shorts that he called Plastigrams. In 1935, he and J. A. Norling made similar items, which MGM bought and distributed as Pete Smith's *Audioscopiks*.

Between 1928 and 1932, Edwin H. Land solved the 3-D problem far more skillfully, and he made *Bwana Devil* possible twenty years later.

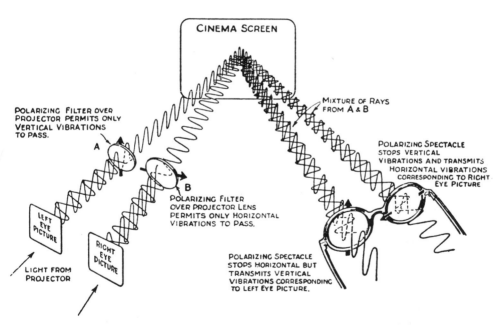

3-D THROUGH POLAROID FILTERS. In the method used for *Bwana Devil* a pair of cameras took simultaneous pictures from points roughly corresponding to the right and the left eye. Edwin H. Land's filters were used in the projectors and the spectacles worn by the moviegoer. The movement of a wave of light in only one direction is somewhat like the pattern made by shaking a rope. (*From Spencer and Waleys The Cinema To-day.*)

Land found a way of manufacturing a cheap polaroid filter. Such a filter passes rays of light—or, rather, waves—that vibrate in only a single plane, or direction. On his two projectors, one for each eye, Land used pairs of Polaroid filters with the planes of light set at 90° angles from one another. With the aid of Polaroid spectacles matched to those planes, the spectator could see movies both in depth and in color.

By grace of Polaroid, European producers made at least three stereocopic productions between 1936 and the beginning of World War II, the first one in Italy and the others in Germany. At the New York World's Fair during 1939 and 1940, the Chrysler Coroporation showed several million visitors advertising films in 3-D—the first year in black and white, the second year in color. The most scientific development of 3-D came in 1951, when Nigel and Raymond Spottiswoode and L. P. Dudley showed some exceptional short subjects at the Telekinema of the Festival of Britain.

The 3-D Boom and Bust

Hollywood had ignored these excellent demonstrations of 3-D in color. I doubt if many producers drove the few miles to the University of Southern California when Land put on his show there during the middle thirties. But *Bwana Devil* was another matter. The story was miserable. Lions and spears jumped out of the screen in an astonishing fashion, and so did tables. Yet, because the people of Los Angeles left their television sets in droves to flock to this curiosity, the studios began to jump, too. They wedded cameras and mirrors and polaroid filters, and turned them loose on some amazing trash. As a local wit put it, Hollywood was suffering from an attack of three-dimensia praecox. (A Los Angeles newspaper printed advertisements in two-color 3-D, and furnished glasses; film fans saw stereo stills in *3-D Movie Magazine*.)

A few studios tried 3-D on some good material—*Kiss Me Kate*, for example, and *Dial M for Murder*. But, at the end of 1953 when MGM prudently offered *Kate* in the old dimensions as well as in depth, it found that the picture did better as a "flattie." Warners never released the stereoscopic version of Hitchcock's 1954 murder mystery; by the time it was finished, so was 3-D. Maybe the public didn't like to wear spectacles. Maybe it just got tired of a novelty. Maybe the puerile stories of almost all the thirty-eight 3-D films made in 1953–54 killed the goose that had laid a few golden eggs. In the big cities, *This is Cinerama* proved that peripheral vision was far better than stereoscopy with polaroid glasses.

There is still a future for 3-D, though a limited one. It lies in the field of science films for the classroom and the laboratory. It ought to have a future, too, in animation, but it won't. Disney made two excellent 3-D shorts. For the Festival of Britain, Norman McLaren of the Canadian Film Board turned out two amazingly beautiful films of abstract shapes moving in space; the critic Arnheim said that it seemed "as though Art were streaming from the skies." Unfortunately, once the 3-D feature disappeared, no theater would pass out polaroid glasses so that audiences might watch a five-minute short.

35mm Supreme for Sixty Years

In the case of Cinerama and its various wide-screen rivals, a lot of technical matters crop up besides peripheral vision. They involve the width of the film, the various shapes of the picture on the screen, and how these shapes are made.

From the Dickson–Edison peep show to the advent of Todd-AO, practically all film in the commercial theaters was 35 millimeters (about 1⅜ inches) wide. Inventors of projectors built their machines so that they could use Edison films. Inventors of cameras adopted the same width so that their films could be run in the 35mm projectors.

Edison Standardizes the "Frame"

When Edison settled on the width of the film he also settled on the width and the height of the picture within it. Thus he standardized the shape, or proportion, of what we now call the "frame." For a time, there were slight changes when a sound track had to be added, but by the middle thirties the ratio of width to height had gone back to just about what Edison set up in the early nineties. This ratio was roughly 4 to 3. It endured for sixty years.

This meant that a screen 20 feet wide would be 15 feet high. In 1952, this was about the size of the screens in most of America's 15,000-odd "hard top" theaters—excluding about 3,000 drive-ins. Of course, some larger theaters had room for larger screens within their wide prosceniums, but even the Roxy's was for some years only 24 by 18 feet. The film itself imposed a limitation that had nothing to do with the size of the proscenium. If the big first-run houses blew up the tiny photographs too much, the images on the screen became far too grainy.

One theater that experienced little difficulty with the changing screen ratios was the Radio City Music Hall in New York. Since its opening in December 1932, the theater has been equipped with a screen measuring 70 x 40 feet, which it claims is the largest indoor screen in the world. By adjusting the screen's masking, and changing lenses and masking plates on the projectors, the theater was able to present both wide screen and CinemaScope ratios with comparative ease.

The Wide Screen and "Aspect Ratios"

The wide screen of the fifties upset sixty years of standardization. All of the new processes changed the shape of the picture that the public saw on the screen.

Instead of the old-fashioned proportion of 4 to 3, the Cinerama screen came out almost 9 to 3. Hollywood—which is as crazy as science for six-bit words and phrases—calls the shape of the Cinerama screen an "aspect ratio of 2.62:1." Several other ratios have appeared in print, and because of the deep curve of the Cinerama screen, the figure for most spectators may be as low as 2:1. With *The Robe* late in 1953, Fox started CinemaScope at 2.66:1 and then reduced it to 2.55:1. Other studios set ratios of 1.85:1, 1.75:1, and 1.66:1. Remember that the old screen proportion was only 1.33:1.

At first, the Hollywood producers made all those changes of shape without changing the width of the film from 35mm. That was economically attractive. Some theaters bought wider screens, if they could get them into the proscenium, but there was no purchase of new projection equipment other than a pair of lenses and masking plates. (Stereophonic sound, at first compulsory with CinemaScope, brought considerable added costs, as I shall explain in another chapter.)

Many Hollywood studios, however, continued to shoot more than half their productions in the old ratio of 1.33:1. Yet on the screens of most theaters, the pictures came out wider than before. They were often as wide as 1.85:1, though never as wide and shallow as CinemaScope. How was this done? It was merely a matter of the theaters' cropping off the top and bottom of the pictures by means of masks in the projectors. Some of the best and most popular films of 1953 through 1955 were shot at 1.33:1 and then cropped—two winners of Oscars, *On the Waterfront*, and *Marty*, as well as *Sabrina, The Country Girl, Summertime* and *Not as a Stranger*. Of course cropping a picture could hurt the composition. To make sure that heads and feet weren't cut off in the projection of these films, cameramen had to "compose loosely." This meant keeping the action well away from the top and bottom of the frame.

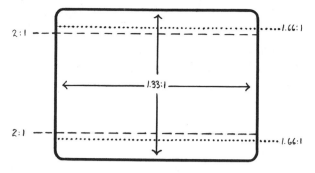

ANY RATIO YOU PLEASE. The majority of films are still shot on 35mm stock with normal lenses. The cameraman keeps the action far enough from the bottom and the top of the frame so that when the projectionist uses the proper mask in the projector, the result will be a well composed, wide picture. There are horizontal lines etched on the finder of the camera to guide the operator.

CinemaScope and Its Problems

CinemaScope, which introduced the wide screen to Hollywood in 1953, tried a different trick on 35mm film. This was more ambitious than merely cropping. On the camera, it used a special lens that took a scene a little more than two and a half times as wide as it was high, and squeezed it onto the 35mm negative. A similar lens on the projector swelled the scene out to its original width. This kind of lens is called "anamorphic," from the Greek meaning "form anew." It was first perfected by two Germans, Ernst Abbe and Carl Zeiss, back in 1890, but

CROPPING IN CAMERA AND PROJECTOR. A close shot in 1.33:1 would normally be shot as in the left sketch. The director, however, knowing that the image would be cropped by a mask in the projector to achieve a 1.85:1 ratio, would sacrifice some of the man's hat and have him raise the gun higher. (*Sketch by Delmer Daves.*)

THE CINEMASCOPE SQUEEZE. Above is the scene covered by the camera. Chrétien's anamorphic lens (also called hypergonar) squeezes it lengthwise, and normal shapes appear narrower in the negative. On the projector, the same kind of lens expands the image on the print to the true proportions of the scene.

at that time they could use it only for still photography. During World War I, Henri Chrétien devised a periscope for tanks, and used a semi-cylindrical lens to give the driver a 180° view of the terrain. When the war was over, he began to develop it for motion pictures. In 1927, Chrétien patented and demonstrated the lens that was to make Cinema-Scope possible.

There was one serious trouble about Chrétien's process as Hollywood applied it to 35mm film, as well as a general difficulty about Chrétien's squeeze. The old 1.33:1 frame was sharp enough on the screens of 1950. But when it was pulled out on the wide screen to almost twice the width of the normal image, it was rather grainy.

VistaVision—Invented in 1919

Paramount found an ingenious method to get rid of graininess, and also to provide a picture that was not only wider than the old 1.33:1, but higher than CinemaScope could be when projected in any but the very largest theaters. Like the other "new" processes, this one goes way back in film history—as far as 1919. One of Paramount's technicians, Loren L. Ryder, remembered an application in that year for a patent on a wide-screen method, which the studio had eventually bought from its inventor, E. W. Clark, in 1926. This involved a camera that lay on its side and ran 35mm film sidewise instead of vertically. The studio did nothing with it in the late twenties, when Paramount and other companies were briefly seeking a wider picture through film up to 70mm in width. In 1953, Ryder dug up the old horizontal process, and it became VistaVision. Vista-Vision put one image on two frames of 35mm film, just as Leica cameras had used double frames since the nineteen-twenties. This increased the width of the negative picture by more than one-half and also doubled its area. The result was a sharper picture when the image was reduced and printed in the normal position across 35mm film. Far more important, VistaVision gave us a higher as well as a wider screen. The values of VistaVision were gloriously apparent in *Strategic Air Command* (1955), but unfortunately Paramount gave up using the process for reasons of economy.

Fortunately, however, other technicians have developed double-frame photography, while some studios have preferred 55mm and 70mm negatives and prints. Technicolor put out its Technirama and then its Super Technirama-70. Both used a double frame with an anamorphic squeeze. The earlier process could produce a CinemaScope type of print on 35mm or a double frame print for road shows in specially equipped theaters. The newer method could imitate 'Scope or 'Vision and also be unsqueezed onto 70mm film at a 2.20:1 ratio. Fox developed 55mm photography for *Carousel* (1956) and *The King and I* (1956). MGM came back with a process they called Camera 65 for *Raintree County* the next year. When Todd-AO introduced unsqueezed 70mm prints with *Oklahoma!* in 1955, and followed this with *Around the World in 80 Days* in 1956, the success of Mike Todd's comedy-spectacle opened the way for really wide film. But more of Todd-AO later.

Cinerama and Its History

Cinerama did another wide-screen trick with 35 mm. It used the old width of film in its three cameras and three projectors, but each frame was half again the height of a normal one. Then, when three different parts of each scene were projected side by side on a screen, the ratio was about 2.62:1.

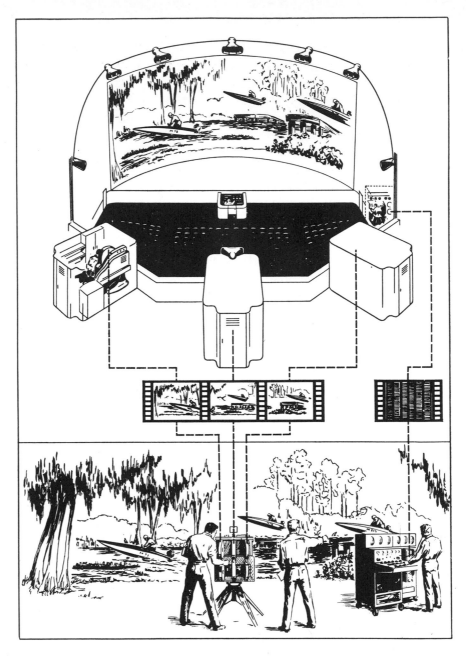

FROM CAMERA TO SCREEN WITH CINERAMA. This early sketch of the Cinerama process reveals how the image was evolved. Three lenses photographed different parts of a single scene. Three projectors threw three images—somewhat taller than they were wide—onto a curved screen. (*Courtesy University of California Press.*)

This use of more than one camera and more than one projector takes us back historically once again. In the middle thirties, Fred Waller, the man who was to invent Cinerama, began working on the problem of peripheral vision. To his dismay, he discovered that if he wanted to make the audience see things out of the corners of their eyes, he would "need a screen a whole block wide." And this was for the auditorium of an "ordinary theater," not the broader and deeper Strand or Music Hall.

Fortunately, Waller began to work in 1937 with the architect Ralph Walker on a unique exhibit for the oil industry at the New York World's Fair. Walker's idea was to fill with motion pictures the inside of a domed building. Still concerned with peripheral vision, Waller saw immediately that the way to get rid of a block-long screen was to use the curved surface of a half dome. To cover all this with movies, Waller had to use eleven 16mm projectors, though he figured that five 35's would be enough. Thus, in 1938, came something called Vitarama. But the oil men would have none of it, and, with the coming of war, Waller and Walker turned their half dome and multiple projectors into the Flexible Gunnery Trainer.

When peace came, Vitarama became Cinerama. The dome turned into a curved screen. Five film projectors shrank to three. They threw the illusion of depth across the inside of half a hollow cylinder. Before Waller died in May, 1954, he had witnessed the commercial triumph of peripheral vision over 3-D with glasses. If he had lived another nine months, he would have seen the first film, *This Is Cinerama,* close a remarkable run in New York. It played for a little more than 122 weeks to 2,471,538 people, and it took in $4,707,688 at the box office. Eleven other cities in the United States and five abroad had seen it. Then followed other travelogues of much the same sort.

The Problems of Cinerama

In terms of the art of the film, something was lacking in all the Cinerama shows. There was no human drama because there was no story. In a sense, *This Is Cinerama* went back to the material that silent pictures had first shown. It gave us an airplane and a roller coaster instead of a railroad train, Niagara Falls instead of breaking surf, the Edinburgh tattoo instead of the Kaiser's troops, opera at Milan and a whole ballet instead of an umbrella dance. There were the same gondolas, of course, though far more colorful. Replacing the incomparably beautiful voyage across the United States by air in the first show, *Cinerama Holiday* gave us one long travelogue, mildly animated in a human way by a Swiss couple and two young Americans who traded scenes in the Old World for scenes in the New. Were the men of Cinerama afraid that its deeply curved screen, which bent horizon lines, was unsuited to a dramatic story, or were they merely playing it safe with spectacular travelogues?

There were also financial and optical problems. Cinerama used considerably more film stock than normal 35mm features. Installing the three projection booths and the screen cost about $75,000 per theater; many seats had to be sacrificed. Furthermore, there was the problem of matching and blending the three segments of the picture. It was difficult to get three prints that matched perfectly, or three arc lamps of the same brilliance. Thus, one blue sky was usually a shade darker or lighter than its neighbor. The joining of the shots, however, was fairly well-handled by what were called "jiggolos." These were saw-toothed masks that vibrate between each pair of images, making the edges fuzzy, and wiping out any obvious overlap.

Todd-AO—Offshoot of Cinema

Cinerama had hardly opened when one of its important backers withdrew from the venture and began to look for some way of solving the problems of fiction, finance, and projection that I have mentioned. He was Mike Todd, producer of Broadway musicals, night-club shows, and outdoor spectacles. He wanted one projector, one piece of film, and a screen that could fit into the proscenium of the larger theaters. According to *Life*, he went to Brian O'Brien of the American Optical Company and said: "Doctor, I want you to get me something where everything comes out of one hole." The result was Todd-AO—and *Oklahoma!*, produced by Arthur Hornblow, a Hollywood veteran and at one time a stockholder in Cinerama.

Because Todd-AO cameras used a 65mm negative, the scenes in *Oklahoma!* were as sharp as VistaVision's. Spectators toward the middle of the auditorium and not too far back got a certain illusion of depth in most scenes. In two scenes this illusion was almost as emphatic as in Cinerama. When the Todd-AO camera moved through the field of corn "as high as an elephant's eye," and when it rode on the runaway surrey careening widly through the woods, the spectator got much of the sensation of the roller coaster ride in *This is Cinerama*.

O'Brien's projector used a 70mm print, though it could also handle the old width. It could be installed in the regular booth—no more loss of seats on the ground floor. The screen was about twice as wide as it was high. There was still some bending of horizon lines, but not too much.

In 1955, the National Theaters Corporation announced another solution of two of Cinerama's problems. This was Cinemiracle. There would still be three projectors and three films, but one booth on the floor would be enough. Mirrors were to throw the right and left hand images on the screen. Also the cameras were to have an "electronic" substitute for the jiggolos. After one production, *Windjammer* (1958), essentially a travelogue, the company stopped production.

Cinerama Undergoes Some Changes

In 1962, ten years after its debut, Cinerama presented its first fiction films. The first, *The Wonderful World of the Brothers Grimm*, seemed ill-suited to the medium. But the second, *How the West Was Won*, with its wide landscapes and well developed action sequences, proved to be considerably better.

However there were still criticisms of the three panel system of presentation. In an attempt to confound these criticisms, Cinerama evolved a different system of photography and projection using only one camera and one projector. The system made its debut with *It's a Mad, Mad, Mad, Mad World* (1963). The film was shot in Ultra Panavision, a 65mm process with a slight anamorphic squeeze, and special projection lenses increased the image size. The result resembled normal Ultra Panavision more than Cinerama.

In the spring of 1964, Cinerama took to the road. In Britain, the first of a projected fleet of fifty mobile theaters began to tour the cities and resorts unable to house a Cinerama "hard-top." In Los Angeles, one of Cinerama's travelogues opened in a drive-in. But what about other earlier processes—processes often more spectacular than those I have mentioned? And what about the effect of the wide screen on motion picture Art?

Chapter
31

The Wide Screen—
1900, 1930, 1952

Two hundred men and women stood or sat in the basket of a balloon. Above their heads hung the lower part of the huge gas bag and about them were all the proper rigging and ballast. The great craft was still at anchor. Then, suddenly, the captain of the balloon announced: "Ladies and gentlemen, we are about to leave the garden of the Tuileries. Cast off!"

The balloon seemed to ascend as hand-colored film in ten motion-picture projectors beneath the basket threw on a circular wall some 330 feet in circumference the vista of Paris of 1900 falling away below the spectators. Then came "a minute of obscurity" (was there a "fade" in the film?), and the officer announced: "We are about to land in the Great Square of Brussels." After that, the balloon took its passengers to England, the Riviera, Spain, Tunis, the Sahara, and back to Paris for their final descent. On the trip, the happy balloonists saw such spectacles as a bullfight, a carnival, cavalry charges, a storm at sea, and a desert caravan.

This Is Cinéorama

This show, called Cinéorama—please note the "o"—came to Paris sixty years ago. As a matter of fact, its inventor had developed and patented his equipment in 1897 when practical projectors were hardly more than a year old. Here in Raoul Grimoin-Sanson, we have another of the many Frenchmen, from Lumière and Méliès to Chrétien of CinemaScope, who

THE WORLD'S WIDEST SCREEN—1900. A contemporary drawing of
Cinéorama at the Paris Exposition. The hand-colored motion picture thrown on the circular wall of the building by ten projectors beneath the audience apparently shows the descent of the
balloon in Brussels. (*Courtesy University of California Press.*)

have contributed so notably to the technical development of motion pictures. Like Méliès, Grimoin-Sanson had been a magician, and the magic
of Cinéorama, just as with any feat of necromancy, came from the union
of imagination with high technical skill.

Cinéorama was a three-day wonder. The police appeared and closed
the show. A workman had fainted when the arc lights of the ten projectors heated the booth—just below the audience—to over 100° Fahren-
heit. The authorities remembered the tragic fire at the charity fete three
years before, and dared not risk another holocaust. Cinéorama had to
go. As for Grimoin-Sanson, he gave up motion-picture work, and turned
his attention from the overheating of projection booths to the cooling
of ice chests with chopped cork.

Grimoin-Sanson's claim that the builders of the projection booth had
failed to follow his designs gains some support from the technical ingenuity with which he solved his major problem. He locked together
ten 70mm cameras to take his panoramic views, and according to reports

of the times, his cameras and his projectors were so nicely adjusted that the edges of the separate shots matched closely on the screen. Since each frame of film was almost square, Grimoin-Sanson's 330-foot picture was more than 30 feet high. Here was a screen with a proportion of 11 to 1, as against the oblong shape of 1.33 to 1 that dominated motion pictures until 1953. The "o" in Cinéorama takes on a peculiar significance when we realize that, at the turn of the century, Paris saw two of the half-cylinders of our present-day Cinerama brought face to face. There, in 1900, was the ultimate in wide screens. It dwarfs CinemaScope and Todd-AO, as well as Cinerama.

Walt Disney's Circarama

Cinéorama also dwarfs the only other circular movie that I have come across in the records of more than half a century. This is Circarama, devised for Disneyland by the father of Mickey Mouse. It is Lilliputian in comparison with Grimoin-Sanson's show, yet ingenious and effective.

The audience walks in under the lower edge of a circular screen, and gazes up at a panorama of color film that takes them from New York

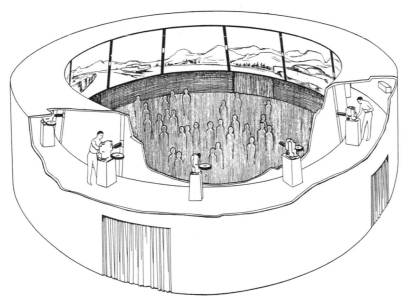

DISNEY'S CIRCARAMA. In this sketch of an ingenious adaptation of the Cinéorama principle of 1900, the upper level is cut away to show the projectors placed between the segments of screen and shooting over the heads of the spectators standing below. (*Courtesy Walt Disney Studios.*)

harbor, through Times Square, and on to many of the nation's beauty
spots including Vermont, the Glacier National Park, the Grand Canyon,
and other sights of the Southwest. The screen, 8 feet high and 130 feet
in circumference, is divided by dark vertical strips into eleven panels.
Through small openings in the strips, eleven synchronized 16mm projectors throw their films on the panels opposite. The strips break the
complete illusion of one great, encircling movie, but they serve to hide
any failure of the tiny 16mm frames to match at their edges. Since 1955
Disney has installed more advanced Circaramas in Brussels, Moscow,
Turin, and elsewhere, sometimes with 35mm projection. A Russian version, called Circlorama, opened in London in the spring of 1963. *Russian
Roundabout*, a twenty minute travel film, was the attraction.

Special exhibits featuring wide and multiple screens have appeared
at numerous trade fairs and so forth, but have not been adopted by the
cinema industry for commercial exploitation.

France—Pioneer in New Processes

Between Cinéorama and Circarama lie a surprising number of attempts
to change the size and the shape of the screen. Most of them were
French, and most of them are forgotten.

At the Paris exhibition of 1900—well named *L'Exposition Universelle*
—there was not only a screen so wide that it was round, but also other
film shows which broke experimental ground.

Visitors heard via the phonograph, as well as saw, three exhibits of
talkies, one of them graced by the great Bernhardt and Coquelin. Mar-
éorama set its audiences on the bridge of a steamship and took them
out of the harbor of Marseilles, into a storm at sea, and on to Algiers;
this show anticipated by four years the American *Hale's Tours* that
seated the spectators in a railroad car. Finally, Paris saw pictures on a
screen 70 feet wide and 53 feet high. When Lumière was asked to create
an *écran géant* for the exposition's Galerie des Machines, he began by
installing a screen 100 by 80 feet—as high as a six-story house. Alterations
in the building before the fair opened forced him to reduce his screen
to 70 by 53 feet—still twice the height of ours today. By immersing the
giant cloth in a tank of water he was able to make it translucent and
managed to show his films to a gigantic audience of 25,000 people at
a time, half of them on one side of the screen and half on the other.
So far, the largest screen appears to have been the one that the engineer
and inventor Lorenzo Del Riccio set up at Columbus, Ohio, in 1919,
for a summer conference of the Methodist Church; it was 165 by 135
feet.

LUMIÈRE'S GIANT SCREEN AND FILM OF 1900. While the French pioneer was installing a 70 by 53 foot screen at the Paris Exposition, he began to experiment with a 75mm film. Here is a view of part of the grounds. For some reason he never showed such views on his giant screen but had to be content with grainy 35mm pictures. (*Courtesy Jean Vivié.*)

70mm Films from 1896 to 1900

Between the last years of the nineteenth century and the depression of 1929, more than a dozen men besides Lumière and Del Riccio tried to alter the movie image in one of three ways. They increased the size of the screen or the size of the film, still keeping the old 1.33:1 ratio. Or they changed the shape of the picture by increasing the width of the frame.

In the eighteen-nineties, many Europeans were imitating the Dickson-Edison camera because it hadn't been patented abroad. Curiously enough, some of them didn't adopt the 35mm width; some used film as narrow as 12mm and some as wide as 80mm. When they began to develop projectors, they found it wise to adopt 35mm because they wanted to use Edison's films.

In 1896, after New York had seen the first large-screen projection, Léon Gaumont developed a 60mm camera from a patent by Georges Demeny and projected a ballet at the huge Théâtre du Châtelet in 1896–97. In 1900, Lumière shot scenes at the Paris Exposition on 75mm film, but he never showed these pictures publicly. Soon Mutoscope, renamed Mutoscope and Biograph, was able to use the more economical 35mm film, and American moviegoers saw no more giant screens until 1926. Then came the astonishing but brief sensation of a gargantuan experiment by Paramount.

Magnascope Distends the Screen

The trick was nothing more than projecting the old 35mm film with a lens that threw a larger picture. Simple as it was, the "process" developed by Del Riccio acquired the impressive name of Magnascope. Early in 1925, an Eastman Theater in Rochester, New York, tried this out on Paramount's feature film *The Thundering Herd*. For the scene of the buffalo round-up the screen opened up from about 20 by 15 feet to about 40 by 30. At the end of 1924 (almost two years before Paramount was ready to exploit Magnascope on Broadway) the Italian director Arturo Ambrosio had already used just such a lens to blow up the hand-colored scene of the burning of Rome at the close of his *Quo Vadis?*. The first use of Magnascope in New York, at the end of 1926, was for only two scenes in *Old Ironsides*. When the frigate *Constitution* appeared, sailing toward the audience, and later, when the battle with the Barbary pirates began, the black cloth masking the top and sides of the screen drew up and away, and the spectators saw the picture grow to what seemed twice its former size. They also saw the picture grow grainier, and perhaps that was why Magnascope was used only in single, exciting episodes of a few pictures released before 1930. After long neglect, the device turned up again to make the storm sequence more impressive in David Selznick's *Portrait of Jennie* (1948).

From Vignettes to Split Screens and Back Again

Two pictures on the same screen is a hoary device. There were a few even before 1903 when Edwin S. Porter showed his fireman dreaming of wife and child vignetted in the upper corner of the scene. Splitting the picture from top to bottom, so as to show different shots at the same time, seems to be a newer trick. Like the vignette, it was used for a long time only in an episode or two, never for an entire film/In 1927, Murnau put two scenes side by side in *Sunrise* to show different aspects of vacation time. The next year, in *Les Deux Timides*, René Clair printed three bed scenes in the same frame to make a comic point. *This Is Cinerama* indulged in one spasm of triple vision. At a point in *It's Always Fair Weather* (1955), Stanley Donen split the wide screen of CinemaScope into three panels in order to cover the divergent activities of his three heroes. Two years later, in *Funny Face*, Donen again used the triptych effect, this time on the VistaVision screen, to show his three principals touring Paris. *Wonderful To Be Young*, one of Britain's top money-makers of 1962, split the CinemaScope screen into eight panels to show some young people preparing for a night out. *The Music Man* (1962) was not only pleasantly old-fashioned in plot and atmosphere but it also revived the vignette to good effect, despite the size of the Technirama screen.

The Amazing Triptych of Abel Gance

In 1927, an enterprising French director astonished Paris with the last word in splintered images. Instead of splitting one screen into three parts, Abel Gance used three screens. Placed side by side and covering an area of about 50 by 12½ feet, they sometimes showed the audience a single long picture, but more often two or even three different scenes at the same time.

In *Napoléon Bonaparte*, Gance had intended to tell the life story of the emperor, but after five years of preparation and many months of shooting, he had produced a film eight hours long—which had to be drastically cut for public presentation—and he had got Napoleon no further than the conquest of Italy. With the triple cameras and triple projectors developed by the noted French technician André Debrie, Gance was able to show huge audiences at the Paris Opera House a production that was as bizarre and unprecedented as it was sometimes confusing. A French critic has said that the camera work was "extravagantly mobile" and, at times, even subjective. The confusion in the minds of

GANCE'S TRIPLE SCREEN. Three projectors threw *Napoléon Bonaparte* upon a screen four times as wide as it was high. Sometimes a picture of an army on the march or in bivouac stretched across the entire screen. Sometimes the head of Napoleon or a symbolic figure occupied the middle section of the triptych, while other scenes appeared at right and left. The scenes at the sides were often identical, but reversed as if in a mirror. Here was the widest aspect ratio—about 4.2:1—ever shown to the public. (*From Paul Raibaud's* Promoteurs et réalisateurs du spectacle cinématographique sur écran large.)

many spectators was due not to how Gance photographed his scenes, but, rather, to how he showed them on the three screens.

At the beginning, Gance used only the central screen, but, with the scene in the French Convention, his triple projectors spread a single vast image out and across all three. Gance had other tricks up his cinematic sleeve. Sometimes he threw a single image on the middle screen, while he used the others for shots that were related in time or through symbolism. For instance, in the center he might show the head of Napoleon or a triumphant eagle, while at the sides he projected the Grande Armée moving outward in mirrored shots.

Aesthetically, Gance's triptych was much more daring than Waller's Cinerama. Theatrically, it was much less effective. Waller let his audiences enjoy peripheral vision. Gance asked his to do a kind of peripheral thinking. That is a very difficult process in the movie theater. There, all in all, speed is of the essence, and the hurrying film allows little time for reflection. The visual effects that Gance created were extraordinary, I'm sure, but at times the audiences in Paris—and still more in other Continental cities where *Napoléon Bonaparte* was shown—must have been as baffled as American moviegoers would be if, watching a foreign film, they tried to read two or three different lines of translated dialogue placed side by side.

In 1935, Gance showed parts of his old triptych film on a single screen, adding new shots and also stereophonic sound. Twenty years later, he was still enamored of what he called Polyvision, but the only director who seems to have imitated him was Claude Autant-Lara. He used Chrétien's lenses to squeeze three images onto a single frame for *Construire un Feu* (1928), and thus cover a screen about the shape of CinemaScope's.

The Wide Screen At The Turn Of The Century

The wide screen (by this I mean a single screen broader than usual but relatively low) might have come to New York in the mid-nineties if the Lathams and Rector had been either a little more enterprising or a little more practical. In their cameras they used film half again as wide as Edison's, and the pictures they took were twice as wide as they were high. On March 17, 1897, having left the Lathams, Rector used 11,000 feet of 60mm film in his Veriscope camera to record the Corbett-Fitzsimmons fight, and soon he was showing his pictures on a screen at the New York Academy of Music in a ratio of two to one. There seems to have been no talk of the advantages of the wide film. Rather, the width and the shape that the Lathams and Rector adopted may have been intended to avoid a patent infringement.

Not so with a later inventor, the Italian producer Filoteo Alberini. In 1910, he became fascinated by what the French called the *premier plan* of American films. It was a kind of "medium shot" that cut off the legs of the actors and emphasized torsos and heads. Alberini wanted to retain intimacy and yet at the same time put the actors against a fuller and wider background. The next year, he patented a camera, the Panoramica, to do this. It had a pivoted lens that swept across each frame of a 70mm film. The result was an image close to the shape of CinemaScope's—about 2.52:1.

Old Processes Used Today

Alberini didn't have even the brief success of the Lathams, but he tried again along other lines, and so did a surprising number of inventors between the beginning of World War I and the end of the silent era. The men of those days tried to achieve the wide screen by a number of different methods. Some of these were improvements on older processes. All of them roughly resemble one or more of the processes introduced since 1952, as I have described them in the last chapter.

The wide film of the Lathams and Rector was the basis of the first of many experiments after Alberini's. In 1914, Edwin S. Porter, director of *The Great Train Robbery*, abetted by Adolph Zukor of Famous Players, tried to create the kind of broad image that we now see highly developed. The next year, however, a fire destroyed the films and equipment of

WIDE FILM FROM A PANORAMIC LENS. At some time after 1910, the Italian technician Filoteo Alberini developed a camera with a lens that swung across a 70mm film. This produced an image 23 by 58mm, with an aspect ratio of 2.52:1. The picture shows us a glassed-in motion picture studio of the silent days. (*From Paul Raibaud's* Promoteurs et réalisateurs du spectacle cinématographique sur écran large.)

Porter and Zukor, and then World War I diverted their attention to America's golden opportunity of monopolizing film production.

In 1916 came the first attempt, so far as I know, to create an impression of an elongated screen by cropping the height of the image in the projector—the method used since the middle nineteen-fifties. While Griffith was directing *Intolerance* in 1916, he allowed E. W. Clark to make some experimental shots with wide film. Using a wide-angle lens, he added a third more coverage at the top and sides of each frame. Apparently Clark cropped his print and kept his figures full size on a screen a third larger than usual. However, no company took up his idea, and he began developing, in 1919, the process ultimately to be known as Vista-Vision.

Two Projectors Instead of One

Between the time when Cinéorama put ten images side by side and when Cinerama did this with three, there were other attempts to widen the screen by using more than one projector. An American named John D. Elms invented a camera with two lenses that took pictures on a couple of 35mm films. In 1922 he demonstrated the projection of two frames side by side, but he didn't solve the problem of joining the edges smoothly. Fifteen years later, Henri Chrétien did the trick more successfully and far more spectacularly by mating two projectors equipped with his CinemaScope lenses. But another fifteen years had to pass before Hollywood studios began to use Chrétien's lenses, and they never adopted his twin projectors that, in 1937, covered the widest screen since Cinéorama.

It was at a Paris exposition devoted to the wonders of electricity that Chrétien thus combined in 1937 the process later called CinemaScope with the use of multiple projectors common to Cinéorama, Gance's triptych, and Cinerama. Using two linked cameras, like Cinerama's three, and adding his anamorphic lenses, Chrétien squeezed onto two black and white 35mm films wide views of hydroelectric plants. Two projectors with his special lenses "unsqueezed" the two films side by side to cover a concrete wall on the outside of the Palace of Light. To make the edges of his pictures seem to match, Chrétien, like Waller with Cinerama, used saw-toothed masks, but the Frenchman's were stationary instead of moving. At Chrétien's evening shows, Parisians saw one continuous picture on a screen 200 feet long and 33 feet high. Nothing so wide and nothing so huge in square footage had been shown commercially since Grimoin-Sanson's Cinéorama. Though each little frame of 35mm film was multiplied more than 1,200 times in width, and al-most 7,000,000 in area, the French film historian and technician Jean Vivié reports that the results "were most satisfactory."

Moviegoers came close to seeing the double screen covered by twin projectors in *Gone With the Wind* (1939). David O. Selznick toyed with the idea when he began production by burning down the back lot settings at the RKO-Pathé studio for the scenes of the destruction of Atlanta. He photographed the holocaust with two cameras and showed the combined shots to his backers, but he found that they were all too sure that the film would be successful without adding double screens in the theaters showing the film.

Enter the Wide Screen, 1929

Before we consider the virtues and faults of our present-day 'ramas, 'scopes, and 'visions, let us review the abortive labor of Hollywood to fill America's theaters with wide screens in the late nineteen-twenties. Today this is all but forgotten, yet if the depression hadn't come along, something very like Todd-AO would have been with us for all these years.

Hollywood hadn't learned too much about making talkies before some of the studios added a new complication by trying to go a step further than Paramount's Magnascope. Some say that the film companies went for the wide-screen film because they had watched the theaters buy millions of dollars' worth of sound equipment from the manufacturers of radios and phonographs, and the movie producers thought they could turn an honest and rather large penny by forcing the theaters to buy a new batch of projectors and screens, this time from corporations controlled by the producers.

At any rate, the studios began experimenting with ways of producing a large picture without any more grain than 35mm film in normal projection. This turned out to be a wide film throwing a wide image on a wide screen. Various studios used various widths of film. Fox and MGM adopted 70mm. At first, Paramount engaged André Debrie to develop a 65mm process, then had its own technician Del Riccio provide 56mm cameras and projectors. First National—merged with Warner Brothers —tried 65mm. RKO turned to 63mm, which George Spoor and P. John Berggren had been working on for quite a number of years. When prints from the wide negatives were projected, the aspect ratio ran from 1.87:1 to a little more than 2:1. The odd part about this revolution in film shape—and all the money and effort that went into it—is that very

THE WIDE SCREEN OF c.1929. Here are three frames from a number of features that were produced or planned as the country was slipping into the depression. The films were all shot on wide film, not squeezed and then blown up. Top, a baseball game on Movietone's 70mm; below, a Paramount test on 63mm; finally, MGM's spectacular western *Great Meadow* on 70mm.

few wide films were actually released. The few that were shown played only in New York and Los Angeles. Fox led off with its Grandeur films. In September 1929, it showed two shorts and a feature, *Fox Movietone Follies of 1929*, on a 28- by 14-foot screen at the Gaiety Theater on Broadway. The next February came *Happy Days*, 42 feet wide and 20 feet high, at the Roxy. Fox's final wide film of the year was *The Big Trail*. In 1930 and 1931, First National went wide and handsome on *Kismet* and *The Lash*, and MGM on *Billy the Kid* and *The Great Meadow*. Paramount's Magnafilm never got beyond two shorts. In most cases, the studios shot the pictures with both a wide-film camera and the regular 35mm. MGM shot *Billy the Kid* on 70mm, reduced it to 35mm, and provided lenses by which at least one New York theater blew the picture up to giant size. Except for this film and the three films from Fox, First National's *Kismet* seems to be the only other production shown in wide-screen form.

1931—Exit the Wide Screen

Before these showings, things looked promising for a time and also a little messy. How to standardize wide film and equipment? Would it be 70mm or 65mm or 56mm? The depression solved that problem, but a bit belatedly. The news of October 1929 was slow in reaching the ivory towers and tin ears of Hollywood. The *Film Daily Year Book* of 1930 editorialized:

> Double width films on screens that fill the proscenium arches are forecast for the larger theaters long before this year comes to a close. With color to play with, the enlarged screen is ideal for the four- and five-thousand seat houses. It takes the wide screen to properly set off color, so these two major developments of 1930 promise to go forward hand in hand.

But before the year was out, the tiny boom of the big screen was over. Word came that the exhibitors wouldn't play ball. They had bought new projectors for the talkies, but that was during the Harding-Coolidge prosperity. They simply couldn't find the money for more new equipment. The theaters and the producers had met something worse than the competition of television in 1952. The audience was broke.

At Last Film-Makers Debate a New Process

There were three interesting side issues to the wide screen of the late twenties. It is ironic that Waller, the man who was to develop Cinerama, reported to his Paramount employers: "I think its value is only a novelty one." Critics, as well as producers, felt something stereoscopic about these broad pictures. And the men who were actually making Hollywood pictures began to debate just exactly what was the best shape for the screen.

In many arts, new mechanical techniques have been developed by the artists for their own purposes. But it was mainly scientists, plus a few still photographers, who created the movie process; and they hadn't the least idea of where it was going. In the case of the talkies, it was scientists, again, who developed the new technique. Sound and dialogue didn't come because of any demand from the men who directed and wrote pictures. Indeed, a great many of them objected to the change. It was significant of a new and healthier attitude among the film-makers —a sense of responsibility and even power—that when the producers set their technicians working on the wide film, the directors and the cameramen at last started to talk about what was going to happen to

STAGE   BROADWAY   SCREEN

VARIETY   PRICE 25¢

Published Weekly at 154 West 46th St., New York, N. Y. by Variety, Inc. Annual subscription, $10. Single copies, 25 cents.
Entered as second-class matter December 22, 1905, at the Post Office at New York, N. Y., under the act of March 3, 1879.

VOL. XCVII. No. 3   NEW YORK, WEDNESDAY, OCTOBER 30, 1929   88 PAGES

WALL ST. LAYS AN EGG

Going Dumb Is Deadly to Hostess In Her Serious Dance Hall Profesh

A hostess at Roseland has her problems. The paid steppers consider their work a definite profession calling for specialized technique and high-power salesmanship.

"You see, you gotta sell your personality," said one. "Each one of we girls has our own clientele to cater to. It's just like selling dresses in a store—you have to know what to sell each particular customer.

"Some want to dance, some want to kid, some want to get soupy, and others are just 'mush-faced' hams."

Girls applying for hostess jobs at Roseland must be 21 or older. They must work five nights a week. They are strictly on salary. No salary going with the job and the house collecting 18 cents on every $5 cent ticket. To keep her job, a girl must turn in at least 100 tickets a week during the cold season and 50 in the summer months. In a dull week girls buy their own tickets to keep up the record.

If a partner wishes to sit out a dance, he must pay for the privilege. "Sitting-out time" sells at eight tickets an hour, or $2.08. It's usually a poor sport who will come across with less than $3, many kicking in heavier for a little genial conversation.

The girl who knows her professional dancing trade will keep an alert eye open for potential "sitter-outers," ascertain their hobbies and talk herself into a whole string of tickets. In this way she not only earns money easily, but saves wear and tear on her evening dresses and slippers.

Big money rolls in if she has a good line. One of the most successful girls at Roseland takes this part of her work so seriously that she reads up on current events (sports and stock market included) and has a smattering of current literature and art.

"There are two types of hostesses at Roseland," she said, displaying high brow leanings. "They are the 'mental' and the 'physical.' Surprisingly enough the physical ones are not those who make the most money. One customer will buy three tickets from them at the most. They rely on their sex appeal and go dumb between dances—and that's the surest way to lose a partner, going dumb.

Mental Girls

"The 'mental' girls, being good conversationalists, can wise-crack flippant, sympathize with . . . know how to salt the . . . them like it . . ."

Hank on Winchell

When the Walter Winchells moved into 204 West 55th street, late last week, June, that's Mrs. Winchell, selected a special room as Walter's exclusive sleep den for his late hour nights. She shushed the Winchell kidlets when her husband dove in at his usual eight o'clock the first morning.

At noon, Walter's midnight, his sound proof room was penetrated by so many high C's he was awake with but four hours of dreams and a grouch. Investigated at once, after having signed the lease of course.

Right next door, on the same floor, is the studio of the noted vocal instructor, Kinney. Among his pupils are Ona Munson, Irene Delroy and Marjorie Peterson. They love Winchell like you love carbolic acid.

And Miss Munson is reported to have requested that an amplifier be started hereafter when she runs up the scale.

Demand for Vaude

Springfield, Ill., Oct. 29.
Petitions requesting Publix theatres to resume vaudeville in Decatur, Ill. are in circulation in that city.

Petitions specify that vaudeville at one or more of the three larger Publix houses would furnish employment to a number of Decatur musicians and stage bands and provide larger variety of local entertainment.

Paul Witte, Publix manager in Decatur, states that he believes vaudeville will find a place in Decatur before the season is over.

Pickpocketing Dying Out

Chicago, Oct. 29.
Some 1,000-odd pickpockets used to make Chicago . . . men shows . . . are no more. A co. . . the hands of . . . men shows . . . bottles. . . . In . . .

DROP IN STOCKS ROPES SHOWMEN

Many Weep and Call Off Christmas Orders — Legit Shows Hit

MERGERS HALTED

The most dramatic event in the financial history of America is the collapse of the New York Stock Market. The stage was Wall Street, but the onlookers covered the country. Estimates are that 25,000,000 people were in the market at the time.

Tragedy, despair and ruination spell the story of countless thousands of marginal stock traders. Perhaps Manhattan was worst hit in the number of victims. Many may remain broke for the rest of their lives, because the money that disappeared via the ticker tape was the savings of years.

Many people of Broadway are known to have been wiped out. Reports of some in show business losing as much as $300,000 is not hearsay. One caustic comment is that was that the theatre is enough of a gamble without its people to venture into Wall street.

Prominent showmen, several identified with the picture industry

(Continued on page 64)

FILTHY SHOW OF SHUBERTS GOOD FOR SCREEN

Chicago, Oct. 29.
Shubert's latest musical of their "Night" series, now in Chicago, is so filthy that one of the cast admits embarrassment while in the . . . 'rmance.
. . . 'cond act of this scramble . . . 'dway Nights," an . . . ' on page 63)

Kidding Kissers in Talkers Burns Up Fans of Screen's Best Lovers

Talker Crashes Olympus

Paris, Oct. 29.
Fox "Follies" and the Fox Movietone newsreel are running this week in Athens, Greece, the first sound pictures heard in the birthplace of world culture, and in all Greece, for that matter.

Several weeks ago, Variety's Cairo correspondent cabled that a cinema had been wired in Alexandria, Cleopatra's home town.

Only Sodom and Gomorrah remain to be heard from.

HOMELY WOMEN SCARCE, CAN'T EARN OVER $25

No homely ones on Broadway! And now it looks as if Crosby Gaige may have to postpone production of "One Beautiful Evening" because the Main Stem is devoid of the non-beauts necessary for the casting of the show.

Arthur Lubin, caster for the producer, for several weeks has been trying to land the right type of women. A most unusual piece, the drama has an all-women lineup, and, although as many as 72 are needed, all must be homely—and middle age or over, except for two who can be young.

Vera Caspary wrote the play and it centers about conditions at a club for girls where requirements of residence demand that the girls must not earn over $25 per week in order to live under its roof. That's why they must be homely.

Ads for Exe . . .

Newspap . . .
'tial an . . .
a . . .

Boys who used to whistle and girls who used to giggle when bathing scenes were flashed on the screen are in action again. A couple of love stuff seriously and devoted but the talkers are reviving the ha ha for film osculators.

Heavy loving lovers of silent picture days accustomed to charming audiences into spasms of silent ecstasy when kissing the leading lady are getting the instead of the heartbeat. The company accompaniment is making laugh.

Such a picture romancer as John Gilbert is getting laughs in place of the sighs of other days, and the flaps who still think he's grand are getting sore. One little flap had to be quieted by an usher when making a commotion during a Gilbert picture at the Capitol, New York. The person sitting next to her, like many others in the house, too, Gilbert's passion lightly. The girl jumped to his defense and started to bawl out the Gilbert derider.

Not only has Gilbert received this bird lately, but all of the other matinee screen players who specialize in romance. Charley Farrell in "Sunny Side Up" draws many a giggle from his mush stuff.

In the silents when a lover would whisper like a ventriloquist, lips apart and unmoved, and roll his eyes passionately, preparatory to the clinch and then kiss, it looked pretty natural and was believable. The build-up to the kissing now makes a gag of the kiss.

When the kiss is with serious intent, the laughs are out of order. It's burning the impressed female fans to see their favorite kissers kidded when kissing.

In Reverse

Seems the only type of love stuff received as intended since advent of the talkers in the comedy love scene. The screen comics are becoming the heavy lovers and the heavy lovers comedians.

The normal kiss, delivered the usual smack, sounds like scenes in the early them rolling in the ai . . . 'oning down the . . . ' noiseless . . .

WIDE SCREEN—R.I.P. As *Variety*, the "Bible of Show Business," recorded on October 30, 1929, the coming of the depression curbed Grandeur and other wide-screen films. More than twenty years later, another financial calamity, the competition of television, broadened the screen again. (*Courtesy Variety.*)

Whistlers in the Dark

Prosperity is in the air. In that prosperity the motion picture industry, of course, will share.

—Will Hays, *The Film Daily Year Book*, 1929

The motion picture industry looks to the future with the confidence which is warranted by a steadily improving product and a steadily increasing attendance at our theaters.

—Hays, *The Film Daily Year Book*, 1930

The motion picture industry enters 1930 in the most prosperous condition in its comparatively short but eventful history.

—Jack Alicoate, *The Film Daily Year Book*, 1930

Let us look back on 1930 for a moment. It was an exacting and depressing year for business generally and a trying and irritating twelve months for this industry. . . . In spite of chaotic conditions in general, with the whole world seeming to be upside down, the motion picture industry gave a splendid account of itself in point of earnings. . . .

The motion picture industry enters 1931 probably on a safer and saner basis than at any time during the past ten years. . . . 1931 promises much in the way of improvement to the world at large. To this industry it will no doubt mark the rising of the curtain on the greatest era of prosperity the motion picture has ever enjoyed.

—Alicoate, *The Film Daily Year Book*, 1931

the art that they worked in. The Academy of Motion Picture Arts and Sciences held meetings, and Eisenstein, newly arrived in Hollywood, sounded off.

The Proper Shape—Square, Round, or Oblong?

A few directors had worried about being confined to the four by three (1.33:1) oblong, and a few had tried to do something about it within the old camera. For instance, in *The Birth of a Nation*, Griffith occasionally framed the bottom and the top of the screen to emphasize horizontal movement; and in a scene in *Intolerance*—the plunge of a soldier from the towering ramparts of Babylon—Griffith tried to concentrate on the man's fall and to increase the apparent height of the walls by masking in the sides of the scene until he had a tall, narrow picture.

Eisenstein, too, wanted a tall frame for some scenes and a wide one for others. He wished, he said, "to intone the hymn of the male, the strong, the virile active vertical composition . . . a vertical perception

led our hairy ancestors on their way to a higher level." Skyscrapers and
chimneys expressed this. But he liked the horizontal, too. It suited "big
trails," "fighting caravans," "covered wagons," and "the endless breadth
of 'old man rivers.'" He toyed with a circular frame that could be made
into rectangles of different shapes. He was ready to settle for a square
that could be similarly reshaped.

At an Academy meeting in September, 1930, Eisenstein became ecstatic: "I think this actual moment is one of the great historical moments
in the pictorial development of the screen . . . Gee, it is a great day!"
In one respect, however, Eisenstein was definite and, perhaps, right.
He was against "the dull proportions of the present standard film size."

For the benefit of the Academy, artists and technicians reported on
the virtues of "dynamic symmetry," "the whirling square," or "the golden
mean," which an art authority named Jay Hambidge had proved was
the basis of Greek architecture and ceramics. This perfect proportion
came out at about 1.62:1. There were statistical studies of 250 great
paintings dealing with action or emotion, and someone reduced the giant
screen of Rubens to quite a series of graphs. But all they found was
what they were looking for; they had to choose only a few out of thousands of paintings.

After a lot more research and argument, members of the Academy
decided that the screen might be safely stretched out to 2:1 but that
the best ratio lay between 1.6:1 and 1.8:1. Hambidge was in by a nose.
Few Academicians stood up for the old frame that had lasted more
than thirty years.

The "Dynamic Frame"—Many Shapes from One

Twenty-five years after Eisenstein's plea for a screen that could show
different scenes in different shapes, an American achieved this in England. (We must note, again, that a Frenchman appears to have made the
first experiment. It was Autant-Lara with his Mobilia of the late nineteen-
twenties, but his attempt seems to have been unsuccessful.) With the
financial aid of the British Film Institute's Experimental Production
Committee and Associated British-Pathé, Glenn Alvey had the opportunity, which America had denied him, of demonstrating his Dynamic
Frame. Using VistaVision and Technicolor, he shot a thirty-minute film
version of H. G. Wells' fantasy *The Door in the Wall* (1956). He used
masks—technically called mattes—to change the shape of the screen
image on his negative. He could move the horizontal pairs and/or the
vertical ones at the same time or separately, and thus change the shape of

the picture. The screen could seem tall and narrow or low and wide. Whatever shape he used could shrink or expand.

Derek Prouse credited the Dynamic Frame with the virtue of "the elimination of meaningless space." He described how the changing shape fitted the dramatic mood of the various scenes. When the child, in a tall and narrow shot, opens the door "and advances into the magic garden, the slowly expanding view becomes subjective and conveys astonishment and strangeness." At one point, "the child, wandering in the garden, sits down on what—in the small-size frame—one takes to be a garden seat. He starts up violently; and the screen, expanding to full size, swiftly reveals that he has sat on the foot of a huge monster." Obviously, as Prouse points out, the shape of every shot must be planned in the script before shooting. Also, the Dynamic Frame seems best fitted to fantasy, the musical, or melodrama.

Differing Views of the New Look

When Cinerama, 3-D, and CinemaScope changed the look of the screen, the Academy held no meetings, but individual film-makers were fairly voluble. There was a good deal of objection outside of the industry, and a lot of cheers from Hollywood's publicity men.

Before 3-D suffered a natural demise, some critics complained that adding a third dimension to color photography would bring the film too near a reproduction of reality to be truly creative. Goethe had said: "It is through the limitations of an art that the master shows his genius." Half a dozen years before 3-D raised its ugly head and thrust it through the screen, the astute English film critic Roger Manvell inveighed against the "three-dimensional, all-talking, all-smelling, all-tasting, all-feeling chaos which is the inartistic affair called the experience of life." "It is wrong," he wrote, "to try to make art too life-like."

An exhibitor disposed of 3-D rather neatly when he advertised an old-fashioned flat film with these words:

> Do You Want a Good Movie—
> Or A Lion In Your Lap?

Samuel Goldwyn put the bee on size, shape, and depth when he said: "The only important dimension is the story." But naturally enough, the studio that introduced CinemaScope had a somewhat different point of view. Twentieth Century-Fox saw the "new look" as "one of the greatest technological advancements" since sound. (Its eyesight hadn't been quite so sharp when Chrétien offered his newly patented process almost thirty years before.) At first it looked as if Fox thought it was selling a combination of 3-D and Cinerama. Its booklet declared that "actors seem to walk into the audience, vehicles roar into the front rows . . . audiences are taken for breath-taking rides on roller-coasters." Then Fox got round to the idea of "audience participation," and had to go back to the Attic theater for something to match CinemaScope. The spectators, the pamphlet asserted, "are made to feel part of the exciting action—the goal of the earliest Greek dramatists—instead of merely watching it." Of course no Athenian playgoer, even if he had a front-row seat, ever got so intimate a view of an actor. One of Fox's producers said, according to *Life*, "Here was Lauren Bacall on a couch! . . . She filled the screen! She was sixty-four feet long"—a slight exaggeration.

Is the Wide Screen Too Wide?

Some of the attacks of Hollywood film makers against the wide screen were a bit off line. For example: "Who wants to see a nuance as big as a house?" Many of the hostile didn't notice that wide screens were, at most, only a couple of feet taller than the old ones, and usually a little shorter. As you will see later, the width of a theater proscenium limits the height of CinemaScope quite as much as it does its breadth. Therefore, full heads couldn't be much larger than before; and, because of cutting and composition problems, single-face close-ups weren't used so frequently.

No, the real point of attack had to be width, not height. The more astute critics and directors inveighed against a "letter slot" screen. George Stevens, who made *A Place in the Sun* and *Shane* without benefit of CinemaScope, called the new shape "a system of photography that pictures a boa constrictor to better advantage than a man." Also, as he put it, "no screen is larger than its smallest dimension."

The defenders of the Fox process and of Todd-AO might have pointed out that the average stage setting for a play is also twice as wide as it is high, but this would have brought them up against a nasty and embarrassing fact. On the stage, we don't see an actor twenty feet high or an actress stretched across a forty-foot couch. As we concentrate on one player, then turn our eyes and even our heads to watch another, we are conscious—but not too conscious—of the three dimensional setting behind them. The scenery is not competing with the actor for the audience's attention. Faces and bodies, furniture and walls, don't share the single surface of the screen.

A STAGE SET IS OF CINEMASCOPE "ASPECT RATIO." This scenic sketch by Robert Edmond Jones for the Broadway play *The Devil's Garden* is typical of most proscenium openings of legitimate theaters, which are more than twice as wide as they are high. (*From* The Living Stage.)

What about Stories?

What did the wide, wide screen—not a slightly wider one like Vista-Vision's—do to the story? Some critics of the first CinemaScope productions were rather bitter. Remembering how the early movies thrived at British fairs, Walter Lassally wrote in 1955, "Today, with the emphasis on novelty, noise, and spectacle, the cinema is on its way to returning to its birthplace, the fairground . . . the present situation is bound to split the industry to some extent into circus and cinema, with main emphasis on the former." At the time, there seemed to be no question that the wide screen would be given over to historical spectacles, big Westerns, musicals, and melodramas with outdoor chases. It was rather amusing to note the success of costume pictures, at least for a time, and then recall that only a few years earlier some exhibitors had found them "poison at the box office." A gloomster among the critics said that in the future the public would see intimate films only on television. Though the first four years of CinemaScope gave us no outstanding dramas of intimate action, we had plenty of such films made in VistaVision or on the old negative cropped to 1.85:1.

Is the New Shape Pleasing or Distracting?

Apart from the vital matter of the story, the moviegoer must ask and answer three fundamental questions if he wants to judge the value of CinemaScope, Ultra Panavision, or any other process that gives us a screen at least twice as wide as it is high. Is the long, narrow screen pleasing whether we sit in the last row or the first? Is a third of the screen a complete waste, even a distraction, when a story deals with tight personal drama instead of visual pageantry? Have we lost some of the important values of direction and editing that film makers developed through years of work with the screen that was almost square?

The answer to the first question—is the shape of the wide screen pleasing?—will be largely a matter of the moviegoer's personal taste and sensitivity. Like Alexander Pope, he may prefer a work of art in which "no monstrous height, or breadth, or length appears."

As to whether things and people toward the sides of the screen distract attention from the main action, there seem to be two attitudes. They are "Yes, and we must do something about it," and "Maybe the audience likes to be distracted." Directors and cameramen who have worked for the wide screen realize the danger of distraction. For example, after the shooting of *Oklahoma!* in Todd-AO an article appeared in which the photographer, Robert Surtees, explained how he tried to concentrate attention on the central action by using static objects in the foreground or filling the side areas of the screen with shadows. When Twentieth Century-Fox first hailed the virtues of CinemaScope in a booklet, it was quite conscious of the problem which directors and cameramen were to face. The studio saw the nettle and grasped it boldly. In a rather remarkable statement, it tried to turn a failing into a virtue:

> The medium enchances the importance of background material, both as regards sets and actors. Their increased size on the big screen permits of closer scrutiny of them *if the viewer chooses to look at them. As a result more actors will be used in all scenes in order to fill the screen* [my italics].

Cutting and Directing on the Wide Screen

The skills in directing and cutting developed through twenty-five years of the silent screen weren't destroyed by the talkies. They were modified, but they were also built upon and improved. Has the two-to-one screen done violence to what had become a supple and perfected technique?

Since the advent of the wide screen, we have noticed many changes in directing and cutting and listened to many a wailing Cassandra. For example, Richard Kohler wrote in 1955: "Unless the present trend is wisely deflected, aesthetic rights gained in a half century of struggle will be cut, literally, into long narrow ribbons, with the public cajoled into applauding the butchery." Such pessimism seems to have been largely unfounded. Long, long ago, when the anamorphic lens was hardly more than a few years old, Arnheim said that the introduction of color, stereoscopy, and the big screen would make the camera "an immobile recording machine," and every cut would be a mutilation. We would go back to a fixed camera and an uncut film. The result would be a kind of stage play without intermissions.

At first, there seemed to be something in this gloomy view. Productions in CinemaScope had some of the static quality of the "ice box" films of early sound days. The camera moved, of course, but, if it panned at all, the distortion of lines and masses near the sides of the screen became obvious. In a scene between three or more people there were fewer cuts—and there always will be, I think. This is partly because rapid cutting is disturbing on the wide screen, and partly because the new screen can hold a wider group of actors than the old one. From the start, there were two-shots, as well as group shots, in CinemaScope, but over-shoulder shots came into use rather slowly. Inserts are harder to handle. The montage, with its series of many rapidly dissolving images, seems quite impossible. In sum, CinemaScope and the other processes do not and cannot use as many setups and cuts as the narrower screen.

It seems clear that pictures shot for the wide screen have lost—perhaps, had to lose—some of the rich variety of angles, as well as visual movement, that we had grown to expect from films. Again, Fox tried to make the best of a bad bargain. It declared that CinemaScope gave a movie "the life-like fluidity of the stage." So far as the theater is concerned, this was a grotesque statement, and self-contradictory. Also it implied that other films are neither lifelike nor fluid, which is rank absurdity. Certainly there can be no question that some early CinemaScope productions—*How to Marry a Millionaire* (1953), for example—seemed much more like stage plays than movies.

Incidentally, the wide screen has put new demands on the actor. In two ways he has become more like the player in a Broadway production. Because scenes are shot in fewer setups, he must learn far longer stretches of dialogue. Also, when the camera is centered on other actors in the set, he may have to play in pantomime because he is not off-screen as he might have been on the narrower film.

Proscenium Problems

One very serious problem about CinemaScope was how to fit it into the average proscenium. In the great majority of America's 15,000 "hard top" theaters the proscenium opening was too narrow or too low to permit projection in correct ratios. In houses with such narrow prosceniums, the height of a picture in CinemaScope has to be less than the height of a picture on normal film; or else the sides of the shots have to be cut off with masks, and then the wide screen isn't really wide. However, Cinema-Scope—used by other producers besides Fox—did pretty well. In spite of architectural difficulties, up through 1960 there were more than 18,000 theaters in the United States and Canada equipped for CinemaScope and some of the other processes, and 30,000 more abroad.

TV and Wide Films

What about the relative shapes of theater and TV screens and the adapt-ability of wide-screen film frames to home viewing?

Few people remember, or even know, that a camera lens takes a round picture, and that this shape was masked down to a rectangle for both snapshots and the screen. More people, perhaps, realize that the viewing end of the television tube would have been round if its makers hadn't decided to imitate the shape of the old motion-picture screen. Whether or not they adopted this shape so as to be able to show films, it is ironical that the wide-screen productions Hollywood made in order to fight TV competition can never be sold to television as they stand; CinemaScope simply won't fit the home screens. But in the early sixties, TV paid Fox and other studios to reedit and reprint CinemaScope pictures to fit their screens. This entailed laboriously and expensively crop-ping every scene in the negative to 1.33:1 proportions. It meant selecting and using only about a half of each wide scene. This portion may be from the right of the original shot or the left or the middle. Such editing for TV won't be what the director and his cutter originally achieved. The composition of the individual scenes will be very far from what the cameraman conceived. The results are far more disastrous than cropping 1.33:1 frames to fit a 1.85:1 ratio, or cutting off the ends of CinemaScope pictures in a theater with a narrow proscenium.

Chapter

32

New Ways with Sound and Distribution

You may picture the screen of Cinerama moving out from behind the proscenium to encircle and absorb its spectators like a gigantic amoeba surrounding the consuming bits of algae. To complete the assimilation, Cinerama enveloped its audience in sound. To the three dimensions of peripheral vision it added the three dimensions of stereophonic sound. The voices of its people and the noises about them could come from any one of five banks of loudspeakers along the back of the screen, and the roar of a plane or the song of a choir from above or behind the audience. While films in 3-D were going through their brief career of boom or bust, CinemaScope was adding a similar kind of sound to its wide screen; later other large screen processes followed suit.

Two Ears at the Movies Instead of One

In the world of reality we hear with two ears just as we see with two eyes. We experience the perspective of sound quite as much as the perspective of sight. In a complex and rather mysterious way, our two ears tell us that a voice or a noise is to the right or the left or even behind us or overhead. Until a few years ago, however, you might say that we used only one ear in a movie theater. All sounds came from a single spot behind the screen, and what our two ears heard was exactly the same. Today in all theaters that play Cinerama or Ultra Panavision, and in many that offer CinemaScope, there are three to five sets of speakers

489

behind the screen and several in the auditorium. The first group reproduce words from about the areas where the actors stand, and, if one of them moves across the screen, loudspeakers make his speech seem to move with him. Other speakers along the three walls of the auditorium and even on the ceiling bring us a great variety of sounds. We may hear the galloping hoofs of horses at our left or right before a troop of cavalry appears on the screen. We may hear the roar of an airplane passing overhead to land on a runway in the picture. In *This is Cinerama*, we heard the choir singing behind us, then at each side and finally in front of us as the choristers entered the setting. In *Around the World in 80 Days*, we saw the backs of two characters who were looking off across the ocean, and then we, too, took a look at the horizon while their voices spoke behind us.

Three Ways to Make Sound in 3-D

How sound can be reproduced from black and white areas on a film, let alone from magnetized bits of metal on a tape, is very difficult for the layman to grasp. The workings of stereophonic sound are only a little less mysterious.

There are three basic ways of adding three-dimensional sound to a motion picture. One way, used by Cinerama, CinemaScope, and other large-screen processes, is to record dialogue, music, or natural noises with three to five microphones at different places in a set. These tracks are transferred onto a release print or, in the case of Cinerama, onto a separate piece of film. The sound from each track goes to a separate speaker behind the screen or to a group of speakers in the auditorium. All the backstage speakers actually carry the same sound, but the dialogue from one will be louder than from the others because one of the recording microphones had been nearer one of the actors.

Another method also uses a number of microphones and a number of speakers, but it also has what is called a control track. This carries a pattern of electronic cues. Their job is to increase the volume of one or more of the speakers. Walt Disney introduced a process of this sort for *Fantasia* in 1940.

The third method—now discarded—did tricks with the same old sound track that had been in use since the talkies came in. The sound was recorded by a single mike, printed on a single track, and the projector sent the same sounds to all the speakers when required. This method —called Perspecta—had economic advantages, but its lack of quality finally eliminated it.

Stereophonic Sound 80 Years Ago

Like the other "new" processes, three-dimensional sound is an old one, revived and very much amplified and refined through new equipment. It goes back as far as 1881, and the scene is another one of those Paris expositions where talkies, Cinéorama, and CinemaScope had their first showings. Eighty years ago there were no electronic microphones, no loudspeakers—and no movies. Yet a Frenchman named Clément Ader reproduced directional sound. He did this through the enterprising use of an invention that was then only five years old—the telephone. Ader placed twelve transmitters along the footlights of the Paris Opera. Wires from the transmitters ran a mile and a quarter to rooms in the Electrical Exhibition, where they were connected with 48 receivers. Each listener held to his ears a pair of receivers, one that gave him the sounds from the right and one from the left side of the stage. Hearing a somewhat louder sound in one ear or the other, he was able to "place in space" the voices of the singers and to hear the strings of the orchestra to the left and the timpani to the right.

France Provides the First Stereophonic Talkies

America came close to pioneering with stereophonic movies at the New York opening of the Grandeur film *Fox Movietone Follies of 1929.* Someone got the bright idea that the dialogue could be switched from a righthand speaker to one at the left through a monitoring device. After a rehearsal on September 16, 1929, Fox abandoned this rudimentary approach to 3-D sound. And thus the palm passed to France.

Though Léon Gaumont seems to have been the first to suggest printing two different sound tracks on a film, the ever-enterprising Abel Gance was the first to patent a method for bringing 3-D sound to the screen. That was in 1932. He and his fellow-inventor André Debrie were too impatient to wait for a Paris exposition at which to exploit their process. Yet it took three years to perfect the invention and provide a film for the Paramount Theater in Paris to show. Gance reedited portions of the film about Napoleon that he had shown on a triptych screen in 1927, and he added some new shots and directional sounds. Instead of using a photographic control track, Debrie cut notches in the edge of the film, and these signals shunted the sound into various loudspeakers. Dialogue and noise came from around the audience as well as from behind the screen. Oddly enough, Gance gave up his triple screens—so well suited to stereophonic sound—and confined the picture to an area only a third as wide.

99 *Loudspeakers for Disney's Fantasia*

It was in 1940 that Walt Disney brought to the screen the first thorough and ambitious use of stereophonic sound.

As early as 1927, the Bell Telephone Laboratories had begun experimenting with 3-D sound, but without the use of film. In 1933, they were content to transmit over wires from Philadelphia to Washington the music of an orchestra picked up by three microphones and heard over three similarly placed speakers. A little later, the Bell organization developed a control track to amplify any one or all of the sound recordings. When the volume of one or another of the speakers is thus increased, this system gives us the fullest effect of directional sound. Increasing two or more gives us a greater tonal range and less distortion than we would get if a single speaker were amplified to produce the same amount of sound.

Working with Leopold Stokowski, Disney applied this system, with some trimmings, to his feature cartoon *Fantasia*. The orchestra was recorded on three tracks. These, along with a control track, were printed on a separate film interlocked with the picture projector. (The picture film had the usual composite sound track, which could be used if a sound machine broke down.) Fantasound, as the process was called, employed three speakers behind the screen, and in a Los Angeles showing, ninety-six small speakers around the auditorium. These last were coupled to one or another of the speakers in the rear of the screen. The speakers in the auditorium gave a greater sense of directional sound than could be got from behind the constricted screen of that day.

No 3-D Dialogue on the Narrow Screen

In *Fantasia*, there was no attempt to make speech come from one side of the screen or move across to the other. This may have been because Disney and Stokowski were only interested in what could be done to make the recording and reproduction of an orchestra truer and more beautiful. Or they may have recognized that the screen of 1940 wasn't wide enough for the effective use of directional dialogue.

Warner Brothers seemed to agree. Those pioneers of the talkies soon put three speakers behind the screen to "spread" the music score, but they sent all the dialogue through the middle speaker. This system recorded voices and music on a single track, and then used a control pattern to bring in the side speakers and thus increase the volume of the orchestral accompaniment. After making two productions, *Santa Fe Trail* (1940) and *Four Mothers* (1941), in what was called Vitasound, Warners gave up. Perhaps our entry into World War II—with its box office prosperity—delayed further experiments. At any rate, more than ten years were to pass before anyone tried to put 3-D dialogue behind the screen.

3-D Sound in Britain and America—1951 to 1953

The Festival of Britain's Telecinema added 3-D sound to its 3-D shorts in 1951. It neglected, however, one future development—the wide screen. This may seem a curious omission, for, without the wide screen, directional dialogue can't be wholly effective or worth the trouble and expense. But we must remember that audiences at the Telecinema heard only a monologue or narration, and never dialogue scenes. (The Telecinema did, however, send sounds such as bird calls around the auditorium.) When Warner Brothers tried 3-D in 1953 with *House of Wax*, the passages of 3-D dialogue may not have been effective, but this horror film created an eerie atmosphere from the noise of off-screen footsteps and of creaking doors.

Wide Screen for Stereo-Sound

It was all but inevitable that Cinerama, with its almost cycloramic screen, should go for stereo sound in a big way. Like the productions at the Telecinema, it was a very special sort of show, and its producers weren't making a film for general release. So, again like the British venture, Cinerama used a separate film just for sound. But, whereas the Telecinema had four tracks, Cinerama had seven. Five covered the width of the screen, and one went to the auditorium. The seventh combined the other six and could be used if any speaker failed to deliver sound.

Hollywood had to be more practical. Fortunately, there was little trouble about additional loudspeakers for the larger theaters. They were already using two or more hitched together in order to amplify the single sound track. But the producers didn't want to ask the theaters to buy an extra projector to handle a special sound film, and they didn't want to spend money on a separate sound print for every picture print. So, while some producers used Perspecta Sound for a time, CinemaScope put four tracks—three for behind the screen and one for the auditorium—onto 35mm stock. Todd-AO managed to have six, five for behind the screen, by printing on 70mm after shooting on 65mm. As demonstrated in *Oklahoma!*, Todd-AO had the most perfect and most engulfing sound; at the Rivoli Theater in New York, it used nineteen speakers in the auditorium.

Even though CinemaScope put picture and sound track on a single film, it wasn't able to persuade all the theaters to go stereophonic. At first it tried to force them to install extra equipment if they wanted to show CinemaScope productions, but the resistance was too great. After a valiant struggle to add to the screen something that TV didn't offer, Fox had to give up. It was forced to permit the use of "mixers" to put all the tracks through one loudspeaker, and then to supply prints with a normal composite track. By the end of 1962, of the theaters in the United States and Canada equipped for CinemaScope, less than 25 percent were said to be equipped for sterophonic sound.

Magnetic Tape for Sound Recording

Other things more remarkable, perhaps, than 3-D sound and 3-D pictures and the anamorphic lenses that squeeze and expand CinemaScope have happened to motion pictures in the last ten years. And still more remarkable things are impending. These are tied up with the magnetic recording of both sound and picture and the development of electronic TV cameras for film production.

At that highly productive Paris Exposition of 1900, a Danish engineer named Valdemar Poulsen demonstrated that voices could be recorded on steel wire and then reproduced. Between 1928 and 1931, German technicians worked at substituting for solid metal a strip of paper with minute steel particles embedded in it. By the late 30's they had developed a tape with a plastic base and a coating of minute pieces of iron oxide. This was used as a cheap and easy means of recording thousands of wire-tappings.

For motion pictures as well as television, magnetic recording has a number of advantages. It is superior to the ordinary film track in tonal range. In moments of silence, it has little or no "ground noise"—the peculiar sort of buzz produced by the graininess of film. A magnetic track can be duplicated several times without seriously affecting the quality of the original.The sound can be quickly erased, and the tape reused several times. All in all, magnetically recorded sound is as superior to photographic sound on film as sound on film was to sound on phonograph discs.

This time there was no Hollywood resistance and little delay. As soon as the war with Germany was over and we learned how she had improved magnetic tape, Hollywood technicians were as ready to try it out as were the makers and users of electronic equipment.

Magnetic Sound on Film

Hollywood soon learned that a strip of iron oxide could be laid on film. But, like the talkie process and CinemaScope lenses, magnetized film was first developed outside Hollywood. And so was its use on release prints.

During the twenties, scientists talked about recording magnetic tracks on film. In 1947, the Du Pont company gave RCA some samples ready for use. A couple of years later, Warner Brothers experimented with magnetized film. By April, 1950, Paramount was using it for all sound recording. At the end of the next year, approximately 75 percent of Hollywood production had fallen in line.

At first, the sound was transferred to photographic tracks for projecting. Then in 1952, through the enterprise of Hazard E. Reeves, *This Is Cinerama* led Hollywood by using magnetic sound tracks for the first time in a commercial theater. The next year Twentieth Century-Fox adopted this system for release prints of CinemaScope.

Putting the Picture on Magnetic Tracks

After the development of magnetic sound, the next step was to try to put the pictures, too, on a magnetic track. The Hollywood studios again lagged behind, but an industrial corporation, Bing Crosby Enterprises, pioneered. So did the manufacturers of television and electronic equipment. The Crosby people demonstrated the recording and reception of black and white TV images in November, 1951. Two years later, the Radio Corporation of America added color. While RCA went ahead rather cautiously, other processes appeared. In 1956, Ampex taped Douglas Edwards' newscasts and, later, *Climax* and live shows of *Playhouse 90*, and these tapes were used for delayed showings. They replaced kinescope films—motion pictures of live shows made from the TV tube—because tape gives a better image than a "kine."

Shortly before RCA put pictures on tape in 1953, TV seriously invaded the field of film production. Inventors devised cameras that photographed scenes and sound directly on film—not through a kine—at the same time that a live show was being broadcast. First came the British Cyclops of 1948. In 1955, the Allen B. Du Mont Laboratories demonstrated a device called Electronicam, in which a film camera and a television camera worked together through the same set of lenses. While the TV image and sound went over the air, Electronicam recorded the scene on photographic film. This device was used on the Jackie Gleason program. Al Simon's Video-Film camera did much the same thing. Devices like Electronicam could put a live show on the air and make a kine of it, while at the same time each camera preserved a film of all shots. The films from all the cameras in use could be edited to follow the pattern of the kine.

Savings from Ampex and Multiple Cameras

What does all this mean to Hollywood and to film production all over the world? The advantage of pictures on tape is largely financial. The lighting of scenes can't be as good as in a Hollywood film because film close-ups, over-shoulder shots, and medium shots are individually lighted to achieve finer photography than from the over-all lighting of a long shot.

Let us consider the advantages of shooting films for television with two or three ordinary cameras at the same time. Though directors don't shoot a whole show in continuous action, they put the actors through an entire scene without interruption. There is no stopping for different setups as in normal film-making. The cameras may run simultaneously, and the cutter will throw away the parts of the scene he doesn't want to use in the finished print. Or the director may "cut in the camera" by starting and stopping each machine so as to cover only the parts of the scene that he intends to use. If the director does this, he saves film, but he risks having to go back and shoot added scenes. In either case, the pictorial product is inferior. When three angles are shot at the same time, they can't be as well lighted—let alone as well acted—as when rehearsed, shot, and lighted one at a time.

Recording a television show on tape by the Ampex system, which provides no film images, can save money in a somewhat different way. The director can shoot with one or more cameras, but he needn't record all the scenes in continuity. After he has finished any scene he can have it "played back" immediately from the tape recording instead of waiting for the overnight development of what Hollywood calls the "rushes." He can decide at once whether or not the "take" is satisfactory or should be retaken. He won't have to repeat the scene until he guesses it is right. (I have known a Hollywood director to make forty-two takes, while the producer chose the first one to use in the finished film.)

TV As Distributor and Exhibitor

The television set is a new kind of screen. It may be one thousandth the size of the screen in a theater, but it serves a similar purpose. Of course what the home viewer looks at is the end of a tube, but he never calls it a tube until he has to buy a new one. To him it is the "TV screen." It always has been. And yet it was a long time before we began to realise that the television set, like the screen in the theater, was actually bringing us moving pictures—not moving pictures in the Hollywood sense but, nevertheless, pictures that moved.

In the beginning, much of what we saw on the little screen didn't look very much like the kind of moving pictures we were used to. The thing flickered. It turned negative. It slithered into diagonal patterns like a futurist painting. Some of what we saw when the set was behaving itself looked like a bad newsreel of fifty years ago. The rest seemed to be a pre-Griffith picture crossed with a talkie. It was only when Hollywood sold its old features down the river, and started to make short and hasty films for TV that some of us began to realise that the sets in our homes were a new way of distributing moving pictures of a real event or an imaginary one. They were bringing into the sitting room things that we used to have to go out of it to see. These included entertainment features and shorts, documentary and educational films and newsreels.

This new system of distribution—competitor of film exchange and movie theater—had one unique feature. This was simultaneity. Instead of waiting for the newsreel shots of a World Series or a national convention to be developed, printed, edited, printed again, and then sent to the theater and projected, we could see them on our home screen at the very moment that the television cameras were shooting them. The same thing could happen with actors in a play. Here was the ultimate in distribution —swift and complete and instantaneous.

From 5,000 Sets to 50,000,000

Thirty years ago it would have taken a prophet from Sinai to foretell the miracle of the growth and financial triumph of this electronic magic lantern. How to broadcast programs until there were sets? How to sell sets until there were programs to hear and see? The fact that the well-heeled radio companies took over television in America wrought the miracle—along with some disasters.

At any rate the babe was born in the thirties, and after the war was over she grew mightily. The nickelodeons and movie theaters multiplied with rare rapidity, but they never matched the rabbit-like proliferation of television sets. One statistician guesses that there were 5,000 home sets in 1946, twice as many the next year, 5,000,000 in 1950, and more than 50,000,000 in 1960. Broadcasting stations grew from nine, in 1946, to more than five hundred.

Film Almost from the First

Film came to television quite early. Broadcasters and producers bought single scenes from film libraries to use as inserts. Thus a shot of Paris or Hollywood, storm clouds or waterfalls, could establish a locale or an atmosphere for the following scene. Presently studios were taking film shots of their actors crossing Fifth Avenue, boating during vacation time, or watching a steamer depart.

Television stations soon began to broadcast old shorts and B pictures made by minor Hollywood producers. By 1949, Rank, Korda and Eagle Lion had sold almost a hundred and fifty of their films to American television. Many a feature was mercilessly butchered to fit a fifty-minute time slot.

In the late forties minor independent companies began to make short films especially for the home screen. Among the first awards of the Academy of Television Arts and Sciences was an Emmy for *The Diamond Necklace* from the *Your Show Time* series, as the best film made for television in 1948. *The Lone Ranger* and *The Life of Riley* were other popular series on celluloid. The major studios began to get into the act in 1951 when Columbia's Screen Gems unit began to make half-hour films for television. MGM, Warner Brothers and Twentieth Century-Fox followed four years later. By 1960, Hollywood was spending over $150,-000,000 a year in making TV films.

From 1955 to 1958, Hollywood dropped almost nine thousand pre-1948 features into the eager lap of its competitor. In 1960, the majors began selling their post-1948 films; United Artists was already doing so. Walt Disney retained his films—animated live action—but put on his own television shows, much to the advantage of his studio. Some of them included his old shorts or snatches from his feature films and also a revival of complete features. Other programs were very effective trailers for his theater screen productions. For a while his program advertised the coming of Disneyland. And always Disney found sponsors to pay for almost all of it.

At first television had bought the plots of Broadway hits and best-selling novels and borrowed stories that were in the public domain. Soon Bill Boyd, Roy Rogers, and Gene Autry were happily riding the TV range in their old Westerns. The new medium fondly embraced some old Hollywood stars and set them to "introducing" TV programs. After contributing the pre-1948 features, the major studios fastened the titles of some old successes—*How To Marry a Millionaire, Lassie, National Velvet*—onto a series of new plots good for twenty-five minutes each. Somewhere along the line, television latched on to the funnies from *Superman* to *Popeye*, sometimes in live action, sometimes in animation.

Why Film Took Over Around 1957

The cold fact of the matter was that 80 percent of TV's evenings—what they call Prime Time—was filled with film. Even Hollywood features had begun to move down from the late show and up from the earlier hours. Forgetting the features, why were the half-hour and hour shows being made on film instead of taped from live performances? It wasn't a matter of economy. Half-hour films made for television in two and a half or three days cost upwards of $50,000, live dramas half as much.

No, economy will not account for the triumph of the film, but economics did—the economics of this programming-cum-sponsor business. Single-shot dramas, with a different story and different actors every week, were full of imponderables. Would the viewers come back, or would there be a somewhat different audience, and maybe a smaller one? The television producers, just like the producers of Hollywood features or Broadway plays, had to guess at the entertainment value of scripts and casts before rehearsals started; so did the sponsor's agency. The half-hour films from Hollywood had two great advantages. They came in series. They involved the same actors and the same kind of plots. If the viewers liked the first one they saw, they would come back for more. Further, the film producers showed a sample called a "pilot." The network, the agency, and sponsor could see the show before they bought it.

Small Virtues, Larger Faults, in Hollywood

The directors who grind out films week after week for television have to work at a terrific pace compared with the men who make feature films. They shoot a half-hour show in about three days, an hour show in six days and an hour-and-half show in ten days. Yet the results are technically excellent. The camera-work ranges frcm good to exceptional, and the editing comes close to the best Hollywood standards. There is some skipping on the number of set-ups, but not very much. When I saw the rushes of a three-minute scene in *Gunsmoke* involving dialogue as well as a fight, I counted at least eighteen different camera angles. Only a third of them were "one take" set-ups. The rest had been photographed from two to six times before the director was satisfied.

If these films have had a defect—particularly the series of Westerns, gangster and detective films, and situation comedies—it has been mainly in the scripts. The blame rests partly on the producers, who pay too little money to attract the best writers, while they will give a TV-made star a Hollywood salary and often a share of the profits from the series in which he appears. In addition, creating a compact dramatic script complete with "intervals" for commercials is no easy task. Television has, however, provided some well produced filmed series in *The Alfred Hitchcock Hour, Ben Casey, Naked City* and *The Defenders*. Documentary films which in the past have had very poor distribution are now being seen on television with an audience potential of millions. However, when F.C.C. Chairman Newton N. Minow charged the medium with being "a vast wasteland," there were few who disagreed with him.

The Possibilities of "Pay as You See"

Is there a way out of this "wasteland" through Pay-TV? I think there is.

The argument against Pay-TV—the argument of the broadcasters and their sponsors—is that the present service is free. Aside from paying for your set and for keeping it in working order, which of course you would have to do with Pay-TV, you are paying your share of a commercial when you buy Kellogg's Special K or a Mercury.

The argument for Pay-TV is simple, though double-barreled. It brings the box office into the home. Those who pay for something become more critical; that is obvious enough. But there is a more important point. Pay-TV will be a tool of self-education through repeated experience. To prove this I must close by being personal.

A Box Office Educates

When I was about fourteen I discovered the fifty-cent gallery of the three legitimate theaters in St. Louis, which were part of our huge touring system. Every Saturday of the season, through my four years in high school, I saw a play. At first my favorite productions were farces like *Mrs. Temple's Telegram* and such melodramas as *Raffles, The Amateur Cracksman,* and *The Squaw Man.* I didn't really enjoy Shaw's *You Never Can Tell* or Sudermann's *Magda.* I was disappointed, and a bit shocked, when Nora of *A Doll's House* slammed that door. I wasn't too enthusiastic about *The School for Scandal.* But as I saw more and more farces and melodramas, they began to please me less; conversely I started to enjoy better and subtler plays—Shaw's *Caesar and Cleopatra,* for example, and Langdon Mitchell's high comedy of divorce, *The New York Idea.* By the time I went to college I was ready for *Hedda Gabler,* Percy MacKaye's poetic tragedy *Jeanne d'Arc,* and Maeterlinck's *Sister Beatrice.* Now the reason my taste improved—without benefit of books on dramatic theory—was that I had sat through the good plays that were somewhat beyond me. I had paid my fifty cents, and I wasn't going to leave the theater till the final curtain.

A generation later, I watched my son have the same experience with the movies. Through two years and a couple of hundred films, his taste and judgment improved and he even developed an interest in film technicians and film techniques. But when it came to radio, he got no experience of good music. He simply tuned it out. He had practically no contact with Beethoven and Brahms, Chopin and Wagner, until I bought a Capehart and played record after record, saying nothing about the merit of the music. When he too went to college, he bought a season ticket to the Boston Symphony concerts.

"Free" television, like radio, cannot educate by experience. The viewers simply tune out the programs that they aren't quite ready to appreciate. With Pay-TV, or so it seems to me, we shall be seeing its programs as we see plays and movies. We shall have a box office again. It will be best, of course, if there is a slot to drop coins in. But even if the toll is obscured a bit in a monthly bill, it should have a helpful effect. And the pay-as-you-see viewer can hardly be expected to tolerate commercials.

Bronson Alcott—who begat Louisa May, who begat *Little Women*—wrote: "Observation rather than books, experience rather than persons, are the prime educators." I wish he hadn't mentioned books. But books, even this one, may help a bit. At least I have to hope so.

Index

Numbers in italics denote illustrations; the abbreviation (f) identifies films.

503